RAISING PRODUCTIVITY

RAISING PRODUCTIVITY

Ten Case Histories and Their Lessons

FREDERICK W. HORNBRUCH, Jr., M.E.

Corporation Consultant

McGraw-Hill Book Company

New York   St. Louis   San Francisco   Auckland   Bogotá   Düsseldorf
Johannesburg   London   Madrid   Mexico   Montreal   New Delhi
Panama   Paris   São Paulo   Singapore   Sydney   Tokyo   Toronto

Library of Congress Cataloging in Publication Data

Hornbruch, Frederick W.   date
    Raising productivity.

    Includes index.
    1. Industrial productivity—Case studies.
    2. Management—Case studies.   I. Title.
    HD56.H66   658.5   77-4294
    ISBN 0-07-030350-9

1234567890   DODO   786543210987

The editors for this book were Robert A. Rosenbaum and Joseph
Williams, the designer was Elliot Epstein, and the production
supervisor was Teresa F. Leaden. It was set in Century Schoolbook
by Monotype Composition Company, Inc.

Printed and bound by R. R. Donnelley & Sons Company.

To my wife, Helen,
who, often alone while I pursued
higher productivity, provided
invaluable guidance and help
in putting it all together

Contents

4
IMPROVING PRODUCTIVITY IN A GOVERNMENT BUREAU
49

Government Employees Respond Constructively • Standards Organization and Training • Average Employee Performance 91 Percent • Standard Data for Office Operations • Office Machine Standards • Typing Standards • Bureau Brochure on Work Measurement • What about Government Employees?

5
TOOL DESIGN RESPONDS TO PLANNING AND CONTROL
69

Seven Tooling Functions • Need for Centralized Control • Plan and Schedule the Work • Measure the Effectiveness • The Plan in Operation • The Fundamentals Involved

6
REPLACING OUTDATED SYSTEM RAISES PRODUCTIVITY
77

Old System Outdated and Beyond Repair • Company Was a Large Job Shop • Vital Concepts for New Plan • Selection and Intensive Training of Timestudy People • Installing the New Plan in the First Department • Expanding the Plan into the Machine Shop • Move on to Fabricating and Assembly Departments • Foremen Rewarded for Controlling Costs • The Consultant's Summary • What Was Learned

7
TRIPLE THRUST CREATIVITY BUILDS A BUSINESS
97

Injecting New Ideas into an Old Subject • Eureka! Eureka! • Selling an Idea Is Not Easy • A New Company Is Formed • Product Proliferation • The Marketing Strategy • Talented Employees Produce Results • The Basic Business Policies • The Changing Involvement • Effective Employee Relations • The Computer Program • Incentive Compensation • Inform Employees • The Achievements • Some Thoughts Related to the Achievements

8
GROUP PARTICIPATION IMPROVES OPERATIONS
113

Multi-Flex Corporation, Illinois

New Management Needed • Innovations Needed to Stimulate Participation • Employees Respond to FTP • Recognition Inspires Employees • Keep Employees Informed • Action Gets Results • The Results • The Reasons Behind the Results

9
COMPUTER OPERATES ON HOSPITAL COSTS
131

The ECH-TMIS Team • What MIS Does at ECH • Patient Admission to Discharge • Installation of MIS, A Critical Period • Accuracy and Reliability • The Overall Results and Management Engineering • Productivity and Cost Improvement • The Principles Involved

10
ASSEMBLY METHODS AND STANDARDS ACHIEVE GOALS
151

Assemble Machines in West Germany and Belgium • The Assembly Layout and Flow • Decision to Install Work Measurement • Timestudy Training • The Standard Data Approach • Use Charts to Set Time Standards • Provisions for Setup and Extra Work • The Time Standards Are Applied • The Program Moves to Belgium • Momentum Maintained

11
BANKING ON HIGH PRODUCTIVITY
169

Management's Philosophy of Management • Modernize with Methods Research • Training Managers • Quality Assurance Is Paramount • Analyze the Big and the Small • Commercial Banking Improves • Check Processing Improves • Trust Operations and Services Improve • Overhead Value Analysis • Corporate Personnel Policies that Produce • A Summary

12
ORGANIZING THE HIERARCHY FOR HIGHER PRODUCTIVITY
195

More Ideas for Implementation • Organized Motivation • Streamline the Organization • Do Not Overstaff • Keep Organization Levels to Minimum • Designing the Organization • Organization Dynamics • Position Descriptions Vital • A Master Set of Position Descriptions • Member, Board of Directors • Executive Committee • Audit Committee • Chairperson of the Board and Chief Executive Officer • President and Chief Operating Officer • Secretary and Legal Counsel • Vice President of Marketing • Vice President of Finance • Vice President of Operations • Vice President of Technology • Vice President of Administration • General Manager of Operating Unit

Preface

Productivity is fundamental to progress throughout the world. No war, no treaty, no discovery, no single invention can match the achievement of a people who are inspired to produce. This inspiration is not something that just happens by itself or is there for the taking. It is achieved by planning, organizing, and working to create a climate, an environment, that encourages people to want to improve their ability to be productive.

This book is intended to bring to the reader's attention some of the motivating forces that influence people constructively in the pursuit of higher productivity. The case histories used to illustrate a variety of ways for increasing productivity— not 2 or 5 percent, but 25, 50, 100 percent and more—are all actual successful programs that produced extraordinary results. The examples are taken from domestic and international businesses producing a variety of products and services, ranging from pot cleaners, electric cords and cables, coated papers and films, zippers, flexible lines and fittings, appliances, automotive parts, aerospace components and accessories, instruments, tools, machinery, calculators, and computers to federal government bureau operations, hospital administration, publishing, and banking. The principles involved in these achievements have universal application. The one principle common to all is that someone high in management provided the guidance and the initiative to make it happen.

Management leadership, then, is vital to continually increasing productivity. Management must provide the initiative by establishing sound policies and programs that are pointed toward high productivity, high pay, high control, and high profits. How to organize and manage a business to achieve these goals is described and illustrated in terms of basic functions, policies, plans, programs, and controls.

This book represents the thinking and experiences of the author gained by working as an engineer, executive, and consultant and by associating with prominent people in the management profession. The author is deeply indebted to Phil Carroll, Arthur A. Rath, Alexander Strong, Dr. Lillian M. Gilbreth, Dr. Harold

B. Maynard, J. Keith Louden, Harold F. Smiddy, Sinclair Weeks, John B. Clark, Richard L. White, Floyd B. Odlum, David A. Stretch, Radu Irimescu, Gail M. Melick, Eugene R. Croisant, C. Chester Jung, P. Kay Schwartz, Mitchel Flaum, Edward R. Hall, Herman A. Peterson, Otto Kraus, James Matarese, Jr., Barclay Kingman, Spencer DeMille, W. Kirk Phillips, Minford Smith, Robert J. Young, Dieter E. A. Tannenberg, George Roxburgh, James G. Bralla, Dale G. Seymour, Samuel C. Berry, and John J. Fleming.

In addition, the author has been influenced by the work and thinking of Frederick W. Taylor, Henry L. Gantt, Frank B. Gilbreth, Charles E. Bedeaux, and Lyndall F. Urwick. Also, the author is grateful for the constructive criticism generously offered by his two sons, Frederick W. Hornbruch III and Harlan R. Hornbruch.

Frederick W. Hornbruch, Jr.

1

Productivity = $\dfrac{\text{Results}}{\text{Time}}$

The productivity of a nation or a company is difficult to measure, because so many interrelated variable factors influence the end result. It is quite easy to say productivity is output divided by input. But what is "output"? The quick and ready response is products and services. This would be simple enough if a common denominator were available for totaling the products and services, but such is not the case. Farm products are measured in bushels, pounds, short tons, long tons, and dozens. And a bushel of wheat may not be equal to a bushel of corn in value to the user. Also, the quality of the wheat may be high and that of the corn poor. Mineral products are reported in tons, pounds, and ounces. Even here a pound is not a pound—steel versus gold, for example. In manufacturing, output is reported in units, but one pencil is not equal to one automobile. In fact, one Ford may not equate to one Chevrolet, especially if one is a basic model and the other is equipped with all possible options. Services are even more elusive to measure and total. What is the worth of the contribution made by a government employee, an artist, an architect, a surveyor, a policeman, a plumber, an astronaut, a surgeon? How do you measure the work of Einstein, Salk, Pasteur, Edison, and the Wright brothers? Does one bank clerk equal two repairmen or vice versa? Who really knows?

Let's look at "input." Here again the variables are staggering. In order to produce most anything, many things are needed—for instance, people, capital, land, facilities, machine tools, mineral deposits, energy resources, ingenuity, creativity, climate, electric power, organization, enthusiasm, national pride. When we think of people do we mean only those employed or total people or perhaps only those between the ages of 16 and 65 or all over 16? Are local, county, state, and federal employees included in the input, or do we consider only the people employed on the farms, in the mines, and in the factories? How about the construction employees, the repairmen, the mail carriers, the people prepared to defend our freedom? In their way, aren't they also a part of the input and the output?

1

THE NEED FOR WORTHWHILE OBJECTIVES

Productivity can be more correctly stated as the relationship between achieving a result and the time it takes to accomplish it. Hence

$$\text{Productivity} = \frac{\text{results}}{\text{time}}$$

Time is a good common denominator. It is the one measurement that is used universally and, fortunately, it is beyond the control of people. An hour is a specific interval of time on this planet, which makes it an exact common denominator. What each of us does with our allotted hours is another matter, and that is what determines how productive we are. If you mow an acre of lawn in 1 hour while it takes me 2 hours, your productivity is twice mine. The result may be equally important to you and to me because we both have pride. We want our property to enhance our sense of well-being, and we feel good when we view the newly mowed lawn. It is our way of contributing to the appearance of our town. The value of this contribution, however, is largely aesthetic. No one will eat better, no one will be healthier, no one will be more adequately clothed or sheltered by this effort. The result is an intangible, but we think it is important. It's entirely possible that we have gained some tangible benefits, too. Perhaps by keeping the lawn mowed we have eliminated a fire hazard. And so, the results can be intangible or tangible or both. It doesn't matter so long as the result is important to us. Thus, as individuals, we need to set worthwhile, meaningful objectives for ourselves and our families—objectives toward which we are willing to think and work to achieve because they are important to us. We are talking about worthwhile, meaningful objectives because our objectives in total make up the progress and the standard of living we enjoy as a nation. If a person's objective is to destroy or kill or steal or go on welfare or get something for nothing, he or she is not making a contribution to the results achieved by his or her country. As a matter of fact, such a person is detracting from the results. That individual is part of the problem and, certainly, is not part of the solution to how to increase productivity.

Thus, setting good objectives is of paramount importance when we seek to increase productivity. Once we know what results we wish to achieve, then time becomes important. The less time it takes to realize our objectives, the more productive we are. In other words, direction is more important than speed, and together they determine our productivity. Improving productivity means compressing more good results into a unit of time. There appears to be no limit to the ways by which we can continue to reduce the time it takes to achieve our objectives. But increasing productivity is largely an individual matter. The operator producing 100 pencils per hour who finds ways to improve this output to 150 pencils per hour immediately knows his or her productivity has increased 50 percent. The improvement may have been gained by applying more effort, or a simpler method, or better tools, or a faster machine. When each individual finds ways to do more in less time, the total result for a company or a country is that there is more of everything for everyone. This must be a continuous process in order to continue to progress. Measuring the improvement in productivity on an individual basis is straightforward and quite correct. When we try to measure the achievement of a country, it becomes much more difficult.

GNP AND THE IMPLICIT PRICE DEFLATOR

The United States of America has developed a measure of productivity that utilizes dollars of gross national product as the common denominator for *results* (output) and people in the labor force (in some instances man-hours) as the measure of *time* (input). From the foregoing discussion it is evident that this measure of productivity leaves something to be desired. However, it is the best measure developed to date, and the United States government goes to great lengths to define and refine the data that provides the measure of productivity for the nation. The following definitions of the three major factors used to calculate productivity in the United States will provide some understanding of the data that is used and the adjustments that are made. These definitions are from the *Dictionary of Economic and Statistical Terms,* published by the U.S. Department of Commerce, Social and Economic Statistics Administration in November 1972.

1. Gross national product

GNP is the market value of the output of goods and services produced by the nation's economy. GNP is a "gross" measure because no deduction is made to reflect the wearing out of machinery and other capital assets used in production. . . .

GNP expresses in dollars the market value of goods and services produced by the nation's economy within a specified period of time. It is almost always estimated for a calendar or fiscal year, or for a quarter of a year expressed at an annual rate.

Raw materials, components, and intermediate products are not counted separately in GNP. However, their value is included in the value of finished goods sold to consumers and governments, in investment goods sold to business, or in inventory accumulation.

GNP is a "gross" measure. It is generally considered the most comprehensive single measure of economic activity.

2. Implicit price deflator

The implicit price deflator is the price index for gross national product. The index is the ratio of GNP in constant prices. It is a weighted average of the price indexes used to deflate the components of GNP, the implicit weights used being expenditures in the current period. All expenditures are valued in prices of the base year—now 1958—to obtain the constant dollar GNP.

Because it is so comprehensive, the implicit price index is generally regarded as the best single measure of broad price movements in the economy as a whole.

3. Employed and unemployed persons

Employed persons comprise (1) all civilians who, during a specified week, did any work at all as paid employees or in their own business or profession, or on their own farm, or who worked 15 hours or more as unpaid workers on a farm or in a business operated by a member of the family, and (2) all those who were not working but who had jobs or businesses from which they were temporarily absent because of illness, bad weather, vacation, or labor-management dispute, or because they were taking time off for personal reasons, whether or not they were paid by their employers for time off, and whether or not they were seeking other jobs. Excluded from the employed group are persons whose only activity consisted of work around the house (such as own home housework, painting or repairing own home, etc.) or volunteer work for religious, charitable, and similar organizations.

Unemployed persons are those civilians who, during a specified week, had no employment but were available for work and (1) had engaged in any specific job-seeking activity within the past 4 weeks, such as registering at a public or private employment office, meeting with prospective employers, checking with friends or relatives, placing or answering advertisements, writing letters of application, or being on a union or professional register; (2) were waiting to be called back to a job from which they had been laid off; (3) were waiting to report to a new wage or salary job within 30 days.

PRODUCTIVITY IS RELATIVE

The intelligent application of the three factors provides a measure of productivity that is reasonably consistent from period to period. And it is the relative value of productivity that is of most interest. The change in productivity is the principal concern. While many things can influence the change in productivity, the basic consideration is labor productivity. Comparing labor productivity among nations introduces additional variables. There are differences in the definitions used, in the methods by which the statistics are obtained, and of course, in currency valuations. One simple, though significant, example, is that the number of employed people is used for labor input. It is recognized that man-hours are a better measure of labor, but most countries do not compile man-hour indices. Also, comparisons of productivity among countries can be made in two relevant ways. One is to evaluate the "level of productivity" at a given time. The second is to analyze the "trend in productivity" over a time period. The latter is more significant. This measure shows how dynamic a country is and offers an indication of the degree to which productivity is affecting inflationary forces.

THE PRODUCTIVITY OF NATIONS

Now let's look at some statistics relating to productivity and population in the United States and several other major countries around the world. This information was obtained from data and reports issued by the United States government's Department of Commerce, Department of Labor, Department of Agriculture, and the National Commission on Productivity and Work Quality. Exhibit 1-1 entitled "Relative Productivity per Person, 1950–1972," shows the comparative level of real gross national product generated in six countries per member of their population in relation to that achieved in the United States during this 23-year period. Interestingly,

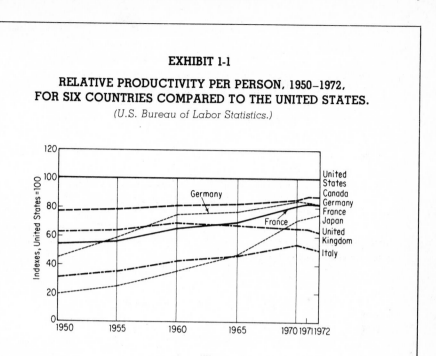

EXHIBIT 1-1

**RELATIVE PRODUCTIVITY PER PERSON, 1950–1972,
FOR SIX COUNTRIES COMPARED TO THE UNITED STATES.**

(U.S. Bureau of Labor Statistics.)

five of the countries—Canada, Germany, France, Japan, and Italy—increased their output per capita faster than the United States. Only one country, the United Kingdom, did not. On a per capita basis, while productivity improvement has the greatest influence on the trends, the proportion of the population in the labor force and the hours per employed person combine to affect the results. In this chart Canada, Germany, and France have been gaining steadily on the United States and have improved their real GNP per person to better than 82 percent of that of the United States. In fact, Canada by 1972 was at 88 percent. Japan has made the most spectacular gain, coming from 20 percent in 1950 to 75 percent in 1972. The United Kingdom has held at 63 percent, while Italy has improved but is still only at the 51 percent level.

A more meaningful measure of productivity improvement is the real gross national product per employed civilian. This relates the output for a country to its labor force. Exhibit 1-2 shows the relative productivity per employed civilian, 1950–1972, for the same six countries in relation to the United States. Compared on this basis, Canada stands out, and by 1972 its labor force was producing at 90 percent of that of the United States. France and Germany gained significantly, with France coming from 46 percent in 1950 to 80 percent in 1972 and Germany moving from 38 percent to 75 percent in the same period. Japan and Italy increased their output, too, and by 1972 were at 62 and 60 percent respectively. The United Kingdom gained very slightly on the United States throughout this 23-year period, coming from 56 percent to the 59 percent level.

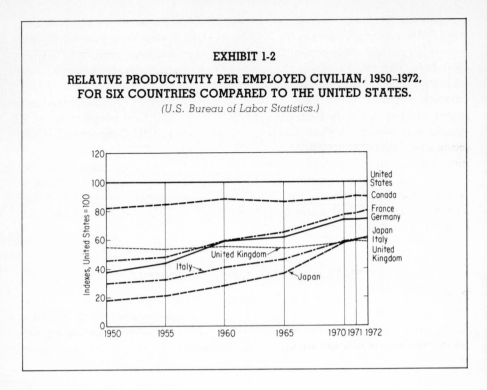

EXHIBIT 1-2

**RELATIVE PRODUCTIVITY PER EMPLOYED CIVILIAN, 1950–1972,
FOR SIX COUNTRIES COMPARED TO THE UNITED STATES.**

(U.S. Bureau of Labor Statistics.)

Exhibit 1-3, entitled "Growth in Productivity per Employed Civilian, 1950–1972" is similar to Exhibit 1-2. However, in this case the output by each country's labor force is related to its output in 1950. Thus, this chart reveals the rate of change taking place through 1972. Japan dramatically increased its productivity 441 percent. Germany and Italy improved 221 percent, France increased 178 percent, Canada 75 percent, and the United Kingdom 69 percent. The United States showed only a 60 percent gain over 22 years.

ATTRIBUTES IN IMPROVEMENT

Exhibit 1-4, entitled "Annual Contribution to Real Economic Growth, 1950–1972," is an attempt to separate the economic growth in these seven countries into two parts, as follows:

1. Growth attributable to increased output per employed civilian

2. Growth attributable to increased labor force

In all seven countries improvement in the output per employee was the major contributor to economic growth. As shown in Table 1-1, increased employment was the minor contributor.

All the foregoing statistics are in total. Now let's look at the contributions made by the principal sectors in the labor forces in these same countries. Exhibit 1-5 reveals the annual improvement in productivity per employed civilian, by sector, 1950–1972. This chart portrays the average annual rate of change in productivity achieved in agriculture, industry, and services. Industry includes mining, manufacturing, and construction. Services contains the output and input of all other employed civilians, including employees of federal, state, and local governments. It is significant to note that without exception the increase in productivity in the services sector was the lowest, averaging less than 2 percent per year during the period from 1950 through 1972. The industry sector did a little better, averaging nearer to 3 percent per year. The agriculture sector was by far the best, averaging almost 6 percent improvement in productivity per year. These figures take on added significance when the shift from agriculture to services is considered. This steady trend is shown in Table 1-2.

PRICE INCREASES AROUND THE WORLD

Productivity and employment have increased in all seven countries. However, prices have increased too. Exhibit 1-6, entitled "Implicit Price Deflator for GNP, 1960–1972," gives some idea of the way in which prices have skyrocketed during this period. Statistics of this sort are used to convert the actual gross national product for

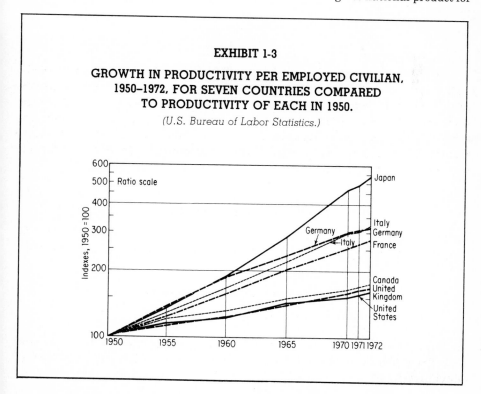

EXHIBIT 1-3

GROWTH IN PRODUCTIVITY PER EMPLOYED CIVILIAN, 1950–1972, FOR SEVEN COUNTRIES COMPARED TO PRODUCTIVITY OF EACH IN 1950.

(U.S. Bureau of Labor Statistics.)

EXHIBIT 1-4

ANNUAL CONTRIBUTION TO REAL ECONOMIC GROWTH, 1950–1972, BY INCREASED PRODUCTIVITY PER EMPLOYEE AND INCREASED EMPLOYMENT IN SEVEN COUNTRIES.

(U.S. Bureau of Labor Statistics.)

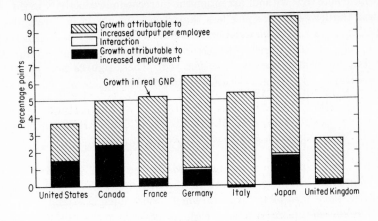

TABLE 1-1

| Country | % Contribution to real economic growth | |
	Increased productivity	Increased employment
Italy	99	1
France	92	8
United Kingdom	89	11
Germany	84	16
Japan	82	18
United States	60	40
Canada	52	48

each country into the real gross national product. The United States and Canada have fared better than other countries on price increases, but even prices in the United States increased 41 percent and in Canada 45 percent in this 12-year period. Germany's prices increased 61 percent, France's 70 percent, United Kingdom's 73 percent, Italy's 75 percent, and Japan's 76 percent. Inflationary trends accelerated sharply after 1972. By 1975 prices in the United States were 84 percent higher than in 1960. And the price levels in other countries had increased even more: Canada 97 percent, West Germany 96 percent, France 121 percent, United Kingdom 168 percent, Italy 164 percent, and Japan 163 percent. The normal increases in productivity in these countries were negligible by comparison.

AGRICULTURAL PRODUCTIVITY COMPARED

Productivity on the farm has improved sharply since 1950, but it is a lopsided improvement when viewed on a worldwide basis. The farmers in the United States,

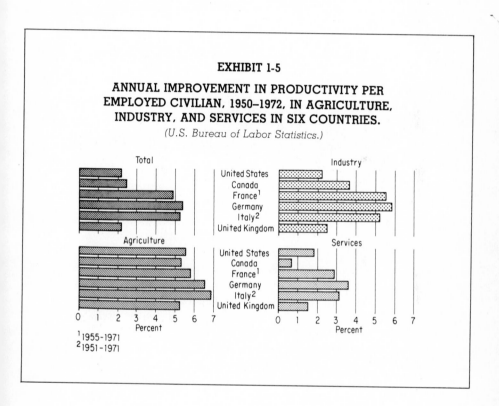

EXHIBIT 1-5

ANNUAL IMPROVEMENT IN PRODUCTIVITY PER EMPLOYED CIVILIAN, 1950–1972, IN AGRICULTURE, INDUSTRY, AND SERVICES IN SIX COUNTRIES.

(U.S. Bureau of Labor Statistics.)

[1] 1955–1971
[2] 1951–1971

TABLE 1-2
Percent Distribution of Civilian Employment by Economic Sector, 1950 and 1970

	1950			1970		
Country	Agri-culture	Industry	Services	Agri-culture	Industry	Services
United States	12.3	33.7	54.0	4.5	33.2	62.3
Canada	22.9	34.6	42.5	7.7	30.3	62.0
Germany	22.7	43.1	34.2	9.0	49.5	41.6
Italy	44.6	29.9	25.6	19.5	43.0	37.6
Japan	43.1	23.5	33.4	16.9	35.6	47.5
United Kingdom	5.3	46.5	48.2	2.9	45.0	52.2

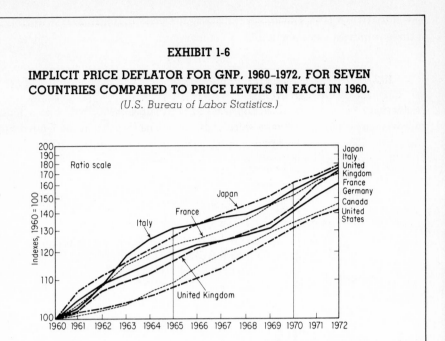

EXHIBIT 1-6

IMPLICIT PRICE DEFLATOR FOR GNP, 1960–1972, FOR SEVEN COUNTRIES COMPARED TO PRICE LEVELS IN EACH IN 1960.

(U.S. Bureau of Labor Statistics.)

Western Europe, and even the other developed countries far outproduced those in the less developed countries and in Communist Asia. See Exhibit 1-7, entitled "Relative Productivity per Person in the Farm Population, 1970." This chart reveals some startling comparisons. Compared to the United States, the countries in Western Europe realize an output per farmer of 21 percent of that of the United States; Communist Asia only 1 percent; the entire world 3 percent. Exhibit 1-8 shows some of the reasons for these results. This chart for 1970 compares agricultural land, fertilizer usage, and tractors per person in the farm population. In the case of agricultural land per person, the world rate is only 6 percent of the United States. For fertilizer usage, the world is 3 percent and for tractors in use 2 percent. Thus in many ways the true story of the United States' greatness in recent years lies in its farmers. Agricultural employment decreased from 6.7 percent of the total noninstitutional population in the United States in 1950 to 2.3 percent in 1974. This represents not only a decrease in the proportion of farmers to the total population but also a reduction in farm employees from 7,160,000 in 1950 to 3,436,000 in 1973, a decrease of 52 percent. During this same period output increased to the point where farm products now substantially exceed our needs and have become a major item for export. This occurred despite the fact that the total population in the United States grew from 152,271,000 people in 1950 to 210,300,000 in 1973, an increase of 38 percent. Farm products in recent years have helped significantly to give the United States a more favorable trade balance. The productivity of America's farms has

EXHIBIT 1-7

RELATIVE PRODUCTIVITY PER PERSON IN THE FARM POPULATION, 1970, FOR THE WORLD COMPARED TO THE UNITED STATES.

(U.S. Department of Agriculture.)

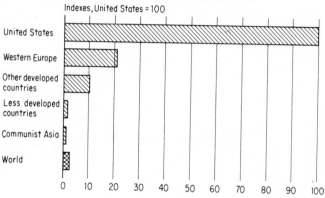

EXHIBIT 1-8

RELATIVE USE OF LAND, FERTILIZER, AND TRACTORS PER PERSON IN THE FARM POPULATION, 1970, FOR THE WORLD COMPARED TO THE UNITED STATES.

(U.S. Department of Agriculture.)

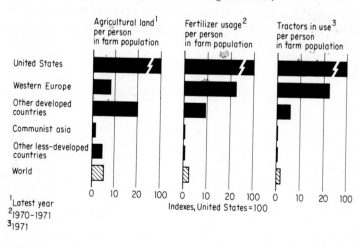

[1] Latest year
[2] 1970–1971
[3] 1971

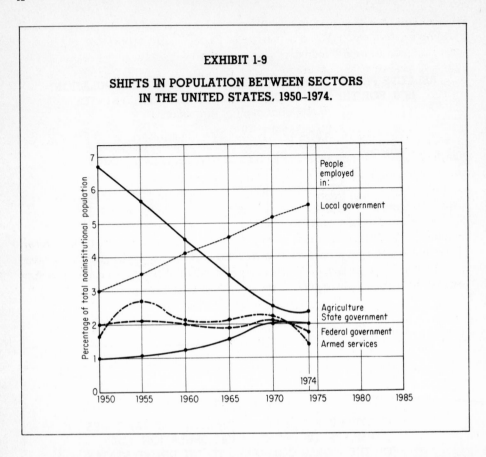

EXHIBIT 1-9

**SHIFTS IN POPULATION BETWEEN SECTORS
IN THE UNITED STATES, 1950–1974.**

increased steadily and dramatically, due to mechanization, research, fertilizer, and the removal of governmental restrictions on acreage and crops. Thus, there is every evidence that the American farmers are doing their part to feed the world and to control inflation.

POPULATION SHIFTS AMONG SECTORS

The population shift from 1950 through 1974 in the United States from the agriculture sector to the services sector bears further analysis. Exhibit 1-9 reveals what has occurred. Expressed as a percent of the total noninstitutional population, the people engaged in the armed services increased in 1955 and again in 1970, but by 1974 the total of 1.5 percent was the same as in 1950. The people employed in the federal government declined from 2.0 percent in 1950 to 1.8 percent. But the state government employment increased from 1.0 to 2.0 percent, and the people working for local governments climbed from 3.0 percent in 1950 to 5.6 percent in 1974. The farm population during this same period fell from 6.7 to 2.3 percent. Thus, the gains in productivity in agriculture essentially resulted in greater employment in the government portion of the services sector. This is an undesirable trend largely because the annual rate of increase in productivity in the services sector is so low in comparison with agriculture and industry. There seems to be little or no question but that state and local governments are too costly. We must reverse this trend if the United States is to make substantial gains in productivity in the future.

UNIT LABOR COSTS IN THE UNITED STATES

Now let's look at the private economy in the United States (see Table 1-3). This does not include federal, state, and local civilian employment. The statistics do show, however, what has taken place since 1967 in agriculture, manufacturing, and all other sectors, such as mining, construction, transportation, and other services.

Here again, while unit labor costs in farming increased 33.7 percent and in manufacturing 24.8 percent since 1967, *the increase in all others was 60.5 percent.* More emphasis has got to be given to increasing productivity in the "all others" area.

In this 7-year period, 1967 through 1974, the annual rate of change in output per man-hour from year to year in the private economy was as follows:

1968	+2.7%
1969	+0.4
1970	+0.8
1971	+4.0
1972	+3.4
1973	+2.6
1974	−2.7

This averages to +1.9 percent per year, a very discouraging gain in relation to that needed to control inflation.

TABLE 1-3
The Private Economy in the United States, All Indices 1967 = 100

Index in 1974	Total	Farm	Manu-facturing	All others
1. Output—gross product (Adjusted by implicit price deflator)	122.6	115.1	131.5	118.3
2. Input—man-hours	109.7	86.0	101.8	115.9
3. Output per man-hour	111.7	133.8	129.2	102.1
4. Compensation per man-hour	164.0	178.9	161.2	163.8
5. Unit labor costs	146.8	133.7	124.8	160.5

POPULATION RELATIVITY

The United States is entering a period that promises to be very different from anything experienced since World War II. Exhibit 1-10, entitled "Growth in Population
in the United States, 1950–1990," shows the actual increase in total population in
the United States from 1950 through 1974 and that forecasted through 1990. The
trend portrays a steady increase. Exhibit 1-11, showing the population relativity in
the United States, 1950–1990, is quite another matter. Those babies that were born,
fed, cared for, and educated during the fifties and the sixties began entering the total
noninstitutional population, 16 years old and over, during the sixties. By 1980 they
will all be in this group. Thus, in proportion to the total population, the people 16
years old and over will increase significantly. This is good if we can find ways to keep
them gainfully employed producing worthwhile products at higher and higher levels
of productivity. In this way much more product can be made available, and the

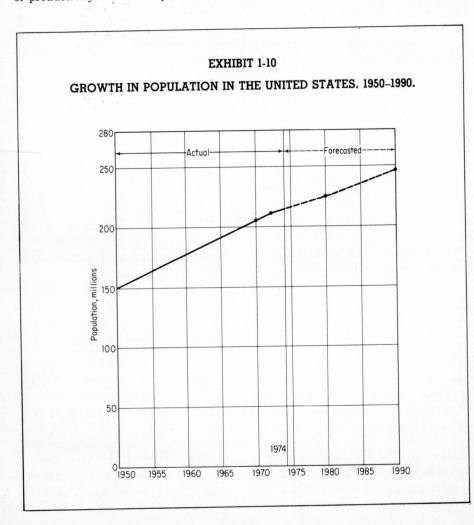

EXHIBIT 1-10

GROWTH IN POPULATION IN THE UNITED STATES, 1950–1990.

EXHIBIT 1-11

POPULATION RELATIVITY IN THE UNITED STATES, 1950–1990.

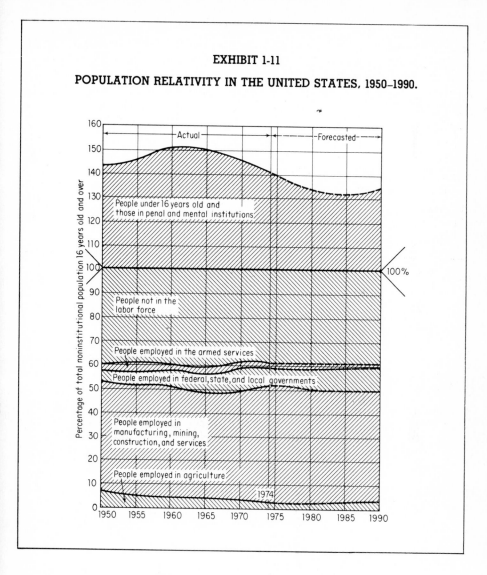

standard of living in the United States, and perhaps the world, can increase notably. On the other hand, if these additional people add to the unemployment rolls or if they are allowed to become an unproductive part of the labor force, then without much doubt the standard of living will decline.

Exhibit 1-11 expresses the number of people of various segments of the total population in the United States as percentages of the total noninstitutional population. The actual percentages are shown by years from 1950 through 1974. Forecasted percentages cover the period from 1975 through 1990. For example, in 1974 the percentage distribution by groups was as shown in Table 1-4.

TABLE 1-4

Population group engaged in	% of total noninstitutional population, 16 years old and over (1974)
1. Agriculture	2.3
2. Manufacturing, mining, construction, and services	47.8
3. Federal, state, and local government	9.4
4. Armed services	1.5
5. Not in the labor force	39.0
6. Total noninstitutional population, 16 years old and over	100.0
7. Under 16 years old and those in penal and mental institutions	41.0
Total	141.0

During this entire period the percentages that make up the total noninstitutional population, 16 years and over, vary somewhat but not by any large amounts. In other words, the people employed, including those in the armed services, has and is expected to remain fairly constant at 61 percent of the total noninstitutional population. However, the group under 16 is expected to drop from a peak of 51 percent to a low of 34 percent by 1980. Keep in mind that the population in total continues to increase about as it has in the past 25 years. Thus these percentages indicate a substantial gain in the number of people available for work. Can we put them to work? Can we make them productive? Can we inspire them to increase their productivity each year by large amounts? We have got to find ways. Too much is at stake.

THE CASE HISTORIES

The next several chapters provide examples from actual cases wherein the productivity of the employees was increased by exceptional amounts. The cases largely have been taken from industry. However, the principles involved have universal application. The good work done in agriculture and manufacturing must be continued and amplified. Services is the area in which much improvement must be gained, however, in order to make it possible for the United States and the world to increase productivity at rates that will stop inflation and provide an ever-increasing standard of living.

Raising productivity is concerned directly with people. How to effectively achieve the desired improvement takes know-how. One can gain this knowledge by personal experience, a slow and lengthy trial-and-error process, or one can use case histories to facilitate the learning process. In addition, improving productivity must be a continuing program. Even the best technique in time loses its allure and capability for arousing people to further achievements. Change is needed. Obviously, the changes must be constructive and should induce new inspiration and ever higher goals to be attained. Again, case histories can bring a variety of programs into the thinking, planning, and actions of the leaders who want to move their organization, their people, and themselves ahead. Case histories, then, can substitute the experiences of other leaders, other businesses, other services as background for the decision makers and the leaders of men and women.

The following case histories are designed to serve these purposes. In these case histories, programs for increasing productivity have been organized, individuals have been trained, and the desired results have been achieved. An executive, a manager, or an engineer can never have too many productivity-improving ideas at his or her calling. Managerial talent comes to the forefront when one deliberately and decisively chooses a way to inspire an organization to produce better and more. One exercises managerial ability to the utmost when directing an organization to implement such a program successfully. And managerial know-how is proven when one finds new ways to keep the organization interested and stimulated in achieving new and higher level results in the future. These case histories are intended to trigger the imagination of today's leaders.

The case histories run from the simple and quick to the complex and intensive. Each has its value, each its lessons. The concepts and practices exemplified in the cases have application to small and large, new and old organizations. Each of the ten case histories was selected for its special contribution as a proven way to *raise productivity through organized motivation.*

2

Team Enthusiasm Increases Output

In February 1944, Columbia Machine Works, Incorporated, New York, was busy producing ferrous and nonferrous castings, forgings, precision machined parts, and assemblies. Some of this production was sold to utility companies, but the major portion went to the Army and the Navy. In fact, the elevation, azimuth, and range units for the first radar installed in the United States Navy battleships were manufactured at this plant. The company had a small core of skilled employees, but because of the rapid expansion demanded by wartime conditions, the plant had been filled with recent graduates, homemakers, automobile salesmen, real estate and insurance people, store clerks, taxi drivers, and retirees. These employees were good, intelligent people, but for the most part they had little or no factory production experience. The management and supervisory staff took the usual steps of indoctrinating and training these employees to perform production operations. The plant was struggling to meet military specifications and schedules, but shipments were being made and the company was operating profitably.

Early on the first Monday in February, a Navy captain arrived and asked to see the general manager. At this point the factory was in production on radar contracts, making a variety of wave guides, power meters, and frequency meters. The dimensional and operating tolerances and the surface-finish requirements on these products was most exacting. Needless to say, many problems were encountered in production. After being closeted with the Navy captain for about an hour, the general manager called in his staff.

THE IMPOSSIBLE DEMAND

After a brief introduction, the general manager asked the Navy captain to explain his mission to the staff. Essentially, the Navy needed frequency meters. Two other sources had not produced any of this new type frequency meter and it was questionable if they ever would. This company was behind schedule but was the only source producing some of the instruments. The Navy wanted the company to increase its schedule threefold immediately and then be committed to producing to this accelerated schedule without fail. The Navy captain went on to explain that the first radar units had proven so successful in combat that this radar equipment was vital to winning the war. The Navy just had to have the new frequency meters! The staff's reaction was the same as the general manager's. Triple production literally overnight! It can't be done! The production manager explained the problems with tools, parts that didn't fit, the shortage of skilled assemblers, the lengthy training required. The chief engineer cited the engineering changes that were involved and the problems relating to calibration of the instruments. The quality manager talked of the need for additional gages and calibrating equipment and reviewed the high amounts of rework and scrap and the number of parts that had to be submitted to the material review board for disposition. The industrial relations manager pointed out that it was impossible to hire skilled employees and next to impossible to find anyone to add to the payroll. The Navy captain listened patiently but remained adamant that it had to be done. He concluded the meeting by suggesting the staff take time to find a way to accomplish the task and indicated he would return the next afternoon.

EMPLOYEES' IDEAS SOLICITED

The general manager and the staff literally dropped the problem in the production manager's lap. The production manager, in turn, groping for a solution, decided to call a meeting of all the assembly employees and supervisors. They were the people who were intimately involved in trying to meet the current schedule, and maybe they would have some ideas as to what could be done. The situation was carefully explained to these employees. Their immediate reaction was the same. Impossible! It can't be done! But as the discussion continued, some ideas for increasing output were presented and then a few more. Finally, one of the key assemblers asked if the group could meet by themselves that afternoon. Permission was granted, even though it meant losing production for most of the shift. Several key assemblers stayed well into the evening on their own time to check ideas with the second shift.

THE EMPLOYEES RESPOND

The next morning the group had a long list of things that needed to be done. To a man (and many of the assemblers were women) they were convinced the schedule could be trebled in time to meet the Navy's request, provided immediate action was taken on the items on the list. What did they want—three times as many people? Not at all! They asked for some additional people, but the majority of their ideas had to do with getting parts to eliminate delays, design changes to facilitate assembly, a rearranged assembly sequence to utilize the capabilities of the more skillful assemblers, transfer of skills to the newer employees, special tools to speed up assembly operations, a closer working relationship with inspectors, and most of all, a chance to show what they could do.

Obviously, the meeting that afternoon with the Navy captain went very well. The captain was satisfied the Navy would get the frequency meters it desperately needed. The production manager was confident the company was committed to a program supported by people who would make it happen. The general manager was pleased because the Navy captain and the production manager had reached agreement. Further, the program as planned would increase sales, decrease costs, and generate more profit.

A WINNING TEAM

The assemblers and their supervisors enthusiastically began to reorganize the assembly operations and train employees. Previously, the assembly of a frequency meter was made in four steps plus a calibration check. Each operation was complicated and included filing, fitting, and matching parts with considerable disassembly and rework. The assemblers divided the assembly work into ten operations and then set up four groups over two shifts to assemble and final inspect the instruments. Each group was aware constantly of its quality and its production. The supporting departments supplied the engineering changes, the tools, and the parts needed. Gradually, as improved parts began to flow from the machine shop and the subcontractors, the assemblers increased their output.

In February, 28 assemblers struggled to produce 95 acceptable frequency meters, a ratio of 3.4 units per assembler. By August, 42 assemblers produced 342 instruments, a ratio of 8.1 units per assembler. This is an increase in productivity of 138 percent and an increase in shipments of 260 percent. Exhibit 2-1 graphically portrays the results achieved by the assemblers.

To be sure, this was accomplished in wartime when it should be easier to arouse a group to action, but the employees and the company thought they were doing their part before the request for more was made. What really happened? The conditions that motivated the employees to improve were as follows:

1. *The request was a real challenge.* The Navy didn't ask for 5 or 10 percent more. It needed 200 percent, and this made everyone think hard about the problem.

2. *The employees were invited to contribute to solving a major company problem.* This released a wealth of stored up ideas and energy.

3. *The recommendations were approved quickly and decisively.* The management staff made no attempt to dilute the enthusiasm that had been generated. In fact, the staff took action to provide the service necessary to support the program.

4. *The assemblers become a team with an important mission to be accomplished.* They actually enjoyed being members of a winning team and worked hard and thoughtfully to achieve their goal.

5. *The team combined their individual know-how, skills, and ideas into a total program.* This brought about better understanding and a willingness to accept change.

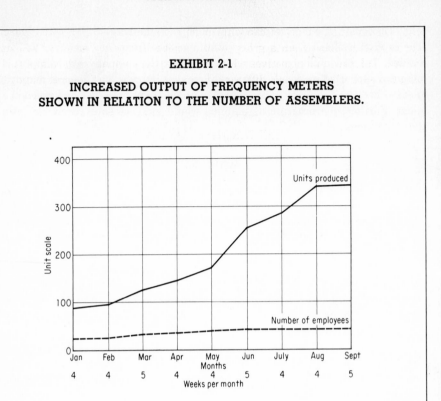

EXHIBIT 2-1

INCREASED OUTPUT OF FREQUENCY METERS SHOWN IN RELATION TO THE NUMBER OF ASSEMBLERS.

THE GAINS

What did the company realize and learn from this successful program?

1. Productivity increased approximately 138 percent.

2. Output increased more than 250 percent with only a minor capital investment.

3. Employees enjoy work if it can be made interesting and exciting enough.

4. Complex operations should be simplified.

5. Employees can be ingenious when given the opportunity.

6. Training time can be reduced substantially when essential factors are explained and understood.

7. People work best when they have high attainable goals to achieve.

8. Active participation and high productivity go together.

Joseph Meister, an excellent manager, who preached and practiced good management throughout his business career, once said: "Individual and group responsibility are essential. No driver can whip energy from a team forever, but a leader can inspire endless effort from a group with a vision before it. For they then have a purpose and goals and objectives which release energy—something to aspire to and achieve—and, it's funny how different things can be when we have a purpose."

SET A CHALLENGING GOAL AND
LET THE EMPLOYEES ROLL

3
Engineering Analysis and Training Get Results

Manufacturing slide fasteners, or zippers as they are more universally known, is a high-quality mass production business. The product, produced and sold by the millions but used one by one, not only must function reliably but is invariably expected to outlast the material to which it is attached. Its appearance must be attractive to the point where it virtually is unnoticed in the garment or product where it is used. Slide fasteners are produced in a variety of styles and colors and in an almost endless number of sizes and lengths to accommodate the differing requirements for dresses, trousers, jackets, coats, wallets, briefcases, bags, suitcases, tarpaulins, and other applications. The specifications for the civilian, industrial, and military markets are quite different and must be adhered to in volume manufacturing. It is a very competitive business.

At first glance, a slide fastener appears to be a simple device, and in turn, it would seem that it should be easy to make. Not so! The Crown Fastener Division of Coats and Clark, Incorporated, operating in Rhode Island, was struggling with curved, wavy, and snaky fastener chain; with fasteners that were too stiff, and hard to join or close; and with fasteners that would not meet the "pull" tests. These problems affected productivity throughout the plant and caused the yield to be much too low. Thus, unit costs were unpredictable and were considerably higher than the competitive price levels would support.

A HIGH-SPEED DIE-CASTING OPERATION

Most of the difficulties in production could be traced back to the machines that formed the scoops or to the tape on which the scoops were die-cast. The scoops are the little metal or plastic segments or teeth that join as the slide fastener is closed and separate as it is opened. The process used by this company for forming and securing the scoops on the tape was a zinc die-casting operation performed on special-purpose, patented, high-speed casting machines. Originally, the dies contained a single cavity, meaning that a single scoop was formed around the bead on the tape each time the dies closed and molten metal was injected into the closed dies. Later, the dies were enlarged to contain three cavities. Ultimately, the machines and the dies were developed to cast a full inch of fastener chain. For the smallest size scoop, the 1-inch dies contained fifteen cavities. Each of these improvements in the casting process was accompanied by a new set of production problems.

Perhaps a brief description of the casting operation will help to present a visual image of the action taking place. *As the dies open, the tape is advanced.* When this advance is incorrect or inconsistent, the spacing between sets of scoops being cast will cause difficulty in joining two pieces of cast chain and can impair the appearance of the final fastener. *Then, when the dies close around the bead on the tape* if the bead is too large in relation to the recess in the die, the dies will not close completely. This allows molten metal to flash out between the die faces, jams the machine, and ruins the casting. This section must be cut out of the fastener chain at a subsequent operation. If the bead on the tape is too small, the molten metal flows around the bead between the scoops. Again, this faulty section must be discarded.

The molten metal is contained in a gas-fired pot located at the rear of the machine. This molten metal is fed through a pumping mechanism, called a *gooseneck,* to a nozzle. *The instant the dies close, the nozzle moves forward and seats at a precise point on the rear surface of the closed dies. Then, the molten metal is injected into the die cavities.* When the nozzle does not seat squarely or in the proper position on the die surfaces, molten metal flashes out between the nozzle and the dies and insufficient metal enters the die cavities. In addition, the temperatures of the molten metal in the pot, the gas-flame-heated nozzle, and the water-cooled dies are critical too. When the combination of temperatures is not compatible, the molten metal drips out of the nozzle as it recedes from the dies, or the scoops are not fully formed. Both conditions require stopping the machine for correction, and misformed scoops result in rejected fastener chain.

All this action—dies opening, tape advancing, dies closing, gooseneck advancing, nozzle seating, molten-metal injection—*takes place at a speed of three hundred injections per minute.* Thus, the speed of the machine, the machine settings, the alignment of the dies, the condition of the tape, the temperatures, the pressures, and the timing functioning in combination either operate to produce good fastener chain or result in a variety of conditions that require correction.

The machines were operating so poorly that the president of the company called in a firm of consulting engineers to study the operation and to devise an incentive plan that would encourage the chain casting employees to improve their output. The consultant assigned to the project worked closely with the company's chief industrial engineer and his timestudy people in taking studies on the machines. After several studies, it became apparent that, in spite of the efforts of the operators and fixers (setup men), and continual attention by the toolroom foreman, toolmakers, and department supervisor and shift foremen, the conditions affecting the operation of the machines were so variable and so unpredictable that the timestudies were useless. Accordingly, it was decided that an engineering analysis of the operation of the machines should be made.

MACHINE CASTING OPERATION ANALYZED

A machine was selected for analysis. An experienced fixer (setup man) was assigned to operate this machine under controlled conditions determined by the consultant, the department supervisor, and the timestudy people. A list of all known operating variables was compiled. The machine was set up and operated with all variables held constant except the one variable factor under analysis. This variable was measured and calibrated to its extremes. From the results an operating range was selected for the factor with knowledge of the effect when the limits of the range were exceeded. For example, when the air pressure operating range is 130 to 150 pounds per square inch, a pressure below 130 results in porosity and half-casting and for a pressure above 150 unnecessary pressure causes pounding of the dies. In this manner factual data was obtained relating to each of the variables. This information was then tabulated as shown in Exhibits 3-1 and 3-2.

One more variable that had to be controlled was the diameter of the bead on the tape. Tests made with a range of bead sizes revealed that the relationship between the bead diameter and the recess diameter in the dies had to be held within 0.005 inch for good operation. Immediate steps were taken to measure and sort the tape into groups by bead size so that each lot of tape could be matched to the dies. Also, action was taken to control the manufacture of future tape within bead size limits compatible with good operation of the casting machines. This increased the cost of the tape slightly, but this added cost could be readily offset by a significant gain in fastener chain quality.

OPERATING PROCEDURES ESTABLISHED

From the tests, operating instructions were compiled (see Exhibit 3-3). These instructions described the conditions for each reason for machine stoppage and listed both the possible causes and the probable corrections based on their frequency of occurrence as learned from the engineering tests. The reasons for machine stoppages were classified as follows:

1. *Stopped casting*—Machine continues to run but metal does not flow through the nozzle.

2. *Nozzle smears*—Metal escapes between nozzle and dies, resulting in spitting and flash on end of gate.

3. *Flash and webbing*—Excess metal at parting line of dies or metal on tape.

4. *Jams*—Machine stops automatically because of interference between dies.

5. *Porosity and half-casting*—Scoops porous or partly formed.

6. *Curvature*—Tape curved after casting and curved or wavy after joining.

7. *Off length*—Cast length exceeds permissible tolerances.

8. *Positioning*—Castings are staggered or improperly positioned in relation to one another or to bead.

9. *Miscellaneous.*

EXHIBIT 3-1

SAMPLE MACHINE ADJUSTMENTS NECESSARY
FOR EFFICIENT, HIGH-QUALITY PRODUCTION.

OPERATING RANGES FOR CHAIN CASTING MACHINE SETTINGS			page 1 of 4
Machine settings which may be adjusted within the specified range during operation to improve performance.			
Variable	Nominal Setting	Operating Range	Condition when Range is Exceeded
1. Air pressure	140 lbs./sq. in.	130–150 lbs./sq. in.	Below 130—porosity, half casting Above 150—unnecessary pressure
2. Nozzle pilot flame	1/8″	1/16″–3/16″ length of blue tip extending beyond end of pilot. End of pilot to be located 1/4″ from center of back edge of nozzle.	Below 1/16″—half casting, porosity, stop casting. Above 3/16″—smear, porosity, jam
3. Volume of metal in pot	1 1/2″	1 1/4″–1 3/4″ distance between level of metal and top of pot when metal is stationary. High level—front lip of pot. Low level—outline of lower portion of gooseneck begins to show through metal.	Below 1 3/4″—half casting. Above 1 1/4″—overflow

(continued)

ACTION TAKEN TO IMPROVE QUALITY

Further engineering studies were made to determine what corrective action was needed to improve quality by minimizing curved, wavy, and snaky chain. Two sample runs were made with the casting machines set up and operated in accordance with the operating instructions established from prior tests. The conclusions reached from the results of studies after processing the fastener chain through secondary operations of trimming, joining, bonderizing, and drying were as follows:

1. Chain which is curved or snaky when joined results from variable spacing between successive castings and not from the amount of reverse curvature in the chain as cast.

2. Chain that is wavy when joined results from insufficient spacing between successive castings or excessive reverse curvature as cast.

3. The spacing mechanism must be in good operating condition. This unit is a vulnerable part of the machine in that sticking pistons, weak springs, or worn feed finger pins or locking pins usually cause variable spacing which leads to curved, wavy, or snaky chain. A periodic maintenance procedure should be established for servicing this unit.

4. The stripping angle in the dies must be located accurately, and the spacing-ring thickness must be correct within 0.001 inch.

5. The tape must leave the roving can freely. Variable spacing will result if the tape occasionally is tangled or snarled even slightly.

6. The bonderizing conveyor operation materially reduces the amount of curvature, waviness, and snakiness by stretching the joined chain.

DECISIONS MADE FOR REDUCING MACHINE DOWNTIME

In addition to machine stoppages that were corrected by the operators and the fixers, there were major downtime items that were handled by the toolmakers and the department mechanic. These major items included repairing leaking die terminals, spacing mechanisms, and goosenecks; installation of new dies and grinding, lapping, and polishing dies; changeover from one type of chain to another. The machines were taken off allocation during the time such major repairs or changes were being made.

EXHIBIT 3-2

SAMPLE SETUP INSTRUCTIONS ISSUED TO STANDARDIZE CONDITIONS AND IMPROVE OPERATION OF THE MACHINES.

OPERATING RANGES FOR CHAIN CASTING MACHINE SETTINGS   page 3 of 4

Machine settings which are to be made during setup and are not to be adjusted during operation.

Variable	Nominal Setting	Operating Range	Condition when Range is Exceeded
7. Vertical position of gooseneck piston	One turn up	1/2–1 1/4 turns up from point where metal just will not flow.	Below 1/2 turn up—porosity, half casting. Above 1 1/4 turns up—porosity, half casting.
8. Rotary position of gooseneck piston	Center of slot.	± 1/8 turn	Beyond 1/8 turn right-smear, jam, flash. Beyond 1/8 turn left, half casting, porosity.
9. Strokes per minute	300 R.P.M.	300 ± 5 R.P.M. 1/2 turn variable pulley is equal to a change of approximately 8 R.P.M.	Below 295—loss of production. Above 305—excessive vibration.
10. Nozzle rest timing	3″ Chord	1″–4″ chord length measured between point on cam where follower is just released from cam and point where cam just engages follower.	Below 1″—smears. Above 4″—possible interference between nozzle and dies.

(continued)

EXHIBIT 3-3

OPERATING INSTRUCTIONS USED TO TRAIN EMPLOYEES.

PROCEDURES FOR CORRECTING CHAIN CASTING MACHINE STOPPAGES   page 1 of 7

The following reasons for casting machine stoppages have been listed in their approximate order of importance from the standpoint of occurrence. The following symbols are used to denote responsibility for corrective action:
"O"–Operator; "F"–Fixer.
The operator is limited to corrective actions marked with an "O". The fixer can carry out or report all corrections necessary.

A. STOPPED CASTING—Machine continues to run but metal does not flow through nozzle due to:

Condition	Cause	By	Correction
1. Cold nozzle	1. Pilot flame too low.	O	1. Open gas valve to increase flame.
	2. Pilot dirty or clogged.	F	2. Clean or replace pilot.
	3. Pilot too far from nozzle.	O	3. Readjust position of pilot.
	4. Nozzle rests too long against dies when machine is stopped.	O	4. Open dies and wait until nozzle reheats.
	5. Contact surface on nozzle too large.	F	5. Grind nozzle to reduce area of contact surface.
2. Nozzle hole diameter reduced	1. Oxidation in nozzle hole.	O	1. Clean nozzle hole with .029″ diameter drill (No. 69), brush off.
3. Cold metal in pot	1. Metal added too fast. (Metal should be added to rear of pot when burner goes off.)	O	1. Stop machine with dies open until pot temperature returns to normal, brush off nozzle.

(continued)

This downtime, too, was excessive. Several decisions were made by the department supervisor and the toolroom supervisor to reduce this loss of production. They included:

1. The die-blocks were to be sealed with peened-in aluminum plates to stop water leakage.

2. The water terminals were to be clamped to the die-blocks to reduce breaking of solder joints.

3. Sets of dies were to be prepared in die-blocks and stocked ready for installation in the machines.

4. Goosenecks were to be prepared or repaired and stocked ready for installation in the machines.

5. Work trays were to be installed on the machines to provide a convenient place for the fixers or the operators to lay tools and parts when correcting stoppages.

6. An assortment of spacing rings was to be assigned to and maintained at each machine.

7. Sample quality standards were to be prepared by the quality control department and displayed in the casting department for reference use by the inspectors and the casting fixers and operators.

NEED FOR ORGANIZATION AND TRAINING

From the foregoing it is obvious that this chain casting was a complex operation involving many interrelated variables. It is just as clear that the chain casting was out of control and that only systematic engineering analysis and standardization could make it possible to reduce the operating problems to acceptable levels. In other words, the chain casting employees would need to be highly organized and trained in order to become highly efficient. The consultant and the timestudy people working with the department supervisor and the shift foremen prepared job specifications for the operators, fixers, shift foremen, and the department mechanic, instructor, tool crib attendant, clerk, remelt man, metal man, and sweeper. These job specifications* are contained in Exhibit 3-4, "Job Specifications—Chain Machine Operator"; Exhibit 3-5, "Job Specifications—Chain Machine Fixer"; Exhibit 3-6, "Job Specifications—Indirect Employees."

A training program was started. A new position of instructor was established, and a competent person from within the company was selected to serve in this capacity. The department supervisor, the shift foremen, and the instructor were required to study the job specifications, the operating ranges for chain casting machine settings, and the procedures for correcting chain casting machine stoppages. This material was discussed in detail until the entire group had a thorough understanding of how the information was to be used for training the operators and the fixers. There were thirty-nine machines in the department. These machines were being operated by thirty employees over three 40-hour shifts. An operator and a fixer were assigned to an allocation of six or seven machines, depending upon the type of chain being cast. The shift foremen and the instructor worked closely with the operators and the fixers in training them on-the-job. This training was concentrated on one allocation at a time. There were no classroom sessions. All the instruction was given at the machines. This was down-to-earth, practical instruction with follow-up at the point where the problems arose and the corrective action took place.

STANDARD TIME DATA

As soon as several allocations completed the initial training, the consultant and the timestudy people began to take timestudies. Standard elemental time data was compiled from the timestudies. Each basic element was defined, and the time for each element was the result of analysis of the values recorded by several timestudy

EXHIBIT 3-4

CASTING DEPARTMENT
JOB SPECIFICATIONS—CHAIN MACHINE OPERATOR

"Operating Ranges for Chain Casting Machine Settings" and "Procedures for Correcting Chain Casting Machine Stoppages" are part of these specifications.

The Operator is to take directions from the Machine Fixer. The Operator under normal circumstances should make only those adjustments on the machine outlined in "Procedures for Correcting Machine Stoppages."

If after a trial it is not possible to run the machine, he should notify the Machine Fixer and then is to follow directions given by Fixer.

The Operator's inspection duties are the most important part of his job. He should inspect every running machine on his allocation at least every 30 minutes.

Under no circumstances should a machine be allowed to run in a faulty condition, *no matter how many machines have already been shut down.* Once the Operator or Inspector has shut down a machine, it should not be started up until the fault has been remedied. After an Inspector's fault has been remedied the Operator should immediately return the lot ticket for Inspector's O.K.

The responsibility for the routine taking of samples for trimming and joining has been allocated to the Inspection Department so the Operator will take a sample only at the beginning of a lot on #1 and #2 chain, or when there is any question as to the quality of work coming off any machine, or when any major adjustment or change has been made to a machine.

An experienced Operator should be able to tell, in most instances, whether a chain will join satisfactorily without actually taking a sample and joining it.

The Operator should notify his Fixer and Shift Foreman if it becomes necessary for him to leave the Casting Department for any other reason than to go to the washroom.

Keeping in mind that the Operator's principal responsibility is for inspection and quality, the Operator's duties are as follows:

Operation

1. Inspection
   a. Measure at least 3 successive gap spacings and gauge the chain with a view to detecting any variations or incorrect lengths due to machine being off gauge, at the same time inspect for flash on tape or on chain, missing scoops, soiled tape, and uneven spacing. (At least every 30 minutes)
   b. Using a glass, inspect scoops for: Excessive or too heavy flash, cracked scoops, cut bead, dies out of line, rough casting, porous casting, half-casting. (At least every 30 minutes)

    c. At the start of the shift the Operator will make a thorough inspection of the chain to see that it meets all specifications. (At start of shift)

    d. If necessary, after an inspection, the Operator should remedy the fault as outlined in "Procedures for Correcting Machine Stoppages" or shut down the machine and notify the Machine Fixer. After such a correction has been made the Operator should immediately reinspect the chain. (As necessary)

2. General

    a. When a machine stops at a splicing or at a cut out, pull the tape through the machine to clear the cut in the flat of the tape, and start the machine. Introduce any loose ends that are not spliced and start the machine. (As necessary)

    b. Clean the front of the machine. Clean around the spacing device, the tape feed, the die beds, and under the dies. (As necessary)

    c. Add metal to the pots, and maintain the proper level in the pots. (As necessary)

    d. Patrol the machines between cleanings and inspections to anticipate any orders running out, to watch for any splices, or to observe the general running of the machines. At all times the Operator should give visual attention to the warning lights and to the tape feed to tell if a machine has stopped or has stopped casting. (As necessary)

    e. Mark the necessary data pertaining to this shift on the back of the lot ticket when the lot was started by a previous shift or allocation. (One per shift)

    f. Skim pots as needed. (As necessary, at least twice per shift)

    g. At start of shift clean nozzle hole with .029" diameter drill (#69) and brush off nozzle. (At start of shift and as necessary)

    h. When trouble is encountered which is apparently attributable to the tape, the Operator will stop casting and inform the Fixer. If after investigation the Fixer agrees that the tape is at fault, then with the Foreman's approval the Operator will remove order from machine, mark stopping time on back of lot ticket and place ticket in barrel with uncast tape, make out a slip Form F-11B and place with the cast part of the order in the other barrel, tie the two barrels together and try a new order. The part order is then to be tried later on some other machine in allocation. Operator will attempt to run all part orders resulting from above conditions on some machine in allocation. If the trouble continues, the Operator will report the condition to the Fixer and Shift Foreman. (As necessary)

    i. At the end of the shift, cut the chain off, and place the shift production slip (Form 11B) in with the work produced by this shift. Then place a divider to separate the production from that production that will be produced on the next shift. Record stopping time on the lot ticket. (1 per shift)

3. Handling of orders

    a. While the current order is still on the machine, handle the next order from the stock room to the machine, handling orders for 2 or more machines at the same time. Never have more than 1 order at a time waiting at a machine,

---

EXHIBIT 3-4 (Continued)

    casting #1 or #2 chain, and not more than 2 orders for the #3 or #4 chain. (1 per 2 orders)

b. Get the timing chain for the next order from the racks to the machine shortly before the current order is due to run out. (As necessary)

c. Find the end in the next lot and pull the last end from the machine, not allowing *any more waste* than is necessary. Introduce the new end and change the timing chain. Remove the last lot, place an empty can, and start machine. (1 per order)

d. Mark the finishing time and other necessary data on the lot ticket, and place the lot ticket with lot. Move the lot aside. (1 per order)

e. Mark the starting time and necessary data on new lot ticket, using same starting time as was used on stop time of previous order. Make out the shift production slip (Form F-11B) giving the necessary data. Place the shift production slip and the lot ticket in the holder on the machine. (1 per order)

f. Inspect and gauge 3 consecutive lengths in a new order. Readjust to scoop gauge as necessary, and check with gauge after each adjustment. Take a sample on #1 and #2 chain only. Measure 3 consecutive chain lengths and spacings with flexible rule on chain lengths up to 36″. Only one chain length is required to be measured on lengths over 36″, as a check on timing chain. (1 per order)

g. Return the timing chain from the previous order to the racks. (As necessary)

h. When Operator is satisfied that work meets specifications he should take the lot ticket to Inspector's carriage. After making necessary tests, inspector places ticket in cardholder on machine or if tests are unsatisfactory notifies Operator. (1 per order)

i. Move completed lots to Trim and Join Department handling one at a time for #1 and #2 chain and handling two at a time for #3 and #4 chain. (1 per order)

---

people from observation of several allocations of machines over the three shifts. For example,

    Element A7. *Start a machine.* 0.10 Standard Expected Minutes. Reset spacing device, tape, and timing chain; lower shield, position light, turn on air valve, turn on motor switch, and move clutch lever to right.

    Element B11. *Brush out.* 0.20 Standard Expected Minutes. Pick up brush, pull tape from between dies, brush off nozzle and flash around dies, set brush aside.

These basic elements, numbering 320, then were combined into 106 major elements of work required to run the machines. This involved establishing the method for performing each major element and determining whether each basic element could be carried out while the machine was running (internal), or that the machine had to be stopped while the element was performed (external). This

EXHIBIT 3-5

CASTING DEPARTMENT
JOB SPECIFICATIONS—CHAIN MACHINE FIXER

"Operating Ranges for Chain Casting Machine Settings" and "Procedures for Correcting Chain Casting Machine Stoppages" are part of this specification.

The Chain Machine Fixer is under the supervision of the Shift Foreman and is in charge of the allocation. The Operator is to take direction from the Fixer. However, the Fixer does not have disciplinary authority over the Operator.

The Machine Fixer is responsible for the mechanical adjustment and repairs on his machine. It is entirely his job to correct any machine found to be producing faulty work. Under normal circumstances, he should never allow the Operator to make any kind of an adjustment to the machines other than those indicated on "Procedures for Correcting Machine Stoppages." The *only* exception to this rule is that the Shift Foreman or Fixer can direct an Operator to make additional adjustments, under an abnormal condition, when so many machines are shut down that the Operator no longer has a full time job inspecting, servicing, and cleaning the few machines that are running. However, under no circumstances should an Operator be required to make these additional adjustments to such an extent that the Operator's own duties will suffer in consequence.

The Machine Fixer is equally responsible with the Operator for the quality of the work produced by his machines. Thus, it is a function of the Machine Fixer to familiarize himself with every phase of the Operator's job, so that he can make sure that the Operator assigned to his section is properly performing his duties. The Fixer should report to the Shift Foreman any Operator improperly performing his duties.

When all machines on the allocation are running satisfactorily the Machine Fixer should aid the Operator, particularly in inspecting the work coming off the machines.

In the making of adjustments, the Machine Fixer should be guided by the Casting Department procedures as posted in the department, and according to the departmental instruction as issued by the Shift Foreman and the Casting Department General Foreman.

At the start of a shift, and before commencing to correct any machine that is already shut down, the Machine Fixer is required to inspect the chain on every machine that is running, to check the flow of water through the dies and the general running condition of the machines including check with 100 scoop gauge on type 1 and type 2 machines.

At least once during every shift, Fixer should thoroughly lubricate all moving parts of machine and every two hours the Machine Fixer is required to check and,

EXHIBIT 3-5 (Continued)

if necessary, to adjust the flow of oil to lubricate the piston, the spacing device, and the master air valve.

Fixer is not to alter speed of machines unless ordered to do so by Shift Foreman.

Electrical difficulties or adjustments to instruments should not be made by the Fixer but should be reported by him to the Shift Foreman who will call for the Maintenance Department. The exception to this will be that a blown fuse will be replaced once before notifying the Maintenance Department.

The Machine Fixer will keep the down time record and the Shift Foreman will keep a record of parts used per machine. The Machine Fixer should notify the Shift Foreman whenever it becomes necessary for him to leave the Casting Department for any reason other than to go to the washroom.

The Machine Fixer is to perform Maintenance Tasks #1, 2, 3, 4, 5, & 6 as specified in the Maintenance Task Manual once each week during the day shift on Friday. The Fixer is to report all conditions requiring the attention of the Toolroom or Maintenance Department to the Shift Foreman for repair. Maintenance Task #1 is to be performed on the type 1 machines only.

The Machine Fixer should call to the attention of the Foreman any fault which cannot be remedied in the routine manner, any machine that gives trouble consistently due to some mechanical fault, or any machine that continually goes out of adjustment.

Instructions on Starting Up Machines after Shut Down

A. After referring to down time sheets, Fixer will arrange to start best machines first.

B. Each man doing one machine at a time.
    1. Put pot in place and light nozzle pilot.
    2. Open air and water valves.
    3. Brush nozzle, oil machine, pump metal through nozzle and start.

Instructions on Shutting Down Machines

A. Fixer will record condition of each machine on down time as follows: good, fair or bad.

B. Each man doing one machine at a time, start shutting down machines 15 minutes before end of shift as follows:
    1. Stop machine with dies open and shut off air and water valves.
    2. Skim pot. Turn off burner switch and nozzle pilot.
    3. Brush out.
    4. Pull back pot.
    5. Oil dies.
    6. Blow off machine with air line and wipe machine clean.

EXHIBIT 3-6

CASTING DEPARTMENT
JOB SPECIFICATIONS—INDIRECT EMPLOYEES

The Chain Casting Department is under the supervision of the General Foreman, and in his absence the Shift Foreman is in charge.

Shift Foreman

The Shift Foreman is included in the Indirect Standard. He is in full charge of chain casting machines operating on his shift and is responsible to the General Foreman. It is the responsibility of supervision to enforce all rules and regulations of the company.

The Shift Foreman is responsible for the men on his shift in reference to performance, quality of work, and discipline.

The routine duties of a Shift Foreman are as follows:

1. Review each allocation daily to make certain that the Fixers and Operators are performing their duties in accordance with the job specifications.

2. Instruct Operators and Fixers in the proper operation of the machines and assist in correcting major mechanical problems within the department.

3. Check and approve the replacement of dies, nozzles, goosenecks and spacing units as required. Shift Foreman will record die numbers in die record book.

4. Check and approve any work to be done to the dies by the Fixers as required, and lap out bead recesses.

5. Record attendance daily and forward to department clerk.

6. Rearrange shift personnel to fill vacancies due to absenteeism. In general, men from the spare allocation are to be transferred to fill in on the full allocations.

7. Distribute any new parts or supplies required by the allocations in the absence of the tool crib attendant.

8. When the Fixer reports any machine requiring toolroom or maintenance work to the Shift Foreman, the Shift Foreman will check the machine to make certain that the condition is as reported. He will then record the request on the Requisition Form in duplicate, describing the condition and the time the Fixer first reported the condition. One copy of this requisition will then be forwarded to either the Toolroom or Maintenance Department as required. When the Toolroom or Maintenance Department have completed their part of the job,

EXHIBIT 3-6 (Continued)

they are to report to the Shift Foreman that their work is completed. The Shift Foreman then will check the machine and if it meets with his approval, it is to go back on allocation immediately. The total off-allocation time will be equal to the elapsed time between when the Fixer first reported the condition and the time that the Shift Foreman approves the work completed by the Toolroom or Maintenance Department.

In the event that Toolroom or Maintenance Department help are not available, i.e., 2nd or 3rd shifts, the Shift Foreman will follow the above procedure except that in some cases the Shift Foreman may make the correction to the machine. The off-allocation time will be computed as though the Toolroom or Maintenance performed the work.

The Shift Foreman is to record each off-allocation time on the Weekly Department Off-Allocation Summary. The Fixer is to record the off-allocation reason and time on the Downtime Record at the machine. The Shift Foreman is to check and make certain that the recorded times on the Requisition Form Off-Allocation Summary and the Downtime Record are identical.

9. The Shift Foreman is to check to make certain that the weekly maintenance tasks are carried out according to specifications. He is to summarize and record, in duplicate, the condition of each machine in the department and forward a copy of this summary to the Toolroom. The maintenance tasks are to be performed by the day shift on Friday of each week so that the Toolroom can repair faulty machines over the weekend.

10. Review faulty chain rejected at the joining operation and refer it back to the responsible allocation. Prepare Scrap Work Report, from the Report of Faulty Work Tickets (Form F-154). The Improvement of Chain Casting Quality is dependent upon close cooperation between the Casting and Trim & Join Departments.

11. Check allocation sheets at the beginning of each pay week to make certain that the allocations are being run according to plan.

Department Mechanic

The Department Mechanic is directly under the supervision of the General Foreman. He will prepare dies, goosenecks, nozzles, and spacing units, in accordance with the job specifications.

Instructor

The Instructor is under the supervision of the General Foreman.

In general, the trainees are to be trained on machines in the spare allocation. The approval of the General Foreman is required in case it becomes necessary to assign trainees to one of the full allocations. His duties are as follows:

1. The instructor will acquaint the new employees with company rules and regulations and all safety devices.

2. Instruct new employees in the performance of the Operator's duties as shown in detail in the Job Specification for the Operator.

3. Train Operators in the duties of a Fixer as detailed on the Job Specifications for a Fixer.

4. Use any available time in assisting the Department Mechanic in preparing dies, nozzles, goosenecks, spacing units, etc.

Tool Crib Attendant

The Tool Crib Attendant is under the direct supervision of the General Foreman.

His duties are as follows:

1. Distribute all parts and supplies in the tool crib and keep inventory records.

2. Check tape stock daily in Tape Room and on the Casting Department floor. Prepare Tape Inventory Report and forward a copy to Tape Issuance and to Production Planning.

3. Check machine speeds and pot temperatures twice each week, and as required. Record values on proper forms and submit them to General Foreman.

4. Prepare the following weekly reports:
    a. Chain Casting Die Report
    b. Die Inventory and Order Report—Chain Casting
    c. Die Inventory and Order Report—Parts Casting
    d. Core and Trim Punch Inventory and Order Report—Parts Casting

Department Clerk

The department clerk is directly under the supervision of the General Foreman. His duties are as follows:
1. Maintain all departmental records, other than parts inventories.
2. Tabulate yardage cast on each die on Die Life Report.
3. Collect and file Casting Machine Downtime Reports and Casting Production Records at the end of each pay week.
4. Perform any miscellaneous duties requested by the General Foreman.

Remelt Man

The Remelt Man is directly under the supervision of the General Foreman. He will remelt lots according to the established Remelt Procedure. He will pick up parts casting scrap. He will weigh and record against the proper lots numbers for all remelt metal.

EXHIBIT 3-6 (Continued)

Metal Man

The Metal Man is directly under the supervision of the General Foreman. He will get the metal from an approved lot and weight, and record the weight. It is his job to break up the bars, using the rotary breaker, and distribute the metal to the casting machines, keeping the bins on the machines filled during the day shift. It is also his responsibility to see that the metal trucks are full before leaving at night. (The metal trucks are placed in the aisles of the casting machines. On the last 2 shifts the Operator must replenish the metal supply of any machine on his allocation, taking the metal from the trucks.) He will clean all trim and join scrap by running it through the magnetic separator. He will handle all cast parts to the Parts Stock Room.

Sweeper—Day Shift

The Sweeper works on the day shift and is responsible to the Shift Foreman on days. He covers the Chain and Parts Casting machines.

The duties of the Sweeper are as follows: Cleans oil out of the drip pans on chain machines daily; takes parts to raw parts stock room and returns empty parts barrels to Parts Casting Department; sweeps floor twice a day; brings lunch to men in the department; cleans lower part of machines not covered by Job Specifications; empties dross from pans; and cleans windows and light shades.

---

separation of elements into internal and external was very important. Both categories affect the amount of work an operator or a fixer must devote to servicing a machine. However, in addition, the external elements reduced machine efficiency and output because the machine must be stopped during the time the external work is done. Obviously, in the analysis the objective was to classify as many elements as possible and practical as internal. Exhibit 3-7 is an illustration of how the time for a major element was developed from the methods analysis and the basic elemental time values.

As soon as the major elements were determined, arrangements were made to take frequency studies. This required observing the operation of several allocations of machines around the clock for one week. The purpose of these frequency studies was to determine how often certain random type major elements occurred so that this data could be reduced to occurrences per 8-hour shift per machine per operator and per fixer by type of chain being cast. Some elements such as inspection were to be performed on a periodic basis specified by quality control. Other elements, like die life, were taken from departmental records. Exhibit 3-8 is an example showing the consolidation of the internal and external times for each major element extended by its occurrence per 8-hour shift for both the operator and the fixer. In total, then, this reveals how much time in minutes the operator and the fixer would be expected to devote to running each machine on #1 chain at the expected machine efficiency. Similar results were calculated for each type of chain.

During the frequency studies machine attention times and machine interference times were recorded and later analyzed. Machine attention occurs when all machines on an allocation are running and the operator and the fixer observe the machines in order to anticipate what major elements of work should be done next to keep the allocation performing at the expected output level. Machine interference is the time when machines, in addition to the one the operator or the fixer are working on, are stopped and waiting for service. In other words, machine attention adds to the work the operator and the fixer must perform to run an allocation of machines properly. Machine interference subtracts from the output of the machines and, therefore, reduces machine efficiency.

EXHIBIT 3-7

EXAMPLE PORTRAYING DEVELOPMENT OF A MAJOR ELEMENT.

ELEMENT NO.	ELEMENT DESCRIPTION	INTERNAL			EXTERNAL			TOTAL
		Std. Exp. Min.	Occur.	Total Exp. Min.	Std. Exp. Min.	Occur.	Total Exp. Min.	Exp. Mins.
100	Stopped casting— brush out			.23			.43	.66
A-28	To machine				.06	1	.06	
A-6	Stop machine				.07	1	.07	
B-11	Brush out				.20	1	.20	
A-7	Start machine				.10	1	.10	
E-7	Check operation	.23	1	.23				

EXHIBIT 3-8

EXAMPLE SHOWING HOW OCCURRENCE OF MAJOR INTERNAL AND EXTERNAL ELEMENTS WAS CONSOLIDATED INTO WORK REQUIRED TO RUN ONE MACHINE.

CHAIN CASTING STANDARD CONSOLIDATION   page 1 of 4
Chain No. 1   Machine Type 3   All calculations per machine per 8 hour shift.

Element No.	Element Description	Standard Expected Minutes		FIXER Expected Minutes			OPERATOR Expected Minutes		
		Int.	Ext.	Occ.	Int.	Ext.	Occ.	Int.	Ext.
	STOPPED CASTING								
100	Brush out	.23	.43	.74	.17	.32	3.00	.69	1.29
101	Adjust pilot	.23	.54	.25	.06	.14	.50	.17	.27
102	Clean or replace pilot	.23	5.40	.03	.01	.16	–	–	–
103	Adjust position of pilot	.23	.90	.11	.03	.10	.07	.02	.06
104	Open & wait for nozzle to heat	.23	1.00	.15	.03	.15	.12	.03	.12
105	Clean nozzle—using drill or wire	.23	.94	.07	.02	.07	.07	.02	.07
	NOZZLE SMEAR								
106	Pry out hard metal	.35	2.45	1.50	.53	3.68	2.70	.95	6.62
108	Replace or shorten gooseneck spring	.71	4.51	–	–	–	–	–	–
109	Adj. Vert. Alignmt. of nozzle	.35	4.35	.09	.03	.39	–	–	–
110	Adj. Hor. Alignmt. of nozzle	.35	2.60	.21	.07	.55	–	–	–
111	Check alignmt. of dies with pick	.35	2.77	.32	.11	.89	–	–	–
112	Stone nozzle	1.50	9.43	.08	.12	.75	–	–	–
113	Emery nozzle	.35	2.22	.15	.05	.33	–	–	–
114	Grind nozzle seat, surface of dies	.81	18.77	.08	.06	1.50	–	–	–
115	Adjust pilot	.35	.54	.13	.05	.07	.25	.09	.14
116	Adjust position of pilot	.35	.90	–	–	–	.02	.01	.02
117	Brush out	.35	.43	1.05	.37	.45	1.87	.65	.88
	Total page 1				1.71	9.55		2.58	9.39
	page 2				4.21	17.37		2.47	2.30
	page 3				3.65	11.26		3.85	4.01
	page 4				5.49	3.46		32.32	1.78
	TOTAL				15.06	41.64		41.22	17.48

PERCENT NORMAL WORKING TIME AND MACHINE EFFICIENCY

Exhibit 3-9, entitled "Chain Casting Standard Calculation," portrays how the internal and external expected minutes for the operator and the fixer with the expected machine attention and machine interference times were used to calculate the number of machines for a full allocation and the corresponding percent normal working time (% NWT) per machine. The % NWT is the portion of an operator's or a fixer's time that was expected to be needed in order to run one machine efficiently. A full workload or assignment equals 100% NWT.

EXHIBIT 3-9

CHAIN CASTING STANDARD CALCULATION

Chain No. 1   Machine Type 3
All calculations per machine per 8 hour shift

	Fixer	Operator	Total
A. ALLOCATION AND % NWT			
1. Internal expected minutes	15.06	41.22	56.28
2. External expected minutes	41.64	17.48	59.12
3. Subtotal	56.70	58.70	115.40
4. Machine attention allowance (10%)	5.67	5.87	11.54
5. Lunch allowance (15 ÷ 7 mchs.)	2.14	2.14	4.28
6. Total expected minutes	64.51	66.71	131.22
7. Machines per allocation =	7.4	7.2	7.3

$$\frac{480 \text{ minutes}}{64.51}$$

USE			7.0
8. % NWT per machine			13.7
USE			14.3
B. MACHINE EFFICIENCY			
1. Fixer external expected minutes			41.64
2. Operator external expected minutes			17.48
3. Subtotal			59.12
4. Machine interference (5% × 480 mins.)			24.00
5. Lunch allowance (15.00 mins.)			15.00
6. Total expected minutes			98.12

7. % Machine efficiency = $\dfrac{100(480 - 98.12)}{480}$ 79.6

8. % Expected tape yield			x.95
9. Net % machine efficiency			75.6
USE			76.0

The expected tape yield of 95 percent shown in Table 3-1 for machine efficiency means that for every 100 yards of tape going into a machine, it was expected that 95 yards of acceptable fastener chain would be produced. This was significant since the tape was a relatively costly item. For the group with the smallest fastener length, the machines per allocation, the % NWT, and the machine efficiency were as shown in Table 3-1. This information, then, was used to calculate the time standards per 100 fasteners for the different chain types and the many fastener lengths being processed. All the time standards were based on a machine speed of 300 injections per minute.

USE WAGE INCENTIVES TO GAIN AND MAINTAIN MOMENTUM

The company now had the basis for standard costs provided the chain casting employees could be encouraged to regularly produce quality chain at the specified level of productivity. A wage incentive plan was developed to achieve this. The consultant, in conjunction with the general manager, the department supervisor, the chief industrial engineer, and the timestudy people, designed the plan to

provide a sound, simple and effective basis for rewarding the Chain Casting Department employees in relation to the quantity and quality of work produced. The plan is based on the standard expected minutes of work required per shift to set up and operate a machine under specified conditions with provisions for machine attention and machine interference. The standard expected minutes of work per shift per machine then is converted to a percent normal working time (% NWT). A 100% NWT is equivalent to a full job.

The department supervisor in accordance with orders and conditions might make up machine allocations as follows for example:

Allocation letter	Chain no.	% NWT per machine		Number of machines		% NWT per allocation
A	1	14.3	×	7	=	100.0
B	1	14.3	×	5	=	71.5
	2	12.5	×	2	=	25.0
						96.5
C	2	12.5	×	8	=	100.0
D	2	12.5	×	4	=	50.0
	3	11.1	×	2	=	22.2
	4	10.0	×	3	=	30.0
						102.2
E	1	14.3	×	2	=	28.6
	3	11.1	×	6	=	66.6
						95.2

TABLE 3-1

Chain type	Machines per allocation	% NWT per machine	% Machine efficiency	% Tape yield expected
1	7	14.3	76	95
2	8	12.5	77	95
3	9	11.1	79	95
4	10	10.0	80	95

The production bonus paid to the operator and the fixer on an allocation will be in direct proportion to the extent to which they better the standards. Bonus will be paid only on productive time. The guaranteed base rate per hour will be paid for off-allocation time and for idle time resulting when less than a full job is assigned to an allocation as indicated by the allocation's total % NWT.

The hourly base rates guaranteed to the employees are to be equivalent to an employee performance of 100% The expected performance is 133%. At this performance the employee would earn a 33% bonus for the time on standard.

In addition, a tape yield bonus of 1% of the employee's hourly base rate is to be paid for each 1% tape yield above the base percentage for the time on standard.

Off-allocation time—Downtime will be allowed and paid at the operator's and the fixer's guaranteed hourly base rates under the following conditions:

1. When a machine is taken off allocation by the department supervisor because of lack of dies, metal or tape; or toolroom personnel unavailable and conditions of similar nature.

2. When a machine must be repaired by other than assigned personnel, the fixer is to report to the shift foreman. The off-allocation time is to start at the moment the fixer first reports the condition to the shift foreman provided after checking the machine the shift foreman agrees that the corrections should be made by other than assigned personnel. The off-allocation time is to end when the other than assigned personnel report to the shift foreman that their work is completed.

Over-allocating—Assigning machines to an allocation to a total %NWT in excess of 105% NWT is to be limited to only those employees who have consistently demonstrated their ability to produce at the expected performance and the expected tape yield on a full allocation. These employees may be permitted to take on additional machines only so long as they continue to produce at the expected performance and the expected tape yield on the over-allocation. This provision is necessary since it is possible to increase earnings at the expense of machine efficiency by over-allocating.

It is company policy to maintain the time standards consistent with the amount of work required at the expected employee performance of 133%. The expected minutes of work have been developed for each of the major elements of work required to be performed in the operation of the chain casting machines. These time values will be changed only when a change is made in method, product, tools, material or design. Production conditions will be checked every six months, or as conditions warrant, to determine the average number of occurrences for each of the major elements of work. The number of machines for a full allocation, the %NWT per machine, and the time standards will be increased or decreased in accordance with changes in time values and occurrences.

LOOK AT THE RESULTS

This entire program from initial studies through to design and approval by the management of the wage incentive plan took place over a 4-month period. It was started early in March. The standards and the wage incentive plan were first applied in the chain department during the second week in July. The tabulation in Table 3-2 shows the progress that was achieved by the chain casting department in total. These results are department averages. Some allocations were below and some were above these overall averages.

Thus, within a period of 4 months, March to July, productivity was increased gradually by as much as 88 percent. This improvement was achieved by thorough engineering analysis, simplified instructions, standardization, and training. With

TABLE 3-2

Week ending	Machines per allocation	Employee performance, %	Tape yield, %	Off-allocation, %	Increase in productivity, %
Reference Period					
3/7	7.0	72	82.9	42.0	0
Development Period					
6/27	7.0	82	88.0	15.2	76
Development Period					
7/4	7.0	89	88.2	16.7	88
Incentive Period					
7/11	7.0	92	89.4	11.5	110
7/18	7.4	94	90.2	9.6	131
7/25	7.8	105	90.1	8.8	177
8/1	7.8	100	88.8	5.8	168
8/8	7.8	104	89.4	13.4	158
8/15	7.8	116	91.2	5.7	220
8/22	7.8	115	91.1	12.0	196
8/29	7.8	113	90.7	4.9	213
9/5	7.8	112	90.0	4.0	210

the application of time standards and wage incentives early in July, further improvement in productivity took place. By the sixth month, productivity had increased more than 200 percent, the operators and the fixers on the average were earning a bonus of 14 percent, and the casting direct labor cost per fastener was reduced 63 percent.

The consultant's report summed up the program in this way:

> Thus, considerable progress has been made in the Chain Casting Department since last March. For the most part this is the result of the effort and the enthusiasm with which the management and the department supervision have tackled the problems which were encountered. The department appears to be well on its way to highly successful operation. Continued effort and attention by the management and the department supervision will insure reaching this goal.

By October, the employees were earning a 24 percent bonus, productivity had increased more than 230 percent, and the unit direct labor cost for casting continued to show a reduction of 63 percent.

The management concepts that served as the foundation upon which this very substantial increase in productivity was based are:

1. Employees at all levels welcome help when they know it is constructive and will be to their benefit.

2. In general, complexity and opportunity go together, and the key that unlocks both is *thorough analysis*.

3. Organization and training are necessary for effective teamwork.

4. The use of time standards and the % NWT principle is fundamental when multiple machine assignments are contemplated.

5. The separation of internal and external elements of work is necessary for optimum machine efficiency.

6. Wage incentives amplify and maintain the benefits gained through methods improvements and standardization.

7. Management direction and support are vital to the success of every major project.

ESSENTIAL CONTROL IS NECESSARY
FOR HIGH PRODUCTIVITY

4
Improving Productivity in a Government Bureau

"From April 9, the date control reporting was begun, through December 31, the Production Planning and Standards Office has established and applied work standards in four divisions. During this period 226,124 hours were worked on jobs covered by standards at an average performance of 91%." Prior to the installation of the time standards, the overall average performance of the employees was approximately 60 percent. This means the employees increased their productivity 52 percent and by doing this saved the American citizens 117,000 payroll hours of cost to run the United States government. And this was only the beginning of a program designed to improve operations in the Bureau of the Census, Department of Commerce, the United States of America.

The consultant's report continued:

Current hours worked on standard are approximately 4500 per week, of which roughly one-quarter are hours worked on census programs; the balance represent hours worked on current or continuing programs. At present, approximately 200 employees are working under measurement, either part or full time. In the coming year, the Production Planning and Standards Office will concentrate largely on compiling data and applying measurement to the current programs.

The Bureau currently lists approximately 1100 full time employees on the Salaries and Expenses Appropriation. In the original survey report, it was estimated that approximately 48% of this number were working on operations subject to direct measurement, which would indicate a probable maximum of 21,000 hours per week. Presently, standards coverage applies to about 21% of these estimated potential hours.

GOVERNMENT EMPLOYEES RESPOND CONSTRUCTIVELY

How did the government employees react to timestudies and to measurement? They improved their productivity 52 percent on the average. Relations between the production planning and standards personnel and the employees and the supervision in the operating departments were good. The consultant's report added:

> In a brief ceremony on January 6, eighteen operators from the Machine Tabulation Division received the first production incentive awards for sustained superior performance over measured standards (performance exceeding 100%). The awards, some of which were quite substantial, came as a surprise and excited considerable comment. We anticipate that this action will stimulate further operator interest in better performance.

It did!

Productivity improved significantly throughout all divisions of the Bureau, covering a wide variety of work performed. For example, the card-punching operations for economic censuses were completed at 60 percent of the budgeted costs and verifying at 81 percent. Combined, the two operations were finished at 65 percent of budget, an overall improvement in productivity based on actual costs versus budgeted costs of 54 percent. The consultant's report highlighted the following additional areas:

1. Standards were used in the Agriculture Census tabulation performed in Washington since the operation began in February. Performance climbed from 40% to 110% and coverage from 20% to 90% by May (an increase in productivity of 175%). These levels were maintained to September when the section started on the third and last major phase of the census, the tabulation of economic areas, and began to override its workload. Several additional tabulations were performed during this period of adjustment and coverage dropped to about 80%; the performance, on the average, remained unchanged at 110%.

2. Standards were applied to the Foreign Trade card-punching section late in August. This section had a pre-measurement performance level of 70%, the highest we have yet encountered. Performance has climbed to 80% on the average in December and to 93% in January. Coverage is approximately 90%. [This represents an increase in productivity of about 33%.]

   During the first week in December, standards were applied to the tabulation side of the Foreign Trade Section on a single machine basis; that is, one operator per machine. Response has been satisfactory with performances now approximating 100% and coverage holding at about 95% (an increase in productivity of 35%). Preparation now is being made to shift to a multiple machine assignment basis by February. These multiple assignments will vary by machine types and the nature of specific jobs, but in the main, will range from two to four machines per operator. [This would more than double productivity.]

3. The Census Operations Division is a central processing center for major censuses. The operations in this division on which standards were set were largely the coding and editing of Economic Census schedules, plus a few miscellaneous operations such as manually collating census forms, mail opening, envelope filling, and label typing.

Initially, performances against standard in this division were in the area of 55% to 65%. In the twenty-nine week period from mid-April through October, the time worked on standard in coding and editing operations totalled 54,583 man-hours at an average performance of 87% (an increase in productivity of 45%).

4. Standards were applied in the Foreign Trade Division in the Document Control Section in August, and have since been extended to cover import coding. Standards for export coding will be applied in January. In addition to coding, operations now performed on standard include filing, adding machine operations, and document sorting, blocking and numbering. It is anticipated that all areas in this division subject to direct measurement will be covered by June. Performances have reached approximately 90% of standard, but coverage is still low, averaging about 65%. [Here again productivity had increased about 50 percent during the time on standards.]

5. Standards were applied to the typing pool August 8 on typing of Agriculture Census preliminary releases, a repetitive tabular typing operation. Performance climbed from a pre-measurement level of 55% to approximately 80% by November (a 45% increase in productivity). Coverage was increased in the same period from 60% to 75%. The Chief of the Administrative Service Division has reported the release phase of the operation was completed four to six weeks ahead of schedule. Additionally, the section was reduced by four people to fifteen operators. Two more recent applications have been made, one in Personal Services Correspondence typing and Agriculture Tables Tabular typing. Performances currently are 64% and 44%, with coverage of 100% and 46%, both respectively.

Studies are now being made in the Accounts and Payroll Section and application of standards in this area is tentatively scheduled for March. These operations include adding machine and calculator work, and auditing and verifying vouchers.

6. Studies of Field Office operations have been underway for about two months, mostly in the Baltimore Office. Standards have been developed for the majority of the routine field office coding, verifying and editing functions on sample survey enumeration forms as well as telephone enumeration. The standards now are being checked out in the New York, Pittsburgh, Chicago, St. Louis and Jackson offices. Visits have been made to the Richmond and Charlotte offices. These standards, which should be ready by April, will be applied and administered by the Field Division. In addition to standards, the methods, procedures, and work space layouts are being analyzed and will be standardized in all offices.

7. During its first year, the Production Planning and Standards Office has developed a standard data manual for nearly all tabulating machine operations. Additionally, considerable information has been accumulated from timestudies of coding and editing operations and miscellaneous clerical functions. This information, in data form, is now being consolidated into a clerical standard data manual which, it is anticipated, will be applicable to a large percentage of Bureau clerical jobs and will greatly speed future standards applications.

The consultant's report ended with an acknowledgment as follows:

The Production Planning and Standards program has, in our opinion, made excellent headway since its inception about sixteen months ago. We wish to express our sincere appreciation for the cooperation and interest in the program by the Director, the Executive Staff, the Division Chiefs and their supervisors which made this progress possible. We feel sure the program will continue to move forward to the satisfaction of all concerned.

And it did!

STANDARDS ORGANIZATION AND TRAINING

Now let us look at the size of the organization that was required to install the measurement program in the Bureau of the Census. The authorized positions of the standards side of the Production Planning and Standards Office were as shown in Table 4-1.

TABLE 4-1

Position	Grade
1 Production planning and standards officer	GS-15
1 Production standards chief	GS-13
1 Production standards analyst	GS-12
2 Production standards analysts	GS-11
6 Production standards analysts	GS-9
4 Production standards analysts	GS-7
5 Trainees (added later)	GS-5

Thus, a group of fourteen timestudy people, plus a supervisor and with the guidance of the consulting engineer, took the timestudies, made the analyses, built the standard time data, set the work standards, and applied the measurement program. The installation was made in a sufficient variety of divisions and sections to establish the program as an integral part of Bureau operations. These people were all selected from within the Bureau. They were trained carefully and thoroughly in sound timestudy techniques. They learned how to be proficient in element breakdown, in using a stopwatch, in rating performance, in applying rest factors, in standardizing methods, in setting work standards, in working with Bureau employees and supervisors, and in the application and administration of time standards to Bureau operations. They developed standard time data and set time standards for setup and for production. The standards were comparable to those used in industry. In fact, the Bureau of the Census is a large factory, but in this case it is a large paperwork operation.

AVERAGE EMPLOYEE PERFORMANCE 91 PERCENT

The results that were achieved by way of improvement in employee productivity were similar to those obtained in industry when work measurement without incentive is used. As a matter of fact, the Bureau did better than usually is realized in industry. Normally, the average performance of employees on work measurement is in the 80 to 85 percent range. Bureau employees on standard averaged 91 percent performance. These employees had some incentive, although it was very modest compared to the usual wage incentive plan. The employees knew that their performances automatically became part of their personnel records and that this information would be used in the decision-making procedure when merit increases and promotions were under consideration. Also, the Bureau effectively used the Special Awards Program authorized by Congress for rewarding government employees who during a fiscal year make extraordinary contributions to the improvement of government operations.

STANDARD DATA FOR OFFICE OPERATIONS

The standard time data and the standards covered many of the types of operations encountered in offices anywhere. For example, coding, editing, key punching, verifying, sorting, collating, tabulating, calculating, filing, retrieving, typing, print-ing, mail opening, envelope filling, auditing and verifying vouchers, operating accounting machines, and other office work. Exhibit 4-1 shows how the standard time data was arranged for ready reference. This is a page taken from the Bureau's manual on key punching. The elements in this manual are grouped into the following classifications:

1. Setup elements
2. Work unit elements
3. Document handling and related elements
4. Machine elements
5. Miscellaneous elements

Each element in the standard data is assigned a specification number for easy identification and reference and is precisely defined as shown in Exhibit 4-2. This is important because these elemental time values expressed in decimal minutes are used over and over by the standards analysts setting standards in different divisions, sections, and units throughout the Bureau. These element definitions are equally important when the time standards should be modified to accommodate changes in methods, documents, procedures, and machines. The time values shown are in normal minutes. A rest factor of 15 percent must be added to convert the normal minutes into standard minutes. The rest factor is needed to allow for fatigue, personal needs, and very small unavoidable delays that occur over an 8-hour day.

EXHIBIT 4-1

SAMPLE PAGE SHOWING HOW ELEMENTS WERE IDENTIFIED AND COMPILED IN THE STANDARD DATA.

Element Specification Reference Number		Normal Time
	DOCUMENT HANDLING AND RELATED ELEMENTS (CONTINUED)	
38	Turn over 14″ × 17″ document for additional punching—per document	.0360
39	Scan and turn over 14″ × 17″ document—per document	.0500
40	Document 14″ × 17″ aside (no turn over)—per document	.0350
41	Turn over schedule 11″ × 17″ or 11″ × 25″ lengthwise—per page	.0400
42	Turn over tabulations—per tabulation	.0500
43	Turn tabulation fold—per fold	.0300
44	Turn over document 8 1/2″ × 11″, thick, heavy paper, 6-16 pages—per document	.0600
45	Turn over document 8 1/2″ × 11″, ordinary weight paper—per document	.0400
46	Turn and scan 8 1/2″ × 11″ document, 1-10 pages—per card	.120
47	Scan 2 page document 8 1/2″ × 11″ and turn over—per document	.0400
48	Document 8 1/2″ × 11″, 11″ × 17″ and 11″ × 25″ aside, no turnover—per document	.0300
49	Close 8 1/2″ × 11″ (folded) schedule and turn over—per schedule	.0500
50	Turn document horizontally—per document	.0180
51	Turn over document of IBM card to 5″ × 8″ card size—per document	.0300
52	Document of IBM card to 5″ × 8″ card size aside (no turn over)—per document	.0200
53	Turn page—per page	.0400
54	Auto-duplicating switch, off and on—per occurrence	.0300
	MACHINE ELEMENTS	
55	Self detected error—per card	.0087
56	Load feed hopper, 024—per card	.001290
57	Unload stacker, 024—per card	.000234
58	Auto card feed and eject, 024—per card	.00420
59	Rubber band around IBM cards—per card	.000865
60	Jog and sight check IBM cards—per card	.000740
61	Remove cards from partially full cardboard box of cards, or from wood box from which wedges have been removed—per card	.000260

OFFICE MACHINE STANDARDS

Exhibit 4-3 is a typical setup standard for getting ready to run a job on an electronic statistical machine. Exhibit 4-4 reveals the details that make up three production standards that may be run on this type of machine. And Exhibit 4-5 shows how the individual weekly performance record was compiled for each employee operating machines of this type. This record also provides for computing the employee's percent performance and percent coverage. These calculations then are summarized for the entire section.

EXHIBIT 4-2

SAMPLE PAGE ILLUSTRATING THE PRECISE ELEMENT DESCRIPTIONS CONTAINED IN THE STANDARD DATA.

42	Grasp IBM or Univac tabulation; turn over, face side down, place on operator's work table at left.
43	Turn IBM or Univac tabulation by fold. Tabulation is positioned in front of operator on reading table. Tabulation approximately $15''$ by $12''$ of varying thickness and weight.
44	Grasp document; turn document over, face side down, place on operator's work table at left. (Schedule is 8 1/2″ by 11″ of heavy paper; contains varying number of pages (6 to 16); held together by small chain on left hand side.)
45	Grasp document; turn document over, face side down on reading table. (Document 8 1/2″ by 11″, 11″ by 17″, and 11″ by 25″, of ordinary paper weight.)
46	Document 8 1/2″ by 11″, turn and scan. Turn and scan by page (1 to 10 pages) per card.
47	Scan 2 page document (8 1/2″ by 11″). Grasp schedule, scan, turn, scan, aside on work table at operator's right.
48	Grasp document; place aside on reading table. (No turn over.) (Document letter size, 11″ by 17″, and 11″ by 25″.)
49	Grasp document; close document; turn document over, face side down on operator's work table at her left. (Document letter size.)
50	Grasp document; turn horizontally on reading table. (For additional punching from face of document only.) Document 8 1/2″ by 11″.
51	Grasp document; turn over for additional punching. (Document card size and weight.) Document is positioned in front of operator on reading table.
52	Grasp document; place aside on reading table. (No turn over.) (Document card size and weight).
53	Turn page—self explanatory.
54	Auto-duplicating switch off and on—self-explanatory.
55	Self-detected error—begins when operator discovers error, traverses the card to the eject position and is removed and thrown away by the operator.
56	Load Hopper (024)—Release pressure plate in back of hopper; pick up cards from reading table (approximately 300), fan, jog, and place in hopper face forward (9's down); slide pressure plate against cards. Increase in size of reading table to 23″ by 31″ doesn't affect time. Standing up to load hopper is compensated by ease in releasing pressure plates and inserting cards.
57	Unload Stacker (024)—Remove completed cards from stacker (approximately 300); set cards aside on reading table.
58	Auto card feed and eject begins when machine feeds from hopper to punching position. Ejection occurs when new card enters into punching position.
59	Secure IBM cards with rubber band—Pick up approximately 200 IBM cards, jog cards to align, pick up rubber band, place rubber band around IBM cards, set cards on reading table. IBM cards measure 7 3/8″ by 3 1/4″.

EXHIBIT 4-3

ILLUSTRATES ELEMENTS REQUIRED TO
COMPLETE A SETUP STANDARD.

IBM TYPE 101 ELECTRONIC STATISTICAL MACHINE

SET UP

For each job assigned on the 101 machine, the operator is given an allowance to get the machine and supplies ready for doing the job. This allowance is called the "Set Up". The element breakdown of this standard allowance is presented below. Although the element pattern may not be the same on every job, the minutes provided should adequately compensate the operator when working under normal conditions.

STANDARD PER SET UP

Element Specif. Ref. No.	Elements	Normal Minutes
512	Change wiring boards (get and away)	.7900
1	Turn on power switch	.0400
520	Get supply of tabulation paper	.9000
2	Insert paper and adjust in rollers of both carriages	.4400
3	Synchronize carriages	.1700
4	Check carriages for correct location	.1700
5	Set switches (3)	.0600
505	Position portable truck (or rack)	.4600
506	Position file box	.0600
508	Remove wedges	.1320
6	Cards from file box to machine top	.0630
502	Sight check (final), 10 pockets at .038	.3800
533	Cards from machine top to file box or rack (final), 10 pockets at .080	.8000
7	Get work assignment; receive instructions and procedures; turn in work upon completion of assignment; recordkeeping	2.0000
		6.4650
	× 1.15 P., F. & D. factor	7.4347
	Use	7.4

In the case of power machine operations, the production standards analysts were given very specific instructions, for example:

A power machine operation involves two major functions—the cycling action of the machine, and the necessary physical activities of the operator. The standards provide for the entire running time of the machine and only that part of the operator's activities which must be performed while the machine is idle, such as positioning the sensing brush for the next column sort or emptying the machine stackers at the end of a column sort before starting the next sort.

The manual activities which can be done only when the machine is stopped are identified as "external elements"; the remaining necessary manual activities which are performed while the machine is running are called "internal" elements.

EXHIBIT 4-4

SHOWS HOW THREE PRODUCTION STANDARDS WERE SET FROM THE STANDARD DATA.

IBM TYPE 101 ELECTRONIC STATISTICAL MACHINE

PRINT LINE
(Continuous Each Sheet)

The standard writeup shown below is for those operations in which printouts occur on every line and generally are continuous from one tabulation sheet to the next. Since the number of print lines per tabulation sheet is known, we have included the tabulation sheet elements with the print line elements so that a count of the print lines only is required when using these time values. The 101 machine can be wired for any width of printing on the tabulation sheet. We have, therefore, provided standard time values for printing three different widths as shown on the following writeup.

CONTINUOUS PRINTING (every line)
STANDARD PER PRINT LINE

Element Specif. Ref. No.	Elements	External Normal Minutes	ACTUAL MACHINE TIMES (Minutes)		
			Print Up To 1/2 of Tab Sheet	Print From 1/2 to 3/4 of Tab Sheet	Print Full Width of Tab Sheet
13	Print tabulation line		.14500	.21800	.29000
14	Carriage return (cards feed simultaneously with carriage return when printing full width)		.01000	.01500	–
14	Carriage return (final) at .02; occurrence 1/28 lines				.00071
525	Manually advance tabulation paper between sheets: Initial space .0350 4 additional spaces at .0025 .0100 Occurrence 1/28 lines .0450	.00161			
15	Line up tabulation paper: 2 carriages at .125, .2500; Occurrence 1/224 lines	00112			
503	Start machine at .0210; Occurrence 1/28 lines	00075			
		.00348			
	× 1.15 P., F. & D. factor	.00400			
			.15500	.23300	.29071
	× 1.15 Machine factor		.17825	.26795	.33432
	× 1.05 Personal factor		.18716	.28135	.35104
	Externals		.00400	.00400	.00400
	External and Machine Time		.19116	.28535	.35504
	Use		.19	.29	.36

EXHIBIT 4-5

AN EXAMPLE OF THE COMPILATION OF AN EMPLOYEE'S WEEKLY PERFORMANCE AND COVERAGE ON STANDARD.

U. S. DEPARTMENT OF COMMERCE
BUREAU OF THE CENSUS

INDIVIDUAL WEEKLY PERFORMANCE RECORD

Operator's name and number *Dorothy Jones*   Week ending *Nov. 11*

Unit of Measure	UNITS PRODUCED					Totals of Units Produced	Time Value	Time Earned
	Monday	Tuesday	Wednes.	Thursday	Friday			
Set Up	1					1	7.40	7.40
Test-Initial	1					1	7.00	7.00
Test-Additional	1					1	5.70	5.70
Work Unit	4					4	2.70	10.80
1000 Cards	45.267					45.267	3.27	148.02
Variable Printing:								
A. Per Line	582					582	.35	203.70
B. Per Line							.28	
C. Per Line							.18	
Per Tab Sheet	97					97	.22	21.34
Continuous Printing:								
D. Per Line							.36	
E. Per Line							.29	
F. Per Line							.19	
Note: Per Sheet count not required; it is included in Per Line values.								
Rejects:								
Per Occurrence	5					5	.55	2.75
Problem Cards:								
Per Occurrence							.70	
Per Card							.55	
	/////	/////	/////	/////	/////	Time Earned----		Total: 406.71
Time On Standard------	360					-------		Total: 360.0
Time Non-Standard-----	120					-------		Total: 120.0
Leave-----		480	480	480	480	-------		Total: 1920.0

COMPUTING PERFORMANCE: 406.71 ÷ 360 × 100 = 113
                        Time Earned   Time On Standard   % Performance

COMPUTING COVERAGE: 360 ÷ 480 × 100 = 75
                     Time On Standard   Total Available Time   % Coverage

Careful analysis must be made of a machine operation to determine the amount of physical activity which is required, and to distinguish accurately between "external" and "internal" elements. Most of the elements are performed over and over during the course of a machine operation. The decision as to whether they are "external" or "internal" elements, and how many times they occur in either case, depends usually upon the time of their occurrence in the operation.

TYPING STANDARDS

Typing has almost universal application in government, business, industry, and commerce. Several examples of the arrangement of the standard time data for typing illustrate how it was used to set work standards for the typing-pool employees. The time values shown are normal minutes. The rest factor of 15 percent must be added to convert the total normal time into standard minutes. It is better practice to include the rest factor in each elemental time, because some elements may be more fatiguing and, therefore, require higher relax. However, in office work 15 percent is adequate. Rarely is heavy lifting, pushing, or pulling required. The Bureau preferred to apply the rest factor to the total normal minutes. Exhibit 4-6 lists the machine elements and their time values for operating both electric and manual typewriters. Exhibit 4-7 covers manual elements for paper insertion, while Exhibit 4-8 shows the time values for correcting typing errors. In Bureau work, a typing error rate of 1 character per 1000 characters was included in the standards. Exhibit 4-9 reveals how some of the elemental times were consolidated into major elements of work. And Exhibit 4-10 is an example of the computation of the standard for a specific typing job. In this case, the production standards analyst determines the method, selects the necessary elements and their frequencies of occurrence, makes the computations, and adds up the total standards. Exhibit 4-11 illustrates how the information was consolidated into a simple table for setting standards for typing letters on an electric typewriter in a wide range of lengths and number of copies. Anyone can set a standard from this table. All that need be known is the number of lines in the body of the letter and the number of copies desired. This particular table contains 98 preset standards. This, of course, facilitates the application of the standards and ensures consistency, because the methods have been standardized.

Thus the Bureau of the Census is equipped to set and apply setup and production standards on virtually every kind of office operation. The time standards "are used to measure individual and group employee effectiveness and serve as a basis for cash awards under the Census Bureau's Incentive Awards Program. The operation time is used in the construction of operational work plans, for production scheduling and staffing, and for determining budgetary requirements at the project level."

BUREAU BROCHURE ON WORK MEASUREMENT

The Production Planning and Standards Office prepared and published a brochure entitled "Measuring a Good Day's Work." This booklet was designed to explain "basic facts about production standards for supervisors." It brings out pertinent

EXHIBIT 4-6

ELEMENTAL TIMES FOR USING ELECTRIC AND MANUAL TYPEWRITERS.

CENSUS BUREAU STANDARD DATA (ELEMENT LEVEL)

Office Machines—1600

Typewriter General Elements—1601

Element Description	Decimal Mins.	
	Electric	Manual
Turn switch on or off	.008	. . .
Set one margin	.041	.054
Set two margins...........................	.072	.106
Key strokes (no carriage return)—Per stroke	.004	.005
Carriage return	.009	.018
Advance additional line after carriage return.......	.003	.007
Depress tabulator key	.007	.009
	Electric or Manual	
Clear all tab stops	.040	
Set one tab stop (carriage manipulation).........	.043	
Set one tab stop (depress space bar c. 5 times)	.027	
Back space, initial	.008	
Each additional back space	.003	
Set line spacer.............................	.025	
Depress space bar	.003	
Depress carriage release lever..................	.026	
Depress variable line spacer button	.024	
Raise or lower paper bail......................	.012	
Open paper release lever	.017	
Close paper release lever	.011	
Position carriage by hand:		
To exact line within 1″ or 6 lines..............	.038	
To exact line and to exact space on line.........	.068	
Constant value for each additional line..........	.014	
To exact space on same line.................	.046	
Scan page after typing.......................	.061	
Remove sheet(s) from typewriter	.027	
Remove carbon from assembled papers and aside	.051	
Separate carbon from letterex for erasing in		
typewriter—each carbon....................	.040	

information that supervisors and their employees need to know in order to gain their acceptance and their willing cooperation. After all, the time standards are only of real value when the employees strive to meet and beat the standards. In this way productivity is increased and operations are stabilized at a higher level of output. This makes planning projects easier and the results much more predictable. Several interesting paragraphs from the Bureau's brochure are as follows:

We haven't mentioned all the benefits that you will get from standards. There are many. Most important, you will have a constant, accurate, and fair measure of the productivity of each of your employees. This measure will be used to determine which employees do better work and are entitled to rewards. It may also be used to show employees how good their work is. Performance speaks for itself. How can Susie Jones argue that she worked harder or better than Jane Smith if her performance is 75 percent compared to Jane's 98 percent? You also have an expert

---

EXHIBIT 4-7

ELEMENTAL TIMES FOR ASSEMBLING AND INSERTING PAPER IN TYPEWRITERS.

CENSUS BUREAU STANDARD DATA (ELEMENT LEVEL)

Office Machines—1600

Typewriter Paper Assembly Elements—1602

Element Description	Decimal Mins.	
	Letterex	Loose Carbons
Assemble papers, insert and align in typewriter (electric or manual):		
Original and 1 copy....................	.284	.325
2 copies....................	.292	.389
3 ”	.300	.453
4 ”	.308	.517
5 ”	.363	.628
6 ”	.371	.692
7 ”	.379	.756
8 ”	.387	.820
9 ”	.473	.993
Add for each additional copy..............	.008	.064
Duplimat	.144	
Single typed sheet	.142	

EXHIBIT 4-8

METHOD DESCRIPTIONS AND ELEMENT TIME
VALUES FOR CORRECTING TYPING ERRORS.

CENSUS BUREAU STANDARD DATA (ELEMENT LEVEL)

Office Machines—1600
Typewriter Error Correction Elements—1603

Element Description	Decimal Mins. Per Error		Decimal Mins. Per Stroke	
	Paper in Typewriter	Paper on Desk	Paper in Typewriter	Paper on Desk
Erase and correct error:				
Duplimat	.314	.456	.0003	.0005
Single typed sheet	.515	.632	.0005	.0006
Original and 1 copy	.739	.775	.0007	.0008
2 copies	.921	.918	.0009	.0009
3 ”	1.103	1.061	.0011	.0011
4 ”	1.285	1.204	.0013	.0012
5 ”	1.467	1.347	.0015	.0013
6 ”	1.649	1.490	.0016	.0015
7 ”	1.831	1.633	.0018	.0016
8 ”	2.013	1.776	.0020	.0018
9 ”	2.195	1.919	.0022	.0019

Method: Paper in typewriter—Reach and grasp platen knob, depress carriage release, move carriage left or right, advance paper, raise paper bail, pick up eraser, erase original and copies, separating carbons and inserting cardboard or paper behind each erasure spot above copies, brush erasure from each sheet, place eraser and insert aside, lower paper bail, turn knob to return to proper line of type, depress carriage release, move carriage to several spaces in front of erasure, space to beginning of correction, type correction.

Paper on desk—Includes all erasure motions, insert each copy in typewriter, careful alignment to correction area, type correction, remove each copy and place aside on desk.

analysis of every step that is taken in performing the work of your unit; this information is tailor made for training new employees and for standardizing work methods. Unnecessary activities will become apparent in the analysis of the operations, and you can eliminate them. Devices for saving time and labor will also occur to you and to the analyst, and these may be installed. Improvement in the use of space and machines will also result. And, of course, as we mentioned earlier, you can use the standards to plan and estimate personnel needs. The scheduling of your work can be vastly improved. You can set more accurate deadlines, and you can be more confident that you will meet them.

Here are some suggestions on how you can help make standards work in your unit and get the full benefit from them.

1. Explain to your employees exactly what the standard is based on, so that they will understand the method, the elements, and the time allowances.

2. Answer your employees' questions about the standards program. If you don't have all the answers, the standards analyst will be glad to help you.

EXHIBIT 4-9

METHODS AND TIME VALUES FOR MAJOR TYPING ELEMENTS.

CENSUS BUREAU STANDARD DATA (ELEMENT LEVEL)

Office Machines—1600
Typewriter Constant Grouped Elements—1604

Element Description	Decimal Mins.
Typing Constants (electric typewriter):	
Type name and address on envelope (letter-size)	.521
Type date, address, and salutation on letter	.708
Type complimentary close, signature, title, and organization on letter	.467
Type date, "To", "From", and "Subject" on memorandum	.936
Type routing data (originator's name, typist's initials, routing of copies)	.323
Type page number for second or succeeding pages	.085

Method: Type name and address on envelope—Includes all necessary motions beginning with "pick up envelope" and ending with "remove envelope from typewriter and close paper release lever"; does not include place envelope aside.
    Type date, address, and salutation on letter—Includes all necessary motions beginning with "reach to platen knob" and ending with "advance carriage to location for typing body of letter."
    Type complimentary close, signature, title, and organization—Includes all necessary motions from "advance carriage to line for typing complimentary close" and ending with typing of organization.
    Type date, to, from, and subject on memorandum—Includes all necessary motions from "reach to platen knob" and ending with "advance carriage to location for typing body of memorandum."
    Type routing data (originator's name, typist's initials, routing of copies)—Includes all necessary motions beginning with "advance carriage several lines" and ending with typing of routing designation on carbon copies; includes remove and place aside letterhead on desk.
    Type page number for second or succeeding pages—Includes all necessary motions from "reach to platen knob" and ending with "advance carriage to line for typing balance of sheet."

EXHIBIT 4-10

STANDARDS SETTING SHEET FOR TYPING
SINGLE LETTERS AND MEMORANDA.

Normal Time Computation Form—Single Letter or Memorandum			
Description of Typing: Letter; original and 4 carbon copies, one envelope	Decimal Mins.	Frequency	Allowed Mins.
Assemble papers, insert and align in typewriter (1602)	.308	1	.308
Turn switch on or off (electric)	.008	2/1	.016
Set margins (1601)			
Type date, address, and salutation on letter	.708	1	.708
Type date, "To", "From", and "Subject" on memorandum	.936		
Type routing data	.323	1	.323

Compute total strokes in body of letter or
memorandum:
    Average width of lines typed (inches)   6
    Multiply by strokes per inch
        (elite 12, pica 10)   12
            Total strokes per line   72
    Multiply by number of lines of typing   25
                                            1800			

Selected time value per stroke: Electric	.004	1800/1	7.200
Manual	.005		
Carriage return in body of typed sheet (lines typed): Electric	.009	25/1	.225
Manual	.018		
Scan page after typing	.061	1	.061

Compute total strokes for error allowance:
    Envelope . . . . 90 X 1 :   90
    Date, etc. on letter . . . . . . .123 X 1 :   123
    Close, etc. on letter . . . . . . 81 X 1 :   81
    Date, etc. on memorandum.127 X__ :   ___
    Routing data . . . . 55 X 1 :   55
    Page number . . . .   1 X__ :   ___
        Total strokes in body
        of typed sheet   1800
                                          2149			

Selected time value for error correction (1603)	.0013	2149/1	2.794
Separate carbons from letterex for erasing	.040	4/1	.160
Type page number for second or more pages	.085		
Type complimentary close, signature, title, and organization on letter	.467	1	.467
Remove sheet(s) from typewriter	.027	1	.027
Remove carbons from assembled papers and aside	.051	1	.051
Type envelope	.521	1	.521
LIST OTHER ELEMENTS AS REQUIRED:			
Total normal minutes			12.861

EXHIBIT 4-11

PORTRAYS HOW ELEMENTAL TIMES WERE CONSOLIDATED INTO A SIMPLE CHART TO STANDARDIZE AND FACILITATE SETTING AND APPLYING TYPING STANDARDS.

TYPEWRITER WORK STEP—TASK STANDARD DATA

Typing Letter—0600 A

Electric typewriter—elite type

Number and Type of Copies	Decimal Mins. per Letter							Add For Loose Carbons
	No. Lines and Strokes in Body of Letter (Average width of lines—6 inches)							
	5	10	15	20	25	30	35	
	360	720	1080	1440	1800	2160	2520	
Duplimat	3.47	5.11	6.75	8.39	10.0	11.7	13.3	. . .
Single sheet letter	3.61	5.32	7.03	8.74	10.5	12.2	13.9	. . .
Letterex:								
Original and 1 copy	3.99	5.77	7.55	9.33	11.1	12.9	14.7	. . .
2 copies	4.17	6.03	7.88	9.74	11.6	13.4	15.3	.02
3 "	4.36	6.29	8.22	10.10	12.1	14.0	15.9	.04
4 "	4.55	6.55	8.55	10.50	12.5	14.5	16.5	.05
5 "	4.79	6.86	8.93	11.00	13.1	15.1	17.2	.06
6 "	4.91	7.01	9.12	11.20	13.3	15.4	17.5	.08
7 "	5.10	7.27	9.45	11.60	13.8	16.0	18.2	.09
8 "	5.28	7.53	9.78	12.00	14.3	16.5	18.8	.12
9 "	5.55	7.87	10.20	12.50	14.8	17.2	19.5	.16
10 "	5.74	8.13	10.50	12.90	15.3	17.7	20.1	.18
11 "	5.93	8.40	10.90	13.30	15.8	18.3	20.7	.19
12 "	6.05	8.55	11.10	13.60	16.1	18.6	21.1	.21

Method: Pick up and assemble sheets and carbons, jostle into alignment, insert assembled papers into typewriter and align, type complete letter (including routing), erase and correct errors detected during typing process, remove assembled papers from typewriter, snap out carbon paper, place sheets and carbons aside.

3. See that your employees keep accurate records of how they spend their time.

Workers may show up either too badly or too well because they don't report their activities accurately. An accurate record of comparative performances will benefit both you and your employees. When you use their performances to evaluate them and to recommend cash awards, you must have the fairest base possible.

4. Notify the Management Branch immediately if there is a change in methods. Standards cannot be fairly applied if methods change after standards are set.

5. Look for new ways to use production standards. They can make your job and your employees' jobs easier.

WHAT ABOUT GOVERNMENT EMPLOYEES?

The work measurement program at the Bureau of the Census was installed successfully, and it has continued to be a viable program. The experience brought to light concepts that in some instances were contrary to popular opinion. Some of the ideas that have far-reaching application in governmental and services operations include the following:

1. Government employees are much the same as employees in industry. They have the same ambitions and desires. They are highly intelligent and they are quite willing to turn in a good day's work. Their productivity pattern is the same as that of people in industry.

2. Government, office, and services employees, like factory employees, work at about 60 percent of standard when there are no production standards. They increase this performance to approximately 80 to 85 percent with measurement. The Bureau of the Census employees reached 91 percent on the average. With standards and wage incentives, all groups increase their average performance to the 125 to 135 percent level. This is a key to stopping inflation. Under wage incentives, the employees earn 25 to 35 percent more, productivity increases more than 100 percent, unit labor costs are reduced by as much as 40 percent, *and the foundation is established for further improvement.* Everybody gains including the taxpayer and the customer.

3. Improvement in government productivity, whether it be federal, state, or local in nature, can equal or exceed that of industry when the principles of scientific management are applied effectively.

4. Congress, state assemblies, and city councils would do well to spend less time making and remaking laws and devote more attention to determining what vital, worthwhile governmental projects are really needed and then require that the effectiveness of every department, division, section, unit, and employee be measured in the implementation of the programs. Current budget preparation gyrations are totally inadequate and tend to result in grossly excessive expenditures.

5. Congress literally has created a working environment for government operations where the "nature of the game" is to obtain a generous budget and then make certain it is all used by the end of the fiscal year. This climate has got to be changed. *But,* it won't be done until Congress changes its attitude, practices, and direction.

6. The stopwatch and time standards, contrary to popular belief, are readily acceptable in government operations provided they are explained properly, are

used and applied fairly and consistently, and are administered by trained technicians who know how to work with people.

7. Standard time data must be developed and used in setting and applying setup and production standards to any activity in order to gain consistency in the standards and to make the administration of a work measurement program economical.

THE NEED FOR PRODUCTIVITY IMPROVEMENT IS GREATEST IN THE SERVICES SECTOR

5

Tool Design Responds to Planning and Control

The Philadelphia Division of Bendix Corporation, Pennsylvania, manufactured aircraft instruments and components. All were intricate precision products requiring close dimensional and operating tolerances and strict adherence to aviation and military specifications. The floor area of this one plant exceeded 1 million square feet. The plant had complete capability for producing these products. The machine tools and related equipment were the very best and latest available and were maintained in excellent working condition. All operations performed in the plant were well tooled for high-volume production and were complete with gages and checking fixtures. The facilities for polishing, buffing, plating, anodizing, painting, and heat treating were modern and adequately controlled. The assembly areas were air-conditioned and well equipped with assembly jigs and fixtures, calibration and test apparatus, and auxiliary equipment. This was a well-tooled company producing highly technical, precision products in volume.

Tooling a new product and retooling to accommodate engineering and methods changes were invariably slow and late in relation to the management's plans and the customers' requirements. In fact, tooling programs were considered the bottleneck in the plant. Much management time and effort was directed to this situation. Process engineers, tool designers, toolmakers, tool vendors, and tool expediters were added, but the problem persisted. All programs continued to overrun schedules and budgets. Finally the works manager hit upon a new approach. Why not use the principles of production planning, scheduling, and control to systematize the tooling programs? He assigned a young industrial engineer, who had some production control experience, to study the problem, design a system, and when approved, implement it.

SEVEN TOOLING FUNCTIONS

The industrial engineer surveyed the situation and found there were seven principal functions required to tool a product. They were:

1. *Process engineering*—Deciding how a part, subassembly, assembly, or change was to be made. Then, preparing operation analysis sheets to show the sequence of operations and the work to be done in each operation with the machines, tools, gages, and special equipment to be used.

2. *Tool designing*—Designing the special tools and gages to meet the requirements spelled out on the operation analysis sheets and to simplify the work of the employees performing the operations.

3. *Tool ordering*—Determining how many tools to order, obtaining quotations for price and delivery, and placing orders with vendors, or issuing orders to the toolroom. In addition, setting maximum-minimum points for controlling perishable tools and gages.

4. *Tool expediting*—Contacting vendors and the toolroom to maintain delivery schedules, revising schedules for emergency requirements, and moving tools into the plant or out of the toolroom through tool inspection and into the tool stores ready for production.

5. *Tool inspection*—Inspecting tools to make certain they conformed with tool drawings and specifications.

6. *Tool stores*—Storing tools so that they are readily available and in good condition when required for production.

7. *Tool troubleshooting*—Investigating problems of dimension, tolerance, finish, performance, and tool life associated with using the tools in production.

NEED FOR CENTRALIZED CONTROL

The industrial engineer readily determined that process engineering, tool designing, tool ordering, and tool expediting were the major contributors to the overrun problem. Tool inspection, tool stores, and tool troubleshooting really couldn't perform until the tools were made and these functions could react quickly when necessary. Accordingly, the industrial engineer decided that in order to plan and coordinate the tooling programs it would be necessary to centralize the control of the processing, designing, ordering, and expediting activities. By doing this the load and capacity of each function could be known and used as the basis for scheduling. The status of parts and assemblies being tooled could be known readily and the best routing and dispositions made. Management could be informed by simple, factual reports. Decisions could be made from complete information. This was important because in tooling a product, different problems arise every day. Can a new product be tooled in time to meet the delivery requirements? Will it cause an overload in any tool group? If so, what must be done? Overtime? Use outside vendors? Revise the schedule? What tooling activities can be set back without interfering with production? How about the impact of engineering design changes? When should a tooling change be released to the shop? What provisions need to be made for parts and assemblies in process or in stock? Should the tools be held, canceled, revised, completed?

The industrial engineer designed a plan. This was reviewed in detail with the supervisor of each section involved in tooling the products. The going was rough in the early stages of the discussions. But as the supervisors became more involved, they began to realize the program could help them do a better job. Once this point was reached, they began to offer suggestions for simplifying and improving the plan. The plan was modified to accommodate many of their recommendations. This made it practical and made it a program they would accept and support. The plan, when submitted to the works manager with an explanation of how it had been developed, received immediate approval.

PLAN AND SCHEDULE THE WORK

The final plan centered around a control chart. The engineering drawings for each product or change to be tooled were studied and the hours for processing, tool designing, and toolmaking were estimated for each part and assembly involved. This information in relation to the workload and capacity of processing, designing, ordering, and expediting was used to plan and schedule the work. For simplicity, the control charts, Exhibit 5-1, were printed on blueprint paper and mounted on a series of panels in full display in the tooling department. The due date for each function to be performed on each part was indicated by a symbol, and overdue items were shown by colored pins (see Table 5-1). The operation numbers shown for expediting were taken from the operation analysis sheets. Specific tools and gages were required for performing each operation. An operation was considered completed when all of the tools and gages specified for it were in the tool stores. Each function or operation on the control chart was checked off in red pencil as it was completed. Control was maintained by updating the control chart during the first hour of the day.

After each job was scheduled, the due dates for each part were recorded on a tool schedule card, Exhibit 5-2, along with other needed information. One copy of this card remained at the control chart and the other copy flowed with the work. As each function was completed, the work passed over a control desk where the completion date was recorded on both copies of the tool schedule card. The control-chart copy was used to post the control chart daily. The working copy informed the next function when its work was scheduled to be completed. All information relating to a part was kept as a unit. In this way, as a part or a change progressed through process engineering, tool designing, ordering, and expediting, complete information was available such as:

1. Part or assembly drawing

2. Change request

3. Stock size card

4. Operation analysis sheets

5. Tool drawings

6. Tool schedule card showing the peak monthly production requirement, the annual production requirement, and the schedule dates

EXHIBIT 5-1

CONTROL CHART USED TO PLAN, SCHEDULE, AND CONTROL TOOLING FUNCTIONS.

| CHART NO. 8 | MODEL NO. 2160 | PART NO. | PRODUCT COMPASS | TOOLING DATES AUGUST 1 TO SEPT. 1 |

PART	1 2 3 4 5 6 7 8	PART NO.	JUNE 7 8 9 10 11	22 23 24 29 30 1	JULY 31 1	AUGUST 1 2 3 4 5 6 7
1. MAIN ASSEMBLY	X	E-16001	P			
2. FRAME ASSEMBLY	X	D-16012	P✓			
3. COMPASS FRAME	X	D-16059	P✓	D	O	10 20 / 30 40 50
4. FRAME CASTING	X	C-16081	P✓ PURCHASE			
5. COLLAR	X	B-16096	P✓	O		10 20 30 40
6. STUD	X	B-67502 IN PRODUCTION				
7.						
8.						
9.						
10.						
11.						
12.						
13.						
14.						
15.						
16.						
17.						
18.						
19.						
20.						
21.						

TABLE 5-1

Function	Symbol	Overdue
Processing	P	Green
Designing	D	Yellow
Ordering	O	Brown
Expediting	Operation Numbers	Blue

MEASURE THE EFFECTIVENESS

Thus the work involved in tooling each product or change was separated into the several functions to be performed, the functions were scheduled in detail, and the

EXHIBIT 5-2

TOOL SCHEDULE CARD SUMMARIZES PERTINENT INFORMATION FOR THE MANUFACTURING ENGINEERS AND THE TOOL DESIGNERS, BUYERS, AND EXPEDITERS.

PART _D-16059 COMPASS FRAME_   MODEL _2/60_

CHART
LOCATION _8-3_   BUDGET NO. _80_   PROJECT
DESCRIPTION _NEW RELEASE_

OPERATION	SCHEDULED	COMPLETED	NOTES	PRODUCTION
ENGINEERING		5/20	SHIP 1ST PRODUCT 10/28	PIECES 1ST MONTH
STOCK SIZE	5/22	5/22		500
PROCESS	6/8	6/7		
ORDERING	6/9	6/8		PIECES PEAK MONTH
DESIGN	6/23			3000
FINAL ORDERING	6/25			
EXPEDITING 10	8/1			PIECES PER YEAR
20	8/2			25 000
30	8/4			
40	8/5			PIECES IN STOCK
50	8/6			
60	8/8			
70	8/9			PIECES IN WORK
80	8/12			
	OVER			

status of each visually portrayed on the control chart. For the works manager's information, all of this detail was consolidated into a weekly tool control report, Exhibit 5-3. This report showed when each tooling program was scheduled to be completed and the progress being made by processing, designing, ordering, and expediting in meeting the schedules. The tool control report summarized for each new product and for changes on products in production, the percent of each function scheduled to be completed as of the date of the report, and the percent effectiveness. This is the percent actually completed of that which was scheduled to be completed. The percent effectiveness, then, was reduced to one overall percentage for each function. The effectiveness factor was designed to give a fair indication of the efforts of each group. Thus it caused the group supervisors to plan and follow their work to meet the schedules. In this way management was kept informed about the status of the various projects and the accomplishments of each of the several functions. Irregularities were readily evident, and management needed to take action only to correct those conditions. The major portion of the tooling programs required little or no management attention to details. The tool control report became an important link between scheduling and meeting the schedules.

THE PLAN IN OPERATION

The plan worked and it worked well. The all-important point to keep in mind, however, is that it takes people to get results. A system serves only to organize the flow of ideas and work and to provide the management with a means for control of the people operating the system. When the people know what is required and what they are doing and that management is aware of their accomplishments, it generally follows that they will do their best to achieve the desired results. The program as outlined was started. Within two months of operation these results were realized!

1. Process engineering improved from 83 percent of schedule to 100 percent.

2. Tool designing increased from 69 percent of schedule to 100 percent.

3. Tool ordering rose from 80 percent of schedule to 100 percent.

4. After getting on schedule, these functions thereafter did not fall below 96 percent of schedule.

5. Tool expediting, over a 6-month period, improved from 66 percent of schedule to 94 percent.

6. Three major tooling projects started during the first year of the program were completed on schedule and within budgeted costs.

7. The productivity of the tool department increased significantly. In addition, on-time tools facilitated production.

THE FUNDAMENTALS INVOLVED

Why were these results achieved and maintained? Several fundamental principles were involved. They were:

EXHIBIT 5-3

TOOL CONTROL REPORT INFORMS MANAGEMENT WEEKLY ON STATUS OF TOOLING PROGRAMS.

TOOL CONTROL REPORT

WEEK ENDING 6/12

PRODUCT	MODEL	TOTAL PARTS #	TOOLING COMP. %	TOOLING START	TOOLING COMP.	PARTS (RE: TOOLS) PROCESSED EFF. %	PROCESSED SCH. %	DESIGNED EFF. %	DESIGNED SCH. %	ORDERED EFF. %	ORDERED SCH. %	COMPLETED EFF. %	COMPLETED SCH. %	ENGINEERING HOLD #	CHANGES WEEK	CHANGES TOTAL
1. SUPERCHARGER	1130	135	85	6/1	6/20	100	100	100	86	100	84	99	72			6
2. FLOW METER	4/5	72	30	6/10	7/5	100	100	100	71	100	71	100	11		1	5
3. GENERATOR	848	39		7/10	8/1	100	95	100	52	97	52			3		
4. COMPASS	2160	118		8/1	9/1	100	80	98	16							
5. MISC. CHANGES	—	248				100	65	99	52	100	43	82	35			
6.																
7.																
8.																
9.																
10.																
11.																
12.																
13.																
14.																
15.																
16.																
TOTAL						100		99		99		92				

1. The responsibility for developing and installing the plan was assigned to an individual capable of applying new thinking to an old problem.

2. The supervisors participated in the development of the plan as individuals, not as a committee.

3. The supervisors did their part to make the plan work.

4. The supervisors and the employees knew what was wanted and made every effort to deliver on time.

5. The control chart highlighted potential problem areas every day.

6. The tool control report assigned schedule responsibility to each tooling function.

7. The score was reported each week in simple, understandable terms.

EMPLOYEES PRODUCE MORE
WHEN THEY KNOW THE SCORE

6
Replacing Outdated System Raises Productivity

A large job shop is a very difficult type of business to manage. This is because a wide variety of skills, machines, methods, and processes are required in order to manufacture the many different custom-designed products for which the customers place orders and contracts. The lot sizes usually are small, and many components never repeat. Most jobs have to be designed to meet the customers' specifications and then have to be engineered for production. Thus, in order to be successful, the design engineering and the manufacturing engineering personnel must be exceptionally capable, possessing a wide range of production know-how. Setup time for the manufacturing operations becomes a major element of cost. Very often it takes more time to set up the operations than it does to run the pieces or to make the assemblies. Good estimating of costs and the control of engineering and manufacturing costs are vital to the success of the business. And yet in many job shops these are the weakest functions in the total operation. Usually the estimating is no more than "guestimating" based on rule-of-thumb experience and unreliable past cost records. And control of costs consists of calling almost everything in the shop "direct labor" so that the manufacturing overhead rate is low. By doing this, direct labor contains, in addition to productive time, setup, waiting, poor performances, scrap, rework, extra operations, errors in counts and time charges, engineering changes, looking for tools, machine maintenance, and other overhead costs. Thus, two identical lots of the same item processed through the shop on different occasions may very well have direct labor reported as 1.5 hours and 9.6 hours. The cost accountant and the estimator happily average the two, round out the answer to three or four decimal places, and call the direct labor 5.550 hours. The next identical lot through posts 8.7 hours—much to everyone's amazement. This way of running a job shop does calculate to low manufacturing overhead rates, a distortion that seems to please both the management and the customers. In actual fact, however, it results in high total costs and high prices. There really is no control of costs, because the basis for control is highly variable and grossly inflated.

The management of Rector and Montgomery, Incorporated, of Philadelphia, Pennsylvania, knew this. Years ago R&M had pioneered with the principles laid down by Frederick W. Taylor and Henry L. Gantt, two of the original proponents of scientific management. The company had installed a piecework system based on time standards. The system worked well and R&M prospered. Thirty years later the company employed more than 1400 employees. During this period, the system gradually deteriorated. Eventually costs began to increase, profits started to dwindle, and business became more difficult to book. Finally, the son of one of the founders of Rector and Montgomery was elected a vice president of the company and given the assignment to determine what action should be taken to revitalize the business. He had worked in just about every department in the company. This experience was part of a program for grooming him for the presidency, which he ascended to several years later. From this firsthand experience he acquired an intimate knowledge of the business, he came to know the employees from the sweeper to the president, and he had a good "feel" for what was going on.

OLD SYSTEM OUTDATED AND BEYOND REPAIR

One of his first decisions was that the piecework system had outlived its usefulness and should be replaced. He realized the transition from the old piecework system to a modern cost control system would be difficult to make. The piece rates were inconsistent; many were tight or loose. Employee earnings were variable depending on whether they worked on a "good" piece rate or a "bad" rate. Earnings, however, were not too out of line, because general increases granted during the past several years had been paid as add-ons. In other words, the piece rates had not been adjusted to include these increases. In addition, less than 50 percent of the work in the plant was covered by the piece rates.

The company had a union, and the vice president knew any change in the system would have to be negotiated with the union and, ultimately, would need the acceptance of the employees. He knew he would need expert help to accomplish this. The firm of industrial consultants he selected assigned a capable consulting engineer to the project. The consultant surveyed the company's products, the lot sizes, the production operations, the manufacturing support departments, the employees' earnings in relation to their hourly base rates, and the performances of the employees. He checked the estimating procedures and the methods used to set the piece rates.

COMPANY WAS A LARGE JOB SHOP

In total, the consultant found R&M, indeed, was a job shop. The company specialized in two fields. The minor product line was textile machinery. This included bale breakers, cards, garnetts, blenders, and other special-purpose machines. These were ordered and built one at a time, and in some instances four or five of a type were released for production. The major product line consisted of drying machinery of all types from small soap dryers 4 feet wide by 3 feet deep by 4 feet high to chemical powder dryers $6 \times 10 \times 8$ feet to tobacco dryers $15 \times 60 \times 15$ feet to instant-coffee drying towers $12 \times 12 \times 60$ feet high. All the dryers were custom built. A large quantity order would be for perhaps six tobacco dryers of the same type and size. With the exception of the small soap dryers, all the dryers were erected on the factory floor, checked for operating characteristics, adjacent parts identified and marked for reassembly, dismantled, packed, and shipped for erection in the customers' plants.

The consultant appraised the performances of the factory employees and found that those on piece rates were performing at approximately 70 percent of standard while those on daywork ranged between 50 and 70 percent of standard. He found there were no piece rates in the assembly areas. The bulk of the piece rates applied to machine shop and woodshop departments plus some fabricating operations such as punch press, shear, and power brake work. Many of the piece rates had been set years ago and applied in recent years on a "similar to" basis. The manufacturing operations were specified but with almost no detail. For example, cutting speeds and feeds were not shown, nor the number of roughing and finishing cuts. No piece rates existed for setup work. And the factory supervision had resorted to paying average earnings to the employees when piece rates were not available. Obviously, the incentive plan had been allowed to deteriorate to the point where it was of little or no value to the company or to the employees.

VITAL CONCEPTS FOR NEW PLAN

The consultant's analysis of the situation indicated that substantial opportunities were present for increasing productivity and reducing cost provided certain action could be taken. He reviewed his thinking at length with the vice president, the director of employee relations, and the director of manufacturing. From these discussions a plan evolved, the vital concepts of which included:

1. The plan should provide the opportunity to all factory production employees to increase their earnings substantially, as much as 25 to 35 percent for example.

2. The hourly rates paid to the employees should be evaluated carefully, taking into consideration the experience, skill, responsibilities, and working conditions demanded by each job classification.

3. The hourly wage rate structure should be competitive with the going rates paid in the Philadelphia area for similar job classifications.

4. Standard time data should be developed for all factory operations from time-studies taken in the plant.

5. The timestudy people should be selected from within the company and trained in the techniques necessary to build reliable standard time data.

6. The standard time data should be arranged and compiled into consolidated charts and tables so that, even under the job shop conditions, the coverage of time standards should exceed 75 percent in all departments.

7. The time standards should be set separately for setup (including teardown) and for production per piece or per assembly.

8. The time standards should be guaranteed but they should be changed when bona fide changes in machines, tools, methods, or materials were made.

9. Additional allowances, called expense standards, should be set from the standard time data when extra work is required because of irregular conditions.

10. Under no circumstances should average earnings be paid, since the time standards were the only measure to be used for rewarding the employees for extra output.

11. The new job-evaluated wage rate structure and the new time standards should be applied simultaneously. The existing hourly rates and the piece rates should be maintained in each department until the new wage rates and time standards were ready to be applied.

12. The total program should be engineered soundly and due to the complexities of the operation could be expected to take 2 to 3 years to complete.

13. The new program should be installed on a department-by-department basis so that the benefits to the employees and to the company would begin to be evident at an early date.

14. The midpoint of the hourly rate range for each job classification should be used to convert the standard minutes produced into incentive earnings.

15. Under all conditions the employees should be guaranteed their personal hourly rates plus overtime premiums and shift differentials for all time worked.

16. The employees should clock separately all work done not on time standards, and all waiting and indirect time so that they could be paid their personal hourly rates for this time off standard.

17. The foremen and the indirect employees under each foreman should be given an opportunity to earn incentives also.

18. The factory management and supervision should prepare for the installation of the new program by repairing machines and tools in advance of the application of the time standards in each department.

The plan was written out in detail (See Standard Practice OU-2, Chapter 15) and reviewed by the corporate officers. Following their approval, the plan was submitted formally to the union in a meeting with the shop committee. Aspects of the plan had been discussed informally with members of the shop committee and with some of the foremen prior to this. Several days later the shop committee asked the management to explain the program to the factory employees. This was done in an employee assembly by the vice president and the consulting engineer. The question-and-answer period was lively and constructive. At the next union meeting, the employees voted to accept the entire program.

SELECTION AND INTENSIVE TRAINING OF TIMESTUDY PEOPLE

Upon acceptance by the employees, the director of employee relations immediately posted a notice inviting all employees interested in being trained to do timestudy work to apply to the personnel department. Twenty-one employees were interested. The applicants were asked to complete a record of their work experience at R&M, and this information along with their personnel folders was reviewed by the vice president and the consulting engineer. The applicants were required to take three tests as follows:

1. The Otis Employment Test, a general knowledge test

2. The Bennett Mechanical Comprehension Test

3. The Moore Arithmetic Test

The consulting engineer interviewed all applicants individually. As part of each interview, the consultant explained the program in detail. This was time well spent since, even though only six people were to be selected at the time for timestudy training, there were fifteen employees in the factory who had a better understanding of the program. Also, these employees were told that they would be reconsidered as the program expanded and the need for additional timestudy people arose. The initial group of six selected included one sheetmetal worker, two machinists, two assemblers, and one shop dispatcher. The caliber of those interviewed and selected was so good that this process for uncovering talent was repeated three times over the next 3 years. Their knowledge of the shop was invaluable to the success of the program.

The consulting engineer trained the new recruits by intensive instruction, drill, and tests in how to break down an operation into small elements of work; how to read and snap back a stopwatch properly; how to rate employee performances; how to compile comparison sheets; how to analyze constant and variable elemental time values; how to prepare curves, formulas, charts, and tables into standard time data; how to set time standards for setup and production; and, perhaps most important of all, how to conduct themselves in the shop so as to gain the cooperation of the employees and the respect of the foremen. Phil Carroll's well-known book *Timestudy for Cost Control** served as the text for the program.

INSTALLING THE NEW PLAN IN THE FIRST DEPARTMENT

It was decided to begin the timestudies in the woodshop. The woodshop operations were somewhat simpler than those in other departments, and some of the work was repetitive, such as the making of slats for conveyor aprons. These operations were good for breaking in the timestudy trainees. There were thirty-four different types of operations for which standard time data was established, such as laying out, drilling, ripsawing, planing, joining, sticker shaping, pinning, sanding, and others. Exhibit 6-1 shows the front of the standards record for joining with all of the elements of work for setting up and running the joiner. By selecting the elements required to complete an operation, a time standard can be set for any joining work. The standard setter must think out the method and must select the proper elemental time values, however. Exhibit 6-2 is the back of the same sheet. Here the methods for operating the joiner have been standardized. Almost anyone can set a standard from these

* Phil Carroll, *Timestudy for Cost Control,* 3d ed., McGraw-Hill Book Company, New York, 1954.

EXHIBIT 6-1

SUMMARY OF ELEMENTAL TIME VALUES FOR SETTING TIME STANDARDS FOR JOINING OPERATION.

STANDARDS RECORD   JOINER

Order, Acct. No.	Sheet	Item	Part Desc.		Dwg. Symbol, Part No.	B/P Issue No.
Material & Size				Dept.	Operation No. of	Machine
Date	By	No. of men	%NWT	Std. Min Per Pc. & Job Gr.	StdMin/Setup & JobGr.	
Operation Description					Feed	Speed	Tooling

Ele No.	Name of Element	Std. Min.	Occ.	Std. Min. Allowed	Ele No.	Name of Element	Std. Min.	Occ.	Std. Min. Allowed
306	PU & place on table 4' .050 + .0005L"				801	Clock in & out (65')	2.30		
322	Momentary Inspection of edge	.05			802	Read Instructions	1.00		
					827	Position loaded truck 10'	.36		
315	Walk back with plank .008 + .0005L"				828	Position empty truck 10'	.29		
					829	Move loaded truck 30',	.50		
307	Position part before joining .025 + .00014L"				830	Move loaded truck .04 + .012D'			
323	Cutting Time/inch:				831	Turn Truck 90°	.07		
	Soft wood 1/16"-.0026"				851	Start & stop joiner	.12		
	Soft wood 1/8" -.0031"				845	Get & return tools (80')	1.60		
	Soft wood 3/16"-.0040"				852	Adjust height of table	.30		
	Hard wood 1/16"-.0031"				866	Adjust joiner Str. edge to use different part of knife	.35		
	Hard wood 1/8"-.0040"								
324	Push plank into joiner blade	.015			868	Reposition guard	.035		
325	Return for extra cut, slide over table (1' fwd. 2' back)	.047			869	Check with rule for dimension	.07		
					861	Brush chips aside	.05	3	
					824	Check with keyman	1.00		
326	Set pc. aside .035 + .0005L"				862	Measure with steel tape	.07	3	
					823	Check length of part with rule or Dwg.	.50		
					867	Free board from pile	.075		
	Total					Total			
	Use					Use			

charts. All that needs to be known is the length of the board, the depth of cut, and the kind of wood used. Throughout the program hundreds of charts of this type had to be prepared in order to simplify the setting of standards. In this way greater consistency in the standards was achieved, and the standard setting was fast enough to be economical for job shop operation. Exhibit 6-3 is an example of charts standardizing

EXHIBIT 6-2

TYPICAL CHARTS DESIGNED TO SIMPLIFY AND SPEED UP STANDARD SETTING FOR JOINING.

JOINER
HANDLING

Std. Mins.	Occ.	Std. Mins. Allow.

One Man Operation
Plank 84" & under

Two Man Operation
Plank 85" & over

STD. MINUTES PER PIECE

Length in Inches	No. of Cuts				Length in Inches	No. of Cuts			
	1	2	3	4		1	2	3	4
23.0	.21	.30	.40	.48	85	..32	.47	.62	.76
39.6	.23	.33	.42	.51	105	.35	.51	.67	.83
56.5	.26	.35	.45	.54	127	.39	.56	.74	.91
76.0	.27	.38	.48	.57	151	.43	.62	.81	.99
84.0	.30	.40	.49	.59	177	.47	.68	.88	1.08
					208	.52	.74	.97	1.19

JOINING

Cutting Knife 5/32" thick, 3300 RPM free running
Soft Wood—Bass, Poplar, Pine, Cypress.
Hard Wood—Ash, Maple & Oak.

STD. MINUTES PER CUT

Wood	Soft	Soft	Hard	Soft	Hard
Length in Inches	1/16	1/8	1/16	3/16	1/8
12.	.031	.037			.048
13.	.034	.041			.053
14.	.038	.045			.058
16.	.041	.049			.064
17.	.045	.055			.070
19.	.050	.060			.076
21.	.055	.066			.083
23.	.060	.072			.091
25.	.066	.079			.100
27.	.072	.087			.110
30.	.079	.095			.120
33.	.087	.105			.131
36.	.095	.115			.145
39.	.104	.126			.16
43.	.114	.138			.17
47.	.125	.152			.19
52.	.137	.166			.21
57.	.150	.182			.22
63.	.165	.199			.25
69.	.182	.22			.28
75.	.20	.24			.30
83.	.22	.26			.33
91.	.24	.29			.36
100.	.26	.31			.40
110.	.29	.34			.44
120.	.30	.38			.48
132.	.34	.41			.53
145.	.38	.45			.58
159.	.42	.50			.64
174.	.45	.55			.70
190.	.50	.60			.76
208.	.54	.66			.83

	Std. Mins.	Occ.	Std. Mins. Allow.
Total			
Use			

EXHIBIT 6-3

CHART PREPARED TO STANDARDIZE METHODS AND FACILITATE STANDARDS SETTING FOR LAYOUT AND ASSEMBLY OF SPECIAL CONVEYOR APRONS.

LAYOUT APRONS

Std. Mins. for Layout canvas, Glue belts,
Fasten to table, Free from table, Punch holes.

					No.	Belts						Std. Mins.	Occ.	Std. Allwd.
Apron Length in ft.	1	2	3	4	5	6	7	8	9	10				
3	16.35	18.78	21.22	23.65	26.07	28.52	30.92	33.34	35.82	38.16				
4	17.21	19.88	22.53	25.17	27.85	30.55	33.75	35.85	38.45	41.33				
5.5	18.54	21.57	24.58	27.62	30.62	33.62	36.66	39.72	42.72	45.54				
6.9	19.76	23.11	26.46	29.81	33.16	36.53	39.81	43.21	46.61	49.93				
8.5	21.19	24.91	28.66	32.36	36.06	39.86	43.56	47.26	51.06	54.77				
10.3	22.75	26.93	31.09	35.24	39.39	43.59	47.79	51.99	56.09	60.22				
12.3	24.53	29.15	33.79	38.49	43.09	47.69	52.39	57.09	61.79	66.15				
14.5	26.49	31.74	36.82	41.92	47.12	52.32	57.52	62.72	67.82	72.70				
16.7	28.42	34.09	39.73	45.43	51.13	56.83	62.53	68.23	73.83	79.75				
19.3	30.71	37.00	43.35	49.60	56.00	62.20	68.60	74.90	81.20	87.60				
22.2	33.27	40.28	47.28	54.18	61.28	68.18	75.17	82.38	89.08	96.20				
25.5	36.15	43.87	51.67	59.57	67.17	74.97	82.87	90.57	98.37	106.29				
29.1	39.32	47.89	56.49	65.19	73.69	82.39	90.73	99.69	108.35	117.03				
32.6	42.60	52.03	61.53	71.03	80.53	90.03	99.43	108.93	118.33	127.75				

Add for width of Apron														
Width in ft.	1	2	3	4	5	6	7	8	9	10				
Std. Mins.	.34	.67	1.05	1.34	1.67	2.04	2.34	2.68	3.01	3.35				

Add for punching rivet holes
.023 Std. mins. per hole for total number of rivets

Add for each 6' Apron length beyond first 12'
Number of Belts

	1	2	3	4	5	6	7	8	9	10				
Std. Mins. Per 6' Section	.75	1.14	1.53	1.92	2.31	2.70	3.09	3.48	3.87	4.26				

Add for make apron endless and fasten to table

No. of Belts	1	2	3	4	5	6	7	8	9	10				
Std. Mins.	11.22	12.43	13.64	14.86	16.07	17.27	18.47	19.67	20.90	22.11				

Subtract from total if necessary to set separate Std.
for free from table, punch holes, make endless and fasten to platform

$$\text{Std. Mins} = 11.17 + .20L' + .21W' + 1.33B + .023H$$

W' = Width of Apron in feet
L' = Length of Apron in feet
B = Number of Belts
H = Number of Holes

Total

Use

the layout of conveyor aprons. This is an interesting set of charts because of a controversy that arose.

There were thirty-one people in the woodshop, including direct employees, laborers, clerks, and the foreman. Two of the direct employees who had worked there a long time and were, undoubtedly, the most skillful all around, served as unofficial working leaders. Robert J., was good on the machine work. Kenneth M., the second man, knew the manual operations. As the work orders arrived in the woodshop, the foreman would sort the job tickets and give Bob and Ken the tickets that applied to their types of work. In addition to their productive work, Bob and Ken assigned work to the other direct workers. This was an informal arrangement that made the foreman's job easier. The job tickets showed the piece rate for each operation and were used later to calculate the piecework earnings of the men. The timestudy trainees had been instructed not to look at any job tickets, piece rates, or old cost records. The reason for this was to maintain complete objectivity in their timestudy work. Further, it was important should a question ever arise on this point that the timestudy people honestly could say no reference to the piece rates or past records had been made in setting the new time standards. Thus, the consulting engineer and the timestudy people were unaware of how Bob and Ken were manipulating the payroll.

The new standards were applied on a Monday morning. This event had been announced to the woodshop employees several days before by the foreman. At the beginning of the shift that first Monday, the vice president, the consulting engineer, and the timestudy people met in the woodshop with the employees. The purpose of the meeting was to briefly describe the new job-evaluated rates and the new wage incentive plan, to explain that the new plan would be introduced gradually starting with only six workers, so that the timestudy people could give the employees on standard as much personal attention as necessary, to spell out the timekeeping and counting procedures, and, of course, to generate enthusiasm for performing well on the new standards. For example, it was explained that the standards were set so that a 100 percent performance on standard equaled the job rate, and that for each 1 percent above 100 percent performance the employees would be paid a premium of 1 percent of the job rate. It was pointed out the average skilled employee was expected to perform at approximately 133 percent and earn a 33 percent premium over the job rate for the time on standard. It was made clear this was the average that was expected to be attained ultimately and that individual employee performances would be below and above this average, some as low as 110 percent and a few as high as 160 percent.

The new wage incentive plan got off to a good start. Several employees earned a premium during the first week. This encouraged other employees in the woodshop to want to work on the new standards. However, two employees, Bob and Ken, were not very happy. It quickly came to light that for years they had maintained a bank of completed job tickets. Each week they turned in to payroll enough tickets to let each of the other employees earn a little extra while they inflated their own earnings to the point they thought would be acceptable to the company. The new wage incentive plan effectively stopped this practice. Thus, when Bob and Ken were given the new stand-ards to work to, their initial performances were well below 100 percent. This was a serious turn of events. Up to this point the performances and incentive earnings of the woodshop employees caused employees in other departments to look favorably on the new wage incentive plan. Suddenly, the two most skillful men in the woodshop couldn't make standard. The timestudy people knew from their studies that Bob and Ken could outperform the other employees, but no amount of check studies or explanations would get them to really go to work. The situation was explained to the union shop committee, but nothing changed. Questions about the fairness of the new standards were being raised all over the plant. Finally, in a meeting with the shop committee, the chairperson of the union asked the consulting engineer if he would personally make a check study on Ken laying out conveyor aprons with the union chairperson, vice-chairperson, and the head of the grievance committee present. The consulting engineer agreed, and arrangements for the check were made with the foreman of the woodshop.

The check study was made as planned. Ken performed very well, although he did some extra work that was unnecessary. This was pointed out to the union committee. During the study the chairperson of the union asked the consultant how he rated Ken's performance. About 130 percent was the answer. At the completion of the study, while still at Ken's layout bench, the consulting engineer compared the total standard time allowed for the aprons Ken had produced with the actual time he had taken, made adjustments for the unnecessary work and for the fact that Ken had not used any of the rest factor allowed in the standards, and calculated Ken's overall performance during the study. It was 128 percent! The chairperson of the union called Ken over, explained the results, and said, "Ken, there's nothing wrong with the standards. Just make up your mind to go to work." The very next day Ken's performance was 122 percent and it gradually improved to the 140 to 150 percent range. This had a good influence on Bob, too. Ultimately, he was performing in the 160 to 170 percent range. The two men were the top performers in the woodshop. Now they could prove it. They were earning their extra pay, not manipulating it with a pencil. This single incident had a salutary effect on the rest of the factory employees. The new job rates and the new wage incentive plan were firmly established. The question now was how quickly the program could be installed in the machine shop, the fabricating departments, and the assembly areas.

Exhibit 6-4 itemizes some examples of the increased productivity gained from the installation of the new time standards, and in combination with the new job rates, the decrease in direct labor costs. The overall weighted average showed productivity increased about 112 percent and direct labor costs were reduced approximately 43 percent. The average earned rate per hour of the direct employees increased 10.5 percent during the first four months of the new program. These earnings per hour gradually increased more than 24 percent as the employees' performances improved and the coverage of standards increased. These results were all documented in a report prepared for the vice president by the controller, the manager of standards, and the consulting engineer.

EXPANDING THE PLAN INTO THE MACHINE SHOP

As soon as practical, timestudies were started in the machine shop. One timestudy person remained in the woodshop to set standards and administer the wage incentive

EXHIBIT 6-4

TYPICAL EXAMPLES OF IMPROVEMENTS ACHIEVED
WITH NEW WAGE INCENTIVE PLAN IN THE WOODSHOP.

Type of work & name of item	Ratio of Production on Standard to output on former piece rates	Increase in Productivity, %	Decrease in Direct Labor Cost, %
1. Ripsawing			
Cork	1.36	36.0	21.3
Slat	1.47	47.0	28.3
2. Lathe operations (including straighten, turn, face, groove, counterbore, sand rings, polish, flute, and sling balance)			
Roll	1.54	54.0	32.2
Roll	1.24	24.0	(1.3)
Roll	2.16	116.0	45.7
Roll	2.82	182.0	62.4
Drum	1.65	65.0	38.2
Head	2.48	148.0	51.0
3. Assemble rolls (including cutoff lags, join lags, prepare heads, and assemble)			
Roll	1.24	24.0	15.7
Drum	.92	(8.0)	(1.7)
Cylinder	1.47	47.0	34.9
4. Apron making (including cut off and sand slats, drill slats, prepare belts, lay out canvas, and assemble)			
Apron	1.65	65.0	34.5
Apron	2.37	137.0	54.5
Apron	1.84	84.0	41.5
Apron	3.40	240.0	67.0
5. Woodshop Average	2.12	112.0	43.0

plan. One timestudy person was made foreman of a department, and the other four moved into the machine shop. In addition, four trainees were added to the program. At this point it was decided that the timestudy people and the new trainees needed intensive training in machine shop practice. The chief manufacturing engineer prepared a training program and several of the manufacturing engineers conducted the training sessions. The program included the following:

1. Shop terminology (see Exhibit 6-5)

2. Basic functions of all machine tools and definition and identification of all major working parts of each type of machine

3. Explanation of all standard cutting tools

EXHIBIT 6-5

SAMPLE PAGE EXPLAINING MACHINE SHOP
TERMINOLOGY FOR TRAINING PURPOSES.

SHOP TERMINOLOGY

The following is a list of commonly used Shop Terms with definitions. In most instances these terms explain work to be done and frequently are used in operation descriptions, for example: Bore 3.250" ± .005" dia. to 1.500" ± .005" depth.

F.

Face	—To machine a flat surface as in the Handscrew or Lathe.
Face-plate	—The plate or disc that screws on the nose of a lathe or other machine spindle and drives or carries work to be turned or bored. Sometimes applies to table of vertical boring mill.
Feather edge	—A fine burr or sliver of metal.
Feed	—The advance of the work or the cutting tool expressed in terms of inches per minute or thousandths of an inch per revolution of the spindle.
Fillet	—A nicely rounded inside corner. Fillets are used on cast objects to provide a stronger corner and because corners are hard to cast sharp.
Finish bore	—To bore to blueprint requirements.
Finish cut teeth	—The finishing of the gear teeth to blueprint specifications.
Finish face	—To face to blueprint specifications.
Finish grind	—Smooth grind finish to the size called for on the blueprint.
Finish mill	—To finish a milled face by the use of milling cutters to the blueprint size.
Finish radius	—A radius finished to the size and smoothness called for on the blueprint.
First piece inspector	—An inspector who checks the first piece of the set-up man and the operator in order to make sure that the machine is properly set up. The first piece should be marked with his stamp or tagged to indicate approval.
Fixture	—A device for holding and positioning work while it is being machined or gaged.

(continued)

---

4. Explanation of all usual types of work-holding tools and their basic designs

5. Inspection and measuring tools and instruments

6. Machinability of metals and corresponding feeds and speeds

7. Nonmetal cutting processes such as heat treating, plating, cleaning, anodizing

8. Welding and flame-cutting principles

Again, standard time data was compiled from an analysis of the elemental time values obtained during the timestudies. This data covered all types of machines in the machine shop, including hand-screw machines, bench lathes, turret lathes, engine lathes, drill presses, radial drills, surface grinders, cylindrical grinders, vertical turret lathes, vertical and horizontal milling machines, gear cutters, and others. Exhibit 6-6 shows how these elemental times were combined and arranged on a standards record to facilitate setting setup standards for milling machine operations. Exhibit 6-7 is the back of the same standards record. This was used to set the standard time per piece for the operations and to itemize the cutting specifications in detail. Then all the information was summarized on the front of the sheet, and the standards were issued. Here again, the standard setting procedure was simplified and speeded up considerably by standardizing the methods for various operations regularly performed on a variety of types and sizes of bearings, shafts, journals, gears, sprockets, collars, and similar parts. By doing this, it was possible to further consolidate the elemental time values such as shown in Exhibit 6-8 for setting standards for machining bearings. In this case, all that needs to be known to set both the setup standard and the standard per piece is the material, the bore diameter, and the length of the bearing.

The improvement achieved in the machine shop is shown in Table 6-1.

MOVE ON TO FABRICATING AND ASSEMBLY DEPARTMENTS

Following the successful installation of the program in the machine shop, the new job rates and the new wage incentive plan were extended throughout the fabricating departments and the subassembly, and final assembly departments. The results continued to be good. Productivity increased handsomely in every department, direct labor costs were reduced, and employees' earnings increased. Ultimately, more than 75 percent of the direct labor in this large job shop was worked on standard.

FOREMEN REWARDED FOR CONTROLLING COSTS

Two additional features of the program were the use of a labor analysis sheet (see Exhibit 14-5) and a foreman's bonus plan (see Standard Practices OU-1 and OU-9 in Chapter 15). The labor analysis sheet summarized pertinent operating statistics for each factory department each week. This was information each foreman needed in order to control and reduce labor costs within his or her department. The salaries and wages of all employees in the department including the foreman's salary were reported in relation to the output as measured in standard hours of salable product produced. Thus, the cost per standard hour of salable product showed the foreman what the actual cost was week by week. A reference period cost per standard hour, which was immediately before the new program was installed in the department, and a standard cost per standard hour were shown also. In this way the foreman knew cost-wise where he or she was, how much progress had been made in reducing departmental cost, and how far had to be gone to operate at standard costs. The foremen's bonus plan was designed to encourage each foreman and to reward him or her in relation to the results achieved in improving the operation of the department.

EXHIBIT 6-6

STANDARDS RECORD FOR SETTING SETUP STANDARDS FOR MILLING MACHINES.

	STANDARDS RECORD					MILLING MACHINES		

Part & Operation Description						Dwg. Symbol No.	B/P Issue No.

						Dept.	Opera. No.	Machine No.

Date	By	Material & Size	No. Men	% NWT	S.Mins./Pc.	Job Grade	S.Mins/S.U.	Job Grade

SET-UP ELEMENTS	Std. Mins.	No.	Std. Min. All.	SET-UP ELEMENTS	Std. Min.	No.	Std. Min. All.
GENERAL				Total brought forward			
Change clock time	2.5			MACHINE ADJUSTMENTS			
Get & return tools to crib	4.0			Arbor in main spindle	3.6		
Clean machine 1st No. lub.	2.3			Arbor from rack to table	.5		
1st with lub.	3.8			Spacing collars & arbor nut	3.0		
Subsequent No lub.	1.0			Cutters on horizontal arbor			
Subsequent with lub.	2.0			1 cutter	4.0		
Read blueprint—Job class 8	2.0			2 cutters	7.0		
Job class 6 & 7	4.0			3 cutters	10.0		
Job class 5	6.0			4 cutters	15.0		
Get 1st pc. inspected Class 8	2.0			Set cuts one dimension	3.0		
Class 6 & 7	4.0			two dimensions	6.0		
Class 5	6.0			Taper shank cutter with draw rod	1.5		
TABLEWORK				Taper shank cutter no draw rod	.5		
P&R rack to table by hand				Taper shank cutter in collet	.2		
Fixtures, vises, etc. 0-35 lbs.	.5			Adapter collet & cutter in spindle	1.9		
35-65 lbs.	1.0			Stub arbor in main spindle	1.5		
P&R rack to table by hoist				Cutter on stub arbor	1.5		
Fixtures, vises, etc.	4.6			Arbor adapter bolted to hose	3.5		
P&R jack, blocks	1.0			Face mill cutter bolted to hose	3.5		
P&R support for long pieces	2.0			Arbor or adapter in vert. head	1.5		
Key vise, index head, etc. to table	.5			Cutter on arbor in vert. head	1.5		
Change vise jaws and adjust	3.5			Taper shank cutter in vert. head	1.7		
Clamp to table by following				Vertical milling attachment P&R	11.0		
One bolt & washer	.5			Change feed & speed — belt	1.0		
Two bolts & washers	.9			motor	.5		
One bolt & strap, gooseneck or F.C.	1.4			Set trip dog or table stop	1.0		
Two bolts & strap, gooseneck or F.C.	2.0			Set dial to zero and lock	.5		
Three bolts & strap, gooseneck or F.C.	2.5			LINE UP	.006	.005	
Four bolts & strap, gooseneck or F.C.	3.0				& over	& under	
P&R strap, gooseneck, etc.	1.3			By scale	.15	.20	
Blocks—select end position	.5			By square	1.80	2.30	
C-Clamp—locate & adjust	.5			By surf. gage	1.90	2.40	
DIVIDING HEAD				By level	2.15	2.65	
P&R index plt. & adjust sector	3.8			CHECK 1ST PIECE			
Crank extension handle	1.5			With micrometer	.5		
Swivel head to angle & return	1.5			With height gauge	1.0		
Change gears for spiral work	5.0			With scale	.2		
P&R chuck or face plate	3.0			Try Go & No-Go plug gauge			
Dog center in index head	2.0			Up to 1″ dia.	.2		
Collet in index head	2.0			Over 1″ dia.	.3		
MISCELLANEOUS							
Coolant piping, position & replace	1.0						
Mark with chalk	.5			Total Set-Up			
Shims get & check	1.0						
				Machine Adjustments			
				Place & Remove			
Sub Total				Cutting Standard			
				Total Standard			

EXHIBIT 6-7

BACK OF STANDARDS RECORD FOR MILLING MACHINES USED TO SET PRODUCTION STANDARDS.

Machine Adjustments	Std. Mins.	No.	Std. All.	Place & Remove	Std. Mins.	No.	Std. All
Start & stop machine spindle	.06			Wt. of Floor Table to			
Change feed, engage power feed	.06			Piece to table Jig or Fixt.			
Change speed	.12			0–1 .12			
Change feed & speed	.18			1–5 .13 .18			
Run piece to cutter by hand	.10			6–20 .26 .37			
Set table to dial reading	.27			21–45 .41 .56			
Raise table to depth of cut	.09			46–65 .70 .92			
Raise or lower table to load	.14			Over 65 3.75 4.65			
Change cutter in adapter	1.00			In & out of vise from table			
Run table back to loading position				Wt. of No. of Pieces			
or advance between cuts				Piece 1 2 4 6 8 10 12			

Table Travel	S.Hand Trav.	R.Hand Trav.	Plain Mill	Dup-lex
0–.9	.09		.03	.03
1–1.9	.14		.04	.03
2–2.9	.19		.05	.04
3–4.9	.30	.12	.07	.05
5–6.9	.40	.19	.09	.06
7–8.9	.50	.22	.11	.07
9–11	.60	.26	.13	.08
12–13	.70	.29	.15	.09
14–15	.81	.33	.17	.10
16–17	.91	.36	.19	.11
18–20	1.06	.41	.22	.13
21–24	1.26	48	.26	.15

Place & Remove (right column, continued):

	Std. Mins.
0–1 .08 .13 .18 .23 .28 .33 .38	
1–5 .14 .24 .34 .44 .54 .64 .74	
6–20 .27	
21–45 .42	
T. & L. vise by hand Up to 1 lb.	.06
1 to 5 lbs.	.12
6 to 20 lbs.	.17
21 to 45 lbs.	.23
T. & L. vise by hammer	.27
Hammer pieces into position	.18
4 Jaw universal chuck	.28
Turn work in vise Up to 5 lbs.	.05
6 to 15 lbs.	.08
16 to 30 lbs.	.12
31 to 45 lbs.	.18
"C" clamps hand tightened	.26
"C" clamps wrench tightened	.40
Packing for "C" clamp	.07
U-strap, gooseneck or finger clamp	
T. & L. and move aside	.41
U-strap gooseneck or finger clamp	
T. & L. and remove complete	.55
Hex, square, or allen nut each	.20
two	.34
Short locating screw each	.11
two	.14
Long locating screw each	.22
two	.28
Wingnut or wingscrew each	.08
two	.11
Thumbscrew with pliers each	.17
two	.28
Screw with screw driver	.21
Wedge or shims (per spot)	.25
Jack screws no lock nut	.30
Jack screws with lock nut	.39
Dividing head (see data)	

CLEANING

	Std. Mins.
Brush or wipe piece (dry)	.10
Brush or wipe piece (wet)	.15
Clean off table 0-10 lbs.	.15
11-20 lbs.	.30
Over 20 lbs.	.60
Wash work in kerosene	.65

MISCELLANEOUS

	Std. Mins.
Loosen screw to relieve strain	.10
Loosen clamp to relieve strain	.20
Loosen clamp to relieve strain over 20 lbs.	.40
Stamping per digit	.10
Apply oil on cutter	.07
Chalking for mating parts	.05
Chalking for scribing	.07
Chalking for surface gaging	.15
Scribing par line	.15
Coolant turn off and on	.15

Burring (see data)
Gauging (see data)

Burr with file surf.	1	2	3	4	5
std.	.06	.10	.14	.18	.22
Gage	1/1	1/2	1/5	1/10	
Scale	.20	.10	.04	.02	
Depth Mic.	.40	.20	.08	.04	

Total

Type of Cut	Dia. of Cutter	No. of Teeth	Depth of Cut	Ft. per Min.	Feed	RPM	Approach	Length of Cut	Table Travel	Std. per In.	Cutting Standard
								Total			

EXHIBIT 6-8

TYPICAL CHART DESIGNED TO FACILITATE STANDARDS SETTING FOR SPECIFIC CLASSES OF PARTS AND OPERATIONS—IN THIS CASE, BEARINGS.

DEPT.	DATE	DESC.					DWG. NO.			
81			BEARING				GS #81			

MACH.	BY						PER PC.	S.U.		
13, 22, 23 LT		DIA. 15/16″ – 3 7/16″ C.I. & BRONZE LENGTH 3″ – 7 1/4″					SEE BELOW	EA. 0.0	1ST 12.0	

CHUCK ON O.D.	LENGTH″			BORE DIAMETER″				
FACE SIDE	FROM TO	15/16 1-	1-1/16 1-1/4	1-5/16 1-3/4	1-13/16 2-1/2	2-9/16 3-	3-1/16 3-7/16	H.S.S. TOOL
ROUGH BORE	3- 3-1/4	6.6 6.7	7.2 7.4	7.9 8.2	9.0 9.4	10.6 11.1	10.9 11.4	REAMER
FINISH BORE / DWG.	3-1/2 3-3/4	6.9 7.0	7.7 7.9	8.5 8.8	9.7 10.1	11.6 12.1	11.9 12.4	GROOVE TOOL
CLEAN GROOVES	4-1/16	7.2	8.1	9.0	10.5	12.7	13.0	
	4-3/8 4-5/8 5-	7.5 7.6 7.9	8.4 8.6 8.9	9.4 9.7 10.1	11.0 11.4 11.9	13.3 13.9 14.5	13.6 14.2 14.9	
BORE END								
REAM / DWG.	5-1/4 5-5/8	8.0 8.3	9.2 9.5	10.4 10.8	12.4 12.9	15.2 15.9	15.5 16.2	
BREAK CORNERS	6- 6-1/2 6-7/8 7-1/4	8.5 8.8 9.0 9.3	9.8 10.1 10.5 10.9	11.2 11.6 12.0 12.5	13.4 14.0 14.6 15.3	16.7 17.5 18.3 19.2	17.0 17.8 18.6 19.5	

OPER.			SPEEDS–RPM				FEEDS
FACE	458	458	458	342	199	199	.016
R.BORE	458	342	252	199	148	148	.008
F.BORE	458	342	252	199	148	148	.008
REAM	342	252	199	148	199	199	H
CT'B	458	342	252	199	148	148	.015
GROOVE	458	342	252	199	148	148	H

ADD EXTRA:	PER PC.	S. U.
FOR EACH DIFFERENT BORE SIZE	0.0	18.0

The weekly factors used to calculate each foreman's bonus were as follows:

1. Percent performance
2. Percent on standard
3. Percent excess costs
4. Percent capacity used

TABLE 6-1

	Department				
Factor	Turret lathe	Engine lathe	Milling machines	Drill presses	Cylinder fitting
Ratio production on standard to output on former piece rates	1.32	1.61	1.96	1.31	1.56
Increase in direct labor productivity	32%	61%	96%	31%	56%
Decrease in direct labor cost with new standards and new job rates	16%	29%	46%	29%	34%
Increase in earned rate per hour in first four months*	24%	22%	11%	19%	13%

* The earned rate per hour in time was expected to increase more than 25% as performances and coverage improved.

The foremen did a superb job in improving the operation of their departments. They all earned bonuses every week. For example, the woodshop foreman earned a low of 4.8 percent and a high of 11.4 percent of his base salary during the first year of the plan; 11.9 to 18.9 percent in his second year, and 14.4 to 20.3 percent in his third year. The engine lathe foreman earned 13.5 to 15.9 percent in the first year and 18.9 to 24.3 percent in the second year. The turret lathe foreman earned 18.5 to 20.2 percent in the first year and 23.9 to 28.8 percent in the second year. Thus, the foremen had a vital interest in the new program and were rewarded in relation to the operating results they achieved. These results are tabulated in Exhibit 6-9. This summary shows the productivity of the woodshop employees increased about 150 percent over a 3-year period. The machine shop employees increased their productivity approximately 66 percent in 2 years. These improvements in productivity are based on the reduction achieved in the total cost of departmental salaries and wages per standard hour of salable product produced.

THE CONSULTANT'S SUMMARY

The consulting engineer's report to the vice president summed up the program as follows:

> The management, the plant supervision, the union shop committee, and the Standards Department personnel are all to be commended for their contribution to the successful operation of the New Wage Incentive Plan, and the very substantial benefits obtained since its installation.

> It is important to point out that the reductions in cost represent the combined efforts of the various staff and operating departments throughout the plant since increased productivity, new methods, new tooling, new equipment, more complete engineering information, reductions in indirect costs, and closer and better supervision all contributed to the total result. The Standards Department provided the measurement—the basis for the control of the costs.

EXHIBIT 6-9

OPERATING RESULTS ACHIEVED
WITH NEW AGE INCENTIVE PLAN.

Departments and Periods	Employee Perform- ance, %	On Standard, %	Capacity Used, %	Department Excess Costs, %	Department Cost Reduction, %	Increase in Produc- tivity,* %
1. Woodshop						
Reference	47	0	46	124	0	0
1st Year	129	84	57	36	46	85
2nd Year	138	66	72	15	55	121
3rd Year	135	75	56	0	60	150
2. Machine Shop						
Reference	86	0	61	73	0	0
1st Year	129	49	82	42	20	24
2nd Year	131	75	58	3	40	66

* Based on reduction in total cost of salaries and wages per standard hour of salable product produced.

The progress made has been very gratifying, and demonstrates what can be accomplished when an organization with manufacturing "know how" applies the necessary time and effort to a management program designed to reduce and control costs.

WHAT WAS LEARNED

Some of the conclusions that can be drawn from the Rector & Montgomery experience would include the following:

1. Measurement is needed in job shop operations, perhaps more than in mass production.

2. A wage incentive plan is a delicate management tool. It needs to be handled with expertise and requires continual management attention.

3. The standard hour of salable product produced is the best common denominator for measuring productivity and controlling costs.

4. Formulas, charts, and simplified standard setting procedures are needed to raise the productivity of the standards department too.

5. The training of timestudy people should be intensive and thorough for best results.

6. A major change in wages and output must be soundly conceived, carefully introduced, and properly administered in order to gain full acceptance by the employees.

7. The "pull" of wage incentives is much more effective than the "push" of supervision.

8. Money has more appeal to more people than any other form of incentive.

9. Foremen, like their employees, perform best when they know the score and are rewarded for results.

10. Wage incentives increase the performance of a company and then sustain the increased momentum.

MEASUREMENT IS THE BEST FOUNDATION FOR CONTROL, REWARDS, AND PROGRESS

7

Triple Thrust Creativity Builds a Business

About 10 percent of students really like mathematics, another 10 percent abhor it. The other 80 percent put up with mathematics with varying degrees of boredom, disinterest, and success. That it doesn't have to be this way was proved 10 years ago by the president of Creative Publications, Incorporated. A physical education major who took a mathematics minor in college, he loved sports, enjoyed coaching, and taught mathematics because it was required by the school that employed him. Fortunately he was a very creative person and had a flair for math. Yet he found teaching mathematics almost as dull as learning it. The classrooms were stark—everything was blackboards and white chalk. The problems were old, outdated, and for the most part abstract, and few students were interested in problem solving.

Coaching seemed so much more exciting. Other subjects were made more interesting with a wide offering of materials supplementary to the textbook. These subjects offered posters, films, maps, supplementary books, and interesting historical data. How could mathematics be made a lively, living subject, too? Faced with a need to motivate his students, he accepted this challenge to his ability as a math teacher; he did something about it.

INJECTING NEW IDEAS INTO AN OLD SUBJECT

Working with other teachers in his department, he began to redesign the math curriculum. Together they started building a large mathematics library. The basic strand for the curriculum reorganization was problem solving. By using puzzles, cartoons, and making problems more interesting to students, the usual stigma attached to problem solving was lessened considerably. The school started to participate in every mathematics contest available. Some of the contests even took on a sort of carnival flair in that they included competitive chalk talks, where students would root for the speaker or contestant from their school, interesting guest speakers, refreshments, and the like. Mathematics became a popular subject with many students in this school. In fact, this transformation from a coach to a creative teacher of mathematics was completed the day his school entered 275 students in a citywide junior high school math contest, and the interest in the math contest resulted in the postponement of the city track meet scheduled for the same day.

EUREKA! EUREKA!

As part of his mathematics enrichment program he and another teacher prepared a book entitled *Eureka!*, which contained 233 cartoon characters, 315 problems, 66 geometric designs, all printed in five different colors of ink on nine different colors of paper. The *Eureka* material was field-tested for three years at the Jordan Junior High School, Palo Alto, California, where students responded enthusiastically. For example, in 1968 Jordan had the top score for a junior high school in the United States in the Mathematics Association of America (MAA) contest. Jordan scored higher than 70 percent of all senior high schools participating in the MAA contest. And with more than 50 schools and 430 students competing in a Northern California math contest, Jordan Junior High School was getting results. The students were learning mathematics faster, their comprehension improved considerably, and they enjoyed solving deductive logic, but also a test of standard curriculum concepts. The field testing at Jordan Junior High School was getting results. The students were learning mathematics faster, their comprehension improved considerably, and they enjoyed solving problems. The teachers were enthusiastic too, because their productivity had increased significantly! Teaching mathematics became much more than just a job.

SELLING AN IDEA IS NOT EASY

With this successful background, he decided to offer his material to several of the well-established textbook publishing houses. All turned him down, leery of the limited market and lack of profitability associated with supplementary materials. He formed a partnership with his mathematics secretary and a teaching colleague, and they published two posters, some line designs, and the book *Eureka!* This was proven classroom material that should be easy to sell. Not so. A year later the sales were small, and the potential profitability of this enterprise was of great concern. One partner asked to be released. He bought out the second.

After requesting and being granted a 1-year sabbatical leave by the Palo Alto School Board, he went to the business school at Stanford University in search of a new partner, one who knew something about the financial and business side of marketing a new product. There he met a young man who had graduated from Yale University and was about to receive an M.B.A. from Stanford. Between degrees this man had worked in manufacturing for 3 years with Procter and Gamble. The two men decided to work together to build the math teacher's ideas and experiences into a successful venture.

A NEW COMPANY IS FORMED

In August 1969, Creative Publications was incorporated and begun in earnest in an apartment. Some venture capital was coaxed into the company, but still the working capital was very limited for the things that had to be done. By January 1970, the staff of four people had developed a product line of thirty-seven items. *Eureka* and a new series of math books, *Aftermath,* were the mainstays. At this point the Wells Fargo Bank of Palo Alto was persuaded to lend $10,000 to the company, guaranteed by the signatures of the two officers—the math teacher and the businessman. This money was used to print and distribute a catalog to mathematics teachers all over the United States. The catalog attracted much attention and orders began to flow. Their hard work was beginning to produce results. In fact, the level of productivity of the staff during this first 7-month period probably will never be surpassed. They often worked 14 hours a day, and they were overcommitted in everything. These people were struggling for survival of an idea that was important to them. They made many fundamental business decisions, several of which proved to be correct and yet were contrary to the accepted way of doing business with schools, such as:

1. The catalog was to be the key selling medium. The established textbook companies traditionally sold through sales people and agents.

2. The selling was directed to teachers. The usual practice was to sell to the department chairpersons, curriculum directors, or school boards.

3. Initially, all products were priced below $3 so that teachers could purchase these items out of their own pockets and experiment with them before requesting larger purchases by the school systems. This proved important. Teachers, by and large, are a dedicated group and will devote their own time and money to make learning more interesting to their students.

4. Books were designed to be copied by the teachers. Permission was granted in the books for teachers to make copies of the pages. Traditional publishers did not do this, but teachers needed this kind of material.

5. In addition to their proprietary products, they would sell selected related products of other companies. A selective supermarket approach provided teachers with one place to order a variety of quality products needed for the math classroom.

6. There are tens of thousands of creative teachers, yet most textbook companies were not receptive to ideas presented by teachers in mathematics education. Creative Publications offered this opportunity. As a result, a steady flood of teacher proposals began, thus helping Creative Publications establish an image of the teacher company.

7. The basic purpose of the company was to do "what's best for the mathematics teacher," with the idea that what's best for the teacher is best for the student. Most companies selling to schools were more concerned with profits. Creative Publications reasoned that meeting the teachers' needs and solving their frustrations would eventually lead to a strong and important teacher image.

PRODUCT PROLIFERATION

Before becoming engrossed in the business side of the company, let's look at the productivity of the product development and editorial staff. This staff, headed by the

president, develops new programs, reviews the current line of products, screens all
new product ideas proposed by teachers and all new products submitted by manufacturers and publishers, selects those products that best meet Creative Publications'
objectives for the coming year, and designs the annual catalog. Exhibit 7-1 shows the
steady growth of their proprietary and nonproprietary products from 1969 through
1976. From 16 proprietary and 21 nonproprietary products in 1969 the catalog grew to
208 proprietary and 418 nonproprietary by 1974. During 1974 the entire line of
products was analyzed carefully and thoroughly, and those items not meeting Creative Publications' performance criteria were eliminated. In 1975 the growth process
was resumed but with renewed emphasis on proprietary products. The productivity of
the creative staff is difficult to quantify, because the quality and usefulness factors
inherent in the products developed and selected are so important. In the final analysis,
however, the customers measure this. Did they buy and will they continue to buy the
products? Creative Publications' sales increased steadily from $225,000 in 1970, the
first full year of operation, to $3,511,000 in 1975. This is a compounded annual growth
rate over a 5-year period of 74 percent. During the same 5 years the creative staff
increased the number of products from 99 in 1970 to 533 in 1975, a compounded rate of
increase of 40 percent per year for 5 years. Yes, the creative staff has been very

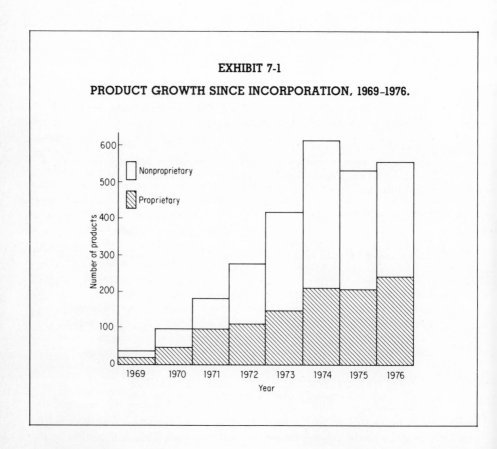

EXHIBIT 7-1

PRODUCT GROWTH SINCE INCORPORATION, 1969-1976.

productive in "serving the teachers of mathematics," and the teachers have welcomed their efforts.

Statistics usually do not reveal the total story of the productivity of a creative effort. A brief look at the way the Creative Publications' product line has been enlarged in scope and depth in 6 years is shown in the mathematics curriculum materials offered in their 1976 catalog. In this catalog Creative Publications reports: "More than 100 new products have been added to this year's catalog. Each year we attempt to provide a more complete and effective selection of quality mathematics materials for classroom teachers."

All the material developed and added since 1969 is based on the original concepts expressed in response to why *Eureka,* the first product, was published in the first place. The answer:

> All mathematics teachers know that they have a good product to sell, but too often the package is dull and uninteresting. *Eureka* is designed so that the package itself will intrigue the student to open it, taste it, and when he has discovered the fun of mathematics to come back again and again to solve the puzzles and to untangle the perplexities of mathematics. Education, we believe, can learn a lesson from the advertisers and from Madison Avenue. Let's make learning more attractive to the student through the bold use of color, design, humor and through personal identification of the student with the cartoon characters. If a student can see something of himself or his world in a problem, perhaps he will find more interest in applying himself to that problem.

THE MARKETING STRATEGY

Creative Publications' total marketing effort is directed to the mathematics teachers. The impact of the catalog on teachers is amplified by advertising in teacher magazines and at Creative Publications' in-house creative teaching center. At this center, teachers are trained in how to use materials to reinforce the regular curriculum interestingly, to handle a wide range of activities in the math class, and to get students regularly involved in problem solving. Without question, the greatest personal exposure Creative Publications realizes is at teacher conventions. Over the last 2 years Creative Publications increased its attendance at teacher conventions by 50 percent while its convention costs per teacher in attendance dropped by 46 percent. In this way the products were made known in a meaningful way to more than 240,000 teachers. All conference materials and displays are designed by, and the exhibits staffed by, Creative Publications employees. The director of educational services schedules plans for these conventions in minute detail and then personally controls all the field activity very carefully. This is typical of the way in which the entire company operates. It takes a tremendously well-organized effort to achieve exposure of this sort, but it's necessary for growth.

TALENTED EMPLOYEES PRODUCE RESULTS

Creative Publications is loaded with talent. This doesn't mean the company has many employees. It does, however, point up the fact that the employees have ability and are dedicated to working well together to get the job done right. The organization includes a working board of directors. This board consists of the president, the vice president, who is also the corporate secretary and treasurer, and three outside members. In addition to the president and the vice president there are ten key people responsible for managing various aspects of company operations. Exhibit 7-2 shows what has been achieved from the beginning in August 1969. In its first full year of operation, 1970, the company reported a loss of $34,600 on net sales of $224,700. It reached a break-even level on net sales of $564,000 in 1971, its second year, and has operated profitably ever since. By 1975 a net profit of $187,000 was earned on net sales of $3,511,000. There are good reasons for this progress.

THE BASIC BUSINESS POLICIES

One reason is the concise, straightforward statement of purpose the two officers prepared for the board of directors. This stated the policies by which they intended to manage the business. It reads as follows:

> This corporate plan is written by the officers of the company for review by the Board of Directors. Its purpose is to provide a written document by which the successful growth of the company can be guided and controlled. It does this by focusing the company's attention and effort on the tasks most critical to its

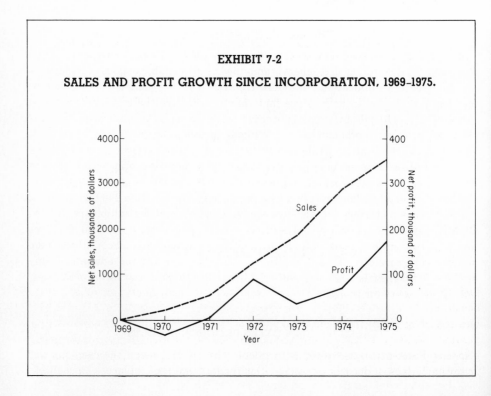

EXHIBIT 7-2

SALES AND PROFIT GROWTH SINCE INCORPORATION, 1969-1975.

success. It facilitates the efficient use of both human and financial resources, and provides a long-run framework against which short-run decisions can be made.

The following summary of goals serves as an introduction to the detailed objectives, strategies, tactics, policies and procedures that Creative Publications is pursuing.

Professional goals

1. *Education*

   To be recognized by educators across the United States as the leading innovative math materials company developing, producing and distributing educational materials and equipment that make teaching and learning mathematics more effective, meaningful and enjoyable.

2. *Business*

   To be recognized by employees and customers as a well-run, well-liked organization of people working toward the common objective of optimizing short and long run profits while achieving the company's educational goal.

3. *Investment*

   To be recognized by investors as a good risk, producing an increasing earnings per share, an increasing positive cash flow and an increasing stock value.

Professional responsibilities

1. *Customers*

   To meet the needs of teachers and learners by helping them more easily and readily learn mathematics and how it plays an important part in life.

2. *Employees*

   To meet the needs of employees and authors by providing them with an opportunity to grow as individuals as they work with and serve other individuals.

3. *Investors*

   To meet the needs of investors by providing them with an opportunity to participate in a worthwhile human endeavor that returns more than invested.

THE CHANGING INVOLVEMENT

Another reason for the progress made by this company is that the two officers understand the nature of the business and the changing management emphasis necessary for continued growth in products and services, and sales and profits. The vice president explained their thinking: Creative Publications has been evolving gradually as an organization from the initial concept into a viable enterprise. In the beginning management involvement was concentrated on creating and making the products. This was necessary to get the business started and to prove out the new concepts. As this initial work took form and shape, the attention of management had to shift to an entrepreneurial phase. This was the period when the emphasis was on establishing an organization and on marketing the concepts and the products. They had to find the market demand for the products and build an organization to meet this demand. The effort was directed so as to do this quickly, thoroughly, and effectively. It had to be done with the future in mind, because this was to be the foundation for further growth. Now the company is entering the third major step in its development—the managerial phase. With products and markets and the organization in place, the emphasis now is to manage the enterprise in a professional manner so that a dynamic, forward-moving balance is maintained. Exhibit 7-3 outlines this shifting emphasis in chart form.

As the vice president described it, this balance must be designed to bring the several important elements of the business together and to keep them working harmoniously in the most effective arrangement. Exhibit 7-4 illustrates this managerial concept. Here the total company is shown as three circles: (1) marketing and product development, (2) business organization, and (3) money. These three facets of the business must work as a well-designed team effort. Each is affected by and, in turn, influences various pressures and needs. The "Customers and Teachers" relate to marketing and product development. The business organization is concerned with "Employees and Professional Services." "Stockholders, Financial Community and

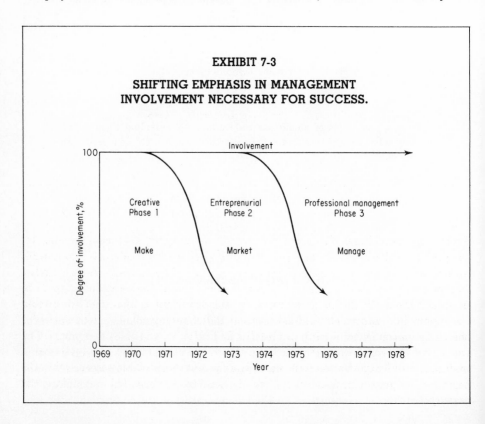

EXHIBIT 7-3

SHIFTING EMPHASIS IN MANAGEMENT INVOLVEMENT NECESSARY FOR SUCCESS.

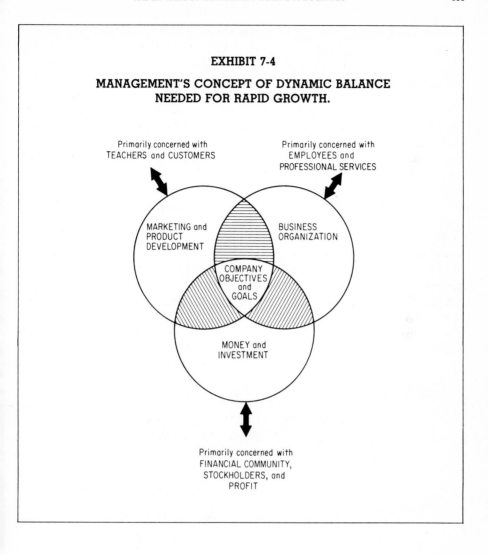

EXHIBIT 7-4

**MANAGEMENT'S CONCEPT OF DYNAMIC BALANCE
NEEDED FOR RAPID GROWTH.**

Primarily concerned with
TEACHERS and CUSTOMERS

Primarily concerned with
EMPLOYEES and
PROFESSIONAL SERVICES

MARKETING and
PRODUCT
DEVELOPMENT

BUSINESS
ORGANIZATION

COMPANY
OBJECTIVES
and
GOALS

MONEY and
INVESTMENT

Primarily concerned with
FINANCIAL COMMUNITY,
STOCKHOLDERS, and
PROFIT

Profit" bear upon the money facet. Instead of pulling apart, management must get the people involved to push together to enlarge their common interests and to work toward achieving common goals. The objective is not to have three concentric circles. In that event everyone would be worrying about the total business. There would be no specialization. With this concept it is management's responsibility to bring about the appropriate balance between functions. This is illustrated by the degree to which the circles continue to overlap uniformly. Thus, this concept is a dynamic, living thing. The officers are expected to utilize the ever-present forces and pressures to maintain equilibrium between the three principal facets of the enterprise so that the three circles grow simultaneously, rapidly, and in balance. This is professional management!

EFFECTIVE EMPLOYEE RELATIONS

A further reason for Creative Publications' progress is that the management really is interested in the employees, and this makes the employees interested in the company. Fringe benefits average about 35 percent of the payroll. This compares favorably with many large, well-established companies. There is an employee booklet to familiarize new employees with policies and procedures. The company operates with a profit plan and budgetary controls. Comparative reports are issued monthly to the key personnel, who discuss the results with the employees in a series of departmental meetings. In these meetings operating plans and problems are discussed and the employees are encouraged to think about the problems and suggest corrective action. Exhibit 7-5 is a typical agenda for a meeting. This exchange produces results. For example, the warehouse/distribution staff rearranged the stock and reduced the walking associated

---

EXHIBIT 7-5

TYPICAL AGENDA FOR DEPARTMENTAL
MEETING WITH EMPLOYEES.

CREATIVE
PUBLICATIONS

P.O. BOX 10328, PALO ALTO, CA 94303   BUSINESS OFFICES — (415) 968-3977   PRODUCT DEVELOPMENT — (415) 968-1101

AGENDA

To: Department 82   FROM: Dan

RE: Agenda Topics for Monthly Meeting   DATE: 12/19/75
                                                   9:30 A.M.

1. Budget and financial information

2. 1976 guidelines for order fulfillment. Please be
    prepared to review 75 and make any necessary changes.

3. Review of 1976 selling prices and product configuration
    changes

4. Questionnaire

5. What's needed for a smooth transition to the 1976 catalog

6. January 2nd?

with filling orders by 29 percent. In packing orders, the cartons are now filled out with Flow-Pack instead of crushed papers, saving about 3 minutes packing time per order. Packers were measured by a composite index that took into consideration the number of orders packed and the dollar volume. A packer pointed out some shortcomings in this measure and proceeded to develop a more meaningful index that also included the boxes packed. This particular proposal was thought out carefully by the employee and was submitted in a concise, well-written report. The idea was adopted. Originally, there was no record of what a packer did or should do. This has been changed. Today it is written in an easy-to-grasp format, which facilitates training and serves as a reference for the experienced packers. In addition, the packing stations have been standardized for layout, equipment, supplies, and method. Interestingly, it was found that more different sizes of carton flats speeded up the packing operation. Now the boxes fit the range of products better. Also, the order gatherers and the packers rotate on a scheduled basis. This eliminates boredom. Through better order handling and inventory control, the year-end physical inventory was completed in 1975 in about one-half the time taken in 1974. At one time the company delivered the packages to the post office. Today, in return for a partial separation of packages, the post office picks up each day's shipments.

In order editing, a rearrangement and changes in order processing made it possible to handle a 5 percent increase in orders entered with a 25 percent reduction in staff in 1975 compared to 1974 operations. Closer attention to customers' orders and better processing of orders reduced errors to about 1 percent of the orders shipped in 1975 and permitted reducing the customer service staff by 50 percent because customer inquiries were reduced by 44 percent.

All the employees are high school or college graduates. Three worked their way into key positions from the warehouse floor. Every employee is given a performance review each 6 months on the anniversary date of his or her employment. This review is made by the department director and the immediate supervisor with the employee. Strengths and weaknesses are discussed and, most important, the employee's goals and ambitions are reviewed. Are the employees responsive to this attention? The answer definitely is positive. One employee quoted Ralph Waldo Emerson when he offered, "Nothing great was ever achieved without enthusiasm."

THE COMPUTER PROGRAM

The Creative Publications' organization likes to tackle major problems too! In 1973, the company installed an on-line, time-sharing computer system. It was a canned package of software adapted to accommodate Creative Publications' special requirements. It used visual data terminals and provided instant response. The system worked but not as well as expected by management. There was excessive downtime interference with the central computer. Order editors encountered difficulty in making corrections. And the hardware and time-sharing was expensive. Finally, the controller was authorized to make a thorough analysis of the situation with recommendations for improving the system and for reducing its operating cost. As a result of the study, it was decided that the functional areas to be covered should remain the same and would be as follows:

1. Billing/order entry

2. Inventory/back order

3. Cash Receipts/receivables

4. Management reports

A new system was designed utilizing the batch concept for input control, instead of the so-called instant response, with easier error identification and correction. In this case the information is prepared daily for input into the computer. On a next-day basis, updated inventory figures are received, as well as daily transaction registers. Input control reports are generated daily as well as monthly. Then, four computer companies were invited to quote. The four proposals were studied carefully. The costs were related to number of transactions per month, and this information was plotted for comparison. Exhibit 7-6 shows the cost differences. The highest cost, curve A, was the instant-response system that was operating so poorly. Curves B, C, and D represent quotations from other companies for the batch-type system. Curve E is the batch-

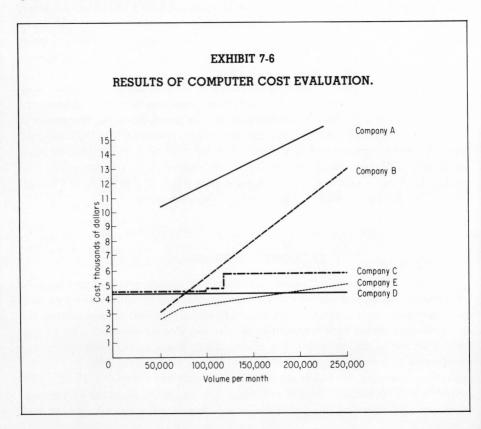

EXHIBIT 7-6

RESULTS OF COMPUTER COST EVALUATION.

concept system that was accepted and installed. The new computer system operated during all of 1975. It is doing the job, the interferences and frustrations are gone, the information the system produces is adequate and timely, and system operating costs are on target. Creative Publications' personnel learned a lesson about computers from this experience and found out how to reduce costs significantly at the same time. One employee said, "The key to success is to keep the system as simple as possible."

INCENTIVE COMPENSATION

Late in 1973, the board of directors of Creative Publications approved the installation of a companywide profit sharing plan. The plan provides for 10 percent of pre-tax profits each year to be awarded as incentive compensation, limited to a maximum of 10 percent of the gross compensation of the participants. The plan is easy to administer. The full impact of the incentive on employee productivity is yet to be determined. In 1975, however, company operations did improve markedly and the employees earned an average incentive bonus of approximately 8 percent. The plan as approved by the board of directors is as follows:

> All employees of the company, employed on or before September 1 of any year and still in the employ of the company on December 1 of that same year are eligible to participate in the company's incentive compensation plan. The amount of incentive compensation is 10% of pre-tax profit as determined by the firm's independent auditors, but in no event more than 10% of the gross compensation of each employee eligible to participate in the plan. Individual incentive compensation is determined by multiplying each participant's total compensation in the year in question by an amount equal to the quotient of total incentive compensation divided by gross compensation. Payment of one-half of the individual compensation is effected on or about December 15 of each year based upon estimates determined by the Board of Directors who administer the plan. In the event the Board errs in its determination, any deficiency will be made up in the second installment of incentive compensation which is paid prior to the next annual meeting of the shareholders. Should the initial payment exceed, however, the total amount which each employee is due under the incentive compensation plan, employees will be required to refund the difference to the corporation. There is a provision in the plan which precludes the company from paying incentive compensation in the event to do so would violate the terms of any obligations or agreements of the corporation. In that event, however, a reserve would be set up for payment of the incentive compensation as soon as the corporation could do so without violating the terms of any obligation or agreement.

> The corporation reserves the right to amend, modify or terminate the plan at any time on the giving of written notice to all employees as specified in the plan. The plan further provides that nothing contained in the plan should be construed to:

> (a) Give any employee any rights whatsoever with respect to shares of common stock of the corporation;

> (b) Limit in any way the right of the corporation to terminate an individual's employment with the corporation at any time;

(c) Be evidence of any agreement of understanding, expressed or implied, that the corporation will employ an employee in any particular position at any particular rate of remuneration;

(d) Require the corporation to segregate or earmark any cash or other property; and

(e) Preclude assignments by employees of their interest in the incentive compensation plan.

INFORM EMPLOYEES

As a management policy and in conjunction with the incentive compensation plan, a financial overview is issued each month to the management team. This is discussed in a meeting of the key personnel. They, in turn, meet monthly with the employees

EXHIBIT 7-7

CREATIVE PUBLICATIONS' MATHEW.

in each of their departments. Additionally, companywide meetings are held quarterly by the officers—one of the advantages of a small company. In this way, all employees are kept informed about the progress being made and, of course, items in need of attention are discussed.

THE ACHIEVEMENTS

Creative Publications in 6½ years has grown from a new concept into a successful business. Its products have improved the productivity of mathematics teachers in the United States of America and in numerous foreign countries. The field testing at Jordan Junior High School in Palo Alto proved this. Jordan students won math contest after contest in California and nationwide. The creative staff of the company has been very productive also. The company's line of products has grown from 37 items to 533, with 100 new products being made available for 1976. Including the two founders, Creative Publications gainfully employed 48 people in 1975, plus several part-time workers. In addition, Creative Publications has a computer service bureau under contract.

Now let's look at the productivity of all the employees including the data processing service. The ratio of sales dollars generated per payroll dollar is the best index available. Table 7-1 shows this ratio for the last 3 years. In addition, the ratio is shown with the data processing costs included.

TABLE 7-1

Year	Ratio $ sales/payroll	Annual productivity improvement	Ratio $ sales/payroll + data processing	Annual productivity improvement
1973	4.64		3.89	
1974	4.90	+ 5.6%	3.95	+ 1.5%
1975	5.66	+15.5%	5.03	+27.3%

Thus, both the employees and the change in the computer system contributed to significant gains in productivity in 1975. This improvement showed up in increased sales and higher profits.

The creative actions of this company have contributed to productivity improvement in general, in three major ways—the triple thrust:

1. Mathematics, a fundamental science, has been made more interesting, and students now learn faster and better.

2. A whole new set of mathematics teaching materials now is available to teachers and students.

3. Professional management is building an organization that has potential for growth and continued gains in productivity and profit.

SOME THOUGHTS RELATED TO THE ACHIEVEMENTS

A review of the events that took place and the management concepts that are used by Creative Publications reveal some ideas that lead to the achievement as follows:

1. Good ideas often are generated out of simply recognizing a need.

2, The marketing concept of management—find a need and fill it—is the key to successfully building a business.

3. A good idea is not of much value until someone works to make it take shape and has the conviction and willingness to see it through.

4. To sell a new product, consumers must be convinced it was created for them.

5. Focusing the purpose and growth of the business on one main idea often gains better consumer respect and acceptance, allowing for more rapid growth.

6. For success, management must have a plan, and the plan must be understood and accepted on all levels in the organization.

7. Management must plan for changing emphasis, especially in a new enterprise as it grows from one phase through another.

8. Every business is subject to internal and external pressures and forces which management must control in order to maintain the necessary balance of growth.

9. Before imposing a computer solution, do a thorough analysis of your needs, plan all manual changes for greatest efficiency, and don't be overwhelmed by gadgetry.

10. Employee interest in a company is directly proportional to management's interest in the employees.

11. Keeping employees informed about the business is a very necessary motivator.

12. Profit sharing technique which can motivate employees in a nonspecific way is a simple basis toward improvements in productivity.

THERE IS NO SUBSTITUTE FOR TALENT,
KNOW-HOW, AND HARD WORK

8

Group Participation Improves Operations

The Multi-Flex Corporation, situated near Chicago, Illinois, had real problems. For 6 consecutive years this company lost more than $1 million per year on annual sales volumes ranging between $12 and $14 million. It had good products, and for the most part the products were well designed and well accepted in the markets the company served. But the company was overstaffed, overburdened with excessive costs, hampered by overly complicated procedures, and slow to respond to customers' needs.

Multi-Flex designed and produced metallic bellows and bellows assemblies for the instruments and controls industry; custom-made flexible metal-hose assemblies, manifolds, ducting, and expansion joints for industrial original equipment manufacturers (OEM); stock products including bulk hose, braid, tubing, fittings, compensators, standard expansion joints, and pipe alignment guides for distributors and agents; and special aircraft and space assemblies for the aerospace market. Thus, the product lines literally covered the spectrum from small, calibrated, precision bellows through flexible products requiring long maintenance-free service life to large, exacting expansion devices used in space rockets, such as the pressure volumetric compensators installed in the LOX and the fuel lines of the Saturn V moon rocket.

The company was settled in a modern plant. The plant consisted of a separate engineering center, a multistory administration building, and a large single-floor factory building. The plant and facilities were excellent and were well suited to the operations carried on by the company. The air-conditioned engineering center contained a model shop and complete hydraulic, mechanical, metallurgical, electrical, and cryogenic laboratories for developing improved and new products, for performing engineering and life tests, for testing materials, and for developing special-purpose machinery used in production to make the flexible metal components. The administration building was spacious, well lighted, and air-conditioned. It housed the purchasing department, the marketing organization, and the finance group. The accounting and cost records were compiled on conventional tabulating equipment. The air-conditioned factory office was adjacent to the production area and contained the production control, manufacturing engineering, tool design, maintenance, and quality control sections. The equipment in the factory had been in service a long time but was being maintained in good operating condition. The "white room" for cleaning, testing, and examining space components was new and well equipped. The machine shop contained automatic screw machines, turret lathes, engine lathes, milling machines, and drill presses. The fabricating departments had power presses, braiders, and special-purpose machinery for producing annular and helical convoluted metal hose and components. The assembly areas were equipped for gas, induction, and electric arc welding of a wide variety of metals in very thin, laminated, and heavy cross sections. These areas, also, contained pressure-testing apparatus and a variety of assembly jigs, fixtures, and gages. In general, then, Multi-Flex had the facilities, the equipment, and the technical know-how to produce its products. What was missing? Why did the company have such a dismal record of losses? True, it was operating in highly competitive markets where there was little or no opportunity for price increases. The year was 1964, which was long before inflationary forces took over. The answer had to be found in the cost of running the business. Productivity had to be increased in order to restore profitability.

NEW MANAGEMENT NEEDED

A new president and general manager was installed. The new president had an engineering background, and most of his experience was in the area of improving operating costs. In fact, he was selected to manage Multi-Flex because of the success he had had in saving a competitor from bankruptcy. The new president immediately recognized that Multi-Flex had talented employees and good products. The solution to the company's problems, then, was to streamline the organization and through a series of programs encourage the employees to apply their talent to running the business more efficiently. This is described more fully in several paragraphs taken from one of the president's reports to the board of directors as follows:

> The past year has been one of change at Multi-Flex. Perhaps the greatest change has taken place in the organization. New functions have been installed, some functions combined, and added emphasis given to others. In general, the Multi-Flex organization has been strengthened and a foundation has been established for more effective operation in the future. We believe it is important to have the right employee in each position and also, to organize the functions so as to achieve the highest degree of coordination.

> One interesting facet of the changes in organization is that the majority of new positions and the changes in staffing have been filled by promoting personnel from within Multi-Flex. The Multi-Flex employees have talent and skill, and equally important, they want to succeed and grow. With this ability and attitude they are very responsive to management direction. Of the thirty-nine key positions in the Multi-Flex organization, fourteen were not changed, one is open, five were filled by recruiting from the outside and nineteen were filled by promoting from within. In every case, the promotions from within were made because we were convinced that the individuals selected would perform better than new employees.

The president's report went on to cite examples of the improvements being made. Those in the marketing area included:

Contract Administration and Program Management have been combined into one department for providing better control of contracts and improved liaison with major customers. The preparation and pricing of proposals and quotations have been centralized. In the past this processing was widely dispersed. The new department is functioning effectively, with better control of pricing and faster and more complete response to customers' requests for quotations.

The Wholesale Sales Department has operated with a Multi-Flex salesman in each of nine territories selling industrial products to distributors and through agents. Plans are under way to accelerate wholesale sales by expanding the nine territories into eighteen. Sales trainees are being selected. They will be given thirty days of in-plant training followed by thirty days of on-the-job experience in the field before being set up in their own territories.

The Field Sales Department sells engineered products to O.E.M. accounts, both industrial and aerospace, through four regional managers supervising seventeen sales engineers. In addition, we have two Product Management Departments, one covering metal hose, expansion joints and ducting and the other specializing in bellows for instruments and controls. These two departments have been extremely active this past year conducting market surveys.

Professional survey reports now are completed as follows:

1. Survey of the bellows market.

2. An evaluation of the new building construction industry.

3. An evaluation of the chemical processing industry—process and service piping market.

4. An evaluation of the cryogenic hose industry.

5. An evaluation of the free turbine and diesel engine industry.

6. An evaluation of the aerospace hose market.

These comprehensive market surveys are being used by Multi-Flex's management to plan marketing and product strategy, to open new markets, and to gain further penetration of current markets.

In the engineering area, the president's report cited the following:

Applications Engineering and Systems Engineering have been consolidated into a Product Engineering Department. A new department, Product Development, has been established and staffed. Multi-Flex now is busily engaged improving its products and developing proprietary products for industrial use. There were no funds budgeted in 1964 for this type of development work. We have provided $150,000 in 1965 and plan to increase the budget for product development to $190,000 in 1966. One recent change in Engineering Services was to combine the Test Laboratory and the Model Shop under one supervisor.

Improvements made in the manufacturing organization were reported this way:

The Manufacturing Division has undergone several major changes all pointed to increasing the technical and managerial capabilities of the manufacturing personnel. The assistant to the Director of Manufacturing manages Plant Engineering and Maintenance in addition to carrying out special assignments. An Estimating Department has been established. Prior to this, estimating was performed by the manufacturing engineers along with their other responsibilities.

Material Control was renamed Production Control with renewed emphasis being given to planning, scheduling, production loading, and shop dispatching. Purchasing now is headed by an engineer, a necessity in our type of manufacturing. The position of Production Superintendent was eliminated and replaced by four section managers, one each for bellows, fabrication, hose and expansion joints, and precision products.

Manufacturing Engineering has been reorganized so that Methods and Standards have been combined and four timestudy trainees added. Attention is being given to the development of standard time data and to specifying better methods and standards for production. An Advanced Manufacturing Engineering Section has been established. It is this group's responsibility to study production methods and processes in order to develop and install significant improvements on a continuing basis. All tool and gage design and specifying have been brought together into a single section also.

In the past, Quality Control was part of the Manufacturing Division and reported to the Director of Manufacturing. On September 1st, a new division, Quality Assurance, was established and its director reports directly to me. This division, consisting of two departments—Quality Engineering and Inspection—has the authority, responsibility and accountability for improving the quality levels in production to the point where sampling techniques can be applied effectively. Quality Assurance is expected to work closely with Manufacturing in identifying quality problems, in analyzing the basic causes of these problems, and in designing corrective action necessary to improve quality, reduce scrap and rework, and to lower the cost of inspection.

Constructive changes in the finance division were started and included the following:

General Accounting, Cost Accounting, Budgets, and Government Audit and Reviews now are consolidated into an Accounting Department. A Systems Department has been added and is engaged in planning computer programs in addition to analyzing, preparing and issuing standard operating procedures. No change has been made in the Credit and Insurance Department and that is good since Multi-Flex's record with bad accounts is excellent. The Data Processing Department has made a successful transition from tabulating equipment to a 1401G computer and is now in the final stages of installing a 357 Data Collection System. The 357 System provides for transmitting factory labor statistics through fifteen stations directly to the Data Processing Department. Also, in preparation for installation is an Estomatic program for extending estimates into prices on the computer. Office Services now is organized to provide more effective control over communications, office supplies and office equipment.

The employee and community relations division played an important part in the changes that were taking place. The president reported the following:

The Employee and Community Relations Division consists of three departments—Placement and Development, Benefits and Services, and Employment and Safety. This division, charged with the responsibility for training, organized the following programs during the past year:

1. Toolroom Apprentice Program.

2. Quality Control Blueprint Reading Course.

3. Clerical Training Program.

4. Management Development Program.

5. Product Training Program for Sales Engineers.

6. Contract Administration Training Program.

The Director of Employee and Community Relations is also director of the FTP program, FIRST TIME PERFORMANCE. This new program is aimed at getting the job—any job—every job—done right the first time, every time. Through FTP we are striving to get each employee to understand his or her job, to complete the job successfully, thoroughly, accurately, and from this gain a sense of satisfaction and a feeling of pride in being an outstanding performer.

INNOVATIONS NEEDED TO STIMULATE PARTICIPATION

Once the organization had been "streamlined," two innovations were important to keeping the employees excited and interested in working together to achieve Multi-Flex's objectives. They were:

1. The FTP program—first-time performance

2. The president's regular quarterly meetings with all employees

These two programs, working in combination, were designed to keep the employees well informed on individual, departmental, and company objectives and progress. This is "group participation" in a highly developed and effective form. The FTP program emphasized "more value." Its underlying premise was that customers want and deserve quality products and services of high reliability at low cost and when promised. It was a total program involving all work by all employees for all products to serve all customers. The basic goals behind the program were to increase productivity, reduce costs, increase reliability of products, improve deliveries, and to encourage the employees to reduce errors and bad work and to complete projects on time.

The FTP program was introduced by the president and the director of employee and community relations during an employee assembly. This was followed by a company open house for the employees, their families and their friends, citizens of the nearby communities, and vendors and suppliers. Invitations to the open house were mailed to the employees' homes and to a limited number of guests, including town officials, Association of Commerce officials, all customer resident personnel, several NASA and CPD people, the editors of local newspapers, and the manager of the local radio station.

The administration of the FTP program was performed by a planning council headed by the director of employee and community relations who reported to the president. The planning council consisted of five FTP managers representing the marketing, engineering, manufacturing, quality assurance, and finance divisions. The entire company was divided into forty logical FTP units averaging less than twenty employees per unit. Each unit was headed by a unit administrator who in turn reported to a FTP manager on the planning council. All these people were management personnel who administered the FTP program in addition to their regular duties. The function of the planning council was to plan the FTP program, develop innovations to keep the program interesting, and select individuals and units meriting special recognition and awards.

Each FTP unit decided upon a measurable factor in its work that needed to be improved. This factor had to be related to the vital function the group was organized to perform and it had to be measurable in readily understandable terms. Each FTP unit was given a 4 × 4 foot scoreboard (see Exhibit 8-1). Each week the results for the unit as measured by its factor was plotted on the scoreboard. These scoreboards were mounted throughout the plant in the work areas of the FTP units. Thus, the performance and the progress being achieved by each unit was on full display for all to see. In addition, a fundamental feature of FTP was to have the employees identify causes of errors and problems—barriers to first-time, error-free performance. The employees were required only to identify the barriers. The regular functional organization was responsible for solving the problems and taking appropriate action to eliminate the barriers. The functional organization was committed to report back within 10 days to the employee who pointed out a barrier indicating the action to be taken to break the barrier. The unit administrators were responsible for making the barrier identification procedure work, for maintaining up-to-date scoreboards, for conducting one 30-minute meeting each month with the employees in their units, and for implementing innovations that would sustain a high level of employee interest in the FTP program.

Another fundamental feature of the FTP program was to give public recognition to individual employees for outstanding performances and extraordinary contributions to the success of FTP. Prizes, bulletin-board announcements, articles in the company newsletter, and presentation of major awards at the quarterly employee assemblies all served to highlight those employees who were contributing importantly to improvement in the operation of the company.

The open house played a significant role in getting the FTP program off to a good start. The employees' families were given escorted tours of the entire plant, souvenirs, refreshments, and FTP brochures. The FTP symbol, Exhibit 8-2, was

EXHIBIT 8-1

TYPICAL FTP SCOREBOARD.

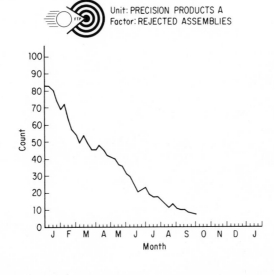

EXHIBIT 8-2

THE FTP SYMBOL DESIGNED TO HELP KEEP EMPLOYEE ATTENTION FOCUSED ON COMPANY OBJECTIVES.

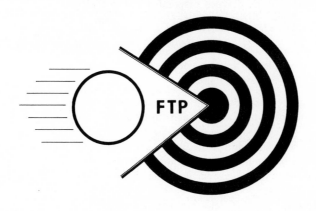

displayed prominently throughout the plant. The brochures set the tone for the entire program. For example, here are two paragraphs taken from the brochure:

> Simple errors made by an assembly worker, a typist, an engineer and a supervisor are seemingly unrelated. In most cases they are corrected easily. Most people hardly think twice about them. It could be said that people have grown accustomed to a standard that accepts a few daily mistakes as the price of being human. Unfortunately, if each person at Multi-Flex makes an "insignificant" mistake each day, the collective result is far from insignificant.

> To err is human—is it a valid outlook? In personal business, no one is willing to accept a 5% error in his paycheck or in his change at the store. No one expects to get into the wrong car 5% of the time. Why, then, should anyone be willing to settle for making errors in 5% or even 1% of his work? FTP is everyone trying to do the job right the first time . . . every time.

The open house was held on a Sunday. The next day, Monday, the employees were asked to sign personal pledges. All employees but one signed the pledge. The personal pledge read as follows:

> Realizing that my work and responsibilities have direct effect on the quality, reliability, delivery, or price of our products, I hereby pledge to our customers that I will accept perfection as my personal target and that I will strive for first-time, error-free performance at all times.

The president and the directors of the six divisions signed a company pledge, and this was mounted and displayed in the Multi-Flex lobby for all to see—employees, vendors, suppliers, and customers. Thus, everyone at Multi-Flex was committed to the success of the first-time performance program.

EMPLOYEES RESPOND TO FTP

Some idea of how the employees responded to the FTP program is revealed in the following excerpts from the minutes of staff meetings:

> The Scoreboard charting is working effectively and in general the Scoreboards indicate the employees are improving their performances. The Barrier Identification Procedure needs stimulation.

> The plan to give recognition to Units demonstrating continued progress was approved. Under the plan a gold star is to be placed on the scoreboards for each measurement factor showing improvement in the current month over the year-to-date average. In addition, the Barrier Identification Procedure is to be facilitated by having the Unit Administrators and the Supervisors work closely with the employees in identifying and describing Barriers to First Time Performance.

> In August 74% of the Scoreboard measurements showed progress. The August results compared with the averages of the first eight months follows:

FTP Factor Progress
August 1965 versus Year-to-Date Average

Division	Improved	No change	Slipped
Marketing	3	1	6
Engineering	8		0
Manufacturing			
Factory	19		5
Office	8		6
Quality Assurance	20		3
Finance	4		2
Employee and Community Relations	2		0
Total	64	1	22

The director of quality assurance reporting on his division's activities stated, "Overall performance compared to the Profit Plan shows expenditures at 86 percent of budget." In addition, significant progress was made in four other areas, as shown in Table 8-1.

TABLE 8-1

Factor	1966 1st half	1967 1st half	Change, %
1. Customer rejections	148	50	−66
2. Returned material	$98,460	$51,461	−48
3. Customer complaints	65	34	−48
4. MRB's (rejected items submitted to material review board)	166	16	−90

RECOGNITION INSPIRES EMPLOYEES

Typical of the recognition given to award winners is shown by the following announcements in the Multi-Flex newsletter:

William N. of Precision Products has won the April FTP award. He was responsible for two improvements in resistance welding. By identifying the problem and proving out a completely new setup on the Sciaky machine, the time required for ply-welding Saturn flex has been reduced to one-sixth of the former time.

In the other instance, he found a way to eliminate an operation. In the past it was necessary to dry hone locomotive manifold parts prior to circle welding the fittings because of the accumulation of oxide resulting from the 900-degree temperature of the annealing furnace. He suggested that a preliminary drying at 300-degrees would properly prepare the units for circle welding. Now the units receive the

900-degree anneal after circle welding and there is no reason to remove the oxide. This results in a net saving of one-half hour of labor for each unit.

William N. selected a $50 Savings Bond as his award.

Exhibit 8-3 illustrates some of the barrier identifications submitted by the employees and the actions to be taken to break the barriers to first-time performance. At least once each month the currently identified barriers were summarized

EXHIBIT 8-3

SAMPLE PAGE PORTRAYING RECOGNITION GIVEN TO EMPLOYEES IDENTIFYING BARRIERS TO FIRST TIME PERFORMANCE.

FTP PROGRAM
BARRIER IDENTIFICATION April 25–May 20, 1966

Dick B., Inspection
Lack of call-out tolerance for buttwelded tube.

BWT book will be brought up to date and commercial tolerances will be included in an addendum to cover tubing not covered by the BWT book proper.

Glady C., Planning & Inv. Control
Doug M., Methods & Standards
(Similar barrier submitted separately.)
Lack of provision for updating working book for raw material and part stock.

Manufacturing Estimating will maintain this working book on a current basis.

Ed C., Tube Fab
Lack of capacity to planish weld in tube over 82".

Barrier arose regarding 92" tube. Operations sheets have been changed to cut into individual lengths prior to planishing. If future orders require planishing of tube greater than 82", up-to-date quotes can be obtained for an attachment which will permit greater length to be handled.

Jim C., Inspection
Need for better cleaning method for small assemblies with convoluted parts.

Use of ultrasonic cleaning is being investigated.

Rita C., Quality Engineering
Difficulty in accurately preparing certificates of conformance from information on packing slips.

C-2 information will be typed on the factory order using standard ditto backing.

Jim E., Shipping
Delays caused by inability of personnel to hear PA system.

Outside vendor will make survey and recommend what steps can be taken to improve system.

Betty E., Bellows Assembly
Decreased production resulting from inadequate turntable.

Permanent tooling is on order to replace temporary tooling used to start job.

(continued)

and posted on plant bulletin boards. In this way, recognition was given to the employees who were trying to improve operations. In addition, other employees were stimulated to think about their jobs too.

KEEP EMPLOYEES INFORMED

The president's quarterly meetings with all of the employees were designed to generate interest and enthusiasm for making Multi-Flex a better place to work. For example, in the April 25, 1966, meeting the president said:

> The purpose of these meetings is to keep you informed, to tell you the good and the bad, and to highlight those areas in need of improvement. By thinking and working together effectively, we can build success into Multi-Flex's future. In doing this we will be building pride and prosperity and fun and security into our own careers.

> We are very pleased with the renewed interest you are showing in the FIRST TIME PERFORMANCE program. The Barrier Identification procedure is working well. Your BI's have been very worthwhile. Keep them coming! Awards have been presented to the outstanding performers. You know who they are. Their pictures have been posted on bulletin boards and printed in the local papers. Turn in your BI ideas. The FTP Planning Council has a good supply of turkeys, hams and FTP lighters, pens and wallets to award to you. The quality of the ideas brought to our attention in the BI's shows you really are thinking about your jobs and are searching for ways to produce better. This is what is needed to make Multi-Flex No. 1 in the industry.

In the January 23, 1967, quarterly meeting, the president reviewed Multi-Flex's operations for the 1966 year. This gives some idea of the operating information that was given to the employees. For example, several significant paragraphs from his presentation were as follows:

> Multi-Flex earned a profit before taxes of 1.1% on sales in 1964, 3.5% in 1965 and 5.5% in 1966. This is progress and this progress is the result of many changes. For one thing, our attitudes changed. We set difficult objectives and we believed we could achieve them. We had confidence. We had faith in our ability to do the job. We were not discouraged when our plans didn't click immediately. We just worked harder and smarter, fully convinced that we were doing the right thing. We worked together. We cooperated. We innovated. We did our best and we succeeded.

> This chart [Exhibit 8-4] shows how orders were booked in relation to the forecasts. For the new members of our Multi-Flex team, let me explain. The vertical scale is percent of forecast; along the bottom line are months and every third month is the end of the quarter. The charts are cumulative. This means that each point indicates the accomplishment from January 1st through that month. We use these charts to keep you informed on the results Multi-Flex is achieving. This information is reviewed with you every three months.

> Incoming Orders are shown on this chart. Orders placed with Multi-Flex by our customers exceeded the forecasts throughout the year and Marketing finished

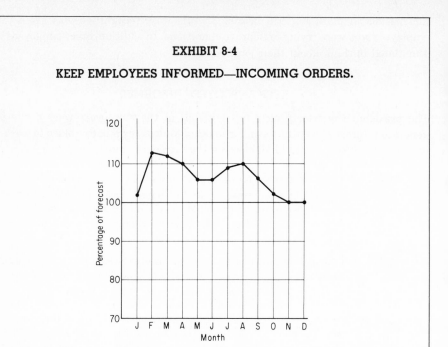

EXHIBIT 8-4

KEEP EMPLOYEES INFORMED—INCOMING ORDERS.

1966 right on target. One interesting fact in this total is that our industrial and aircraft orders were 21% ahead of those booked in 1965. Our Marketing people believe there is only one way to find business, and that is to go out after it, and they have been doing this very successfully.

Net Sales, better known as Shipments [see Exhibit 8-5], trailed the forecast all year and finished at 93% of forecast. It is significant to note, however, that while space business was substantially below 1965 volume, industrial and aircraft production was 14% higher. In fact, during the last quarter of 1966 shipments of industrial and aircraft products were running at a rate of 31% over the 1965 average. It took us the better part of the year to get organized and geared up to this rate of production. Now we need to maintain this level of production and then gradually improve on it in 1967. The demand for our products continues to be good.

Our Backlog of open orders [see Exhibit 8-6] closed the year at 116% of forecast. The backlog totals about four and one-half million dollars, with two-thirds of it in industrial and aircraft orders and one-third in space contracts. A year ago the space contracts dominated the backlog. Today, it is just the reverse. We have every reason to believe we will be able to maintain this backlog volume by balancing a high rate of incoming orders with shipments in 1967.

Here's the chart—Net Profit—that really tells the score [see Exhibit 8-7]. You'll remember we started poorly last January. We had to work all year to make up for

EXHIBIT 8-5

KEEP EMPLOYEES INFORMED—NET SALES.

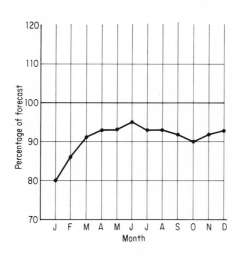

EXHIBIT 8-6

KEEP EMPLOYEES INFORMED—BACKLOG.

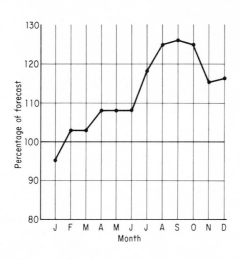

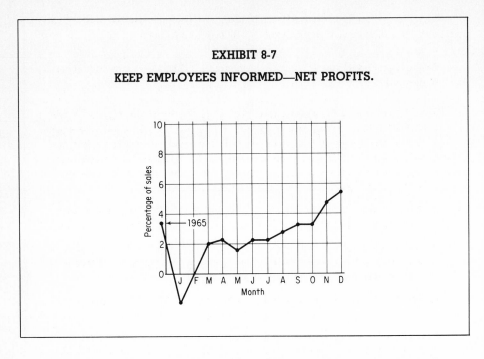

EXHIBIT 8-7

KEEP EMPLOYEES INFORMED—NET PROFITS.

it. During the summer we began to move upward and by the end of the third quarter Multi-Flex's profits were 3.3% of sales. In our October assembly, I indicated that the profits for nine months were at 3.3% of sales and said: "Our goal is to exceed 5.0% by year-end. We are working in the right direction; we have the orders and we can reach this goal by December 31, 1966." Ladies and gentlemen, I am pleased to report that we pushed it up to 5.5% for the year. Congratulations on the fine job you did in 1966 and especially for your splendid performance during the last quarter.

ACTION GETS RESULTS

The Multi-Flex employees were thinking, and many of their ideas were sound. Two innovations were unusually good. One was a recommendation by the marketing group for establishing a fast-response telephone service to handle customers' small orders and emergency requirements. The president announced this new service in the employee assembly on April 25, 1966, as follows:

A new Tel-O-Product Sales Department, better known as TOPS, has been established in the Manufacturing Division. This department began operating in April. TOPS was organized to give customers forty-eight hour service on hose assemblies made from stock components. Customers' orders are accepted, priced and entered directly by this department, completely bypassing the system used for large and more complex orders. Further, it is planned that most of the orders will be completed from inventories located right in the department. Economies gained by simplified handling of orders should improve profit margins. In addition, the forty-eight service feature should increase sales of hose assemblies substantially.

The president cited Tel-O-Products along with other improvements in his report to the board of directors on October 18, 1966, as follows:

Several significant innovations have been made in 1966. These have contributed to the results achieved. They are:

1. A Tel-O-Product Sales Department was placed in operation in April to give forty-eight hour service to customers on hose assemblies made from standard components. Sales of this type have averaged about $5,000 per week in the past. Since April TOP Sales have increased to $10,000 per week in August and in September. This streamlined method of serving customers now is being extended to include standard expansion joint assemblies, also.

2. A sales incentive plan for both O.E.M. and Wholesale sales engineers is working well, with approximately $7000 in initial bonuses earned and paid in July.

3. An Annual Purchase Plan was introduced to distributors in January and was accepted by twenty-three distributors. Also, annual purchase commitments with releases have been established with several major customers.

4. Training programs, utilizing Job Instruction Training (JIT) principles, have been put into effect to instruct and upgrade production employees.

5. Daily and weekly reporting of employee performances were installed in August to direct attention of production managers and their employees toward higher productivity and increased production. Employee performances averaged 74% of standard in 1965, 80% of standard through July, 1966 and then increased to 93% in August and 94% in September, an increase in productivity of 27%.

6. Production schedules have been compiled so as to highlight delivery commitments made to customers and to focus attention and efforts to reducing delinquencies.

7. Production is being facilitated in October as a result of simplified inspection procedures adopted by the DCASR resident team.

The other unusually good innovation came out of several discussions the president had with the advanced manufacturing engineering group. The idea was to automate the production of metal hose. The president submitted a "Proposal for Continuous Tube Mill Facility" to the board of directors for approval in their meeting on October 18, 1966, and then briefly described the proposal as follows:

Multi-Flex owns a U.S. patent expiring in 1981 on a method for helically corrugating metal hose. In addition, patents have been granted in Canada, France and Italy and are pending in Great Britain and Germany. Experimental corrugating heads have been designed, built and used by Multi-Flex and have proven to be highly successful. The hose is of higher quality than current products, tool wear is at a minimum, and for the first time corrugating speeds far exceed welding speeds. The new process makes it thoroughly practical to automatically produce metal hose from coils of strip stock through all operations to the reeling of the finished hose. [Exhibit 8-8 schematically portrays this concept.]

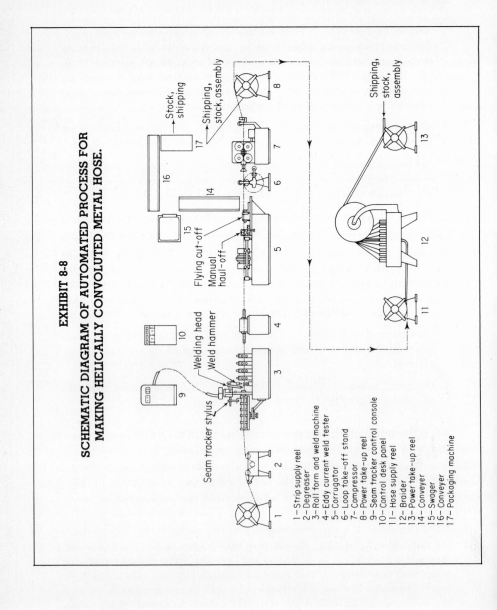

EXHIBIT 8-8

SCHEMATIC DIAGRAM OF AUTOMATED PROCESS FOR MAKING HELICALLY CONVOLUTED METAL HOSE.

Stock, shipping

Shipping, stock, assembly

Shipping, stock, assembly

Flying cut-off

Manual haul-off

Seam tracker stylus

Welding head

Weld hammer

1– Strip supply reel
2– Degreaser
3– Roll form and weld machine
4– Eddy current weld tester
5– Corrugator
6– Loop take-off stand
7– Compressor
8– Power take-up reel
9– Seam tracker control console
10– Control desk panel
11– Hose supply reel
12– Braider
13– Power take-up reel
14– Conveyer
15– Swager
16– Conveyer
17– Packaging machine

It is planned that this automated process in time would replace all other methods for producing metal hose. Phase I covers the design, building and installation of a continuous tube mill at a cost estimated to total $197,000 for mass producing continuous or intermittent hose from 3/16" to 1½" I.D. The economies estimated to be achieved, plus the additional hose sales anticipated, indicate an average rate of return on the investment over a five year period of more than 176% per year. This project is vital to Multi-Flex's future.

The board of directors approved the proposal. Two years later the automated process was operational and began to contribute to Multi-Flex's continued success as projected in the proposal.

THE RESULTS

All the programs and all the enthusiasm generated were directed toward turning Multi-Flex into a profitable ongoing company. This was individual and group participation on a companywide basis. Productivity increased. The production employees whose output was measured by time standards increased their productivity by more than 27 percent. This was readily determined since their average performance against the time standards increased from 74 to 94 percent. And this measure does not include improvements made in methods whereby the time standards were revised and required more output per standard hour. The productivity improvement of all other employees was more difficult to evaluate. No question, it had increased substantially. The problem was how to calculate the improvement. Perhaps the best measure of the productivity improvement would be to calculate it for the total company as shown in Exhibit 8-9. This example relates total costs to

EXHIBIT 8-9

MULTI-FLEX CORPORATION
ANNUAL OPERATING STATISTICS

Year	Net Sales, $	Net Profits (Loss), $	Profit on Sales, %	Added Costs (cumulative), $	Added Costs* on Sales, %	Costs of Sales,† %	Productivity Improvement, %
Base‡	12,923,000	(1,125,000)	(8.7)			108.7	0
1964	14,667,000	161,000	1.1			98.9	10
1965	14,623,000	507,000	3.5	702,000	4.8	91.7	19
1966	12,780,000	701,000	5.5	1,143,000	9.0	85.5	27

* Added cost = Increases in salaries and wages, fringe benefits, local taxes and some overhead items.

† Costs of sales—Adjusted for added costs.

‡ Base year = Average of three years, 1961 through 1963.

Calculation:

$$\% \text{ productivity improvement} = \frac{108.7 - 85.5}{85.5} = 27\%$$

total net sales and then factors in the added cost of increases in salaries and wages, fringe benefits, local taxes, and some overhead items. On this basis total company productivity increased approximately 27 percent over a 3-year period. The simplest measure of the improvement, however, was that a $1 million loss per year was turned into a $700,000 profit.

THE REASONS BEHIND THE RESULTS

Several principles for increasing productivity can be learned from Multi-Flex. They include:

1. Management must provide the initiative and guidance and the programs in order to make worthwhile things happen.

2. Employees at all levels are most responsive when they are well informed about the objectives, programs, problems, and progress of the enterprise.

3. Most people want to do the right thing but they need help and direction.

4. Employees are great problem identifiers and solvers when asked to show what they can do.

5. The management encouraged the employees to identify the barriers to first-time performance, because once a barrier or problem is defined, ideas immediately are forthcoming for its solution.

6. Employees welcome the opportunity to tell the "boss" what's wrong and they will continue to point out barriers if the "boss" acts quickly and constructively to correct the conditions.

7. Work isn't always fun, but people can find work satisfying if it can be made stimulating and meaningful.

8. Pride, teamwork, recognition, achievement are powerful medicines when mixed with an apothecary's care and administrated regularly in strong doses.

9. Synergy is possible only when there is teamwork.

10. Change is necessary in order to maintain employee interest. The best program will become routine and dull in time if it is not improved.

The April 1966 issue of the Multi-Flex newsletter contained some wisdom that is appropriate to completing the Multi-Flex story. It is:

TO LOOK IS ONE THING,
TO SEE WHAT YOU LOOK AT IS ANOTHER,
TO UNDERSTAND WHAT YOU SEE IS A THIRD,
TO LEARN FROM WHAT YOU UNDERSTAND IS STILL SOMETHING ELSE,
BUT TO ACT ON WHAT YOU LEARN IS ALL THAT REALLY MATTERS!

9
Computer Operates on Hospital Costs

Hospital costs have been rising at a sickening pace. Inflation has penetrated into all corners of the hospitals. Staff wages have increased. Just about everything a hospital needs and uses costs more. The new diagnostic machines and laboratory equipment are expensive, not in terms of what they can do but in relation to their impact on the hospital bill. It's very difficult to say what is or is not expensive when human feelings and health and life are the issue. Blue Cross–Blue Shield premiums in Illinois have been raised more than 240 percent in 6 years. This probably is typical of the trend all over and is directly related to costs. Part of the problem stems from the way hospitals are reimbursed. Medicare and the hospitalization insurance plans, like Blue Cross–Blue Shield, seemingly just pay the bill so long as the items shown are covered legitimately by the plan policies. This method of compensation puts little or no restraint on the hospitals. Literally, the hospitals are given a blank check when what they really need is an incentive to reduce costs. It takes a firm board of trustees and a resolute administrator to move against this alarming trend.

The sad joke today is that only the very poor and the very rich can enjoy the best of hospital care. The rest of us can't afford it. This seems funny, not because the statement is grotesque but because it is so true. The very people who are the backbone of this country are the ones who are being priced out of good health care. They have earned the best but now hardly can afford it. Certainly this situation cannot go on much longer. Someone, some group, some hospital, some company must lead the way out of this untenable state of affairs.

The situation is about to become even more acute. Medicare, which was amended to the Social Security Act in 1966, catapulted the federal government into the business side of running a hospital. Since then most hospitals have had to convert their financial and cost accounting programs to computerized processing, a necessity in order to administer the increasingly complex government-dominated reimbursement system. In 1972, a second amendment was added to the Social Security Act. This Professional Standards Review Organization (PSRO) amendment has widened the government's horizon in health services to include "appropriateness of care" in addition to "cost of care." The PSRO requirements for medical audit and utilization review are guaranteed to escalate demands on the clinical side of hospital activities. Reduced to simple terms, the medical audit inquires whether the quality of care was sufficient, while the utilization review asks if the patient is in the appropriate medical facility to receive the care that is needed. Thus, the hospitals will have to perform the required review procedures internally or be subjected to external evaluation. This phase is only beginning. Hospital costs are certain to accelerate their upward trend unless a breakthrough is discovered and implemented on a broad scale.

THE ECH-TMIS TEAM

El Camino Hospital and Technicon Medical Information Systems Corporation, both of Mountain View, California, joined forces several years ago to do something about hospital services and costs. It was perfectly natural that these two institutions would team up to solve these problems. Historically, El Camino Hospital (ECH) has had significantly lower costs than the average of the other Northern California hospitals according to Blue Cross statistics. In 1971, Technicon of Tarrytown, New York, formed the present Technicon Medical Information Systems Corporation (TMIS). TMIS, with its highly developed computer technology, and ECH, with a staff trained and devoted to excellent health care and cost containment, organized a team equal to the challenge. ECH had one additional element that served as an interface between the potentials of the computer and the hospital staff—its management engineering department. The ECH management engineers, through their methods studies and previous work, had earned the respect of the doctors, nurses, and administrators. This was important for both the clinical orientation of the system and for its successful implementation.

First, let's look at El Camino Hospital. It is a general community hospital with 464 beds and 52 bassinets serving patients under the care of their own personal physicians. The hospital is of the nonprofit, tax-supported (district), short-term type. Its facilities are modern, adequate, and in excellent condition. The hospital provides the latest inpatient and outpatient ancillary services, acute cardiac and intensive care, psychiatric facilities, and kidney dialysis. Diagnostic, surgical, and nursing facilities are available for open-heart surgery patients. The hospital also is used by area physicians for diagnostic procedures such as heart catheterization, electromyographic analysis of nerve function, blood gases, and radioactive isotope studies of various body organs. The medical staff consists of about 340 physicians with 170 courtesy medical memberships. Interns or residents are not employed normally. There are 470 full-time nurses, and the total hospital staff averages about 1050 full-time equivalents (FTEs). Traditionally, it has been considered a well-managed hospital. Its average per diem charge and its average length of patient stay since its inception in 1961 have been well below the Northern California area averages. ECH personnel have been working thoughtfully and hard to maintain this tradition. Technicon's Medical Information System (MIS) has helped in this effort. ECH's staff believe quality of service is paramount; their definition of quality is accuracy, timeliness, and completeness of care being given to the patients.

WHAT MIS DOES AT ECH

Computers are not new in hospitals, but MIS was the first computer system designed for direct professional (physicians, nurses) use. It is a system designed by doctors for doctors and by nurses for nurses. The terminology displayed on the video matrix terminal (VMT) is determined by the users themselves and is easily modified. Information can be retrieved or orders generated simply by pointing a light pen at the appropriate place on the video screen and pressing a button. MIS is designed to operate as fast as a person thinks; that is, the system's response to most light pen selections is about one-half second. It is used by everyone in the hospital—doctors, nurses, laboratory technicians, pharmacists, accountants, clerks, and others. In short, it is a hospitalwide, real-time, automated system for quickly and accurately handling clinical, administrative, and financial information. The printers used with the system are designed to be quiet enough to be located in a hospital ward without disturbing patients. The on-line computer provides data upon request at any one of the VMTs in the hospital.

Technicon briefly described MIS this way:

> The VMT's and Multiprinters provide the hospital personnel with the most convenient, comfortable means of communicating. The VMT consists of a television screen, a light pen for rapid selection of information presented on the screen and a keyboard [see Exhibit 9-1]. The VMT is used to send or retrieve information such as medical orders, lab results, diagnostic information, and medications, to name a few. The high speed, quiet Multiprinter [Exhibit 9-1] produces hard copy cumulative Laboratory and Medications reports, x-ray requisitions, laboratory worksheets, medications due lists, pharmacy and specimen labels and patient care plans. Important sections of printouts can be highlighted by large size print or double printing for easy recognition of key data.

> Each person authorized to use the VMT's is assigned a secure four-digit identification code which acts like an electronic combination lock. This code limits each person's access to only information appropriate for his or her work. Only valid codes can gain access to information in MIS. Studies conducted to crack the code have produced some interesting results. MIS has proven to be more secure than conventional manual systems.

Three additional features of MIS are as follows:

1. *Mini medical library*—Physicians with exceptional expertise in a particular field can store this information in MIS for instant retrieval by other physicians. To date there are approximately 1500 pages of "medical library" information in operational use. They cover a variety of subjects including antibiotic-sensitivity surveys, abstracts of recent surgical articles, assistance in interpreting laboratory test results, drug-choice information, advisories on special work-ups such as thyroid disease, hyperlipodemia, and others.

2. *Automated devices for reporting laboratory test results*—Two new methodologies for reporting laboratory test results have been added to MIS to supplement the VMT entry method. An automatic interface has been built to

EXHIBIT 9-1

**TECHNICON VIDEO MATRIX TERMINAL
AND TECHNICON MULTIPRINTER.**

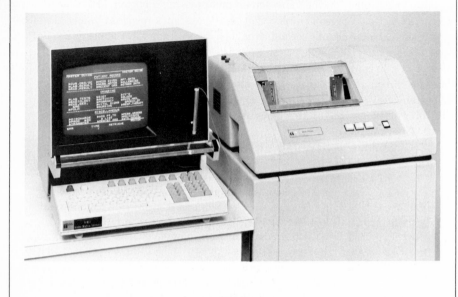

permit direct entry of chemistry and hematology test results from the analyzer, through a minicomputer, into MIS. The laboratory retains full monitoring control over this system and can release or hold results as desired. The second new methodology is a mark-sense card reader and specially designed cards on which the lab technologist can record test results. The cards are stacked in the hopper of the card-reading device and MIS automatically handles the printing and distribution of the test results.

3. *Drug allergy alert*—The pharmacist now receives automatic notification of the patient's drug allergies (printed with the medication label) whenever a medication is ordered.

PATIENT ADMISSION TO DISCHARGE

Now let's quickly follow MIS from the admission of a patient to his or her discharge. This should give a better "feel" for the action taking place. Technicon related the process as follows:

A patient's computer record originates when he is admitted or pre-admitted. Using special VMT displays which are similar in context to conventional Admitting forms, the admission clerk assembles the patient's basic record, consisting of name, age, sex, address, insurance coverage and other vital statistics. The computer stores this information and makes it available to approved hospital personnel.

The physician, upon identifying himself by typing his code into any VMT keyboard, receives a list of his patients on the VMT screen. He selects a particular patient (using the light pen on the video screen) and can then either write new orders for the patient, or review any previous orders and test results. When the physician writes new orders or renews or discontinues previous orders, a New Medical Orders sheet is immediately printed at the patient's nursing station. In addition, all orders are automatically printed as service requisitions in the appropriate hospital departments. Each requisition is uniquely formatted to accommodate each department's needs. For example, a laboratory requisition prints in the form of a worksheet for the specific test ordered, including spaces for all results to be filled in. In addition, the computer periodically prints Specimen Pickup Lists pre-sorted in bed number sequence. For each drug order, the computer automatically prints two documents in the Pharmacy—a prescription record and a gummed label for the medication container. Dietary orders print in the form of a consolidated Diet Orders List, generated just prior to each meal. This Dietary Department printout is in bed number sequence with a separate page for each nursing station.

The computer also generates many follow-on documents as a result of medical orders. These include: Medication Due Lists printed at each nursing station for each hour of the day, Daily Orders Summaries which show both newly written orders and all current orders, Reminder Notices for overdue laboratory work and late medications administration. For all orders which are to be accomplished on a future date, the computer automatically prints requisitions in the appropriate departments on the correct date or dates.

When the laboratory, radiology, or other service department has completed a diagnostic test or examination, the results are entered into MIS via the VMT. Special VMT displays are used for each type of test, and the results are immediately and directly entered by either a light-pen selection technique or by keyboard—depending on which method is more efficient. As test results are entered into the computer, they immediately become available for screen retrieval at any VMT and/or print out at the appropriate nursing unit. In addition, the computer summarizes and prints all laboratory results for each patient at the nursing station. "STAT" (emergency) orders or results receive special immediate processing throughout the system.

Just prior to the start of each shift, the computer prints a Patient Care Plan for each patient. This document combines diet and fluid balance orders, medications to be given, laboratory work, nursing instructions, and patient data such as "wears dentures" or "speaks Spanish." The care plan is used for the shift change report and for giving and annotating care throughout the shift.

Nurse reporting of medications given, intake and output, and other patient data is done via the VMT using special video displays and the light pen.

Every night the computer reviews each patient's record to determine the charges that have accrued for the day (daily hospital service charge, medications given, laboratory tests and others). The appropriate charges for each item are assigned by the computer and the billing file is updated.

After the patient is discharged, the computer goes through the complete patient file and prepares a series of documents, including:

1. A Test Results Summary, which contains all laboratory, radiology, and other test results which were entered into the computer for the period of hospitalization. Two copies are printed—one for Medical Records and one for the physician's office.

2. An insurance form for the physician's office.

3. The patient's itemized bill.

Throughout the patient's stay in the hospital, and at discharge time, the computer has printed a series of documents which now become a part of the chart to be filed in Medical Records. In addition, the patient's complete computer record is retained on magnetic tape at the computer center.

Thus, MIS at El Camino Hospital is a comprehensive data system for patient care and hospital management functions. It uses a large-scale computer and advanced input/output devices to record information at its source and to make this information available throughout the hospital when and where it is needed. Its basic objective is to provide better patient care and more efficient hospital operations through an improved communication system. MIS substitutes computer processing for manual data processing, thus gaining advantages in terms of speed, accuracy, cost, legibility, and completeness and consistency of data.

This application of Technicon's Medical Information System at El Camino Hospital is the most complete design conceived to date for a complex situation involving a broad range of professional variables and people. It works. It is effective and it is efficient.

INSTALLATION OF MIS, A CRITICAL PERIOD

Before evaluating how well MIS functions, let's review how the program was introduced into ECH. In the fall of 1971, a hospital team of four knowledgeable people was assembled—a nurse and three management engineers. This team was given the responsibility for the planning, training, and implementation of the installation. The broad questions to be resolved by the team included:

1. How to train the people who were to use the new system and gain their acceptance of MIS.

2. Where to start the installation.

3. How to coach and reinforce the people involved in bringing the new system on line.

4. How fast to install and expand the new system and assure the success of the total program.

5. How much duplication between the old and the new system was desirable in order to avoid irreconcilable errors and omissions.

Since this was one of the first attempts to automate an entire hospital, the team carefully experimented with trial-and-error methods. They determined the nurses would be the key to the successful implementation of MIS. They wrote lesson plans and then tested them with a group of volunteer nurses. This experience was used to modify and improve the plans and the training techniques they were developing. Gradually, the training media took shape and was finalized. The training was carried out in two steps. First the people were taught in a classroom how to use the video matrix terminals and the data that was available in the new system. Technicon had developed a "practice hospital" that simulated a real hospital's operations for training purposes. This gave the users of MIS a thorough familiarity and foundation in the new techniques. For example, the final project report, dated September 1975, prepared by the management engineering group, described the MIS training program as follows:

> Nursing classes consisted of about seven registered nurses attending five one-hour sessions over a two-week period. The orientation covered the physical mechanics, actual methods of system use (charting, care planning, discharging), projected nurses' role changes and the benefits to be derived from the use of the system. Physician specialties were trained in conjunction with the planned implementation of corresponding nursing stations. It was determined that one two-hour session would be sufficient for a physician to be oriented. The average class size was five. Orientation included an overview, methods of writing orders, retrieving data and the use of computer documents with special emphasis placed on the concept of the physician's personal order sets. Ancillary departments were oriented initially on a group basis within their own departments, with the actual departmental users trained individually according to their needs.

Further, the team decided that two people skilled in the use of MIS should be available at all times in each hospital unit for on-the-job instructions and troubleshooting. They provided for extra nurses to be trained so that nurses trained in MIS could be transferred to the next unit to go on the system without any degradation in the units already operating with MIS.

They carefully selected the first unit to go on line. The prime consideration was that the nurses in the first unit had to be enthusiastic about the potential MIS promised for creative growth in nursing and in the functioning of the hospital. In other words, they selected the unit that had the most dedicated believers in the new way. The team prepared a time schedule for implementing MIS throughout all nursing units and hospital departments. In general, 2 weeks were scheduled for installing MIS in a unit. During the first week, a Technicon representative and a nurse skilled in MIS were in attendance on each shift. The Technicon representative was scheduled to move on to the next point of implementation at the end of the first week. On January 4, 1972, the changeover began at the nursing station 4 West. The admitting department had gone on line a week earlier. Admission data, doctors' orders, and patient information were in the computer ready to go. Parallel operation of the old manual system and the new MIS automated system was carried on for the first day only. This was done to make certain nothing was overlooked. It took from 4 to 6 weeks to establish MIS as a well-running routine in the unit. Technicon engineers and the ECH team worked diligently to solve initial problems as they arose. Equipment reliability and queuing to use the VMTs were the major concern. As soon as critical difficulties were resolved, the program was advanced to the next unit.

A major change was made in the doctor-nurse relationship. Some tensions were created, but gradually the differences were dissipated. With the old system when a medication order was incomplete, a nurse completed it. Under MIS, the doctor had to "write" a prescription completely the first time. MIS would not accept the order unless it specified the drug, dose, route, and schedule of administration. Also, the nurses became proficient sooner than the doctors. One reason for this was that MIS became an integral part of their daily routine, while the doctors used the VMTs 5 to 15 minutes a day on those days when they had patients in the hospital. In time, however, many doctors became skillful, too. Charting was another problem area. This was resolved by revising charting methods and terminology to take advantage of the benefits of automation. Ten months later the entire hospital was operating smoothly under the new MIS program. Much training had taken place, many problems had been resolved. In every case, the ECH team kept the attention of the entire staff focused on "making MIS work."

ACCURACY AND RELIABILITY

Any new system to be of value must be accurate and reliable. This emphasis goes "double" in a hospital. Since MIS was designed to serve a medical environment, accuracy and reliability were given top priority as design concepts. Numerous checking features were built into the system, including:

1. A feedback signal which creates a "bright spot" on the VMT screen on the word being selected by the light pen.

2. Two immediate positive confirmations each time a light-pen selection is made—first, the computer displays a check mark in front of the selected word ($\checkmark$), and second, the computer displays the selected word(s) in a confirmation area at the top of the screen.

3. In addition to the above checks to confirm each light-pen selection as it is made, a final review and confirmation of the entire series of light-pen selections (medical orders) is *required* before the computer will process a light-penned message. When the user signals his or her final confirmation of a computer message, he or she is reviewing a "mirror image" of the message which is already in temporary storage in the computer. This means there is no possibility of a transmission error after confirmation.

4. Checks are made for completeness of information as it is light-penned. If essential data items (for example, schedules) are missing, the computer rejects the entry and explains what data must be added.

5. MIS is based upon the principle that the computer prints documents (requisitions, reports, and other information) at the using location, thus eliminating incorrect routing or pigeonholing of documents.

6. MIS follows up on action items (medications to be given, laboratory tests, and others), and if they are not accomplished on a timely basis, prints a reminder notice.

7. MIS printouts which are most useful at a specific time of day (for example, day-shift patient care plans are needed at 6:30 A.M.) are automatically triggered by the computer clock and are not dependent upon someone remembering to request them.

8. To ensure that no information is lost because of a hardware or software malfunction, MIS incorporates extensive data recovery provisions. These include: first, logging of all computer inputs on a transaction tape; second, the ability to "play back" the transaction tape covering either a short time span (up to 15 minutes) or a long time span (up to 24 hours); and third, the permanent maintenance of all computerized records in a tape library.

9. To reduce the effects of hardware failures, the IBM 370/155 central computer is backed up by an IBM 370/145.

MIS's downtime for all reasons has been reduced 48 percent over the past 2½ years. During the period July–December 1972, downtime averaged 15.18 minutes per day, while for the 6-month period July–December 1974 the total downtime averaged 7.86 minutes per day split to 3.90 minutes on the day shift, 1.46 for evenings, and 2.50 minutes for nights. During this same period the frequency of MIS downtime averaged 1 downtime every 3 days for the day shift, every 5 days for evenings, and every 7 days for nights. The average uptime rose from 98.9 percent in 1972 to 99.3 percent in 1974 to 99.6 percent in 1975.

A primary benefit of MIS has been error reduction. Information-handling errors of all kinds in all areas (laboratory, patient care, pharmacy, radiology, and others) were reduced by one-half, from 7.58 percent under the manual system to 3.70 percent with MIS. At the same time the turnaround time of almost all routine procedures was reduced sharply. Table 9-1 compares typical turnaround times:

TABLE 9-1

Department	Manual	MIS
1. Pharmacy—stat medicines	1 to 2 hrs.	Less than 5 mins.
2. Laboratory		
a. Ordering to results reporting	½ to 15 hrs.	¼ to 4 hrs.
b. Results reporting from automated equipment to nursing unit	1 to 3 hrs.	Less than 5 mins.
3. Radiology—ordering to results reporting	24 to 48 hrs.	11 hrs.

THE OVERALL RESULTS AND MANAGEMENT ENGINEERING

The results achieved at El Camino Hospital from the installation of Technicon's Medical Information System are significant. Errors have been reduced, turnaround times have improved, the productivity of the hospital staff has increased, and hospital costs have been contained. ECH is much more efficient today. Keep in mind, ECH operations and costs compared favorably with the hospitals in its area before MIS. This was not a poor hospital that suddenly responded to attention. ECH was a well-managed hospital that became even better with the introduction of MIS. Many people contributed to the success of the ECH-Technicon MIS project. In a very real sense they were pioneering. They reached out beyond the known and in a series of carefully planned and logically executed steps significantly raised the state-of-the-art of managing a hospital. They have achieved a breakthrough.

The Battelle Final Report, funded by a $1,500,000 four-year Health, Education and Welfare grant, on evaluation of the implementation of Technicon's Medical Information System in a general community hospital, dated December 19, 1975, reviews the entire ECH-MIS project in detail. The report gave special mention to ECH's management engineers as follows:

> The Management Engineering Department played the key role in implementing MIS. Personnel from the department were assigned to all hospital departments to provide implementation support. In effect, the head of each department had a staff assistant in the person of the management engineering representative who supported the department head to attain the best possible operation from MIS through:
>
> 1. Developing of MIS methods that modify or replace manual methods.
>
> 2. Auditing MIS operations to ensure that information is accurate and complete.
>
> 3. Coordinating interdepartmental MIS operations attributable to MIS implementation.
>
> 4. Promoting changes to MIS that improve departmental operations.
>
> 5. Identifying systems problems and transmitting them to Technicon.
>
> 6. Implementing changes to MIS as they occurred.
>
> 7. Assisting in reviewing departmental objectives, responsibilities, and authority.
>
> 8. Performing special studies to obtain cost savings benefits realization, and quality improvement.

Prior to the ECH-MIS program, the management engineering department at ECH had three management engineers. Today, the staff consists of five engineers, one registered nurse, and a secretary. This staff uses time standards, methods analysis, work simplification, work sampling, and statistical analysis to make certain that methods continue to improve and to assure management and supervision that hospital staffs are balanced effectively with the projected workloads. For example, ECH management engineers developed a comprehensive Nurse Scheduling and Allocation System to realize the cost savings potential of MIS. It is composed of five interrelated subsystems as follows:

1. *Workload forecasting*—prediction of future patient load by nursing unit

2. *Scheduling*—assignment of work days by employee to meet forecast demands

3. *Skills inventory*—continuous identification and documentation of special staff skills

4. *Allocation*—adjustment in staffing pattern necessary because of variance between actual and forecast workload, unscheduled employee absence, and temporary special skill needs

5. *Management reporting and control*—operational data summaries to provide nursing administration meaningful control information

The Nurse Scheduling and Allocation System is predicated upon a permanent staff in each nursing unit supplemented by utilizing float and per diem personnel plus assignment of patients to the unit best able to absorb additional load. The foundation for the system is the patient dependency categorization guidelines shown in Exhibit 9-2. From work measurement analyses the relationships between the number of patients in each category and the staff required per shift for proper patient care was developed as illustrated in Exhibit 9-3. Exhibit 9-4 shows how this information is used daily to determine staffing needs in each nursing unit. This is a very significant control in view of the fact that nursing accounts for about 45 percent of the total hospital staff. This is an example of the type of management system being utilized by the hospital to control costs with aid of the MIS system.

The Battelle study concluded that:

El Camino Hospital was successful in translating time saved by nursing and ancillary department personnel into staff reductions using an effective benefits realization methodology. This process was facilitated by the active support of the hospital administration and by having management engineers work cooperatively with nursing administrators, head nurses, and ancillary department heads. Starting with the major workload reductions and procedural changes resulting from the implementation of MIS, the benefits realization teams re-defined job roles, re-distributed the remaining work load peaks and valleys, and improved and standardized methods. New lower staffing levels were defined, agreed to, implemented and monitored for operational effectiveness. A nursing standardization committee was established and worked cooperatively with the benefits realization teams. In many departments, but particularly in Nursing, the introduction of MIS acted as a change agent, or catalyst, to effect improvements that theoretically could have been, but in practice would not have been, implemented without MIS. One change resulted in a major reorganization of the Nursing Department, wherein the responsibility and authority of the head nurse was considerably enlarged, and the nursing administration group reorganized to provide specialized staff support to the nursing units. A workload forecasting and staffing allocation system was developed and implemented to improve matching of

EXHIBIT 9-2

PATIENT DEPENDENCY CATEGORIZATION GUIDELINES.

Area of Care	Category I	Category II	Category III	Category IV
Eating	Feeds self or needs little help.	Needs some help in preparing food for eating. May need encouragement.	Cannot feed self but is able to chew and swallow.	Cannot feed self and may have difficulty chewing and swallowing.
Grooming	Almost entirely self-sufficient.	Needs some help with bathing, oral hygiene, hair combing, etc.	Unable to do much for self.	Completely dependent.
Excretion	Up and to bathroom alone or almost alone.	Needs some help in getting up to bathroom or using urinal.	In bed needing bedpan or urinal placed and removed. May be able to partially turn or lift self.	Completely dependent.
Comfort	Self-sufficient.	Needs some help with adjustment of position or bed (tubes, IVs, etc.).	Cannot turn without help, get drink, adjust position of extremities, etc.	Completely dependent.
General Health	Good—in for diagnostic procedure, simple treatment, or surgical procedure (D&C, biopsy, minor fracture, etc.).	Mild symptoms—more than one mild illness, mild debility, mild emotional reaction, mild incontinence (not more than once/ shift).	Acute symptoms—severe emotional reaction to illness or surgery, more than one acute medical or surgical problem, severe or frequent incontinence.	Critically ill, may have severe emotional reaction.
Treat-ments	Simple—supervised ambulation, pedangle, simple dressing, test	Any Category I treatment more than once/shift, Foley cath. care,	Any treatment more than twice/ shift, medicated IVs, complicated	Any elaborate or delicate procedure, procedure requiring 2

	procedure preparation not requiring medication, reinforcement of surgical dressing, X-pad vital signs once/shift.	I&O, bladder irrigations, sitz bath, compresses, test procedures requiring medication or follow-ups, simple (nonmedicated) IVs, simple enema for evacuation, vital signs every 4 hrs.	dressings, sterile procedures, care of tracheotomy, Harris flush, suctioning, tube feeding, vital signs more than every 4 hours.	nurses, vital signs more often than every 2 hours.
Medications	Simple, routine, not needing pre- or post-evaluation, PRN, medications no more than once/shift.	Diabetic, cardiac, hypophypertensive, diuretic, anticoagulant medications, PRN medications more than once/shift, medication needing pre- or post-evaluation.	Unusual amount of Category II medications, control of refractory diabetics (need to be monitored more than every 4 hours).	More intensive Category III medications, IVs with frequent close observation and regulation.
Teaching and Emotional Support	Routine follow-up teaching, patients with no unusual or adverse emotional reactions.	Initial teaching of care of ostomics, new diabetics, tubes that will be in place for periods of time, conditions requiring major change in eating, living, or excretory practices. Patients with mild adverse reactions to their illness—depressions, overly demanding, etc.	More intensive Category II items, teaching of apprehensive or mildly resistive patients, care of moderately upset or apprehensive patients, confused or disoriented patients.	Teaching of resistive patient care and support of patients with severe emotional reaction.

actual staff to workload requirements. Perhaps most importantly, the introduction of MIS has created a climate wherein nursing and ancillary department staffs accept, adapt to, and support continual change that leads to improved hospital efficiency, effectiveness, and cooperation in a MIS environment.

The MIS program has been accepted by the physicians, the nurses, the technicians, and the administrative personnel at ECH. MIS is a vital, integral part of hospital operations and is used voluntarily by 78 percent of the physicians and by 100 percent of the nurses. In July 1974, an attitude survey was conducted among the nurses at ECH relating to various aspects of MIS. This was followed in August 1974

EXHIBIT 9-3

CHART PREPARED FOR CONVERTING PATIENTS' NURSING NEEDS INTO STAFFING REQUIREMENTS.

STAFF ASSIGNMENT GUIDE

NURSING UNIT _____

NO OF PATIENTS	STAFF REQUIRED PER SHIFT (BY CATEGORY & CENSUS)											
	DAY SHIFT				EVE SHIFT				NITE SHIFT			
	1	2	3	4	1	2	3	4	1	2	3	4
1	.2	.3	.4	.5	.1	.2	.3	.5	.1	.1	.1	.2
2	.4	.5	.7	1.1	.3	.5	.6	.9	.1	.2	.3	.4
3	.5	.8	1.1	1.6	.4	.7	.9	1.4	.2	.3	.4	.7
4	.7	1.1	1.5	2.2	.6	.9	1.2	1.8	.3	.4	.6	.9
5	.9	1.4	1.9	2.7	.7	1.1	1.5	2.3	.4	.5	.7	1.1
6	1.1	1.6	2.2	3.3	.9	1.4	1.8	2.7	.4	.7	.9	1.3
7	1.2	1.9	2.6	3.8	1.0	1.6	2.1	3.2	.5	.8	1.0	1.5
8	1.4	2.2	3.0	4.4	1.2	1.8	2.4	3.6	.6	.9	1.2	1.8
9	1.6	2.5	3.3	4.9	1.3	2.0	2.7	4.1	.6	1.0	1.3	2.0
10	1.8	2.7	3.7	5.5	1.5	2.3	3.0	4.5	.7	1.1	1.5	2.2
11	2.0	3.0	4.1	6.0	1.6	2.5	3.4	5.0	.8	1.2	1.6	2.4
12	2.1	3.3	4.4	6.6	1.8	2.7	3.7	5.4	.9	1.3	1.8	2.6
13	2.3	3.6	4.8	7.1	1.9	2.9	4.0	5.9	.9	1.4	1.9	2.9
14	2.5	3.8	5.2	7.7	2.1	3.2	4.3	6.3	1.0	1.5	2.1	3.1
15	2.7	4.1	5.6	8.2	2.2	3.4	4.6	6.8	1.1	1.6	2.2	3.3
16	2.9	4.4	5.9	8.8	2.3	3.6	3.9	7.2	1.1	1.8	2.4	3.5
17	3.0	4.7	6.3	9.3	2.5	3.8	5.2	7.7	1.2	1.9	2.5	3.7
18	3.2	4.9	6.7	9.9	2.6	4.1	5.5	8.1	1.3	2.0	2.7	4.0
19	3.4	5.2	7.0	10.4	2.8	4.3	5.8	8.6	1.4	2.1	2.8	4.2
20	3.6	5.5	7.4	11.0	2.9	4.5	6.1	9.0	1.4	2.2	3.0	4.4
21	3.7	5.8	7.8	11.5	3.1	4.7	6.4	9.5	1.5	2.3	3.1	4.6
22	3.9	6.0	8.2	12.1	3.2	5.0	6.7	9.9	1.6	2.4	3.3	4.8
23	4.1	6.3	8.5	12.6	3.4	5.2	7.0	10.4	1.6	2.5	3.4	5.1
24	4.3	6.6	8.9	13.2	3.5	5.4	7.3	10.8	1.7	2.6	3.6	5.3
25	4.5	6.9	9.3	13.7	3.7	5.6	7.6	11.3	1.8	2.7	3.7	5.5
26	4.6	7.1	9.6	14.3	3.8	5.9	7.9	11.7	1.9	2.9	3.9	5.7
27	4.8	7.4	10.0	14.8	4.0	6.1	8.2	12.2	1.9	3.0	4.0	5.9
28	5.0	7.7	10.4	15.4	4.1	6.3	8.5	12.6	2.0	3.1	4.2	6.1
29	5.2	8.0	10.8	15.9	4.3	6.5	8.8	13.1	2.1	3.2	4.3	6.4
30	5.3	8.2	11.1	16.5	4.4	6.8	9.1	13.5	2.1	3.3	4.4	6.6

EXHIBIT 9-4

FORM USED TO DETERMINE TOTAL STAFFING SCHEDULE FOR EACH NURSING UNIT.

NURSING UNIT STAFFING SUMMARY

NURSING UNIT:_____   DATE:_____

PREPARED BY: _____

PATIENT DEPENDENCY CATEGORY	NUMBER OF PATIENTS	REQUIRED STAFF		
		DAY	EVENING	NIGHT
1	4	0.7		
2	12	3.3		
3	10	3.7		
4	3	1.6		
TOTAL	29	9.3		

STAFF SUMMARY	DAY	EVENING	NIGHT
SCHEDULED STAFF	9.10		
LESS: UNSCHEDULED ABSENCES (*1)	1.0		
AVAILABLE STAFF	8.10		
LESS: REQUIRED	9.13		
OVER OR (UNDER) (*2)	(1.3)		

(*1) List names and job titles of unsched. absentees

(*2) If (under), list job titles needed.

V. SMITH (RN)   1 RN

_____   _____

_____   _____

_____   _____

_____   _____

with a similar survey of the doctors who were using the system. The results of these two surveys appear in Table 9-2.

TABLE 9-2
Summary of Responses to 1974 Attitude Survey
Relating to Various Aspects of MIS

Category	Number of questions	Response, % Positive	Response, % Negative
Nursing Staff			
1. Training	3	88	12
2. Mechanical	5	97	3
3. Medical chart	13	87	13
4. Nursing care	5	94	6
5. Provision of medication	5	99	1
6. Information transfer	6	93	7
7. General evaluation	21	78	22
8. Interdepartmental	4	95	5
Total	62	88	12
Physician Users			
1. Training	3	90	10
2. Mechanical	5	89	11
3. Placing medical orders	9	66	34
4. Medical chart	10	63	37
5. Hospital practice and patient care			
Impact on patient care	5	62	38
Satisfaction with procedures	4	91	9
6. General evaluation	23	61	39
7. Research and information	3	94	6
8. Post discharge	2	66	34
Total	64	69	31

PRODUCTIVITY AND COST IMPROVEMENT

Nursing hours per patient admitted to the hospital averaged 41.42 at ECH in 1971, the period just prior to the implementation of MIS. For 1973, the first full year of operating with MIS, this average dropped to 35.00 hours per admission. This is an improvement of 16 percent in nursing productivity, and it occurred while the average for other similar hospitals in the Northern California area increased about 1 percent.

Exhibits 9-5 and 9-6 portray the impact of the ECH-MIS program in total on Blue Cross patients. Both exhibits compare ECH with the average for similar hospitals in Northern California. Exhibit 9-5 entitled "Per Diem Charges Compared (Blue Cross Data), 1970–1974," shows the area average in 1971 was $117.88

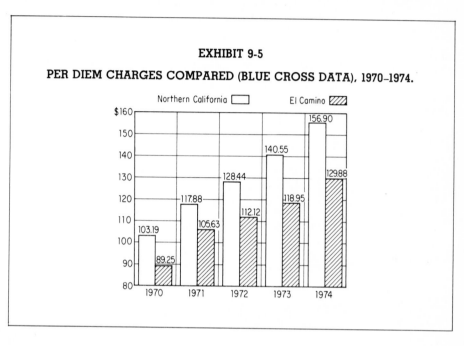

EXHIBIT 9-5

PER DIEM CHARGES COMPARED (BLUE CROSS DATA), 1970–1974.

Northern California ☐   El Camino ▨

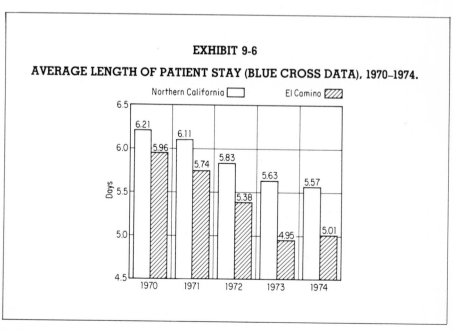

EXHIBIT 9-6

AVERAGE LENGTH OF PATIENT STAY (BLUE CROSS DATA), 1970–1974.

Northern California ☐   El Camino ▨

contrasted to $105.63 for ECH, a spread in ECH's favor of 10.4 percent. By 1974, the area average climbed to $156.90 while ECH's charge increased to $129.88. The spread, still in ECH's favor, increased to 17.2 percent. Thus, ECH was doing a better job of controlling its costs. Exhibit 9-6, entitled "Average Length of Patient Stay (Blue Cross Data) 1970–1974," reveals that in 1971 the area average was 6.11 days versus 5.74 for ECH, a difference of 6.1 percent in ECH's favor. In 1974, the area average declined to 5.57 while ECH had reduced its days per patient to 5.01, a difference in ECH's favor of 10.1 percent. Again, ECH outperformed its contemporaries. These two charts are very meaningful in terms of cost to the patients. Table 9-3 summarizes the combined impact of the daily charge and the average length of patient stay into composite totals as shown:

TABLE 9-3

| | Charge per Patient Stay | | | | |
Hospital	1970	1971	1972	1973	1974
Northern California					
Average	$641	$720	$749	$791	$874
ECH	532	606	603	589	651
Patient saving	$109	$114	$146	$202	$223

In terms of charge per patient, ECH was 15.8 percent lower in 1971 and 25.5 percent better in 1974 than the other hospitals in Northern California. The pioneering and hard work were producing tangible results. The average patient's bill was $223 less or 25.5 percent lower at El Camino Hospital.

THE PRINCIPLES INVOLVED

A review of the Medical Information System developed jointly by Technicon and El Camino Hospital brings to the surface management thinking and principles that have universal application. Application not only in hospital operations but in almost any endeavor—service, commerce, business, government, and manufacturing.

A few of these universal ideas are as follows:

1. It takes considerable management courage to embark upon a pioneering program and a high degree of capability to achieve success.

2. Management support is an absolute necessity in order to implement a new system that reaches into every corner of a business.

3. Thorough planning and meticulous attention to detail are necessary to make a major transition with a minimum of interruption to service.

4. Work measurement is the foundation for transforming potential improvements into actual gains.

5. Computer systems when specifically designed to meet the needs of a business can reduce cycle time, errors, and costs by significant amounts.

6. Employees enjoy a challenge and will respond constructively when management invites them into a program at the very beginning.

7. Computers can be made to react as fast as the human mind can think.

8. Eliminating manual paperwork has to be one of management's prime objectives, because shuffling papers costs too much and is slow and error prone.

A COMPUTER IS A
POWERFUL RESOURCE
IN THE HANDS OF
QUALIFIED PEOPLE

10

Assembly Methods and Standards Achieve Goals

AM International is a manufacturing and marketing division of Addressograph Multigraph Corporation of Cleveland, Ohio. AMI operates around the world through 21 subsidiaries, 87 dealers, 4 international branches, and 15 factories and service centers. All these operations are outside the United States of America and are located strategically to serve markets in Europe, Africa, Asia, Australia, South America, and Canada. The division markets the complete line of Addressograph Multigraph products, which includes copiers; data collecting, addressing, and mailing equipment; duplicators; strike-on and phototypesetters; diazo printers; microfiche cameras and duplicators; data recorders and credit cards; coated papers and films; chemicals and supplies; and a line of products for engineering departments such as drafting tables, desks, and file cabinets. Many of these products are manufactured by AMI, while others are produced in the United States and are exported to AMI's foreign markets.

In the spring of 1972, the vice president for operations of AMI was authorized to establish an engineering center in Liège, Belgium. Its purpose was to develop new products for the international markets and to furnish technical support to the international factories. The engineering center's prime functions, in addition to product development, were as follows:

1. To serve as a control source for all drawings, parts lists, and specifications.

2. To define and qualify foreign parts sources.

3. To provide technical backup for the AMI manufacturing and service operations.

4. To modify products to meet the special requirements of foreign countries.

ASSEMBLE MACHINES IN WEST GERMANY AND BELGIUM

The introduction of the engineering center into AMI activities set the foundation for standardizing the production of machines by types at various factories. It was decided that copiers would be produced at Sprendlingen, West Germany, and data recorders at Liège, Belgium. Plans were developed to install modern assembly methods including line production in these two plants. The first major assignment was to transfer the assembly of the Model 5000 Copier from the United States to Sprendlingen. This was necessitated in part by a need to produce a 220-volt, 50-hertz machine incorporating safety standards that would meet European requirements. The Model 5000 was a sophisticated copier that operated with rolls of coated paper. The machine was controlled by a solid-state electronic system that permitted cutting the paper automatically to almost any sheet length desired between 20 and 36 centimeters. From one to ninety-nine copies could be made with the aid of a two-digit counter. The optical system in the machine was very excellent and produced sharp-image copies. The machine was the fastest copier on the market. All these features combined to make the assembly, adjustment, and final testing of the machine complex.

A thorough analysis was made of costs before finally deciding to move the assembly of the Model 5000 to Sprendlingen. This study projected savings of $1,600,000 per year with an investment, including start-up expenses of $456,000. The indicated return on investment was 351 percent. The savings came from differentials in wage rates, royalty payments, duty tariffs, shipping costs, and methods improvements. A parts sourcing plan was formulated, and a program schedule was established. Designs were completed for rearranging the Sprendlingen plant so as to provide an assembly area including floor space for storing components and hardware and for warehousing finished machines. A four-man planning and coordinating team was established. The members of the team were experienced production engineers who had worked in international operations for a considerable time. The team consisted of the works manager of the Sprendlingen plant, the director of manufacturing operations planning, the director of manufacturing engineering, and a project engineer from AMI. Arrangements were made to train key Sprendlingen personnel in the United States and to provide on-the-line training at Sprendlingen. All assembly methods and tooling were reviewed and revised for volume production. This included a review of all drawings, operation sheets, manufacturing specifications, test requirements, and bills of materials. Procurement sources and schedules for tools, components, and hardware were established, and orders were placed. Essentially, the initial production was to be made with parts supplied by the United States, and gradually sources in England, Holland, Belgium, and West Germany were scheduled to begin supplying the required components. All small and large subassembly, final assembly, and check-out operations were assigned to Sprendlingen. The program was approved in May, and employee training and pilot-run assembly were scheduled to start in October, with production to begin in the first quarter of 1973. A very ambitious program!

The works manager assigned technically qualified personnel to the program. This group included a production supervisor, a line foreman, two manufacturing engineers, two material control people, and two quality control people. The group working closely with the coordinating team layed out the assembly and stores areas, selected the equipment, designed the tools, ordered and procured the tools and the components, hired and trained the employees, made necessary changes, analyzed and solved problems, and supervised the quality and the production of the Model 5000 Copier.

THE ASSEMBLY LAYOUT AND FLOW

The assembly and stock areas were laid out to utilize space and the workforce in the most effective manner. Exhibit 10-1 is a vertical cross-sectional view of the department. On the right side of the assembly aisle there were 7 small subassembly stations plus 20 major subassembly positions. On the left side were 16 final assembly stations. The first final assembly operation involved placing the machine base on a dolly. Thereafter, the dolly progressed through 15 stations of final assembly, optical adjustment, electrical test, mechanical adjustment and check-out, final inspection and tryout, readjustment as necessary, clean, and pack. When the packed machine left the production line, it was delivered immediately by lift truck to a bonded warehouse. The assembly stations were arranged so that the major components used at each work station were stored overhead and adjacent to it. Most of the parts required at each station were fed into the station from the rear by a material handler. Assembly fixtures and special tools when not in use were stored under the bench at the work station where they were normally needed. The entire layout was designed to utilize space fully and to minimize handling and rehandling of components, hardware, tools, assemblies, and machines. Exhibit 10-2 shows the entire assembly area with the stock racks overhead. Exhibit 10-3 is a close-up of a subassembly station.

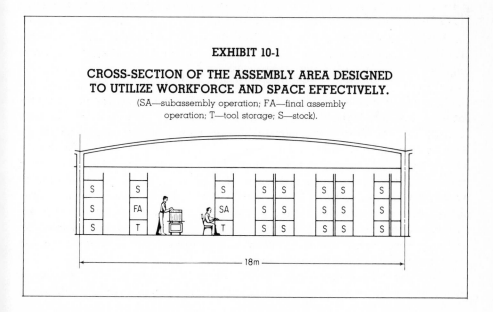

EXHIBIT 10-1

CROSS-SECTION OF THE ASSEMBLY AREA DESIGNED TO UTILIZE WORKFORCE AND SPACE EFFECTIVELY.

(SA—subassembly operation; FA—final assembly operation; T—tool storage; S—stock).

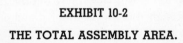

EXHIBIT 10-2
THE TOTAL ASSEMBLY AREA.

These pictures were taken before the racks were filled in order to show the type of construction.

DECISION TO INSTALL WORK MEASUREMENT

In August 1972, the vice president for operations decided that AMI should consider applying work measurement to the assembly operations. This was desired in order to assure that the best-known methods were employed, to ensure high productivity on the part of the employees, and to provide a factual basis for planning and controlling production and costs. A meeting was arranged in September at which the vice president had a consulting engineer conduct a one-day seminar in Sprendlingen on work measurement. The meeting was attended by the vice president and Sprendlingen's managing director, works manager, chairman of the Workers' Council, controller, manager of factory accounting, two manufacturing engineers, a production supervisor, and two foremen. A day later the same seminar was given at the engineering center in Liège, Belgium. This meeting was attended by the vice president and Liège's managing director, controller, and two production supervisors; and the chief engineer, assistant chief engineer, and two manufacturing engineering consultants from the engineering center. Following these two meetings, it was decided to install work measurement and cost controls in both factories.

TIMESTUDY TRAINING

Training in work measurement techniques was started in the middle of November. Five people were trained. Three were selected from within the factory at Sprendlingen by the works manager, and two by the managing director of the Liège factory. The prerequisites for the trainees were that they should speak English in addition to German for the Sprendlingen people and French for the Liège candidates; that they had demonstrated some mechanical aptitude in their work; and that they professed an interest in learning timestudy work. The Sprendlingen group included a manufacturing engineer and two very capable people from the factory, one of whom was vice chairman of the Workers' Council. The two from Liège were both engineers. The initial training was done in a series of classroom sessions—two weeks in November and one week in December. The intensive training consisted of thorough, concentrated, laboratory-type study and drill. Phil Carroll's book *Time-*

EXHIBIT 10-3

A SUBASSEMBLY WORK STATION.

study for Cost Control, served as the text. There were lectures, discussions, instructions, and tests emphasizing the following areas of work measurement:

1. *Mechanics*—Element breakdown, watch reading, relax factors, building and charting standard time data, methods analysis, setting time standards

2. *Performance rating*—Daily drill in performance rating using films and physical demonstrations with measurement and analysis of each timestudy trainee's improvement in ability to rate performance

3. *Employee response*—Conduct for obtaining the employees' cooperation, applying time standards and incentives, encouraging employees to reach expected performances

4. *Supervisory support*—Basic coaching in how to work with and through line supervisors to improve methods, correct workplace conditions, increase standards coverage, and improve employee performances

5. *Management thinking*—Fundamentals necessary for sound work measurement and wage incentives, importance of correct and consistent time standards as the basis for payrolls, costs, and control of production and manufacturing overhead

THE STANDARD DATA APPROACH

By the middle of December, the timestudy trainees were ready to go into the factory to begin the timestudy work. The first information they collected in the assembly department was the weight and the overall dimensions of each component and subassembly. The weight was necessary so that proper relax factors could be applied to the elemental time values obtained from the timestudies. For example, the instructions relating to relax factors read as follows:

Relax Factors are necessary in order to allow for the personal needs of the employee working on standard and to compensate for the fatigue encountered by the employee during the work day. The Relax Factors tabulated below consist of 5% for personal needs plus fatigue percentages related to the force required to lift, carry, push or pull in performing each element of work.

These Relax Factors are used with the NORMAL PACE equivalent to a performance of 100% and defined as dealing 52 cards into four piles in .45 minute.

The Relax Factors are applied to each element of work as follows:

ACTUAL MINUTES × % RATING × (100% + % RELAX FACTOR) =
ELEMENT STANDARD MINUTES

Example 1 Pickup Part   4 lbs. or 2 kg.
.06 × 110% × (100% + 15%) = .076

Example 2 Pickup Part   20 lbs. or 10 kg.
.06 × 110% × (100% + 25%) = .083

* Phil Carroll, *Timestudy for Cost Control,* 3d ed., McGraw-Hill Book Company, New York, 1954.

Force in lbs.	Force in kg.	Relax factor
0 to 8.0	0 to 4.0	15%
8.1 to 16.0	4.1 to 8.0	20%
16.1 to 32.0	8.1 to 16.0	25%
32.1 to 52.0	16.1 to 26.0	30%
52.1 to 70.0	26.1 to 36.0	35%
70.1 to 92.0	36.1 to 46.0	40%
92.1 to 117.0	46.1 to 58.0	45%

Next the parts and subassemblies were classified into readily identifiable groups by type as follows:

Group	Type of parts
A	Extrusions, channels, angle irons, straps. Shafts, spindles, spacers, studs, rollers.
B	Formed sheet metal and formed plastic parts, panels, doors. Switches, counters, locks, fuse boxes, sockets and small assemblies (0–4.0 kg) Cabinets, major subassemblies (4.1–8.0 kg) Cabinets, major subassemblies (8.1–16.0 kg) Cabinets, major subassemblies (16.1–26.0 kg) Lenses, mirrors, lamps, biases, PC boards, instruments. Cartons, boxes, envelopes, instruction sheets, decals, pressure sensitive labels, insulation.
C	Gears, wheels, pulleys, sprockets, bearings.
D	Pins, cotter pins, rivets, screws, bolts, nuts, washers, keys, tru-arcs, buttons, rubber bumpers, grommets, gaskets. Spiral springs, helical springs, leaf springs.
E	Timing belts, vacuum belts, transporting belts, electrical harnesses, cords, chains, lines.

Then the handling of parts was analyzed, and eighteen basic handling elements were defined. These were discussed at length so that each timestudy person knew each definition precisely and could recognize each element instantaneously during the timestudy of an operation. These basic handling elements included the following:

1. *Pickup*—Reach for, pick up and hold part(s), tool(s), or material(s), using either or both hands, from bench, carton, floor, conveyor, skid or other material handling equipment.

2. *Pickup and position*—Reach for, pick up, move, and set down part(s), tool(s), or material(s) into approximate position (on, near, above, below mating part), using either or both hands, from bench, carton, floor, conveyor, skid or other material handling equipment.

3. *Locate, open*—With part or material in approximate position (on, near, above or below mating part), move part, using either or both hands, into a predetermined location that is controlled but not exact.

4. *Locate, 2 point*—With part or material in approximate position (on, near, above or below mating part), move part, using either or both hands, into exact position over 2 pins, into 2 recesses, against 2 surfaces, or over 1 pin to a surface.

5. *Locate, interference fit*—With part or material in approximate position (on, near, above or below mating part), move part, using either or both hands, into mating part or tool to a predetermined location when force is required to overcome the interference fit of mating surfaces.

6. *Locate, 3 point*—With part or material in approximate position (on, near, above or below mating part), move part, using either or both hands, into exact position over 3 pins, or into an irregularly shaped recess.

7. *Align, open*—With part or material located, move part into precise alignment on all required axes or dimensions using either or both hands.

8. *Align, 2 point*—With part or material in approximate position (on, near, above or below mating part), move part, using either or both hands, into exact position over 1 pin to 1 line, or to 2 lines.

9. *Align, interference fit*—With part or material located, move part into precise alignment on all required axes or dimensions, using either or both hands, when force is required to overcome interference.

10. *Align, 3 point*—With part or material in approximate position (on, near, above or below mating part), move part, using either or both hands, into exact position over 1 pin to 2 lines, or 3 lines.

11. *Turnover 90°*—Reach for, pick up, turn part over with adjacent side up, and set down using either or both hands.

12. *Turnover 180°*—Reach for, pick up, turn part over with opposite side up, and set down using either or both hands.

13. *Rotate 90°*—Reach for, pick up, rotate part on longest axis 90° and set part down using either or both hands.

14. *Rotate 180°*—Reach for, pick up, rotate part on longest axis 180° and set part down using either or both hands.

15. *Remove and set aside*—Reach for, pick up, move aside and set down part(s), tool(s) or material(s) on bench, into bin pan, into carton or onto floor conveyor, skid or other material handling equipment.

16. *Set aside*—With part(s), tool(s) or material(s) in either or both hands, set aside on bench, into bin pan, into carton or onto conveyor, skid or other material handling equipment.

17. *Move hole-to-hole*—With part or tool in hand(s) move or slide to next hole or position and locate part or tool exactly.

18. *Tweezers*—Note the use of tweezers with any of the above elements by marking "TWZR" next to the time posted on the comparison sheet.

By January, subassembly operations were in production. The timestudy people began stopwatch studies using the above element definitions and parts classifications. After the actual time values were converted into element standard minutes, the values were posted to comparison sheets. The time values for those elements that were constants were analyzed and a representative value selected for each one. The time values for each variable element were plotted against various dimensions such as weight, length, area, and volume, and analyzed. As soon as sufficient data was plotted for each element, a representative curve was drawn. Each curve revealed how the time for that element varied as the dimension changed. From the curves formulas were developed, for example:

Group A, where the length L, in millimeters, of the part is the controlling dimension.

Pick up part from bench.

$T = .023 + .000040L$

or

Group B, where the major cross-sectional area A, in square centimeters, is the controlling dimension.

Pick up part from bench.

$T = .030 + .0000115A$

USE CHARTS TO SET TIME STANDARDS

All the elemental standard time values and formulas then were compiled in a series of charts. The charts covered all the handling elements plus a variety of elements performed in assembly, such as tighten a nut, use small tools, make adjustments, tap with hammer, clamp, apply grease, oil, clean, and many others. This information, called *standard data,* was used to set the time standard for each operation. The timestudy person developed the method in exact sequence of elements for performing an assembly operation and then selected the proper time value for each element from the standard data charts. Typical charts are shown in Exhibits 10-4, 10-5, and 10-6. Exhibit 10-4 illustrates part handling time values for group A and E parts classifications and covers parts in the 0–4.0 kilogram weight range. At the bottom of the chart are shown factors for heavier parts. Exhibit 10-5 relates to part handling for group B parts. Exhibit 10-6 covers a variety of conditions for assembling and disassembling screws, bolts, and nuts.

Assembling machines can involve considerable walking, either to and from the bench or around the machine as parts and subassemblies are mounted and secured and adjustments are made. The walking time was kept separate from the part handling and other elements. Exhibit 10-7 is a chart that provides elemental standard time values for walking based on the weight carried, the distance walked, and the number of turns required.

EXHIBIT 10-4

STANDARD DATA CHART FOR PART HANDLING—GROUP A AND E PARTS.

PART HANDLING—GROUP A AND GROUP E—STANDARD MINUTES

* Weight 0 - 4.0 kg

L(mm) Length From - To	Pickup Bench	Pickup Floor	Locate Open	Locate 2 Point	Locate Intf.	Align Open	Align 2 Point	Align Intf.	Rotate 90°	Rotate 180°	Remove & SA Bench	Remove & SA Floor	Set aside Bench	Set aside Floor
Constant	.023	.033	.028	.035	.044	.023	.050	.080	.023	.023	.023	.033	.020	.030
Variable (L)	.00004	.00004	.00015	.00023	.00038	.000096	.00038	.00056	.000011	.000054	.000029	.000029	.000023	.000023
0 - 30	.024	.034	.032	.041	.053	.025	.059	.093	.023	.024	.024	.034	.021	.031
31 - 43	.024	.034	.034	.044	.058	.027	.064	.101	.023	.025	.024	.034	.021	.031
44 - 58	.025	.035	.036	.047	.063	.028	.069	.108	.024	.026	.024	.034	.021	.031
59 - 75	.026	.036	.038	.050	.069	.029	.075	.117	.024	.027	.025	.035	.022	.032
76 - 93	.026	.036	.041	.054	.076	.031	.082	.127	.024	.028	.025	.035	.022	.032
94 - 113	.027	.037	.043	.059	.083	.033	.089	.138	.024	.029	.026	.036	.022	.032
114 - 135	.028	.038	.047	.064	.091	.035	.097	.149	.024	.030	.027	.037	.023	.033
136 - 160	.029	.039	.050	.069	.100	.037	.106	.162	.025	.031	.027	.037	.023	.033
116 - 187	.030	.040	.054	.075	.110	.040	.116	.177	.025	.032	.028	.038	.024	.034
188 - 216	.031	.041	.058	.081	.120	.042	.126	.192	.025	.034	.029	.039	.025	.035
217 - 249	.032	.042	.063	.088	.132	.045	.138	.210	.026	.036	.030	.040	.025	.035
250 - 283	.034	.044	.068	.096	.145	.049	.151	.229	.026	.037	.031	.041	.026	.036
284 - 321	.035	.045	.073	.104	.158	.052	.164	.248	.026	.039	.032	.042	.027	.037
322 - 364	.037	.047	.079	.114	.174	.056	.180	.272	.027	.041	.033	.043	.028	.038
365 - 410	.038	.048	.086	.124	.191	.060	.197	.297	.027	.044	.034	.044	.029	.039
411 - 460	.040	.050	.093	.135	.209	.065	.215	.323	.028	.046	.036	.046	.030	.040
461 - 516	.042	.052	.101	.147	.229	.070	.235	.353	.028	.049	.037	.047	.031	.041
517 - 576	.045	.055	.110	.160	.251	.075	.257	.385	.029	.052	.039	.049	.033	.043
577 - 643	.047	.057	.119	.175	.275	.081	.281	.420	.030	.056	.041	.051	.034	.044
644 - 717	.050	.060	.130	.191	.302	.088	.308	.460	.030	.060	.043	.053	.036	.046
718 - 797	.053	.063	.141	.209	.331	.095	.337	.503	.031	.064	.045	.055	.037	.047
798 - 885	.057	.067	.154	.228	.363	.104	.369	.550	.032	.068	.047	.057	.039	.049
886 - 983	.060	.070	.168	.249	.398	.112	.404	.602	.033	.073	.050	.060	.041	.051
984 - 1089	.064	.074	.183	.273	.437	.122	.443	.659	.034	.079	.053	.063	.044	.054
1090 - 1205	.069	.079	.200	.298	.479	.133	.485	.721	.036	.085	.056	.066	.046	.056
1206 - 1332	.074	.084	.218	.326	.525	.145	.531	.789	.037	.091	.060	.070	.049	.059

* Weight 4.1-8.0 kg   Multiply above standard minutes by factor 1.0435
  8.1-16.0 kg   "   "   "   "   "   "   1.0870
  16.1-26 kg   "   "   "   "   "   "   1.1304

PROVISIONS FOR SETUP AND EXTRA WORK

Setup time should be separate from the standard time per part or assembly. Exhibit 10-8 shows how setups were standardized and recorded on a chart for fast standard setting. In this case, special tools and the parts making up the assembly had to be arranged on the workbench for ready access. In addition, hardware items such as standard screws, bolts, nuts, washers, and lock washers were maintained in a central location. The assembler was required to replenish his or her own stock of these items at the workplace. All the standard setter had to know in order to use this chart was the number of special tools involved, the total number of different parts in the assembly, and the number of hardware items required. A setup standard was issued with every production standard.

Also, in assembly work, there are times when the parts do not fit properly or a hole is undersize or has not been deburred properly. When these irregularities occur, extra work is required by the assembler to correct the condition. Whenever conditions were not normal, an expense standard was issued to cover the extra time required for that lot. In every case, a timestudy person verified the condition and set an expense standard from the standard data. In this way, the assembler was given an additional allowance to cover the extra work, and this extra cost was reported to management for corrective action.

THE TIME STANDARDS ARE APPLIED

The first time standards were applied to small subassembly operations during the last week in May 1973. Employee performances were good and averaged about 81 percent. It should be noted that this performance was achieved with work measurement—no wage incentive was involved. With work measurement only, a performance of 85 percent of standard is generally considered good. Gradually, major subassemblies were put on standard, followed by final assembly operations. By September however, while more assembly work was measured, the average performance had dropped to about 68 percent. Part of the reason for this was that the production schedule and the increased output of the employees on standard made it necessary for the supervisor to train each employee to perform a greater variety of operations than was originally planned. This was necessary to maintain balance, flexibility, and flow in the total assembly operation. The works manager, the production supervisor, and the foreman and the two timestudy people worked diligently to improve the performances. By the end of October, the average performance had increased to 91 percent. This level was improved to 103 percent by the middle of April 1974. The total assembly time per machine based on production in the United States was 32.0 man-hours. The total time based on the new methods, new tools, and new time standards in Sprendlingen was 16.1 standard hours plus setup. Thus, when the department average reached 103 percent, the direct employees had increased productivity about 100 percent. Exhibit 10-9 summarizes operating statistics for this assembly department for the period reviewed above—September 1973 through April 1974—and shows that performance increased from 68

EXHIBIT 10-5

STANDARD DATA CHART FOR PART HANDLING—GROUP B PARTS.

PART HANDLING–GROUP B–STANDARD MINUTES

* Weight 0 - 4.0 kg	Pickup		PU & Position		Locate				Align			
A (cm²) Area	Bench	Floor	Bench	Floor	Open	2 Point	Intf.	3 Point	Open	2 Point	Intf.	3 Point
Constant	.030	.040	.033	.043	.030	.037	.044	.050	.025	.050	.080	.100
Variable (A)	.0000115	.0000115	.0000145	.0000145	.000036	.0000445	.000092	.000178	.0000232	.000030	.0000443	.000062
From To												
0 - 30	.030	.040	.033	.043	.031	.038	.046	.053	.025	.051	.080	.101
31 - 50	.031	.041	.034	.044	.032	.039	.048	.058	..026	.051	.082	.103
51 - 90	.031	.041	.034	.044	.033	.040	.051	.063	.027	.052	.083	.105
91 - 126	.031	.041	.035	.045	.034	.042	.054	.069	.028	.053	.085	.107
127 - 165	.032	.042	.035	.045	.035	.044	.057	.076	.028	.054	.087	.109
166 - 208	.032	.042	.036	.046	.037	.045	.061	.083	.029	.056	.088	.112
209 - 256	.033	.043	.036	.046	.038	.047	.065	.091	.030	.057	.090	.114
257 - 310	.033	.043	.037	.047	.040	.050	.070	.100	.032	.059	.093	.118
311 - 366	.034	.044	.038	.048	.042	.052	.075	.110	.033	.060	.095	.121
367 - 427	.035	.045	.039	.049	.044	.055	.080	.120	.034	.062	.098	.124
428 - 497	.035	.045	.040	.050	.047	.058	.086	.132	.036	.064	.101	.129
498 - 571	.036	.046	.041	.051	.049	.061	.093	.145	.037	.066	.104	.133
572 - 651	.037	.047	.042	.052	.052	.064	.100	.158	.039	.068	.107	.138
652 - 743	.038	.048	.043	.053	.055	.068	.108	.174	.041	.071	.111	.143
744 - 842	.039	.049	.045	.055	.058	.072	.117	.191	.043	.074	.115	.149
843 - 950	.040	.050	.046	.056	.062	.077	.126	.209	.046	.077	.120	.156
951 - 1067	.042	.052	.048	.058	.066	.082	.137	.229	.048	.080	.125	.162
1068 - 1197	.043	.053	.049	.059	.071	.087	.148	.251	.051	.084	.130	.170
1198 - 1337	.045	.055	.051	.061	.076	.093	.160	.275	.054	.088	.136	.178
1338 - 1492	.046	.056	.053	.063	.081	.100	.174	.302	.058	.092	.143	.187
1493 - 1667	.048	.058	.056	.066	.087	.107	.189	.331	.062	.097	.150	.198
1668 - 1860	.050	.060	.059	.069	.093	.115	.206	.363	.066	.103	.158	.209
1861 - 2065	.053	.063	.061	.071	.101	.124	.224	.398	.071	.109	.167	.222
2066 - 2290	.055	.065	.064	.074	.108	.134	.244	.437	.075	.115	.176	.235
2291 - 2540	.058	.068	.068	.078	.117	.144	.266	.479	.081	.122	.187	.249
2541 - 2810	.061	.071	.072	.082	.126	.156	.290	.525	.087	.130	.198	.266
2811 - 3110	.064	.074	.076	.086	.136	.168	.315	.575	.093	.139	.211	.283
3111 - 3435	.068	.078	.080	.090	.148	.183	.345	.631	.101	.148	.225	.303
3436 - 3790	.072	.082	.085	.095	.160	.197	.375	.692	.109	.158	.240	.323
3791 - 4185	.076	.086	.091	.101	.173	.214	.410	.759	.117	.169	.256	.347
7920	.121		.148		.389							
* Weight 4.1 - 8.0 kg	Multiply above standard minutes by factor				1.0435							
8.1 - 16.0 kg	" " "		" " "		1.-870							
16.1 - 26.0 kg	" " "		" " "		1.1304							

percent to 103 percent, time on standard rose from 42 to 94 percent, while the total labor cost per standard hour of salable product dropped from DM22.70 to DM15.22, a reduction in cost of 33 percent. During this 7-month period, based on this reduction in cost, overall productivity increased approximately 49 percent. The objectives toward which the department is striving are shown also.

THE PROGRAM MOVES TO BELGIUM

Two timestudy people were trained for Liège. They began to make timestudies in September 1973 on the assembly of two basic models of data recorders. These two people followed the same techniques employed in Sprendlingen for building standard

Turnover		Rotate		Remove & SA		Set Aside			Cartons			
90°	180°	90°	180°	Bench	Floor	Bench	Floor		Pick Up Bench	Turn over 180°	Close Bottom Flaps	
.025	.025	.030	.030	.030	.040	.027	.037		.025	.025	.015	
.0000031	.0000113	.0000032	.0000155	.0000084	.0000084	.0000067	.0000067		.0000064	.0000113	.000048	
.025	.025	.030	.030	.030	.040	.027	.037		.025	.025	.015	
.025	.026	.030	.031	.030	.040	.027	.037		.025	.026	.016	
.025	.026	.030	.031	.031	.041	.028	.038		.025	.026	.017	
.025	.026	.030	.032	.031	.041	.028	.038		.026	.026	.019	
.026	.027	.031	.032	.031	.041	.028	.038		.026	.027	.021	
.026	.027	.031	.033	.032	.042	.028	.038		.026	.027	.023	
.026	.028	.031	.034	.032	.042	.029	.039		.026	.028	.025	
.026	.028	.031	.034	.032	.042	.029	.039		.027	.028	.028	
.026	.029	.031	.035	.033	.043	.029	.039		.027	.029	.030	
.026	.030	.031	.036	.033	.043	.030	.040		.028	.030	.033	
.026	.030	.032	.037	.034	.044	.030	.040		.028	.030	.036	
.027	.031	.032	.038	.035	.045	.031	.041		.028	.031	.040	
.027	.032	.032	.039	.035	.045	.031	.041		.029	.032	.043	
.027	.033	.032	.041	.036	.046	.032	.042		.029	.033	.047	
.027	.034	.033	.042	.037	.047	.032	.042		.030	.034	.052	
.028	.035	.033	.044	.038	.048	.033	.043		.031	.035	.057	
.028	.036	.033	.046	.039	.049	.034	.044		.031	.036	.062	
.028	.038	.034	.048	.040	.050	.035	.045		.032	.038	.068	
.029	.039	.034	.050	.041	.051	.036	.046		.033	.039	.075	
.029	.041	.035	.052	.042	.052	.037	.047		.034	.041	.082	
.030	.043	.035	.054	.043	.053	.038	.048		.035	.043	.090	
.031	.045	.036	.057	.045	.055	.039	.049		.036	.045	.099	
.031	.047	.036	.060	.047	.057	.040	.050		.038	.047	.108	
.032	.050	.037	.064	.048	.058	.042	.052		.039	.050	.119	
.033	.052	.038	.067	.050	.060	.043	.053		.040	.052	.130	
.033	.055	.039	.071	.052	.062	.045	.055		.042	.055	.142	
.034	.058	.040	.076	.055	.065	.047	.057		.044	.058	.156	
.035	.062	.041	.081	.058	.068	.049	.059		.046	.062	.171	
.036	.066	.042	.086	.060	.070	.051	.061		.048	.066	.187	
.037	.070	.043	.092	.063	.073	.054	.064		.051	.080	.205	
	.114						.090					

data. Except for several minor improvements, they proved out the Sprendlingen data. The first time standards were applied in December 1973. The several assemblers who worked on standard during the first week averaged a 93 percent performance. By the middle of January, the entire assembly line was on standard, and the performance of the employees averaged 95 percent. The Liège assembly had been methodized, and the employees were trained well before any timestudies were taken. This made it possible to establish reference costs so that the full impact of the new time standards could be ascertained. Exhibit 10-9 shows this reference cost which was developed by applying the new time standards to the operation of the assembly line for a period prior to taking timestudies. Employee performance averaged 67 percent during the reference period and the total labor cost per standard hour of salable product was 158.0 Fr. During the first week on standard, perfor-

EXHIBIT 10-6

STANDARD DATA CHART FOR TIGHTENING AND REMOVING SCREWS, BOLTS, AND NUTS.

NORMAL SCREWS AND BOLTS

STANDARD MINUTES — N Turns	Tighten Hand	Tighten O.E. Wrench	Tighten Screw Driver	Tighten/Loosen Air Driver	Loosen Hand	Loosen O.E. Wrench	Loosen Screw Driver
CONSTANT	—	.046	.046	.018	.018	.030	.030
VARIABLE (N)	.032	.0073	.0089	.0013	.032	.0069	.0069
1	.032	.053	.055	.019	.050	.037	.037
1.5	.048	.057	.059	.020	.066	.040	.040
2	.064	.061	.064	.021	.082	.044	.044
2.5	.080	.064	.068	.021	.098	.047	.047
3	.096	.068	.073	.022	.114	.051	.051
3.5	.112	.072	.077	.023	.130	.054	.054
4	.128	.075	.082	.023	.146	.058	.058
4.5	.144	.079	.086	.024	.162	.061	.061
5	.160	.083	.091	.025	.178	.065	.065
5.5	.176	.086	.095	.025	.194	.068	.068
6	.192	.090	.099	.026	.210	.071	.071
6.5	.208	.094	.104	.026	.226	.075	.075
7	.224	.097	.108	.027	.242	.078	.078
7.5	.240	.101	.113	.028	.258	.082	.082
8	.256	.104	.117	.028	.274	.085	.085
8.5	.272	.108	.122	.029	.290	.089	.089
9	.288	.112	.126	.030	.306	.092	.092
9.5	.304	.115	.131	.030	.322	.096	.096
10	.320	.119	.135	.031	.338	.099	.099
11	.352	.126	.144	.032	.370	.106	.106
12	.384	.134	.153	.034	.402	.113	.113
13	.416	.141	.162	.035	.434	.120	.120
14	.448	.148	.171	.036	.466	.127	.127
15	.480	.156	.180	.038	.498	.134	.134
16	.512	.163	.188	.039	.530	.140	.140
17	.544	.170	.197	.040	.562	.147	.147
18	.576	.177	.206	.041	.594	.154	.154
19	.608	.185	.215	.043	.626	.161	.161
20	.640	.192	.224	.044	.658	.168	.168
21	.672	.199	.233	.045	.690	.175	.175
22	.704	.207	.242	.047	.722	.182	.182
23	.736	.214	.251	.048	.754	.189	.189
24	.768	.221	.260	.049	.786	.196	.196
25	.800	.229	.269	.051	.818	.203	.203
26	.832	.236	.277	.052	.850	.209	.209

NORMAL NUTS

N Turns	Tighten Hand	Tighten Crank	Tighten O.E. Wrench	Tighten Screw Driver	Tighten/Loosen Air Driver	Loosen Hand	Loosen Crank	Loosen O.E. Wrench	Loosen Screw Driver	Tighten/Loosen Jig Screw Hand
CONSTANT	.046	—	.046	.046	.018	.020	—	.030	.030	.035
VARIABLE (N)	.020	.020	.0073	.0089	.0013	.020	.020	.0069	.0069	.012
1	.066	.020	.053	.055	.019	.040	.020	.037	.037	.047
1.5	.076	.030	.057	.059	.020	.050	.030	.040	.040	.053
2	.086	.040	.061	.064	.021	.060	.040	.044	.044	.059
2.5	.096	.050	.064	.068	.021	.070	.050	.047	.047	.065
3	.106	.060	.068	.073	.022	.080	.060	.051	.051	.071
3.5	.116	.070	.072	.077	.023	.090	.070	.054	.054	.077
4	.126	.080	.075	.082	.023	.100	.080	.058	.058	.083
4.5	.136	.090	.079	.086	.024	.110	.090	.061	.061	.089
5	.146	.100	.083	.091	.025	.120	.100	.065	.065	.095
5.5	.156	.110	.086	.095	.025	.130	.110	.068	.068	.101
6	.166	.120	.090	.099	.026	.140	.120	.071	.071	.107
6.5	.176	.130	.094	.104	.026	.150	.130	.075	.075	.113
7	.186	.140	.097	.108	.027	.160	.140	.078	.078	.119
7.5	.196	.150	.101	.113	.028	.170	.150	.082	.082	.125
8	.206	.160	.104	.117	.028	.180	.160	.085	.085	.131
8.5	.216	.170	.108	.122	.029	.190	.170	.089	.089	.137
9	.226	.180	.112	.126	.030	.200	.180	.092	.092	.143
9.5	.236	.190	.115	.131	.030	.210	.190	.096	.096	.149
10	.246	.200	.119	.135	.031	.220	.200	.099	.099	.155
11	.266	.220	.126	.144	.032	.240	.220	.106	.106	.167
12	.286	.240	.134	.153	.034	.260	.240	.113	.113	.179
13	.306	.260	.141	.162	.035	.280	.260	.120	.120	.191
14	.326	.280	.148	.171	.036	.300	.280	.127	.127	.203
15	.346	.300	.156	.180	.038	.320	.300	.134	.134	.215
16	.366	.320	.163	.188	.039	.340	.320	.140	.140	.227
17	.386	.340	.170	.197	.040	.360	.340	.147	.147	.239
18	.406	.360	.177	.206	.041	.380	.360	.154	.154	.251
19	.426	.380	.185	.215	.043	.400	.380	.161	.161	.263
20	.446	.400	.192	.224	.044	.420	.400	.168	.168	.275
21	.466	.420	.199	.233	.045	.440	.420	.175	.175	.287
22	.486	.440	.207	.242	.047	.460	.440	.182	.182	.299
23	.506	.460	.214	.251	.048	.480	.460	.189	.189	.311
24	.526	.480	.221	.260	.049	.500	.480	.196	.196	.323
25	.546	.500	.229	.269	.051	.520	.500	.203	.203	.335
26	.566	.520	.236	.277	.052	.540	.520	.209	.209	.347

SPECIAL CONDITIONS — Adjust.—Screws or Bolts

N Turns	Dial Gage Al.Key	Feel O.E. Wrench	Eye Allen Key
CONSTANT	.020	.015	.020
VARIABLE (N)	.050	.061	.086
.25	.033	.030	.042
.50	.045	.046	.063
.75	.058	.061	.085
1.00	.070	.076	.106
1.25	.083	.091	.128
1.50	.095	.107	.149
1.75	.108	.122	.171
2.00	.120	.137	.192
2.25	.133	.152	.214
2.50	.145	.168	.235

EXHIBIT 10-7

STANDARD DATA CHART FOR WALKING, TURNING, AND CARRYING.

WALKING (T = .015 + .013 D + .01 t)						STANDARD MINUTES			
Number of turns						Weight carried, kilograms			
0	1	2	3	4	5	0–4.0	4.1–8.0	8.1–16.0	16.1–26.0
0.5						.022	.023	.024	.025
1.0						.028	.029	.030	.032
1.5						.035	.037	.038	.040
	1.0					.038	.040	.041	.043
2.0						.041	.043	.044	.046
	1.5					.045	.047	.049	.051
2.5						.048	.050	.052	.054
	2.0					.051	.053	.055	.058
3.0		1.5				.054	.056	.059	.061
	2.5					.058	.061	.063	.066
3.5		2.0				.061	.064	.066	.069
	3.0					.064	.067	.070	.073
4.0		2.5				.067	.070	.073	.076
	3.5		2.0			.071	.074	.077	.080
		3.0				.074	.077	.081	.084
	4.0		2.5			.077	.080	.084	.087
5.0		3.5				.080	.083	.087	.091
			3.0			.084	.088	.092	.095
		4.0		2.5		.087	.091	.095	.099
	5.0		3.5			.090	.094	.098	.102
6.0			3.0			.093	.097	.101	.105
			4.0			.097	.101	.106	.110
		5.0	3.5			.100	.104	.109	,113
	6.0			3.0		.103	.108	.112	.116
7.0			4.0			.106	.111	.115	.120
			5.0	3.5		.110	.115	.120	.124
	7.0	6.0		4.0		.116	.121	.126	.131
8.0			5.0			.120	.125	.130	.135
		7.0	6.0			.126	.132	.137	.142
9.0	8.0		6.0	5.0		.132	.138	.143	.149
		8.0	7.0			.139	.145	.151	.157
10.0	9.0		7.0	6.0		.145	.151	.157	.164
		9.0	8.0			.152	.159	.165	.172
11.0	10.0		8.0	7.0		.158	.165	.172	.178
		10.0	9.0			.165	.172	.180	.185
12.0	11.0		10.0	9.0	8.0	.171	.179	.186	.194
		11.0				.178	.186	.194	.202
13.0	12.0		10.0	9.0		.184	.192	.200	.208
		12.0	11.0			.191	.200	.208	.216
14.0	13.0		11.0	10.0		.197	.295	.214	.223
		13.0	12.0			.204	.213	.222	.231
15.0	14.0		12.0	11.0		.210	.218	.228	.237
		14.0	13.0			.217	.227	.236	.245
16.0	15.0		14.0	13.0	12.0	.223	.233	.242	.252
17.0	16.0	15.0	14.0	14.0	13.0	.236	.246	.257	.267
18.0	17.0	16.0	16.0	15.0	14.0	.249	.260	.270	.281
19.0	18.0	17.0	17.0	16.0	15.0	.262	.273	.285	.296
20.0	19.0	18.0	18.00	17.0	16.0	.275	.287	.298	.311
	20.0	19.0		18.0	17.0	.285	.298	.310	.322
		20.0	19.0	19.0	18.0	.295	.308	.321	.333

DISTANCE WALKED, meters

EXHIBIT 10-8

CHART FOR STANDARDIZING AND FACILITATING THE APPLICATION OF SETUP STANDARDS IN ASSEMBLY.

SETUP STANDARDS FOR SMALL SUBASSEMBLIES $\qquad$ $(T = 1.70 + .18 t + .18P + .551)$ $\qquad$ STANDARD MINUTES PER SETUP (T)

Number of Special Tools (t)						Number of Hardware Items — Obtained From Stock Bin (I)																				
0	1	2	3	4	5	0	1	2	3	4	5	6	7	8	9	10	11	12	13	14	15	16	17	18	19	20
2						2.1	2.6	3.2	3.7	4.3	4.8	5.4	5.9	6.5	7.0	7.6	8.1	8.7	9.2	9.8	10.3	10.9	11.4	12.0	12.5	13.1
3	2					2.2	2.7	3.3	3.8	4.4	4.9	5.5	6.0	6.6	7.1	7.7	8.2	8.8	9.3	9.9	10.4	11.0	11.5	12.1	12.6	13.2
4	3	2				2.4	2.9	3.5	4.0	4.6	5.1	5.7	6.2	6.8	7.3	7.9	8.4	9.0	9.5	10.1	10.6	11.2	11.7	12.3	12.8	13.4
5	4	3	2			2.6	3.1	3.7	4.2	4.8	5.3	5.9	6.4	7.0	7.5	8.1	8.6	9.2	9.7	10.3	10.8	11.4	11.9	12.5	13.0	13.6
6	5	4	3	2		2.8	3.3	3.9	4.4	5.0	5.5	6.1	6.6	7.2	7.7	8.3	8.8	9.4	9.9	10.5	11.0	11.6	12.1	12.7	13.2	13.8
7	6	5	4	3	2	3.0	3.5	4.1	4.6	5.2	5.7	6.3	6.8	7.4	7.9	8.5	9.0	9.6	10.1	10.7	11.2	11.8	12.3	12.9	13.4	14.0
8	7	6	5	4	3	3.1	3.6	4.2	4.7	5.3	5.8	6.4	6.9	7.5	8.0	8.6	9.1	9.7	10.2	10.8	11.3	11.9	12.4	13.0	13.5	14.1
9	8	7	6	5	4	3.3	3.8	4.4	4.9	5.5	6.0	6.6	7.1	7.7	8.2	8.8	9.3	9.9	10.4	11.0	11.5	12.1	12.6	13.2	13.7	14.3
10	9	8	7	6	5	3.5	4.0	4.6	5.1	5.7	6.2	6.8	7.3	7.9	8.4	9.0	9.5	10.1	10.6	11.2	11.7	12.3	12.8	13.4	13.9	14.5
11	10	9	8	7	6	3.7	4.2	4.8	5.3	5.9	6.4	7.0	7.5	8.1	8.6	9.2	9.7	10.3	10.8	11.4	12.0	12.5	13.0	13.6	14.1	14.7
12	11	10	9	8	7	3.9	4.4	5.0	5.5	6.1	6.6	7.2	7.7	8.3	8.8	9.4	9.9	10.5	11.0	11.6	12.1	12.7	13.2	13.8	14.3	14.9
13	12	11	10	9	8	4.0	4.5	5.1	5.6	6.2	6.7	7.3	7.8	8.4	8.9	9.5	10.0	10.6	11.1	11.7	12.2	12.8	13.3	13.9	14.4	15.0
14	13	12	11	10	9	4.2	4.7	5.3	5.8	6.4	6.9	7.5	8.0	8.6	9.1	9.7	10.2	10.8	11.3	11.9	12.4	13.0	13.5	14.1	14.6	15.2
15	14	13	12	11	10	4.4	4.9	5.5	6.0	6.6	7.1	7.7	8.2	8.8	9.3	9.9	10.4	11.0	11.5	12.1	12.6	13.2	13.7	14.3	14.8	15.4
16	15	14	13	12	11	4.6	5.1	5.7	6.2	6.8	7.3	7.9	8.4	9.0	9.5	10.1	10.6	11.2	11.7	12.3	12.8	13.4	13.9	14.5	15.0	15.6
17	16	15	14	13	12	4.8	5.3	5.9	6.4	7.0	7.5	8.1	8.6	9.2	9.7	10.3	10.8	11.4	11.9	12.5	13.0	13.6	14.1	14.7	15.2	15.8
18	17	16	15	14	13	4.9	5.4	6.0	6.5	7.1	7.6	8.2	8.7	9.3	9.8	10.4	10.9	11.5	12.0	12.6	13.1	13.7	14.2	14.9	15.4	16.0
19	18	17	16	15	14	5.1	5.6	6.2	6.7	7.3	7.8	8.4	8.9	9.5	10.0	10.6	11.1	11.7	12.2	12.8	13.3	13.9	14.4	15.0	15.5	16.1
20	19	18	17	16	15	5.3	5.8	6.4	6.9	7.5	8.0	8.6	9.1	9.7	10.2	10.8	11.3	11.9	12.4	13.0	13.5	14.1	14.6	15.2	15.7	16.3
21	20	19	18	17	16	5.5	6.0	6.6	7.1	7.7	8.2	8.8	9.3	9.9	10.4	11.0	11.5	12.1	12.6	13.2	13.7	14.3	14.8	15.4	15.9	16.5
22	21	20	19	18	17	5.7	6.2	6.8	7.3	7.9	8.4	9.0	9.5	10.1	10.6	11.2	11.7	12.3	12.8	13.4	13.9	14.5	15.0	15.6	16.1	16.7
23	22	21	20	19	18	5.8	6.3	6.9	7.4	8.0	8.5	9.1	9.6	10.2	10.7	11.3	11.8	12.4	12.9	13.5	14.0	14.6	15.1	15.7	16.3	16.9
24	23	22	21	20	19	6.0	6.5	7.1	7.6	8.2	8.7	9.3	9.8	10.4	10.9	11.5	12.0	12.6	13.1	13.7	14.2	14.8	15.3	15.9	16.4	17.0
25	24	23	22	21	20	6.2	6.7	7.3	7.8	8.4	8.9	9.5	10.0	10.6	11.1	11.7	12.2	12.8	13.3	13.9	14.4	15.0	15.5	16.1	16.6	17.2
26	25	24	23	22	21	6.4	6.9	7.5	8.0	8.6	9.1	9.7	10.2	10.8	11.3	11.9	12.4	13.0	13.5	14.1	14.6	15.2	15.7	16.3	16.8	17.4
27	26	25	24	23	22	6.6	7.1	7.7	8.2	8.8	9.3	9.9	10.4	11.0	11.5	12.1	12.6	13.2	13.7	14.3	14.8	15.4	15.9	16.5	17.0	17.6
28	27	26	25	24	23	6.7	7.2	7.9	8.4	9.0	9.5	10.1	10.6	11.2	11.7	12.3	12.8	13.4	13.9	14.5	15.0	15.6	16.1	16.7	17.2	17.8
29	28	27	26	25	24	6.9	7.4	8.0	8.5	9.1	9.6	10.2	10.7	11.3	11.8	12.4	12.9	13.5	14.0	14.6	15.1	15.7	16.3	16.9	17.4	18.0
30	29	28	27	26	25	7.1	7.6	8.2	8.7	9.3	9.8	10.4	10.9	11.5	12.0	12.6	13.1	13.7	14.2	14.8	15.3	15.9	16.4	17.0	17.5	18.1
31	30	29	28	27	26	7.3	7.8	8.4	8.9	9.5	10.0	10.6	11.1	11.7	12.2	12.8	13.3	13.9	14.4	15.0	15.5	16.1	16.6	17.2	17.7	18.3

Total Number of Different Parts in Subassembly (P)

EXHIBIT 10-9

COST REDUCTION AND PRODUCTIVITY INCREASE ACHIEVED IN WEST GERMANY AND IN BELGIUM.

Week ending	Performance, %	On Standard, %	Setup, %	Cost per Standard Hour of Salable Product				Cost Reduction, %	Productivity Increase, %
				Direct Labor	Direct Excess	Indirect Labor	Total Labor		
Sprendlingen, West Germany									
Reference (not available)									
9/ 8/73	68	42	0.6	DM10.60	DM3.32	DM8.78	DM22.70	0	
9/29/73	69	85	1.7	7.93	3.55	7.36	18.84	17	+ 20
10/27/73	91	66	1.7	9.04	0.43	4.05	13.52	40	+ 67
12/ 1/73	86	78	2.0	8.67	1.21	4.67	14.55	36	+ 56
4/ 6/74	95	85	1.6	8.87	0.78	3.97	13.62	40	+ 67
4/13/74	103	94	1.2	8.23	2.28	4.71	15.22	33	+ 49
Objective	100	95	2.0	8.45	0.51	2.42	11.38	50	+100
Liège, Belgium									
Reference	67	36		fr.124.2		fr.33.8	fr.158.0	0	
12/15/73	93	100	0.3	110.6	fr.2.2	37.4	150.2	5	+ 5
1/12/74	95	100	1.2	92.0	6.7	28.4	127.1	20	+ 25
2/16/74	92	100	0.9	86.9	8.7	29.7	125.3	21	+ 27
5/16/74	96	100	0.7	82.4	4.6	30.1	117.1	26	+ 35
Objective	100	95	0.5	80.8	3.2	27.3	111.3	30	+ 43

mance increased to 93 percent, time on standard was 36 percent, and the total labor cost per standard hour was 150.2 Fr. Five months later performance had increased to 96 percent, time on standard was 100 percent, and the total labor cost per standard hour had been reduced to 117.1 Fr., a reduction of 26 percent. This reduction in labor cost is equivalent to a 35 percent increase in productivity. The timestudy people in the meantime studied and applied standards to coating paper, paper converting operations, and credit card manufacture with similar success. By June 1974 all these operations were on standard too.

MOMENTUM MAINTAINED

Thus, in Sprendlingen and in Liège productivity increased substantially, costs were reduced sharply, and the programs achieved sufficient momentum to maintain the gains. Some reasons for this accomplishment and the management principles involved can be summarized as follows:

1. The programs had the full interest and support of management.

2. Work measurement provided the employees and the supervision with fair, consistent goals to work toward.

3. The employees had pride and wanted to be recognized as skillful performers.

4. The standard hour of salable product produced is the best measure of volume to which costs can be related reliably.

5. Standard data is necessary in order to set correct, consistent time standards.

6. Expense standards are necessary to allow for the extra work required when conditions are not normal.

7. Full utilization of space is part of achieving low costs.

8. People in any country, every country, will respond to good management direction.

WELL-COORDINATED TEAMWORK
IS NECESSARY TO GAIN
SUBSTANTIAL RESULTS

11

Banking on High Productivity

"We'll find a way." The Continental Illinois Corporation, headquartered in Chicago, Illinois, really means it. In fact, in many areas it already has found the way. This theme holds a lot of promise. It commits the employees to serving the customers. Employee commitment is not new at CICorp but it is stimulating to have a single sentence that so aptly expresses the attitude of the entire organization. The company is committed to the employees and the employees are committed to the customers. This relationship produces results—the worthwhile kind of achievement that helps the customers, the employees, and the company grow rapidly and soundly.

Continental Illinois Corporation is a one-bank holding company. Its principal subsidiary is Continental Illinois National Bank and Trust Company. Continental Bank operates a full-service commercial banking and trust business. Its subsidiaries engage in banking and financially related activities. Customers are individuals, partnerships, small businesses, companies, institutions, and governmental agencies in the United States and around the world. Continental opened its first overseas branch in London in 1962. Since then it has grown to 129 branches and subsidiaries located in 39 countries. It manages Master Charge for 460 correspondent banks in the Midwest, covering approximately 650,000 card holders. In 1975 CICorp reported earnings before security transactions of $118,997,000 on total operating income of $1,441,240,000, a profit of 8.2 percent. The $118,997,000 represents a 24 percent increase in earnings over 1974. This made Continental Illinois Corporation the leading bank holding company in profit gains in 1975. Continental is the largest bank between the coasts, and with assets of $20,225,633,000 it ranked seventh in size in the United States on December 31, 1975. Exhibit 11-1 reveals the progress made by CICorp in recent years. This exhibit, covering the 5 years 1971 through 1975, shows the income before security gains or losses, as well as its relationship in terms of per employee; the return on equity; the operating income; the compound 5-year growth rate of earnings; and the earnings per share. As the charts show, this is a large, complex, fast-moving business. There are many reasons for Continental Illinois Corporation's success. The key ones are the ability and productivity of the employees.

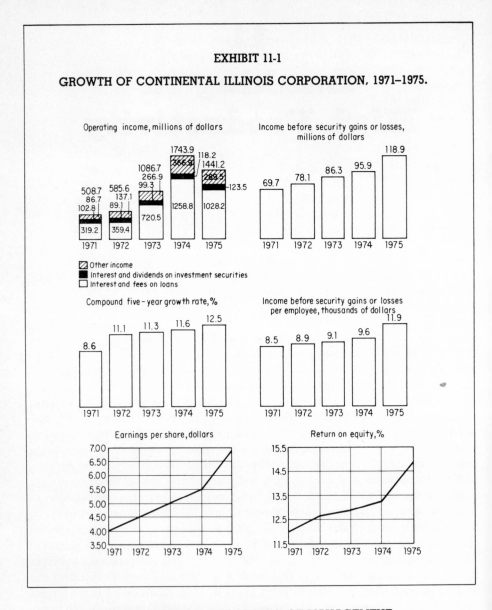

EXHIBIT 11-1

GROWTH OF CONTINENTAL ILLINOIS CORPORATION, 1971–1975.

MANAGEMENT'S PHILOSOPHY OF MANAGEMENT

The foundation for this progress was formulated 14 years ago when the then head of operations of the bank authorized the formation of a methods research department. Many meaningful endeavors emanated from that decision. But, before reviewing what was done, let's explore the management philosophy that maintains, in fact accelerates, the forward-moving momentum the company enjoys. Continental Illinois Corporation really cares about its employees. This thinking and this attention start right at the top. The chairman of the board and the president of CICorp believe management must be concerned and must make the effort to understand its employees and their abilities, their ambitions, their goals, their anxieties, and their frustrations. They believe that efficiency is derived from the underlying philosophy and policies that shape and motivate the organization. The executive vice president for operations and management services expressed it this way. "Employees want to be productive. People thrill to the chase for better productivity. Management must find the means to inspire them." The senior vice president in charge of personnel said: "We get tremendous support from top management. This is important because it has a positive influence on the attitudes of managers and employees at all levels. We instill in our people that while planning is important and must be done thoroughly and well, we reward for implementation and results." The manager of executive placement thoughtfully added: "The selection process is most critical. An organization is only as good as the material it recruits. We go to great lengths to attract the talent we need. Then we help this talent grow. Perhaps the most significant thing is we train our managers to deal head-on with conflict. We have learned that side-stepping confrontation leads to problems. This can be disconcerting and disruptive to an organization. We don't want our managers to allow intolerable situations to arise or to exist. The best way is to deal with and resolve problems before they become issues." The executive vice president summed up CICorp's management philosophy when he quoted his mentor, a retired director of personnel, in this manner, "The basic ingredients of success are nature, nurture and chance." Nature endows people with talent. CICorp carefully searches for the kind of talent it needs. Then, it nurtures and trains this talent so that it expands and grows in strength and stature. Very little is left to chance. Confucius, in response to the question how to build a successful business, is reported to have said, "You must first teach people what you want them to know." When asked for further counsel he replied, "Don't get tired." CICorp believes managers should be trained so that they instinctively apply the philosophy of the company to the decisions they make day in and day out. The chairman and the president know from experience that when given both a philosophy and the freedom to act, managers and employees will outperform and surpass any goals set for them.

The executive vice president for operations and management services is responsible for managing approximately 4500 employees out of the total of 9928 on the payroll. In explaining the ecology of the work environment, he described the influences of manager and nonmanager attitudes and the need for attitudinal direction. He pointed out that when this climate is not healthy, the best tend to seek a more rewarding situation, and a company ends up with the poorest talent. However, when the environment is inspiring and made exciting with overtones for growing, all employees are inclined to be happier, because a basic need is fulfilled—the desire to achieve. This led to a discussion of productivity in general. He pointed out that many managements have failed to increase the productivity of their companies because of preoccupation with the productivity of money rather than the productivity of people. He added that the founders of businesses knew what to do and they did it. Their own money and future was at stake. But as companies grew and management was brought in from the outside, the know-how was lost and the new managers had no real concept of how to go about improving employee productivity. The new managers by and large were skillful at interpreting reports but were not perceptive of what was needed at the workplace. The employees recognized the situation and quickly realized there was no reason to energize themselves beyond the accepted norm. They could hold their jobs and get the same wages as the poorer producers, so why try. All these conditions forced a gradual deterioration in attitude toward improving productivity. The executive vice president summed up the recent history of productivity with, "An organization elicits the behavior it rewards."

Another point was made. There is much evidence indicating a lack of integrity on the part of management in many companies. It is difficult to instill integrity in subordinates when they suspect it is missing at the top. The manager who lives a life of luxury, who has no interest in the stockholders, who flaunts his "power and wealth," can hardly expect his employees to respect his views when he exhorts them to increase their output. What is needed is example, not exhortation.

MODERNIZE WITH METHODS RESEARCH

Fourteen years ago the head of operations of the bank realized that the banking industry was beginning to shift from a low-volume, high-margin business to a high-volume, low-margin service. This transition had serious implications for a business that traditionally was labor intensive. To some degree there had been no pressing need for efficiency. The labor market was adequate. Conditions were good for banks. But the head of operations was concerned about the future. The present executive vice president for operations and management services at that time had worked for the bank about 10 years. The head of operations assigned him to establish a methods research department. The purpose of the new department was to take the principles of scientific management that had been tried and proven in industry and apply them to the bank's operations. The purpose was to trim the organization, increase productivity substantially, and prepare the bank for rapid future growth. The timing was perfect.

The new manager of methods research was well aware of the magnitude of his assignment. He decided to surround himself with believers in the new management concepts. He reasoned that only believers could overcome the obstacles and teach the new programs to the managers and the employees. He hired twelve very bright college graduates who had worked at least 2 years since graduation but not in a bank, who had the potential to grow into managerial positions of importance in the future, who had enthusiasm for producing, and who possessed the following attributes (incidentally, these are the same qualities he looks for in managers today):

1. *Honesty*—Subordinates instinctively know when the boss is not intellectually honest.

2. *Candor*—A manager must be frank and impartial without developing anxieties.

3. *Courage*—Will he look you in the eye and tell the truth and is he willing to hear the truth about himself?

4. *Sense of humor*—Does he have the ability to understand the impact of his work life on his total life and still laugh at himself?

5. *Commitment*—Will he yield to commitment and has he demonstrated a history of high commitment to people and projects?

6. *Discipline*—Are his personal habits and thought processes organized and controlled?

7. *Capacity*—Does he have a high capacity for work and, more importantly, does he possess the capacity to discipline those for whom he is responsible because it is important to their future well-being?

8. *Sense of obligation*—Does he feel obliged to skillfully influence his subordinates so that they grow with the organization and achieve their full potential?

9. *Sense of timing*—This quality is not necessary in a manager, but it is highly desirable since those who possess it become brilliant managers.

The twelve people spent 4 months in discussion with the manager of methods research. They worked well beyond 40 hours a week developing a common commitment to the program they were designing. They explored the philosophy of scientific management. They reviewed the bank organization from the top down through the managerial levels. They talked systems and procedures and management techniques. Gradually, a total program for improving the operation of the bank evolved. They decided better measurement was needed in order to increase employee productivity and to control operating costs. The company just had to know "how long it should take." The manager of methods research called in a consultant to train the people in methods analysis, work measurement techniques, and cost controls. Following this training, the people began stopwatch timestudies in several of the operating departments. From these timestudies they built standard time data and set production standards. They built staffing and cost models. They learned how to cope with the emotional reactions of the department managers when confronted with the results of the studies. They learned how to work with the managers to achieve the results. Essentially, they found that the entire managerial-supervisory corps, some 400 people, had to be retrained in how to get the job done with a tightly manned staff of employees. They used predetermined time values, statistical analysis, reporting analysis, short interval scheduling, process cost models, work simplification— any technique that would help to "eliminate unnecessary work and streamline the remaining work." Their objectives were to:

1. Reduce the processing time of individual operations.

2. Reduce the total time required to perform an assigned function.

3. Reduce the time to train new employees or to cross-train old employees.

4. Improve accuracy and eliminate errors.

5. Improve customer service.

In total, the group developed a common understanding of management based on high productivity performance and adopted an attitude best exemplified by the simple sentence: *It can be done!* They reinforced and helped each other. They were dedicated to the program and gradually their zeal and results penetrated the entire organization. However, some managers had worked in a static environment too long and either could not or would not change to meet the managerial demands of a dynamic operation. The company took great care to relocate these men within the company. They were replaced by managers schooled in the principles and practices of scientific management. These new managers made mistakes but learned quickly from their errors. The manager of methods research directed and managed the total program. The head of operations served as the transitional interface between the new and the old. He was old enough to relate to the older higher levels of management and young enough to know "it had to be." The entire transition took about 8 years to accomplish. However, significant strides were made during the first 5 years of the "modernization program."

Three of the original believers left the bank. The remaining nine are all serving the bank in key managerial positions. The manager of methods research is the executive vice president for operations and management services. And the management corps has ability, depth, and a sound philosophy of management. Today, the bank has the following:

1. A methods research division that concentrates on further improvement in manual and machine operations.

2. A management sciences division that is involved in computer technology and the application of higher mathematics to problem solving, staffing and cost models, queuing theory, and expense projections.

3. A cost and operations analysis division whose major responsibility is to provide reliable cost information to management. The cost information is used to price products and services, transfer costs between divisions and profit centers, measure the cost performances of operating and service divisions in meeting established standards, and assist operating and service division management in budgeting and controlling costs. Interestingly, this division analyzes and determines a normal volume for each product and service. Then, work measurement standards and simulation models are used to develop the required staff and expenses incurred to process the normal volume. The normal volume is converted into total standard direct labor hours required, and this common denominator is divided into the total normal expenses to establish an hourly cost rate. The hourly cost rate when multiplied by the standard direct labor hours required to process each item of output yields the standard cost for each product or service. Thus, the standard hour of salable product or service serves as the measure of volume and the foundation for standard costs, operating controls, and pricing calculations.

TRAINING MANAGERS

Considerable attention is given to the training of managers, supervisors, and staff personnel in the use of the scientific management tools. For example, the following is an outline of a management game which is part of the training program for managers:

> *Overall Objective:* Develop in the student an understanding of labor related costs, their effects on product costs and how labor related costs can be planned for and controlled by planning and controlling your staff through the use of standards and volumes.
>
> *Introductory Lecture:* Communicate to the student the overall objective; the rules of the game; the importance of understanding and therefore planning and controlling labor related costs; the impact labor related costs have on product costs; and the method of determining a required staff to complete specific quantities of work, with minimum labor related costs, using standards and volumes.

1. Discuss game objectives.

2. Discuss the concept and the rules of the game.

3. Define and discuss labor related costs and why they should be planned and controlled.

4. Demonstrate an approach to staffing utilizing standards and volume analysis in order to minimize labor related costs and unit costs.

> *Idle Time, Overtime and Opportunity Costs Lecture:* Communicate to the student and analyze the relationships between regular time, idle time, overtime and holdover costs and the cost ramifications which should be considered when making staffing decisions.

1. Discuss regular time, idle time, overtime and holdover.

2. Present a sample section and determine various unit costs with various mixtures of regular time, idle time and overtime.

3. Present an example and determine various unit costs with various mixtures of overtime, idle and holdover.

4. Discuss all the considerations necessary to determine a staff with a minimum unit cost.

> *Concluding Lecture:* Communicate and demonstrate to the student, using a sample section, how he can effectively utilize the staffing principles which he has been employing in the game to plan and control his own section's staff or labor related costs and therefore plan and control his unit cost.

1. Show the student how to analyze his own sections in order to determine operations, standards, items of output and their volumes.

2. Demonstrate for the student how operation standards are related and item of output volumes analyzed.

3. Utilizing standards and volumes, have the student determine the staff necessary to staff a section and minimize unit costs.

4. Review all the management principles utilized throughout the game and lectures.

Employees about to become supervisors participate in a 3-day seminar entitled "The New Supervisor." This is a series of illustrated lectures and discussions designed to familiarize the neophyte with background information, techniques, and practices so that he or she will be prepared to cope successfully with the new assignment. As was highlighted earlier, not much is left to chance. The new-supervisor program provides basic procedural information about a variety of meaningful subjects from operating routines all the way up to a discussion of the general manager viewpoint. Typical topics are:

1. The role of the supervisor

2. Payroll rules, procedures, and forms

3. Breaking in the new employee

4. Job description, performance appraisal, and salary administration

5. Personnel policies, information, and employee benefits

6. Writing better reports

7. Production control

8. Production skills

9. Problem solving

10. Moving into the new job

Staff employees are given formal training through programs and seminars prepared to develop their skills and keep them informed and up to date. These are in-depth sessions such as the Operations Analysis Training Seminar. The description of this 4-day series of sessions reads as follows: "The purpose of this program is to give a new analyst a general overview of the theories and techniques required in conducting a divisional study. The program is structured to follow the phases of a study, and two days are devoted to extensive time study practice. Two experienced analysts are responsible for teaching the training program."

Thus, training at CICorp is aimed at making certain that the managers, supervisors, and staff are equipped to perform their duties effectively and efficiently. For these reasons much emphasis is given to helping them become skillful in the use of the tools of scientific management. In return for this attention and effort, the bank's costs are controlled, and employee productivity continues to improve.

QUALITY ASSURANCE IS PARAMOUNT

The control of quality is one of management's prime responsibilities. There are two good reasons for this. The bank's customers expect error-free performance, and with the volume of transactions handled daily there just isn't time to track down and correct a large number of mistakes. The executive vice president for operations and management services defined it in this manner:

The term "Quality Control," when applied to many areas within Operations, usually conjures up visions of accuracy reports, timeliness reports and aging reports—and rightly so. These are, in fact, the heart of the quality measures used in Operations. In some instances it is relatively easy to quantify the measures of quality; in other instances a judgment of quality must be almost entirely subjective.

Each division is required and has been trained to follow three quality control steps as follows:

1. To identify the products and services for which low error rates and timeliness are critical

2. To record the error and output rates for those products and services

3. To establish goals for the improvement of error and output rates

The following paragraph illustrates this concept of quality that permeates the organization:

The International Services Division maintains a constant effort in its customer contact area to keep its teller services fast enough to never have more than two people in line at the window at once. Sampling techniques are used in this area to measure how well this objective is met. The Cashbook section maintains a log of the number, size and frequency of teller differences in order to measure Quality in that area, also. Additionally, the same section maintains controls on the accuracy of all IBD bookkeeping entries processed each day, with daily feed back to section supervisors regarding their efficiencies in this area.

At the beginning of each year, each division reviews its quality indices and sets objectives for improvement. Then, progress toward attainment of these goals is measured so that action can be taken in time to assure that they will be achieved during the year. Table 11-1 shows a few examples taken from the bank's records for the year 1975.

TABLE 11-1

Category	Projected	Actual
Stop payments	1 error per 3,150,000 checks processed	1 error per 3,967,378 checks processed
Signature irregularities	2 errors per 3,500,000 checks processed	1 error per 3,570,640 checks processed
International section errors	2.00% of total volume	0.08%
Purchasing requisition turnaround	3 days	2.6 days
Holdover jobs (duplicating)	276	81
Testing system, maintenance time per incident	20 minutes	7.25 minutes

ANALYZE THE BIG AND THE SMALL

Analytical cost studies are continually under way. Nothing is too big or too small to review for economies. For example, paper-conservation studies resulted in implementing measures, such as, reducing paper sizes, printing on both sides, purging various files of obsolete internal reports and publications, and cutting and reusing paper printed on one side for scratch-pad purposes. Over a 12-month period, the bank saved about $37,000 from these economy moves and eliminated the need for purchasing 11 tons of scratch paper. Also, purging mailing files resulted in annual savings of approximately $53,000 in postage, address plates, and printing and duplicating costs.

COMMERCIAL BANKING IMPROVES

The vice president of commercial banking operations maintains close surveillance of unit costs. Cost-reducing efforts in this area have centered on careful balancing of peak loads with part-time employees, methods improvements, and automation. Several examples of significant reductions in unit costs and the related increases in productivity show up in the commercial paying and receiving department's activities as shown in Table 11-2.

Exhibits 11-2 and 11-3 show, respectively, how the vice president of commercial banking operations tracks the performance of the employees against time standards and the performance of a department to total standard cost. These charts are actual results achieved by the safekeeping department from January through October 1975. Overall employee productivity increased by 14 percent during this 9-month period. For both control reports a 100 percent performance is the target. Performance above 100 percent is favorable; below 100 percent means attention must be given to improving output in relation to the time and cost standards. The backup for these charts is a computer printout that permits detailed analysis when necessary.

CHECK PROCESSING IMPROVES

The vice president of check processing operations manages a division of 1550 employees working three shifts. The division's activities are divided into four major

TABLE 11-2
Comparison of 1975 Unit Costs to 1971

Item of output	Unit cost decrease, %	Productivity increase, %
Certified check	31.3	46
Traveler's check	8.2	9
Cashier's check	33.2	50
Check cashed	9.4	10
Deposit	10.2	11
Currency shipment	39.4	65
Total	36.7	58

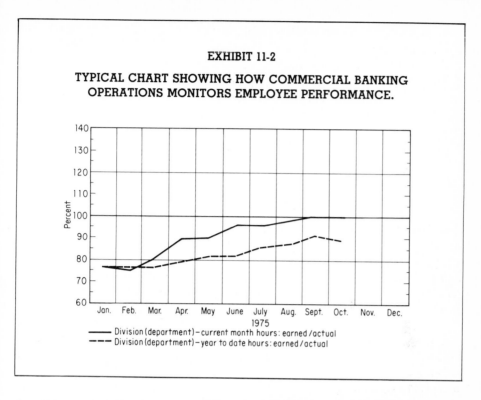

EXHIBIT 11-2

TYPICAL CHART SHOWING HOW COMMERCIAL BANKING OPERATIONS MONITORS EMPLOYEE PERFORMANCE.

—— Division (department) – current month hours: earned /actual
--- Division (department) – year to date hours: earned /actual

departments covering proof transit, document processing, bookkeeping, and remittance banking. This is a high-volume, fast-moving group of operations where no errors in the final information are tolerated and timing equates directly to money. Each day this division processes about 1,800,000 checks. Multiple document handling raises this figure to over 3,000,000 transactions. A check is just a piece of paper until it is presented for payment to the drawee bank. This is why timing is so critical. Over the past 3 years this division's check processing was reviewed and improved considerably. Today the stand-alone systems have been integrated into a network of major systems that communicate with one another and feed information into an on-line accessed information file. The new check processing control system (CPCS) has produced major benefits. These were reported to top management as follows:

1. Prior to CPCS, all rejected items were floated as zero-day availability. Today, because of on-line reject re-entry, Continental Bank has a data base which assures that all checks are floated properly, thus increasing potential annual earnings.

2. Through the implementation of re-entering items through a second high speed sort, rejected items decreased by 250,000 items monthly, also, resulting in increased potential annual savings.

3. Through the elimination of multiple check-flow paths, each Magnetic Ink Character Recognition, MICR, document now is assigned a unique reference

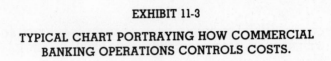

EXHIBIT 11-3

TYPICAL CHART PORTRAYING HOW COMMERCIAL BANKING OPERATIONS CONTROLS COSTS.

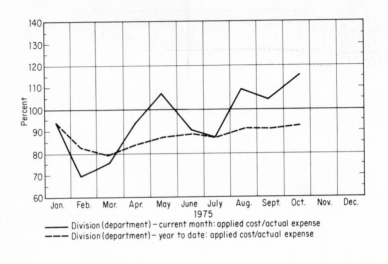

———— Division (department) – current month: applied cost/actual expense

–––– Division (department) – year to date: applied cost/actual expense

number. Accordingly, the time required to respond to customer inquiries decreased by more than 50%.

4. Significant results have been achieved in the percentage of analysis float to uncollected funds. In 1973, the percentage of analysis float to uncollected funds averaged 63%, and during the fourth quarter of 1975 it increased to 88%.

5. Direct sendings to Federal Reserve Offices and correspondent banks were increased 65%, thus providing Continental Bank with one of the very best availability schedules in the country.

6. As a result of increased processing speeds, the holdover of current day deposits was reduced by 79%, significantly increasing potentially available funds.

7. Installation of the new Demand Deposit Accounting System (DDAS), which included on-line access to customer checking account information, had a dramatic effect on productivity in the Bookkeeping Department of the Check Processing Division. The average telephone call for account information was shortened from an average of three minutes to approximately forty-five seconds. For an operation that receives over 2500 calls daily, savings are significant in terms of cost and improved customer service.

8. The unit cost of processing a check, the key measure of cost control for the Bookkeeping Department, actually decreased by over 5% despite rising labor and material costs. Each percentage point change in unit cost is extremely significant in a department that handles 72,000,000 checks or units per year.

Improvements in check processing over the past 5 years, including the introduction of the new CPCS and DDAS systems, have increased employee productivity significantly and from the above, it is clear that the other benefits are substantial too. In addition, processing capacity has been increased dramatically. The search for better and faster ways of doing the job continues, for example:

1. *Encoding equipment*—By converting from a IBM 1260 to a Burroughs S-105, the average overall throughput was increased from 800 to 1000 items per hour. The operator no longer is required to sort. There was a reduction in equipment of 25 percent with accompanying personnel reduction, and training time was reduced from 8 to 3 weeks.

2. *IBM 802*—The installation of this machine in the return-item teller section combined sorting and listing for balance purposes of returns being presented to the bank. It increased output from 200 to 300 checks per hour.

3. *Electronic inserter*—This machine automated the mailing of checks and statements and stuffs envelopes at the rate of 1500 statements per hour.

In addition to the new systems and the installation of latest generation equipment, the division utilizes a variety of techniques for controlling and improving productivity and operating unit costs. These techniques in total compose the daily job of managing the operation and include the following programs:

1. *Work segmentation*—A functional approach to planning operations.

2. *Job simplification*—An analysis of a single function to reduce it to a basic method.

3. *Standardized instructions*—A detailed description of a single task or operation.

4. *Work standards*—The standard for measuring employee output and performance. Provides a form of incentive when used in conjunction with the appraisal and salary review system.

5. *Volume projection*—This is developed by a computerized staffing model based on multiple regression involving forty-seven variables. Managers use this output to plan weekly staffing needs for twelve shifts, with part-time employees assigned for peak load requirements. The projected volume was on target 93 percent of the time in 1975.

6. *Staffing flexibility*—A multishift operation supplemented with part-time people. This staffing policy achieves the following:

   a. Flexibility in handling severe volume fluctuations
   b. Ability to process all available input items on Mondays and other heavy periods
   c. Reliability in meeting check-clearing deadlines
   d. Economy in labor cost considerations

7. *Prejob training*—Vestibule training is required, and all important aspects of a job are explained and demonstrated; motion patterns are learned and practiced. This front-end check helps both the new recruit and the company. The

recruit has an opportunity to determine if he or she likes the work, while the company can eliminate those recruits lacking in aptitude or attitude. The trained recruit is equipped to produce good work at an acceptable performance level.

8. *Cross-training*—Employees trained in one type of operation are trained to perform several additional functions. This provides greater flexibility in planning operations and gives the employees an opportunity to grow in job knowledge and remuneration.

9. *Performance evaluation review techniques*—Operations are reviewed regularly using work simplification principles to eliminate, combine, or rearrange work for increased efficiency and effectiveness.

10. *Job enrichment*—The restructuring of some jobs by combining several functions in order to make the jobs more interesting and more challenging.

11. *Effective management span of control*—Assigning supervisors and coordinators so that they can maintain proper control of their responsibilities, including employee performances and unit costs.

Exhibit 11-4 and 11-5 show, respectively, how well the check processing operations performed in relation to established standards for employee performance and to cost from January 1975 through October 1975. Productivity as measured by

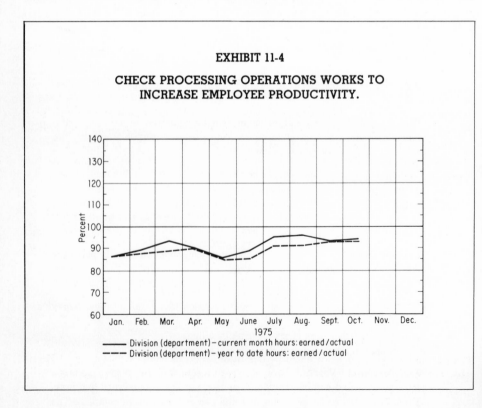

EXHIBIT 11-4

**CHECK PROCESSING OPERATIONS WORKS TO
INCREASE EMPLOYEE PRODUCTIVITY.**

——— Division (department) – current month hours: earned / actual
- - - - Division (department) – year to date hours: earned / actual

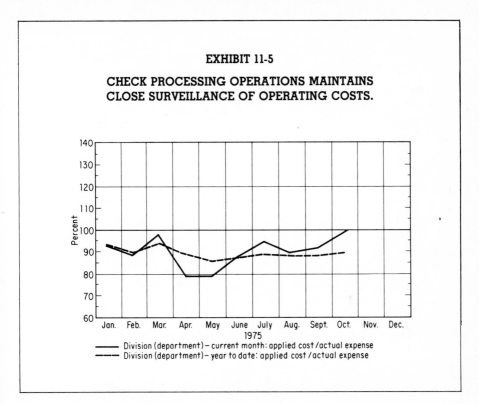

EXHIBIT 11-5

**CHECK PROCESSING OPERATIONS MAINTAINS
CLOSE SURVEILLANCE OF OPERATING COSTS.**

——— Division (department) – current month: applied cost /actual expense
– – – Division (department) – year to date: applied cost /actual expense

performance against standards improved about 9 percent. It's important to note that this is in addition to improvements in methods and systems, since the time standards are changed to reflect those changes as they are introduced into production. Some idea of the impact of new methods on the productivity of the employees can be gleaned from a comparison of the item pass ratio and reject percentages for the months of January 1975 and 1976 as shown in Table 11-3 (productivity increase from year to year shown in parentheses):

TABLE 11-3

Factor	January 1975	January 1976	Future 1977
1. Item pass ratio			
With control documents	2.13	1.78(+20%)	1.50(+19%)
Without control documents	2.03	1.67(+22%)	1.30(+28%)
2. Reject volume	3.5%	1.9%	1.2%

In January 1975, 60 percent of the checks were processed by the old DOS system and 40 percent went through the new CPCS process. By January 1976 all checks were processed by CPCS. The figures shown are actuals except for those projected for the future, when the IBM 3890 will be operable. The IBM 3890 will process checks at the rate of up to 2000 per minute. The above reductions in the item pass ratio show that productivity improved between 20 and 22 percent in one year and that it is expected to increase an additional 19 to 28 percent in the next year. In addition, the volume of errors that had to be corrected was reduced 46 percent in one year with an additional improvement of 37 percent expected in the next year. The new CPCS process is working so well that holdover dollars were reduced 79 percent comparing January 1975 to January 1976. This represents money that can be put to work sooner.

Employee turnover and absenteeism are costly to a company in terms of recruitment, training, performance on the job, and fringe benefits. CICorp maintains a complete set of statistics on turnover and absenteeism. Table 11-4 shows the improvement achieved in these areas over the past 3 years for the four divisions in check processing operations. It is believed the improving trends are due partly to management's efforts and partly to the general economic conditions.

TRUST OPERATIONS AND SERVICES IMPROVE

Now let's take a look at another important activity of the Continental Bank, the trust department. In this department, the vice president for operations, staff services, and corporate services manages trust accounting, trust records, trust securities, trust tax, securities transfer, staff services, employee benefits, and corporate agency, custody, trust, and business development activities. This is a wide range of related activities. The volume operations are measured and controlled with time standards. The reporting system for all transaction activity is automated and computerized fully. It reports among other items, employee performance and cost performance against standard. In 1972, the administrative and operation staff totaled 1450 employees. Since then this staff has been reduced to 1133 at the end of 1975, and the total is projected to 1074 employees in 1976. This 26 percent reduction in staff has been accomplished while maintaining service and improving quality performance during a period when security transactions decreased by approximately 25 percent.

Exhibit 11-6 reveals the improvement achieved in reducing errors for three different quality performance indices. It should be noted that this chart is truncated from 0 to 50. This doesn't change the curves nor the improving trends shown. A downward trend is favorable. It just means that the quality indices are farther away

TABLE 11-4

Division	% Turnover			% Absenteeism		
	1973	1974	1975	1973	1974	1975
Bookkeeping	21.5	18.0	23.5	2.1	2.3	2.1
Document processing	20.0	28.9	16.1	2.2	2.5	2.3
Proof transit	49.0	29.8	11.2	3.1	2.7	2.3
Remittance banking	39.6	42.7	13.8	3.1	2.7	2.4

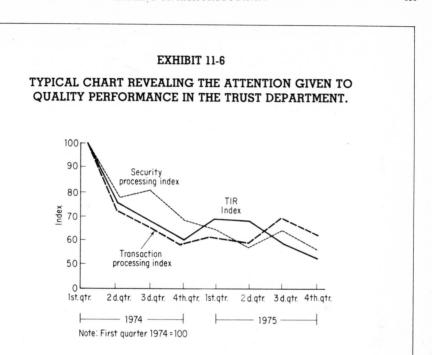

EXHIBIT 11-6

TYPICAL CHART REVEALING THE ATTENTION GIVEN TO QUALITY PERFORMANCE IN THE TRUST DEPARTMENT.

from perfection than the curves appear to indicate. The security processing index shown measures the number of errors of all kinds incurred in the handling of the purchase and sale of securities. The trust investigation report (TIR) covers all inquiries relating to trust accounts. This index covers all customers' questions, some of which arise from errors but also those that seek information, explanation, or clarification. Further analysis of the improving trend reported by the TIR index showed inquiries of all kind were less in total but that reduction in errors accounted for the major portion of the gain indicated. The transaction processing index is an overall measure of all errors made and corrected within trust operations and services. With these definitions of the indices in mind, it is apparent that a significant improvement in operating effectiveness has been achieved. During the 21-month period from the first quarter of 1974 through the fourth quarter of 1975, the security processing index dropped from 100 to 58, a 42 percent improvement. In the same time frame, the trust investigation report (TIR) index was reduced from 100 to 55, a 45 percent improvement, and the transaction processing index was lowered from 100 to 65, an improvement of 35 percent. These improvements are significant because all errors must be investigated and corrected. This is time-consuming and unproductive. In other industries the scrap is discarded. Not so in banking. You just don't throw a stock certificate away. Any reduction in the error rate releases time for other activities.

In addition, in 1975 alone, a total of eighty-two separate actions were taken to improve operating costs. The total net reduction represented by these actions was $422,200. The savings came from the following:

1. Quota and personnel cuts

2. Prevention of future expenditure of clerical time—one time

3. Prevention of future expenditure of clerical time—recurring

4. Elimination of current clerical time expense

5. Elimination of paper, equipment, space, and data processing charges

6. Control enhancement

7. Quality enhancement

8. New or increased revenues (or prevention of fee losses)

Results of this magnitude are difficult to achieve. The vice president explained how it was done. The starting point was a strong, firm conviction that *It can be accomplished!* He and his six managers went through an intensive planning process. They designed a long-range system plan. This was a plan for mechanizing and automating most of the activity. They started with an objective that each system must pay for itself in 18 months or less. Then, they identified job by job where reductions in staff would be made as the automated production machines were introduced. Next, all items of salaries, expenses associated with employees, supplies, space—the controllable and the uncontrollable—were analyzed and budgeted. The budget and reporting systems were set up so that the vice president and his managers could analyze each line item regularly. In fact, they receive daily control reports for the high cost-input items. There is only one purpose for these reports and that is to take action to keep the various programs on target. The entire effort for improvement had to be implemented carefully. The vice president has profit responsibility for the services and must maintain good customer relations. It is bank policy that all services—products—must make or be made to make a contribution to bank profits or be dropped. Literally, the only way to go was to improve operations and reduce costs.

Needless to say, there has been substantial training and cross-training carried on throughout the organization. The result is, however, that in-depth expertise has been developed and the organization now has reached a degree of stability that is conducive to further gains in productivity. The index of total expense per security transaction is an overall measure of the progress made in trust operations and services. This index was reduced from 100 in 1973 to 92 in 1975. This is an overall reduction of 8 percent achieved over a period of 2 years, with inflationary pressures going the other way.

OVERHEAD VALUE ANALYSIS

Recently, CICorp introduced a relatively new management tool to its managers—overhead value analysis (OVA). It is too soon to report results from this program.

However, the OVA program holds substantial promise for reducing overhead costs, especially in those areas that traditionally have been difficult to measure, evaluate, or control. Essentially, overhead value analysis utilizes the concepts of value analysis that have proven so effective in industry for appraising product design from the customer's viewpoint. In the case of OVA, however, the attention is directed to all items making up overhead. The starting point is an objective review by the managers of the services each overhead or staff group provides or uses. This is followed by a penetrating analysis based on managerial judgment to determine if each service is really necessary and the consequences if the quantity and quality of each service are curtailed or eliminated. Following a thorough discussion of pros and cons, the major issues are presented to top management for decision. The program is designed to arouse managers to adopt a questioning attitude toward overhead and to carry through their thinking to overhead-reducing conclusions and actions.

CORPORATE PERSONNEL POLICIES THAT PRODUCE

A business whose theme is "constructive change" solves problems and it creates uncertainties. This is why CICorp managers are trained to identify, deal with, and resolve differences when they arise. The personnel policies have been designed to give the employees confidence that the bank has a comprehensive plan for encouraging their growth and well-being. The plan recognizes that employees have anxieties and frustrations. A program called "Person-to-Person" is available to the employees to provide a confidential, direct line of communications with management. Person-to-Person allows employees to communicate directly with an objective third party about problems in those instances when they do not wish to go through their direct managers. The purpose of Person-to-Person is stated concisely as follows:

> By providing an additional line of communication, the Person-to-Person program is meant to benefit bank management as well as individual employees. It will allow management to take timely action to correct specific problems that might otherwise not have been brought to management attention before reaching a highly critical stage. The program will also help make management more aware of any general conditions and broad trends causing concern among employees throughout the organization.

At first it was used mainly by clerical employees, but today personnel at all levels are using this fast-response service. All kinds of questions are answered. Why is the bank doing this or that? How will this change affect me? How do I get around this situation or problem? Why doesn't the bank do this? Person-to-Person is there and it is serving a purpose.

The senior vice president for personnel and the manager of executive placement described CICorp's personnel policies and the impact these policies have on bank operations and employee productivity. They explained it this way. We take care in selecting recruits. We indoctrinate and train these employees so they can perform well and have a "sense of pride" in their ability. It is Bank policy to appraise each employee on a regular schedule and to discuss the appraisal in detail with each one. We review their development and potential and show interest in their careers. We want to do all we can as a company to help each employee to improve and grow. We counsel them individually and now are developing a program called Life Path Planning to help employees focus on their career goals and options. We cross-train, we transfer, we promote, we counsel, and we try to remedy deficiencies. As a last resort, when a thorough review by management and Personnel indicate that an employee's performance clearly warrants it, we sometimes have to discharge.

Sometimes employees who have performed well in responsible positions over a period of years are not able to adapt to changes in the organization and they become unhappy and unproductive in their jobs, despite the efforts of their managers to help them adjust. In contrast to those situations where employees are terminated for a good cause, in these cases we look first to see whether training or a transfer to another job will enable the person to become a productive member of the organization again. When neither training nor a transfer will help, we feel that it is our obligation to help the employee relocate himself or herself in a more suitable position with another company. To assure that this is done effectively, we arrange for the employee to meet with a professional career counselor. We do everything we can to create an orderly and planned transition for the individual and the work area. This process is called Outplacement. It is supported fully by top management and the department heads as "a necessary, dignified, professional tool of management." Outplacement is intended to help the person involved and to improve the operation of the Bank. It is reported to have achieved both goals in every case.

The senior vice president for personnel sees a need for sophisticated in-house training programs to support the bank's policy of promotion from within. He explained his reasons:

> Emphasis has to be placed upon developing the technically competent or machine-skilled individual. The acquisition of time-saving, modern, business equipment has eliminated many unskilled clerical positions and replaced them with a need for well-trained machine operators. Professional business will continue to seek machine-skilled clerical workers as well as computer—mathematics—business oriented college graduates, thus creating competition in the labor market for the qualified individuals in these categories. Our recruitment units are highly developed and capable of attracting talented people but attention must be paid to what happens to them afterward. Career planning and inter- and intradepartmental transfers for personal and organizational development must be emphasized.

CICorp has developed a series of employee appraisal procedures to bring out the significant features relating to the following levels:

1. Nonexempt employee appraisal

2. Exempt employee appraisal

3. Executive level review: appraisal of performance and assessment of potential

4. Review of development and potential

Exhibits 11-7 and 11-8 are pages taken from the form used to appraise exempt employees. In all cases, the appraiser is given a set of instructions, for example:

One of the most important supervisory responsibilities is to appraise individuals accurately and to record that judgment in terms that can be easily understood. You are being asked to appraise this person because you have direct supervisory

---

EXHIBIT 11-7

SAMPLE PAGE SHOWING FACTORS UTILIZED IN APPRAISING THE PERFORMANCE OF EXEMPT EMPLOYEES.

APPRAISAL OF CURRENT PERFORMANCE

DD — Definitely Disagree
TD — Tend to Disagree
TA — Tend to Agree
DA — Definitely Agree

Behavior Rating

Attitude

Is enthusiastic about work.
Is a cooperative team worker.
Under adverse conditions, the individual still maintains poise.
Lets small problems grow into large ones before trying to solve them.
Contributes significantly to good customer or business relations.

Responsibility

Accepts and seeks responsibility.
Makes prompt decisions when necessary.
Blames others rather than accepting the responsibility for mistakes or delays.
Needs considerable supervision.
Gets things done.

Organization and Communication

Plans work effectively.
Tries to do too much of the work, fails to delegate adequately.
Memos and reports are appropriate and clearly presented.
Communicates well orally.

Analytical Ability

Is highly regarded for both competence and up-to-date technical knowledge.
Is able to learn quickly.
Has difficulty separating the essential from the trivial.
Is resourceful and creative in solving problems.
Is unable to analyze data and conditions to determine the causes of problems.
Judgment is sound and accurate.

Leadership

Opinions are respected by associates.
Is a good coach and trainer.
Does not readily accept new ideas.
Motivates subordinates through fear or pressure.
Subordinates have a high opinion of him/her.
Adjusts rapidly to people and situations.
"Goes to bat" for his/her people.
Subordinates don't like to approach him/her with personal problems.

contact with him and are in a positon to appraise his qualifications accurately. This appraisal will become an important part of the individual's record. Please give it as much care and attention as you would like from those who are appraising you.

The appraisals are important. They are intended to improve employee performance and productivity and to help make the employee more valuable to the bank. The

---

EXHIBIT 11-8

ADDITIONAL INFORMATION REQUIRED TO COMPLETE APPRAISAL OF EXEMPT EMPLOYEES.

The degree to which the employee has achieved major objectives for the year is

_____ outstanding, in the top 10%
_____ well above average, but not outstanding.
_____ satisfactory, in the middle 50%
_____ marginally acceptable.
_____ unsatisfactory.

Overall Performance Rating (check one)

_____ An outstanding performer, definitely in the top 10%.
_____ A highly competent, dependable performer.
_____ An acceptable performer, in the middle half among peers.
_____ A minimally acceptable performer.
_____ An unsatisfactory performer who fails to meet minimum requirements.

Please support your rating by commenting in this space.

_____

_____

_____

_____

_____

_____

This appraisal covers the period from _____ to _____.

I have supervised or worked closely with this individual for _____.
                                                                                    length of time

---

APPRAISAL OF POTENTIAL

Use this space to summarize this person's strengths and special talents.

_____

_____

_____

_____

_____

_____

appraisal results are used to establish salary increase guidelines for the employee and are taken into consideration when promotional opportunities arise. In addition, the employee's base salary is used in calculating his or her profit sharing bonus at the end of the year.

The senior vice president of personnel reports directly to the chairperson and chief executive officer and is responsible for executing specific functions for the corporation. These functions in total are designed to motivate everyone in the organization, and to ensure that CICorp is a good place to work and grow. The functions are as follows:

1. **Affirmative action**

   Structure comprehensive and innovative action programs within both the spirit and the letter of compliance requirements.

2. **Compensation/benefits**

   Develop competitive base, differential, bonus and other direct compensation methods.

   Develop and manage competitive programs such as physical examination, health maintenance, health insurance, life insurance, disability insurance, pension and profit sharing.

3. **Employee relations**

   Design and manage Employee Relations programs, such as travel, discount buying, suggestion system, athletics, to accommodate diverse needs and interests of the total staff.

4. **Management Development**

   Ensure that communication lines to management are open to all employees through various vehicles such as hot line, person to person, suggestion system and objective personnel counselors.

   Design and coordinate tailored training programs to enhance personal skill development and to accelerate upgrading and promotion opportunities for employees of all backgrounds and at all levels of the Corporation.

   Provide the Corporation with guidance and a process for effectively establishing and monitoring manpower succession planning programs.

5. **Organization development**

   Advise management on organization planning and development issues, incorporating outside consultant imputs as required.

6. **Personnel—related public issues**

   Advise Corporation—both management and its employees—on the proper response to personnel issues and developments stemming from legal, regulatory, special-interest groups and legislative pressures—based on a firm commitment to protecting management prerogatives and shareholder interests within the free enterprise system.

7. **Recruitment and placement**

   Develop innovative and competitive recruitment programs within the structure of the Corporation's manpower plans for general employment markets—high school, college, professional and executive.

Incorporate, for management's use, professional and objective tools and chan-
nels for evaluating, assigning, motivating and utilizing the human resource.
Initiate advice and recommendations for reassigning and utilizing employees
for optimum benefit to both the person and the organization. Guide and
manage evaluation and placement processes.

Provide counseling capability to the employees and management encouraging
career development, second careers, pre-retirement, loaned executive assignments, transfers, requests for reassignments, educational assistance, personal
problems.

Assist management in the continuing process of upgrading the caliber of the
staff through providing objective appraisal and ranking systems and selective
use of dignified and professionally-managed out-placement techniques.

A SUMMARY

Thus, Continental Illinois Corporation is among the leaders of the banking industry
in providing opportunity, training, benefits, and rewards to its employees. The esprit
de corps is excellent, employee productivity is high and continues to improve,
up-to-date systems and machines are in place, and the employees work well together
to serve the customers. The excellent earnings are no surprise. Very little is left to
chance.

Here again, let's look at the total operation to highlight the significant
management decisions and principles that have helped to increase productivity at
Continental Illinois Corporation. They are as follows:

1. It takes a corps of believers to introduce major new management concepts into
   an organization.

2. Imaginative personnel programs contribute to improved employee effectiveness and productivity.

3. Management should be more concerned about the productivity of people than
   the productivity of money.

4. The desire to achieve is a basic motivating force.

5. Employees are more responsive to direction when they know the management
   really cares about them.

6. The fundamentals of scientific management, like mathematics, have universal application.

7. The standard hour of salable product or service produced is the best base for
   establishing standard costs and controls.

8. Projected and controlled staffing reduces costs and increases productivity.

9. Vestibule training brings new employees up to speed faster and better.

10. Reducing errors increases time for productive work.

11. The latest-generation business machines are a must for high-volume office operations.

12. Profit sharing helps to increase productivity.

13. The functions of personnel should be structured to fulfill management's philosophy of management.

THE GENUINE MILK OF HUMAN
KINDNESS IS VERY NOURISHING

12
Organizing
the Hierarchy for
Higher Productivity

MORE IDEAS FOR IMPLEMENTATION

The case histories in the previous chapters described what was done and the gains in productivity actually achieved in ten different situations. The theme common to all ten cases is that *productivity was raised through organized motivation*. Building motivation momentum as an integral part of an organization's character takes considerable preparation, painstaking attention to details, and careful implementation. Rarely, if ever, can it be done quickly and easily. The remaining five chapters compose a reference section in which organization, policies, controls, plans, and programs are discussed and illustrated. The purpose here is to provide specific guidance material for those executives, managers, and engineers who intend to increase the productivity of their organizations significantly year after year after year. An organization structure, position descriptions, and standard practices are given. The information is presented to show how to do it and is extensive and intensive. The casual reader may prefer to stop here. This reference material has been designed to be useful for those who strive to improve the efficiency and the efficacy of their enterprises. The final chapter dwells on aspects of management thinking related to productivity improvement in the future.

ORGANIZED MOTIVATION

The most difficult and the most rewarding task confronting an executive and a manager is to manage people successfully toward fulfillment of desirable goals and objectives. Organization, motivation, coordination, and delegation are several of the tools the manager uses to do this. In organizing for higher productivity, motivation takes on a broader meaning. Time and cost are added to the definition. The objective now is to motivate to achieve the result but in less time, or with a smaller workforce, or with less cost, or with higher yield. And productivity improvement becomes the responsibility of each and every employee in the organization. The sales representative, the engineer, the accountant, the clerk, the electrician, the toolmaker, the material handler, and the truck driver should be just as involved as the production employee and the industrial engineer.

To achieve this broad desire to increase productivity, every level of management from the board of directors to the group supervisors needs to: *Establish a business environment that encourages all employees to improve their skills, knowledge, productivity, and value for the progress of the individuals and the company.*

This concept or philosophy should be basic to the thinking that goes into the design of the organization structure and the preparation of the position descriptions. It should start at the top of the company and gather momentum as it is applied throughout the organization. The watchwords are *simplicity* and *effectiveness*.

STREAMLINE THE ORGANIZATION

Whatever happened to the word *streamline*? At one time it was a popular part of business vernacular and thinking. It has always meant a design that offers the least possible resistance to flow. Flow, interpreted in the broadest sense, can mean movement and exchange of fluids (materials), ideas (communications), money (rewards). Streamlining applied to an organization structure denotes designing, redesigning, altering, modifying, simplifying, and testing the arrangement and the relationships in order to make it possible for the organization to function more efficiently. "Streamline" is a concept that should never be allowed to pass into disuse. And yet that is exactly what has happened. As the technological-economic-social-political environment has increased in complexity, many managements have tried to cope with or protect the business from the accompanying problems by adding frills and patches, unnecessary activities, and inflated titles to the organization pattern. An organization structure is much like a fruit tree. If ignored, it develops branches and leaves abundantly but doesn't produce much fruit. What little ripens usually is of poor quality. The fruit grower knows customers are interested only in buying the fruit. So he prunes out the unnecessary branches and twigs and, lo and behold, the tree yields more fruit of larger size and better quality. The fruit grower repeats this process annually, always cutting back to fundamentals, sometimes more severely than normal.

DO NOT OVERSTAFF

Many organizations today are cluttered with unnecessary staff. Unfortunately, not only do these staff functions and personnel add to the cost of operations but in numerous instances they interfere with the line manager's ability to produce. Staff personnel tend to confuse, bewilder, and make line managers defensive and indecisive. Often the staff does not fully understand the conditions about which it is critical or trying to be constructive and, therefore, too high a percentage of its recommendations can be theoretical or ill conceived. Someone in top management should continually evaluate the effectiveness of staff functions and their personnel. Those that are contributing to improving the productivity of the organization should be encouraged to continue. Those that are marginal or unnecessary should be corrected or eliminated. The productivity of the staff personnel should be appraised not only on their own work habits, but also by the degree to which their services help the company to produce and grow. This is not easy to do but is necessary in many companies, since it represents an opportunity for much improvement. Staff positions should provide specialized knowledge or unique services to the organization. There should be both a functional and an economic reason for each position. The staff functions should be required to justify their existence in terms of joint results that are timely, successful, and profitable.

KEEP ORGANIZATION LEVELS TO MINIMUM

The number of levels in an organization also has an important impact on its productivity. It is axiomatic that the more levels the more cost. The excess cost shows up in payroll and fringe benefits, but the real cost is hidden in the slowness with which the company can respond to change. Too many levels and the introduction of "assistant" and "assistant to" positions is almost a guarantee that the organization will be afflicted with corporate arteriosclerosis. Management effort tends to become fragmented or duplicated, coordination becomes more difficult to control, communications are slowed, and decision making is delayed. In these times of accelerating kaleidoscopic change, an organization must be dynamic if it is to maximize opportunities while minimizing costs. In other words, the organization structure needs to be streamlined, not cluttered.

DESIGNING THE ORGANIZATION

An organization structure for optimum effectiveness should be designed to:

1. Translate thinking and planning into constructive timely action
2. Permit the essence of corporate policies, plans, and objectives to flow naturally down through the organization
3. Filter ideas, problems, and conditions upward through managers to corporate officers so that management remains alert to the needs for innovation
4. Avoid duplication and ambiguity in decision-making responsibility
5. Decentralize and delegate authority and accountability for decision making down to the point of action
6. Facilitate serving the customers with value in the most profitable way

Exhibit 12-1, which shows a basic corporate organization structure, outlines the essential functions and committees that are needed to operate virtually any kind of business. It shows the board of directors with its executive committee and audit committee, a chief executive officer and a chief operating officer, which in the case of

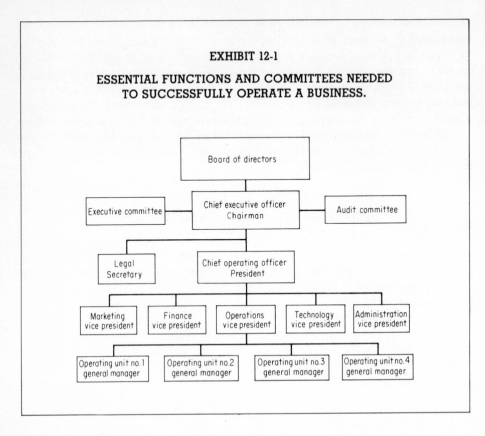

EXHIBIT 12-1

ESSENTIAL FUNCTIONS AND COMMITTEES NEEDED
TO SUCCESSFULLY OPERATE A BUSINESS.

smaller companies may be consolidated, and the basic functions: legal, marketing, finance, operations, technology, and administration. This pattern can be repeated with judicious modification throughout the operating units. An *operating unit* may be a division, a subsidiary, a plant, or a distribution center. This basic organization structure shown in conventional chart form is simple and straightforward. The object is to keep it uncomplicated as the corporation grows and as problem areas and expediencies seem to demand appendages. This chart portrays the structure very clearly, but it is quite static. It really doesn't reveal the action that must take place.

ORGANIZATION DYNAMICS

Exhibit 12-2, which shows a basic dynamic organization structure, is an attempt to give a better picture of this basic organization in action. Here each function is a wheel that must rotate with the other wheels in order to perform its duties. When some wheels run slow or fail to perform or turn contrary to the desired direction, slippage occurs and friction is generated. The organization machine loses efficiency and needs attention. When all wheels rotate in synchronism, the organization machine is most efficient, provided of course that the chief executive officer by example and direction establishes a highly productive, profitable pace.

POSITION DESCRIPTIONS VITAL

The charts outline the organization structure, but to make it work there must be a clear understanding on the part of the people involved as to their individual function and its relationship to other functions and to the total operation. One of the best media for achieving this mutual comprehension is to prepare a *position description* for each function on the organization chart. The description, in order to be comprehensive and effective, should simply and clearly state the following:

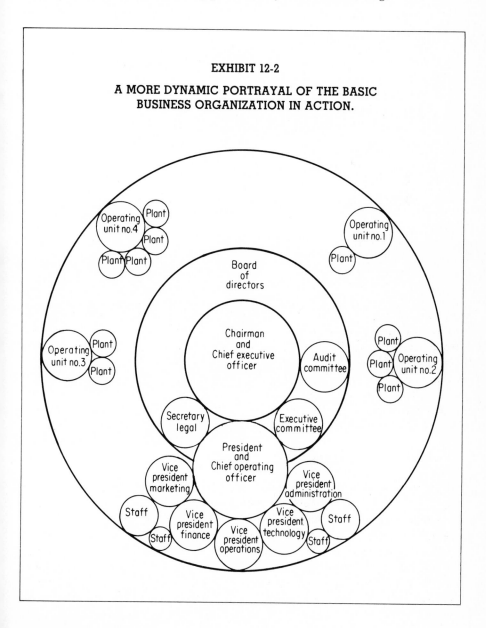

EXHIBIT 12-2

A MORE DYNAMIC PORTRAYAL OF THE BASIC BUSINESS ORGANIZATION IN ACTION.

1. *Scope*—A succinct definition of the function to be performed with its parameters

2. *Organization relationships*—The reporting relationships that have been established

3. *Authority*—The authority granted for implementing the function

4. *Major duties and responsibilities*—A summary of all major duties and responsibilities, set forth so as to highlight and categorize relationships with other functions and business objectives, for the following:

   a. General management
   b. Organization
   c. Business development
   d. Shareholders
   e. Finance
   f. Corporate policy
   g. Public relations
   h. Operations
   i. Mergers and acquisitions
   j. Patents, licenses, and agreements
   k. Marketing
   l. Products
   m. Employee relations
   n. Production
   o. Technology
   p. Long-range planning
   q. Industrial engineering
   r. Others

5. *Accountable for*—The salient factors by which performance of the function is to be measured

When the position descriptions are detailed in this fashion, incumbents can begin to focus sharply on what is expected and how their performance and that of the employees within their function will be appraised. This is an important step toward achieving higher productivity.

A MASTER SET OF POSITION DESCRIPTIONS

The balance of this chapter is devoted to position descriptions covering all the functions shown on the organization charts, Exhibits 12-1 and 12-2. These position descriptions represent a master set, so to speak, that, with modification to accommodate each local situation, can be applied to almost any business venture. All this information from the board of directors and the chief executive officer to the operating unit general managers is designed to provide a streamlined organization that has the built-in capability to achieve higher productivity on a continuing basis.

POSITION DESCRIPTION

Title	Member of board of directors	Group	Corporate
Elected by	Shareholders of the corporation	Issued _____	
Recommended by	Chairperson of the board	Revised _____	

Scope

The board of directors is responsible for determining the philosophies, policies, and goals of the corporation and for seeing that these objectives are carried out by the officers; for electing the officers of the company and specifying their responsibilities; for authorizing the chairperson of the board, the president, and the other officers to act for or on behalf of the corporation in performing delegated responsibilities as prescribed in the corporate resolutions of the board; for establishing committees of the board and defining their responsibilities; and in general for directing the management and control of the business, finances, property, and concerns of the company.

Organizational Relationships

Members of the board of directors are responsible to the shareholders of the corporation. Reporting to the board of directors is the chairperson of the board and chief executive officer.

Authority

The board of directors is empowered to review, consider, decide, and cause action to be taken upon matters affecting the corporation's policies and activities so as to properly protect the rights and interests of the stockholders and other creditors.

Major Duties and Responsibilities

For general management

1. Attend board meetings and carry out functions as prescribed in the bylaws of the corporation.

2. Establish basic policies for the corporation.

3. Provide controls and regulations necessary to properly protect the rights and interests of shareholders and creditors of the corporation.

4. In its discretion, submit for approval or ratification by the shareholders at any of their meetings any contract or act of the board or of any officer, agent, or employee of the corporation.

5. Make all such regulations as are considered expedient concerning the issue, transfer, and registration of stock certificates of the corporation.

6. Create, make, and issue mortgages, bonds, deeds of trust, trust agreements, or negotiable or transferable instruments or securities secured by mortgage or otherwise.

7. Purchase, or otherwise acquire for the corporation, property, rights, or privileges at such price or consideration as is deemed proper, and pay therefore in money, stock, bonds, debentures, or other securities of the corporation.

8. Appoint any person or corporation to accept and hold in trust any property or interest of the corporation.

9. Delegate any of the powers of the board in the course of the current business of the corporation to any standing or special committee or to any officer or agent, and appoint any person the agent of the corporation, with such powers and upon such terms as it considers proper.

10. Adopt, subject to shareholder approval when required by law, and administer any retirement, group insurance, stock option, incentive bonus, or similar plan.

11. Review and appraise, jointly with other members of the board, management's performance, future plans, and programs; and in joint action approve or disapprove them and recommend specific actions to be taken by corporate management in the form of policies, orders, and resolutions of the board.

12. Establish a business environment that encourages all employees to improve their skills, knowledge, productivity, and value for the progress of the company.

For organization

1. Elect the officers of the corporation.

2. Appoint members of the executive committee and other committees of the board.

3. Establish from time to time the salaries of officers and executives, except as power may be conferred by the bylaws upon the executive committee to fix salaries for members of the board or other specified persons.

4. Remove any officer or transfer the powers and duties of any officer to any other person.

5. Confer upon any officer the power to appoint, remove, or suspend subordinate officers and agents.

For finance

1. Publish and submit to the shareholders an annual statement of the financial condition of the corporation, including consolidated income and surplus accounts and a consolidated balance sheet for the preceding fiscal year.

2. Determine the amount and manner of payment of any dividends paid by the corporation.

3. Fix, periodically, the amount of the corporation's working capital, and set aside out of net profits or surplus such amounts as are considered necessary to safeguard and maintain adequate working capital, or as reserves for contingencies, repairs, maintenance, revaluation of profits, equalization of dividends, or for other purposes.

4. Determine who shall be authorized to make and sign bills, notes, acceptances, endorsements, checks, releases, receipts, contracts, conveyances, and all other written instruments executed on behalf of the corporation.

5. Appoint outside auditors upon the recommendation of the treasurer, and provide direct access at all times for reports and recommendations from the outside auditors and the treasurer of the corporation on any matters they may wish to bring to the attention of the board.

COMMITTEE DESCRIPTION

Title	Executive committee	Group	Corporate
Appointed by	Chairperson of the board and chief executive officer	Issued	_____
Approved by	Board of directors	Revised	_____

Scope

The executive committee provides a forum for the discussion and the formulation of policies, regulations, and the handling of broad internal problems on matters which affect the total corporation. This committee is legislative and coordinative in character, assisting each responsible executive to do an effective planning, organizing, coordinating, controlling, and operating job at the level and within the scope of his authority and responsibility. It is the declared spirit of the committee:

That each member is to have the privilege and responsibility of presenting all ideas and problems which he or she feels are important to the corporation. That such ideas and problems should be prepared and organized for effective presentation. That discussion is to be open, frank, and uninhibited, without reservation or concealment, and in full confidence that the whole purpose of the committee is for constructive action in the interest of skillful and effective management. Each member shall hold himself or herself open to constructive suggestions.

Organizational Relationships

The chairperson of the board serves as chairperson of the executive committee.

The president serves as vice chairperson of the executive committee.

The corporate secretary serves as secretary of the executive committee.

All members shall have voting privileges.

There are no alternate members.

Authority

The executive committee is authorized to act for the board of directors between board meetings. Actions taken by the executive committee are subject to review and approval by the board in accordance with the bylaws of the corporation.

Major Duties and Responsibilities

For general management

1. Provides the chairperson of the board with sound, well-considered judgments for shaping the major plans of the business which are divided into four segments:

    a. Long-range strategic planning
    b. Short-range planning
    c. Specific project planning
    d. Emergency action

2. Develops coordination and cooperation by ensuring that all corporate officers and the general managers of the operating units:

    a. Have a clear, objective-oriented plan of action.
    b. Understand the operations and problems of other operating units.
    c. Provide mutual assistance.

3. Establishes basic corporate objectives and policies relating to research, product and process development, product control, production, sales, financing, accounting, purchasing, traffic and office management, and the broad plans for attaining the objectives.

4. Approves operating objectives and corporate and operating unit budgets.

5. Establishes a business environment that encourages all employees to improve their skills, knowledge, productivity, and value for the progress of the company.

For budgets

Evaluates proposed profit plans and recommends a final total corporate profit plan to the chairperson of the board. Direct action resulting from the committee's recommendations is initiated by orders from the chairperson of the board and the president.

For appropriations

1. Evaluates all individual requests for capital appropriations, appropriation deviations, acquisitions, investments, and leaseback arrangements.

2. Reviews and ratifies capital expenditures made by operating units and not requiring prior approval, in accordance with the limits of authority established and delegated to management of operating units by the board of directors.

3. Develops and recommends policies and methods for the preparation of appropriation requests and establishes standards for request evaluation.

For finance

1. Reviews and evaluates the financial structure of the corporation, its financial needs, financing methods, credit terms, borrowing practices, and its financial budgets, for the purpose of recommending to the chairperson of the board adequate programs for attainment of a sound and balanced corporate financial structure which will support an optimum rate of growth and profit.

2. Ascertains and recommends sound short-term and long-term corporate financial objectives, including:

   a. Required rate of capital expenditure.
   b. Required amount of working capital.
   c. Required total operating funds.
   d. Preferred methods of financing.
   e. Return on capital employed.
   f. Required gross profit margins.
   g. Required rate of expenditures for research and development.
   h. Attainable financial ratios.

For planning

1. Advises the chairperson of the board and the president on matters relating to:

   a. Research and development programs to be undertaken.
   b. The type of work and projects which should be solicited and accepted.
   c. General instructions to serve as guides to the operating groups in the acceptance of business; recommendation on specific projects not governed by outstanding general instructions, when such matters are referred to the committee.
   d. The allocation of work among the various geographic areas or operating units.
   e. General policies governing items to be subcontracted.

f. General facility requirements and recommendations as to specific items deemed advisable by the committee or referred to the committee for consideration.

g. Any other matters which the committee considers pertinent.

COMMITTEE DESCRIPTION

Title	**Audit committee**	Group	**Corporate**
Appointed by	**Chairperson of the board**	Issued	_____
With Approval of	**Board of directors**	Revised	_____

Scope

The audit committee is expected to broaden the directors' perspective on corporate financial activities and, thereby, provide the directors with added means for contributing to the success of the corporation.

The audit committee shall develop its own objectives from year to year. The scope of its studies is expected to vary depending upon the results obtained from the committee's review of information and from those areas that indicate need for further analysis. The audit committee shall be sensitive to areas that involve judgment in asset valuation, and assessment of liabilities and decisions relating to the impact of present and future conditions on the finances of the corporation.

Organization Relationships

Reports to the board of directors.

The audit committee shall consist of three corporate directors who are not financial or operating executives of the corporation. The members are to be appointed to the audit committee by the board of directors for a 1-year term expiring at each annual meeting of the corporation.

Authority

The audit committee is expected to maintain a relationship of candor and cooperation in dealing with management and with the auditor. The audit committee may request and it shall receive any information it considers necessary for the fulfillment of its responsibilities.

Major Duties and Responsibilities

1. Reviews the management letter submitted by the auditors and the annual financial statements of the corporation prior to their submission to the board of directors.

2. Examines and considers other matters in relation to the internal and external audit of the corporation's accounts and in relation to the financial affairs of the corporation and its accounts as the audit committee, in its own discretion, may determine to be desirable.

3. Considers the effect on the corporation's financial statement of proposed changes in generally accepted accounting principles.

4. Surveys the quality and the depth of staffing in the corporation's financial and accounting departments.

5. Studies the effectiveness of the corporation's internal control system.

6. Analyzes implementation by the corporation of recommendations contained in the auditors' annual report to management.

POSITION DESCRIPTION

Title	Chairperson of the board and chief executive officer	Group	Corporate
		Issued	_____
Elected by	Board of directors	Revised	_____

Scope

Provides leadership to the board in carrying out its collective responsibility for management of the property, business, and other affairs of the corporation, and assumes overall responsibility for the successful operation of the corporation.

Organization Relationships

Reports to the board of directors.

Reporting to the chairperson of the board are:

The president

The secretary

Authority

Within the limits of sound business practice and the further limitations of the articles of incorporation, the bylaws of the corporation, and the policies laid down by the board of directors, the chairperson of the board and chief executive officer will exercise final authority over all corporate policy matters. In addition, he or she is specifically delegated operating authority to conduct the affairs of the corporation. He may delegate to members of the corporation as much of his authority as may be necessary to formulate policy and maintain a strong, effective organization without loss of essential control, but he may not delegate his overall responsibility for results or any portion of his individual accountability.

Major Duties and Responsibilities

As chief policy and planning officer of the corporation, the duties and responsibilities of the chairperson of the board and chief executive officer extend to any and all activities in which the corporation may engage.

For general management

1. Conducts the affairs of the office in accordance with the Corporate Policy C-1 which defines the responsibilities common to all corporate management positions.

2. Presides at all meetings of the shareholders.

3. Provides agenda for and chairs regular and special meetings of the board of directors in accordance with corporate and statutory requirements.

4. Participates jointly with other members in carrying out directional functions such as:

   a. Election of officers of the corporation and the determination of their duties and compensation.
   b. Appointment of trustees and agents for the corporation.
   c. Creation and issuance of negotiable or transferable instruments and securities.
   d. Approval of the objectives, general policies, principles, practices, and the overall organization plan of the corporation.
   e. Authorization of major capital expenditures.
   f. Authorization for acquisition or disposal of corporate assets.
   g. Approval of loans, investments, and other plans to finance the corporation's operations.
   h. Declaration of dividends and establishment of reserves.
   i. Establishment of the controls and regulations deemed necessary to protect properly the rights and interests of shareholders and creditors of the corporation.
   j. Control and supervision of the operations and financial affairs of the corporation through approval of major programs, profit plans, budgets, and forecasts; review of periodic reports, financial and operating state-

ments, and summary analyses of major operations in relation to authorized programs; and determination of remedial action as required.

k. Performance of all duties imposed by statutory requirements.

l. Revision of corporate bylaws as may be desirable or necessary.

5. Appoints all members of the committees of the board of directors subject to the approval of the board.

6. Serves as chairperson of the executive committee, and as ex-officio member of all other board committees.

7. Presents to the board reports and recommendations from the other officers and committees.

8. Presents proposed changes in basic policies of the corporation for board action.

9. Obtains professional services of a legal, financial, and accounting nature as necessary.

10. Directs the efforts of the secretary in the recording of formal corporate action and the preparation and safeguarding of corporate records.

11. Establishes a business climate that encourages all employees to improve their skills, knowledge, productivity, and value for the progress of the company.

For business development

Subject to approval by the board, the chairperson directs the growth program of the corporation as it relates to the acquisition of companies, new products, and patents, including participation in such activities as the:

a. Formulation of acquisition policies and plans.

b. Evaluation and negotiation of potential acquisitions.

c. Recommendation of related financial measures required.

d. Approval of plans proposed by the president for the integration and operation of acquisitions.

For finance

The chairperson assumes responsibility for the financial condition of the corporation and takes effective action to satisfy its fiscal needs and conserve the assets entrusted to his or her care by:

a. Assuring that each operating unit develops and submits profit plans, operat-ing budgets, and forecasts in keeping with policy requirements.

b. Reviewing and submitting to the board for approval the annual consolidated profit plan, operating budget, and forecast and the proposed capital expendi-ture program.

c. Establishing and adhering to procedures governing corporate expenditures.

For public relations and advertising

The chairperson directs the public relations and institutional advertising programs of the corporation, including participation in such activities as:

a. Formulation of public relations policies and plans, subject to approval of the board when required.
b. Selection and use of various advertising media.
c. Communications to shareholders, employees, industry, and the public.
d. Representation of the corporation in public relations matters.
e. Overall direction of the shareholder relations program and coordinating the shareholder relations activities of the president.

For corporate relationships

1. With shareholders of the corporation

   a. Accountable to the shareholders for the proper execution of the duties and responsibilities and the protection of shareholder interests and rights.
   b. As chief public relations officer, the chairperson assures that the shareholders are kept adequately informed of the affairs of the corporation and that sound relationships and effective communications are maintained between management and the owners of the corporation.

2. With the board of directors

   a. Counsels individually and collectively with the members of the board, utilizing their capacities to the fullest extent necessary to secure optimum benefits for the corporation.
   b. In conjunction with the president, the chairperson keeps the board of directors informed on the condition of the business and on all the important factors of influence.
   c. In conjunction with the president, reviews major activities and plans with the board of directors to assure that both of them have the benefit of the board's thinking and are acting in conformity with the board's views on corporate policy.
   d. Refers promptly to the board of directors such matters as may require the board's decision.

3. With the committees of the board

   a. As chairperson of the executive committee, the chairperson participates jointly with the other members in its proceedings. He or she counsels with the executive committee, in the intervals between meetings of the board, on all matters of interest to the committee, and is guided by the recommendations of the committee in the absence of specific direction from the full board.
   b. Acts as an ex-officio member of all corporate committees and appoints such members of management to committees as he or she deems advisable, except for those appointments made by the board.

4. With the president

   a. Advises, directs, and cooperates with the president as may be required to assure that the policies, orders, and resolutions of the board and directives of the executive committee are carried out.

   b. Reviews all important operating matters with the president.

   c. Keeps the president fully informed and counsels with him or her on those corporate functions which report directly to the chairperson.

   d. In the event of the absence or disability of the president, the chairperson of the board performs the duties of the president.

5. With other officers and executives

The chairperson coordinates his or her efforts with those of other officers and executives toward the goals of the corporation and stands ready at all times to give advice and counsel as may be required or desired.

6. With persons outside the corporation

The chairperson establishes and maintains such outside relationships as he or she considers appropriate in the interest of the corporation, and as chief public relations officer of the corporation maintains contacts with industry, other companies, business associations, the community, the government, the press, and the general public.

Accountable for

The chairperson of the board and chief executive officer is accountable for the fulfillment of the responsibilities, duties, and relationships described herein. The primary measurements of satisfactory performance are as follows:

1. The effectiveness with which the board of directors functions in making its optimum contribution to the benefit of the corporation.

2. The soundness and adequacy of the objectives and policies recommended to the board of directors; the effectiveness with which the policies of the board are executed; and the extent to which the approved objectives of the corporation are realized.

3. The extent to which the assets of the corporation have been conserved and strengthened; the soundness of the financial condition of the corporation; and the extent to which its fiscal needs have been met.

4. The profit results of the corporation as a whole and of the individual operating units.

5. The extent to which the character and quality of the products and services of the corporation assure leadership position and further the reputation of the corporation as a whole.

6. The soundness and success of the corporation's growth program.

7. The extent to which the corporate public relations program achieves public understanding and support for the corporation and its divisions, and the extent to which the policies and operations of the corporation are identified with the public interest.

8. The quality, quantity, timeliness, and continuity of the guidance and support rendered to the president.

9. The cordiality of relations which exist between the chairperson and other persons both within and without the corporation.

10. The example of leadership, good management, high morale, personal conduct, and effective teamwork evidenced by the chairperson in his or her contacts with members of the board of directors, the officers of the corporation, the general managers, and others.

11. The extent to which the corporation carries out its customer, employee, shareholder, industry, government, and public responsibilities.

POSITION DESCRIPTION

Title	President and chief operating officer	Group Corporate
Elected by	Board of directors	Issued _____
With Approval of	Chairperson of the board	Revised _____

Scope

As chief operating officer of the corporation, the president is responsible to the chairperson of the board of directors and chief executive officer for the general direction of all business, operations, or other affairs of the corporation so as to assure realization of maximum profits compatible with the best interest of employees, customers, and shareholders, and for making recommendations to the chairperson of the board with respect to these activities.

Organization Relationships

Reports to the chairperson of the board and chief executive officer. Reporting to the president and chief operating officer are the:

Vice president of marketing

Vice president of finance

Vice president of operations

Vice president of technology

Vice president of administration

Authority

The president and chief operating officer is authorized to take any reasonable action necessary to perform the duties and responsibilities assigned by the chairperson of the board and chief executive officer, provided the action taken is consistent with sound business judgment and the limitations placed upon this authority by:

Federal, state, and local laws and regulations

Corporate policies and procedures

Major Duties and Responsibilities

For general management

1. Operates in accordance with Corporate Policy C-1, which defines the responsibilities common to all managerial positions.

2. In the event of absence or disability of the chairperson of the board, the president performs the duties of the chairperson, and presides at meetings of the shareholders, the board of directors, and the executive committee.

3. In conjunction with the corporate officers, develops and recommends short- and long-range objectives and goals for the operating units relating to marketing, product development, manufacturing facilities, innovations, financial requirements, human resources, and corporate profitability which will take maximum advantage of operating unit potentialities and assure desired growth. Determines that objectives developed and sponsored are in harmony with corporate objectives; and secures their authorization by the chairperson of the board.

4. Makes certain that the corporate officers reporting to him are kept fully informed on matters relating to their respective functions and the effectiveness of their operations.

5. Requires the generation of operating unit plans; evaluates them and submits appropriate proposals to the chairperson of the board; and sees that authorized plans are efficiently executed.

6. Establishes effective means of control to permit appropriate delegation of responsibility and authority.

7. Coordinates corporate activity with business conditions by keeping fully informed regarding the external factors which have a bearing upon the conduct of the business.

8. Keeps the chairperson of the board informed with operating results in all phases of corporate activity.

9. Assists the chairperson of the board in the formulation of corporate policy.

10. Maintains continuing programs for analysis and review of results, recognizes achievements, detects undesirable trends or developments at an early stage and assures that appropriate remedial action is promptly taken.

11. Advises the chairperson of the board in establishing corporatewide performance objectives and in setting specific standards for each of the operating units in important result areas such as marketing, personnel development and utilization, operating efficiency, innovation, physical and financial resources, public responsibility, and profitability.

12. Evaluates the performances of the operating units against established standards and directs and advises the corporate officers and the general managers in the improvement of their planning and performances.

13. Establishes an operating environment that encourages all employees to improve their skills, knowledge, productivity, and value for the progress of the company.

For organization

1. Assures that the corporate officers, general managers, and the functional managers are delegated sufficient authority and are encouraged to operate in an entrepreneurial manner.

2. Makes certain that the necessary limitations of authority are defined and clearly understood.

3. Determines that the general managers are continually developed so that qualified successors are available for key positions when needed.

4. Recommends the appointment, promotion, retirement, or release within his or her area of responsibility of key members of management in cases requiring the approval of the chairperson of the board; and authorizes such actions in cases where the president has final authority.

5. Assures that appropriate salary, wage, and incentive compensation programs and structures are developed and their use properly controlled within the corporation and the operating units subsequent to the approval of the chairperson of the board.

6. Determines that operating units maintain effective relationships with labor organizations and that commitments in union contracts are consistent with basic corporate policies and objectives.

For operations

1. Assures that the vice president of operations develops and implements programs for growth in keeping with the established plans and objectives for overall growth of the corporation.

2. Counsels with the vice president of technology and others involved in the development of new products.

3. Counsels with the vice president of marketing and others involved in the formulation of marketing strategy for the introduction of improved and new products and services.

4. Approves and observes the execution of major contracts of sufficient magnitude to require attention of the president.

5. Participates with the chairperson of the board in programs relating to corporate decisions which determine the expansion or contraction of the product lines of the operating units.

For mergers and acquisitions

1. Maintains alertness for companies which are potential prospects for merger or acquisition and submits findings and recommendations to the chairperson of the board.

2. Arranges for surveys and negotiations, as directed by the chairperson of the board, of potential merger or acquisition prospects.

3. Requires the application of Corporate Policy C-5, which outlines the pertinent information normally to be obtained as the basis upon which to make an evaluation of an acquisition prospect.

4. Encourages the corporate officers reporting to the president to participate in the corporate program for realizing growth through acquisition as well as through internal expansion.

For finance

1. Directs the vice president of finance in the exercise of care, custody, and control of corporate assets and financial activities.

2. Evaluates requests from operating units for capital expenditure appropriations, capital equipment disposal, and when necessary, recommends suitable action to the chairperson of the board; authorizes action of this nature in cases where the president has final authority.

3. Makes certain that authorized profit planning and budgetary procedures are properly prepared and utilized in the operating units.

4. Assists the chairperson of the board in the formulation of corporate policies relating to finance.

Accountable for

1. Meeting the objectives set by the chairperson of the board.

2. Planning for continued growth, diversification, and profitable operation of the operating units.

3. Attaining profit objectives established for the corporation.

4. Achieving a satisfactory return on the gross assets of the corporation.

5. The extent to which the character, quality, and price of the products and service of the operating units assures a leadership position for the corporation.

6. The soundness of the policies and procedures recommended to the chairperson of the board.

7. The quality, quantity, timeliness, and continuity of the guidance and assistance rendered to the corporate officers and the operating units.

8. The example of leadership, good management, high morale, personal conduct, and effective teamwork evidenced in contacts with officers of the corporation and others.

9. The extent to which the operating units make effective use of the services of the staff organizations.

10. The extent to which the corporate officers and the operating units carry out their public, community, and employee responsibilities.

POSITION DESCRIPTION

Title	Secretary and legal counsel	Group	Corporate
Elected by	Board of directors	Issued	_____
With Approval of	Chairperson of the board president	Revised	_____

Scope

Provides legal counsel and service to the corporation.

Arranges for meetings of the shareholders, board of directors, executive committee, and audit committee; and prepares minutes of these meetings.

Signs authorized corporate documents and affixes the official corporate seal.

Maintains custody of corporate deeds, contracts, and other documents of similar nature.

Organization Relationships

Reports to the chairperson of the board. The secretary and legal counsel establishes and maintains working relationships with the following:

Shareholders of corporate stock

Directors of the board

Officers of the corporation

All departments of the corporation

The public

Authority

The secretary and legal counsel is authorized to perform duties as assigned by the chairperson of the board and the president and in accordance with the bylaws of the corporation.

Major Duties and Responsibilities

For general management

1. Operates in accordance with Corporate Policy C-1, which defines the responsibilities common to all managerial positions.

2. Issues proper notice for the meetings of the shareholders, board of directors, and executive committee; makes all necessary arrangements; and prepares the agenda and procedures of such meetings.

3. Attends all meetings of shareholders, board of directors, and executive committee, and acts as secretary, keeping a proper record of the topics discussed, decisions reached, and actions taken.

4. Informs officers and directors of their elections or appointments and keeps a statutory register of directors and their biographies.

5. Notifies affected departments of action taken by the board of directors, providing copies of resolutions or extracts from the minutes where appropriate.

6. Affixes the corporate seal and attests, signs, or countersigns corporate documents when authorized; including contracts, certification of extracts from minutes, and resolutions.

7. Maintains custody of corporate records, including deeds to property, selected original contracts, official minute books, and seals of the corporation and its domestic subsidiaries.

8. Administers the remote storage depositories established for emergency protection of the corporation's vital records in accordance with the corporate security program.

9. Gives formal notice on behalf of the corporation and receives formal notice addressed to the corporation.

10. Provides legal counsel and guidance to the corporation and handles litigation.

11. Develops and coordinates the basic methods, practices, and procedures relating to matters within his or her function.

For shareholders

1. Arranges for the publication of notice of annual meeting, announces any special meetings with shareholders.

2. Coordinates with the treasurer's office all matters pertaining to the determination of shareholder attendance, proxy representation, and shareholder's comments received with proxies.

3. Handles corporate correspondence, including inquiries from shareholders and the public concerning matters of general interest.

4. Maintains current information concerning corporate stock relative to shareholder matters.

For patents, licenses, and agreements

1. Maintains complete records of patents issued to the corporation and current applications pending in the United States and in foreign countries.

2. Assists in the determination of the countries in which patent applications are to be filed.

3. Solicits and negotiates license agreements designed to protect and profitably exploit the corporation's patents, technical know-how, and trademarks.

4. Solicits and arranges license agreements to make available to the corporation machines, processes, and products as directed by the chairperson of the board and the president.

5. Negotiates and prepares other contracts and agreements as directed by the chairperson of the board and the president.

6. Examines contracts in relation to United States and foreign-country regulations, and obtains governmental approval as required.

7. Obtains legal assistance and counsel as may be required in the preparation of applications for patents and trademarks, registrations, licenses, contracts, and agreements.

Accountable for

1. Rendering effective service to the board and the executive committee, in the planning, arranging, and reporting of meetings.

2. Maintaining sound relationships between the corporation and its shareholders.

3. Conforming to the requirements of regulatory bodies governing corporations.

4. Safeguarding corporate records entrusted to his or her care.

5. Providing service to the chairperson of the board and the president in the performance of special assignments.

POSITION DESCRIPTION

Title	Vice president of marketing	Group	Corporate
Elected by	Board of directors	Issued	_____
With Approval of	President	Revised	_____

Scope

Administers, directs, and coordinates the marketing activities of the corporation so as to strategically plan for, develop, and profitably penetrate the markets to which the products, services, and capabilities of the corporation are directed. These activities include sales, advertising and promotion, distribution, and customer service.

Organization Relationships

Reports to the president and chief operating officer. Reporting to the vice president of marketing are the:

Manager of sales

Manager of advertising

Manager of distribution

Manager of customer service

Authority

The vice president of marketing is authorized to take any reasonable action necessary to perform the duties and responsibilities assigned by the president so long as the implementation is consistent with sound business judgment and the limitations placed on this authority by:

Federal, state, and local laws and regulations

Corporate policies and procedures

Major Duties and Responsibilities

For general management

1. Operates in accordance with Corporate Policy C-1, which defines the responsibilities common to all managerial positions.

2. Consults with, advises, informs, and takes direction from the president.

3. Maintains liaison with, and seeks advice and counsel of, the vice president of administration and members of his or her staff.

4. Coordinates thinking and action, and maintains an effective working relationship with other corporate officers toward achievement of corporate objectives and goals.

5. Develops the managers in the marketing organization through direction, guidance, and coaching to help them perform most effectively, both individually and as a team.

6. Establishes high, attainable objectives for the managers and works closely with them to ensure achievement of the objectives.

7. Analyzes and evaluates in a systematic manner and on a regular basis, the efectiveness of the operation of the marketing functions with the managers, and recommends measures and actions for correction and improvement.

8. Motivates managers by providing equitable compensation and benefit structures.

9. Motivates managers through programs of incentive rewards for outstanding achievement and extraordinary contribution to the success of the marketing programs.

10. Promotes and develops effective planning directed toward enlarging the scope and the penetration of the corporation's markets.

11. Supervises managers to make certain that they are functioning within the framework of corporate objectives, policies, procedures, plans, and controls.

12. Assures that provisions have been made for the development and maintenance of marketing policies, procedures, and controls.

For marketing

1. Provides for a selling, advertising, and distribution setup organized to most effectively penetrate and service the markets and the customers for the corporation's products, services, and capabilities.

2. Develops and maintains personal contact with principal customers and prospective accounts.

3. Provides detailed market forecasts for management planning.

4. Provides for the preparation, distribution, and best exposure of advertising and promotional brochures and materials.

5. Coordinates all selling activities throughout the corporation.

6. Approves and executes major contracts within the established limits of authority.

7. Approves all pricing formulas and factors.

8. Maintains proper balance between finished goods inventories and delivery response to the customers.

9. Develops and continues relations with important industries, trade groups, and competitors.

For products

1. Maintains surveillance of competitive products and services and translates this information into new products and product changes needed.

2. Anticipates and maintains sensitivity to customers' needs for products and services.

3. Recommends products and services to be added or deleted from the line.

4. Keeps informed on profit margins by product line and uses this information to stimulate the marketing, technology, and operations organizations to take effective action.

For organization

1. Delegates to the managers adequate authority to properly direct their activities and to accomplish approved objectives and programs.

2. Enforces corporate policy limitations on the authority of the managers relating to such matters as policy, contract commitments, expenditures, actions affecting personnel, and other management variables; and makes certain such limitations are clearly understood and observed.

3. Organizes a system of communications designed to give quick, reliable response to customers' inquiries and wants.

For employee relations

1. Obtains approval from vice president of administration before changing the compensation structures applicable to the marketing organization.

2. Provides for the development and maintenance of effective practices, plans, and programs to implement corporate policies and procedures.

3. Provides for effective communications and coordination throughout all echelons of the marketing organization and with the other functional organizations of the company.

4. Creates a climate through programs and practices that encourages the employees on all levels to improve their skills, knowledge, productivity, and value for the progress of the marketing organization and the company.

For mergers and acquisitions

1. Maintains alertness of companies that are prospects for merger or acquisition and submits findings to the president for consideration.

2. Surveys, as directed by the president, potential merger or acquisition prospects and reports information with recommendations to the president.

3. Utilizes Corporate Procedure C-5, which outlines the pertinent information normally to be obtained in making a merger or acquisition evaluation.

4. Participates with corporate officers in discussions leading to decisions by the chairperson of the board and the president relating to mergers and acquisitions.

Accountable for

1. Meeting objectives set by the president.

2. Achieving a satisfactory rate of return on sales.

3. Attaining the sales volume objectives and market penetration projected for each product line and in total.

4. Planning the continued sales growth and diversification of the corporation.

5. The extent to which the character, quality, and price of the products and services assures a leadership position for the corporation.

6. The soundness of the policies, procedures, and market forecasts recommended to the president.

7. Establishing and maintaining a high level of morale and personnel efficiency in the marketing organization.

POSITION DESCRIPTION

Title	Vice president of finance	Group	Corporate
Elected by	Board of directors	Issued	_____
With Approval of	President	Revised	_____

Scope

Responsible for all financial activities of the corporation including custody and management of liquid assets, directing corporate controller, participating in arranging financing requirements and in acquisition and merger activities of the corporation.

Organization Relationships

Reports to the president. Reporting to the vice president of finance are the:

Corporate controller

Internal audit and systems review personnel

Authority

The vice president of finance is authorized to take any reasonable action necessary to perform the duties and responsibilities assigned to him or her by the chairperson of the board and the president, provided the action taken is consistent with sound business judgment and within the limitations imposed by:

Federal, state, and local laws and regulations

Applicable corporate policies and procedures

Major Duties and Responsibilities

For general management

1. Operates in accordance with Corporate Policy C-1, which defines the responsibilities common to all managerial positions.

2. Administers and directs the financial activities of the corporation.

3. Develops and requires the use of procedures for handling, evaluating, and controlling financial aspects of the corporation.

4. Serves as custodian of the corporation's liquid assets.

5. Assumes responsibility for the purchase and sale of securities, notes and mortgages, and the leasing of property.

6. Provides for the protection of the corporation's physical assets by obtaining adequate insurance coverage.

7. Provides the chairperson of the board and the president with comprehensive and timely financial reports.

8. Formulates and administers credit and collection policies and procedures and the handling of claims for and against the corporation.

9. Determines and maintains satisfactory equity positions and working capital ratios.

10. Arranges for short-term and long-term loans and handles capital financing transactions.

11. Supervises and directs internal audit and systems review personnel.

12. Maintains liaison with outside professional advisers in the banking and accounting fields.

For organization

1. Establishes a sound organization structure for the proper functioning of the financial activities.

2. Delegates adequate authority to corporate controller, and operating unit controllers, to allow proper performance and direction of their activities for the accomplishment of approved objectives.

3. Maintains working relationship with operating unit general managers and controllers.

For finance

1. Selects depositories for corporate funds.

2. Administers the handling of petty cash funds.

3. Assists in the determination of procedures for disbursements, dividends, and interest.

4. Handles foreign exchange transactions.

5. Analyzes and interprets economic trends and conditions and recommends a course of action.

6. Arranges capital appropriations in conjunction with the corporate approved forecast, profit plans, and budgets.

7. Assumes responsibility for the accuracy and validity of financial data submitted in corporate reports such as annual reports, interim reports, and SEC reports.

8. Coordinates and participates in the establishment and administration of incentive compensation programs such as profit sharing, stock option, and pension plans for the corporation.

9. Supervises maintenance of the maximum and minimum limits of inventories and turnover rate.

10. Invests surplus funds of the corporation.

11. Handles confidential payrolls.

12. Purchases, sells, and leases property; handles real estate and handles personal property taxes and assessments.

13. Signs or cosigns checks, contracts, stock certificates, and other related documents of corporate importance.

For employee relations

1. Obtains approval from the vice president of administration before changing the compensation structures applicable to the finance organization.

2. Provides for the development and maintenance of effective practices, plans, and programs to implement corporate policies and procedures.

3. Provides for effective communications and coordination throughout all echelons of the finance organization and with the other functional organizations of the company.

4. Creates a climate through programs and practices that encourages the employees on all levels to improve their skill, knowledge, productivity, and value for the progress of the finance organization and the company.

For merger and acquisition

1. Collaborates with director of corporate planning regarding the financial review and evaluation of merger and acquisition prospects for the corporation.

2. Utilizes Corporate Procedure C-5, which outlines the pertinent information normally considered when evaluating a prospect for merger or acquisition.

3. Participates with other corporate officers in discussions leading to decisions by the chairperson of the board and the president relating to acquisitions.

4. Establishes financial surveillance program for use in connection with new acquisitions so as to indicate operating results to corporate officers.

Accountable for

1. Meeting the objectives set by the president.

2. Participation in the achievement of profit objectives of the corporation through effective planning and financial guidance.

3. Safeguarding corporate assets.

4. Preparation of corporate financial reports.

5. Coordinating and evaluating profit plans and budgetary controls for effective cost reduction and control throughout the corporation.

6. Following sound principles and procedures in all accounting matters.

7. Establishing simple, effective controls for the corporation.

POSITION DESCRIPTION

Title	Vice president of operations	Group	Corporate
Elected by	Board of directors	Issued	_____
With Approval of	President	Revised	_____

Scope

Administers, directs, and coordinates operations and activities necessary to efficiently plan, develop, manufacture, and market products and services for the operating units; the prime objective being to produce earnings that represent adequate returns on the gross assets of the operating units.

Organization Relationships

Reports to the president and chief operating officer. Reporting to the vice president of operations are the:

General manager of operating unit 1

General manager of operating unit 2

General manager of operating unit 3

General manager of operating unit 4

Authority

The vice president of operations is authorized to take any reasonable action necessary to perform the duties and responsibilities assigned by the president, so long as
the implementation is consistent with sound business judgment and the limitations
placed on this authority by:

Federal, state, and local laws and regulations

Corporate policies and procedures

Major Duties and Responsibilities

For general management

1. Operates in accordance with Corporate Policy C-1, which defines the responsibilities common to all managerial positions.

2. Consults with, advises, informs, and takes direction from the president.
   Obtains approval of the president before authorizing any changes in organization structure, general managers, and the salary and wage scales of the
   operating units.

3. Maintains liaison with, and seeks advice and counsel of, the vice president
   of administration and members of his or her staff.

4. Coordinates thinking and action, and maintains an effective working relationship with other corporate officers toward the achievement of corporate
   objectives and goals.

5. Develops the general managers of the operating units through direction,
   guidance, and coaching to help them perform most effectively, both individually and as a team.

6. Establishes high, attainable objectives for the general managers and works
   closely with them to ensure achievement of the objectives.

7. Analyzes and evaluates in a systematic manner, and on a regular basis, the
   effectiveness of the operation of the operating units with the general managers, and recommends measures and actions for correction and improvement.

8. Motivates general managers and their functional managers by providing
   equitable compensation and benefit structures.

9. Motivates general managers and their functional managers through programs of incentive rewards for outstanding achievement and extraordinary contribution to the success of each operating unit.

10. Promotes and develops effective planning directed toward expansion of facilities and plant modernization.

11. Supervises operating unit general managers to make certain that they are functioning within the framework of corporate objectives, policies, procedures, plans, and controls.

12. Assures that provisions have been made for the development and maintenance of operating unit policies, procedures, and controls.

For production

1. Provides for the necessary facilities, machines, and support to ensure and maintain efficient production.

2. Provides for effective production planning, scheduling, and control techniques and practices to ensure producing quality products and services as committed and scheduled.

3. Provides for economical procurement of materials, supplies, tools, machines, and related equipment and facilities.

4. Provides for efficient control and flow of materials with emphasis on line production.

5. Provides for quality assurance systems, procedures, and practices in keeping with the demands of the aerospace, industrial, and commercial markets served.

6. Provides for processes, methods, and production standards designed to increase productivity and production, and to reduce unit costs and manufacturing cycles.

7. Provides for maintaining facilities in good operating condition and for repairing, replacing, discarding, and adding facilities.

8. Provides for automating processes and for the development or procurement of automatic machinery and controls.

For finance

1. Provides for the establishment and maintenance of sound financial and accounting practices in the operating units that fulfill the requirements of corporate policies and procedures.

2. Plans, directs, and works with the general managers to achieve profit objectives established for each of the operating units.

3. Provides for detailed forecasts, profit plans, and operating budgets for the operating units and regularly reviews actual results and the budgets with each general manager.

4. Prepares and submits consolidated forecasts and profit plans for the operating units to the president for modification and approval.

5. Evaluates information on general and specific economic conditions relative to the effect on the products and services of the operating units, and properly uses the data with the general managers to plan and control operations.

For organization

1. Establishes a sound organizational structure for the proper functioning of each operating unit.

2. Delegates to the general managers adequate authority to properly direct their activities and to accomplish approved objectives and programs.

3. Enforces corporate policy limitations on the authority of the general managers relating to such matters as policy, contract commitments, expenditures, actions affecting personnel and other management variables; and makes certain such limitations are clearly understood and observed by the general managers.

For employee relations

1. Obtains approval from vice president of administration before changing the compensation structures applicable to the operating units.

2. Provides for the development and maintenance of effective practices, plans, and programs to implement corporate policies and procedures.

3. Provides for effective communications and coordination throughout all echelons of the operating units and with the corporate organization.

4. Creates a climate through programs and practices that encourages the employees on all levels to improve their skills, knowledge, productivity, and value for the progress of the operating units and the company.

5. Develops and maintains relations with important industries, trade groups, vendors, competitors, local community interests, and other elements of the general public.

For mergers and acquisitions

1. Maintains alertness of companies that are potential prospects for merger or acquisition and submits findings to the president for consideration.

2. Surveys, as directed by the president, potential merger or acquisition prospects and reports information with recommendations to the president.

3. Utilizes Corporate Procedure C-5, which outlines the pertinent information normally to be obtained in making a merger or acquisition evaluation.

4. Participates with corporate officers in discussions leading to decisions by the chairperson of the board and the president relating to mergers and acquisitions.

Accountable for

1. Meeting the objectives set by the president.

2. Attaining profit objectives established for the operating units, individually and in total.

3. Achieving a satisfactory rate of return on the gross assets of the operating units, individually and in total.

4. Establishing simple, effective controls for operating unit activities.

5. Directing operating unit organizations constantly toward operational improvements and effective cost reduction.

6. Establishing and maintaining a high level of morale and personnel efficiency in the operating units.

7. Planning for continued growth, diversification, and profitable operation of the operating units.

POSITION DESCRIPTION

Title	Vice president of technology	Group	Corporate
Elected by	Board of directors	Issued	_____
With Approval of	President	Revised	_____

Scope

Administers, directs, and coordinates the technological activities of the corporation so as to create products and services developed and designed to meet the demands of the markets in which the corporation is engaged. These activities include research, development, engineering design, and quality assurance.

Organization Relationships

Reports to the president and chief operating officer. Reporting to the vice president of technology are the:

Manager of research

Manager of product development

Manager of engineering

Manager of quality assurance

Authority

The vice president of technology is authorized to take any reasonable action necessary to perform the duties and responsibilities assigned by the president so long as the implementation is consistent with sound business judgment and the limitations placed on this authority by:

Federal, state, and local laws and regulations

Corporate policies and procedures

Major Duties and Responsibilities

For general management

1. Operates in accordance with Corporate Policy C-1, which defines the responsibilities common to all managerial positions.

2. Consults with, advises, informs, and takes direction from the president.

3. Maintains liaison with and seeks advice and counsel of the vice president of administration and members of his or her staff.

4. Coordinates thinking and action, and maintains an effective working relationship with other corporate officers toward achievement of corporate objectives and goals.

5. Develops the managers in the technology organization through direction, guidance, and coaching to help them perform most effectively, both individually and as a team.

6. Establishes high, attainable objectives for the managers and works closely with them to ensure achievement of objectives.

7. Analyzes and evaluates in a systematic manner, and on a regular basis, the effectiveness of the operation of the technology functions with the managers, and recommends measures and actions for correction and improvement.

8. Motivates managers by providing equitable compensation and benefit structures.

9. Motivates managers through programs of incentive rewards for outstanding achievement and extraordinary contribution to the success of the technology programs.

10. Promotes and develops effective planning directed toward enlarging and improving the corporation's products and services.

11. Supervises managers to make certain that they are functioning within the framework of corporate objectives, policies, procedures, plans, and controls.

12. Assures that provisions have been made for the development and maintenance of technology policies, procedures, and controls.

For technology

1. Provides for an adequate research, product development, engineering and quality assurance organization with facilities to develop, design, test, and adopt new and improved products.

2. Coordinates all technical activities related to product design and quality throughout the corporation.

3. Provides for continuing evaluation of existing products and services in terms of growth and profit potential, and the redesign or replacement of those not meeting minimum standards of growth and profitability.

4. Provides for continuing analysis, test, and review of competitive products and services.

5. Provides for protection of creative ideas and unique products through patent applications and safeguarding of proprietary know-how.

6. Establishes, throughout the technology organization, an attitude for optimizing both product design and production design in the products.

7. Requires a value analysis of each product line so as to minimize cost and maximize usefulness of the design of the products.

For organization

1. Delegates to the managers adequate authority to properly direct their activities and to accomplish approved objectives and programs.

2. Enforces corporate policy limitations on the authority of the managers relating to such matters as policy, contract commitments, expenditures, actions affecting personnel and other management variables; and makes certain such limitations are clearly understood and observed.

3. Organizes a system of communications designed to give quick, reliable response to customers' inquiries and wants.

For employee relations

1. Obtains approval from vice president of administration before changing the compensation structures applicable to the technology organization.

2. Provides for the development and maintenance of effective practices, plans, and programs to implement corporate policies and procedures.

3. Provides for effective communications and coordination throughout all echelons of the technology organization and with the other functional organizations of the company.

4. Creates a climate through programs and practices that encourages the employees on all levels to improve their skills, knowledge, productivity, and value for the progress of the technology organization and the company.

For mergers and acquisitions

1. Surveys, as directed by the president, potential merger or acquisition prospects and reports information with recommendations to the president.

2. Utilizes Corporate Procedure C-5, which outlines the pertinent information normally to be obtained in making a merger or acquisition evaluation.

3. Participates with corporate officers in discussions leading to decisions by the chairperson of the board and the president relating to mergers and acquisitions.

Accountable for

1. Meeting objectives set by the president.

2. Developing products and services that meet the demands of the markets for which they are designed.

3. The timeliness with which product developments meet marketing objectives of style, function, quality, price, and delivery.

4. Assisting in the planning for the continued sales growth and diversification of the corporation.

5. The extent to which the design of the products and services assures a leadership position for the corporation.

6. The soundness of the policies, procedures, and product development forecasts recommended to the president.

7. Establishing and maintaining a high level of morale and personnel efficiency in the technology organization.

POSITION DESCRIPTION

Title	Vice president of administration	Group	Corporate
Elected by	Board of directors	Issued	
With Approval of	President	Revised	

Scope

Administers, directs, and coordinates corporate staff functions necessary for the efficient operation of the total corporation. These staff activities include organization planning, policies, and procedures, long-range planning, employee relations, industrial engineering, and special assignments.

Organization Relationships

Reports to the president and chief operating officer. Reporting to the vice president of administration are the:

Manager of planning

Manager of employee relations

Manager of industrial engineering

Authority

The vice president of administration is authorized to take any reasonable action necessary to perform the duties and responsibilities assigned by the president so long as the implementation is consistent with sound business judgment and the limitations placed upon this authority by:

Federal, state, and local laws and regulations

Corporate policies and procedures

Major Duties and Responsibilities

For general management

1. Operates in accordance with Corporate Policy C-1, which defines the responsibilities common to all managerial positions.

2. Consults with, advises, informs, and takes direction from the president.

3. Obtains approval of the chairperson of the board and the president before authorizing any changes in the corporate organization structure, key personnel, and compensation programs.

4. Maintains an effective working relationship with other corporate officers and with the general managers.

5. Provides service to and coordinates thinking and action with the other corporate officers and the general managers toward the achievement of corporate objectives and goals.

6. Develops administrative staff personnel through direction and guidance to help them perform most effectively, both individually and as an administrative team.

7. Analyzes and evaluates in a systematic manner, as directed by the president, the effectiveness of operating unit operations and recommends, to each general manager, the vice president of operations, the president, and the chairperson of the board, actions and programs to be considered for improvement.

For corporate policy

1. Directs the preparation and distribution of corporate policies and standard procedures subject to the approval of the chairperson of the board and the president.

2. Invites ideas and recommendations on policy and standard procedure matters from other corporate officers and the general managers.

3. Discusses and reviews new and revised corporate policies and standard procedures with other corporate officers and the general managers to ensure understanding and effective implementation.

For organization planning

1. With the concurrence of the chairperson of the board and the president, directs the design and revision of the organizational structure of the corporation, and publishes the corporate organization chart.

2. Prepares and maintains current position descriptions for all corporate officers and the general managers specifying major duties, responsibilities, and accountability.

3. Assists with the recruitment, transfer, and promotion of key personnel as required.

For long-range planning

1. Directs the collection and evaluation of general and specific information relating to economic conditions.

2. Provides reports indicating industrial trends and proposes action in those product areas having the greatest growth potential.

3. Arranges for the preparation and release of information to corporate officers and general managers which is significant to current planning and operating activities.

4. Arranges for evaluation of strengths and weaknesses within the corporation and for monitoring competitor capabilities.

5. Authorizes a suitable library of information relating to economic or technological changes which may affect the corporation.

For employee relations

1. Provides services for and coordination of corporate activities relating to labor relations, wage and salary administration, employee insurance benefits, and safety.

2. Provides for an effective program of personnel services consistent with sound management and tailored to meet the needs of each operating unit.

3. Provides for programs for management development, recruitment, training, and performance appraisal.

4. Provides policy guidelines for the safeguarding of company personnel, property, and security.

5. Provides for the formulation and development of public relations policies, plans, and programs to identify the corporation with the public interest.

6. Creates a climate through programs and practices that encourages the employees on all levels to improve their skills, knowledge, productivity, and value for the progress of the company.

For industrial engineering

1. Provides industrial engineering services to assist the operating units in the areas of:

   Labor cost controls
   Quality controls
   Production and inventory control systems
   Facility and equipment planning and layout
   Machine utilization
   Office systems and procedures
   Estimating and pricing procedures
   Automation
   Line production techniques

2. Provides direction and industrial engineering guidance to the operating units in formulating, installing, and administering work measurement programs, including methods improvements, production standards, and wage incentive plans.

3. Arranges for proper estimating procedures and authorizes the pricing formulas that are utilized.

For merger and acquisitions

1. Maintains alertness for companies that are potential prospects for merger or acquisition and submits findings to the president for consideration.

2. Surveys, as directed by the president, potential acquisition prospects and reports information with recommendations to the president.

3. Utilizes Corporate Procedure C-5, which outlines the pertinent information normally to be obtained in making a merger or acquisition evaluation.

4. Participates with the corporate officers in discussions leading to decisions by the chairperson of the board and the president relating to mergers and acquisitions.

Accountable for

1. Meeting the objectives set by the president.

2. Constructively influencing the corporation and the operating units toward operational improvement and effective cost reduction.

3. Contributing to the establishment of a high level of morale and employee efficiency throughout the corporation.

4. Planning the organization structure for continued growth, diversification, and profitable operation of the corporation.

5. Communicating corporate policies to all management personnel for effective implementation.

6. Assisting the operating units to achieve their profit objectives.

7. Performing special assignments for the chairperson of the board and the president.

POSITION DESCRIPTION

Title	General manager of operating unit	Unit	Precision metal products division
Appointed by	Vice president of operations	Group	Aerospace components
		Issued	_____
Approval of	President	Revised	_____

Scope

Administers, directs, and coordinates operations and activities necessary to efficiently plan, develop, manufacture, and market products and services, the prime objective being to produce earnings that represent an adequate return on the gross assets of the operating unit.

Organization Relationships

Reports to the vice president of operations. Reporting to the general manager are the:

Controller

Manager of employee relations

Manager of industrial engineering

Manager of manufacturing

Manager of product engineering

Manager of quality assurance

Manager of sales

Authority

The general manager is authorized to take any reasonable action necessary to perform the duties and responsibilities assigned by the vice president of operations, so long as the action is consistent with sound business judgment and except for limitations placed on this authority by:

Federal, state, and local laws and regulations

Corporate policies and procedures

Major Duties and Responsibilities

For general management

1. Operates in accordance with Corporate Policy C-1, which defines the responsibilities common to all managerial positions.

2. Consults with, advises, informs, and takes direction from the vice president of operations before authorizing any changes in organization structure, key personnel, and salary and wage scales.

3. Maintains liaison with, and seeks advice and counsel of, the vice president of administration and members of his or her staff.

4. Develops operating unit managers, through direction, guidance, and coaching to help them perform most effectively, both individually and as a team.

5. Establishes high, attainable objectives for the managers and works closely with them to ensure achievement of the objectives.

6. Analyzes and evaluates in a systematic manner, and on a regular basis, the effectiveness of operating unit operations and applies measures and actions for correction and improvement.

7. Motivates managers and their employees by providing equitable salary, wage, and benefit structures.

8. Motivates managers and their employees through programs of incentive rewards for outstanding achievement and extraordinary contribution to the success of the operating unit.

9. Promotes and develops effective planning directed toward expansion of facilities, plant modernization, and product and service diversification.

10. Directs operating unit activities within the framework of corporate objectives, policies, procedures, plans, and controls.

11. Provides for the development and maintenance of operating unit policies, procedures, and controls.

For production

1. Provides for the necessary facilities, machines, services, and support to ensure and maintain efficient production.

2. Provides for effective production planning, scheduling, and control techniques and practices to ensure producing quality products and services as committed and scheduled.

3. Provides for economical procurement of materials, supplies, tools, machines, and related equipment and facilities.

4. Provides for efficient control and flow of materials with emphasis on line production.

5. Provides for quality assurance systems, procedures, and practices in keeping with the demands of the aerospace, industrial, and commercial markets served.

6. Provides for processes, methods, and production standards designed to increase productivity and production, and to reduce unit costs and manufacturing cycles.

7. Provides for maintaining facilities in good operating condition and for repairing, replacing, discarding, and adding facilities.

8. Provides for automating processes and for the development or procurement of automatic machinery and controls.

For finance

1. Provides for the establishment and maintenance of sound financial and accounting practices that fulfill the requirements of corporate policies and procedures.

2. Plans, directs, and works to achieve profit objectives established for the operating unit.

3. Provides for detailed forecasts, profit plans, and operating budgets for the operating unit and regularly reviews actual results and the budgets with each manager.

4. Evaluates information on general and specific economic conditions relative to the effect on operating unit products and services and properly uses the data obtained to plan and control operations.

For organization

1. Establishes a sound organization structure for the proper functioning of the operating unit.

2. Delegates to the operating unit managers adequate authority to properly direct their activities and to accomplish approved objectives and programs.

3. Provides, in writing, for appropriate limitations on the authority of the operating unit managers relating to such matters as policy, contract commitments, expenditures, actions affecting personnel and other management variables; and makes certain such limitations are clearly understood and observed by the managers.

For employee relations

1. Obtains approval from vice president of administration before changing the compensation structures applicable to his or her operating unit.

2. Provides for the development and maintenance of effective practices, plans, and programs to implement corporate policies and procedures.

3. Provides for effective communications and coordination throughout all echelons of the operating unit organization and with the corporate organization.

4. Creates a climate through programs and practices that encourages the employees on all levels to improve their skills, knowledge, and value for the progress of the operating unit.

5. Develops and maintains relations with important industries, trade groups, vendors, competitors, local community interests, and other elements of the general public.

For marketing

1. Provides for a marketing and distribution setup organized to most effectively penetrate and service the markets and the customers for the operating unit's products and capabilities.

2. Develops and maintains personal contacts with principal customers and prospective accounts.

3. Provides for the preparation and distribution of advertising and promotional brochures and materials.

4. Reviews all requests for quotation, approves all proposals and quotations, and approves acceptance of all customers' orders.

5. Provides the organization and the basis for estimating, approves all pricing formulas and factors, and approves all prices before submission to the customers.

For products

1. Provides for an adequate product engineering and development organization with facilities to develop and adopt new and improved products.

2. Provides for continuing evaluation of existing products and services in terms of growth and profit potential, and the redesign or replacement of those not meeting minimum standards of growth and profitability.

3. Provides for continuing analyses of competitive products.

4. Provides for protection of creative ideas and unique products through patent applications and safeguarding of proprietary know-how.

Accountable for

1. Attaining profit objectives established for the operating unit.

2. Achieving a satisfactory rate of return on the gross assets of the operating unit.

3. Meeting the objectives set by the vice president of operations.

4. Establishing simple, effective controls for operating unit activities.

5. Directing operating unit functional organizations constantly toward operational improvements and effective cost reduction.

6. Establishing and maintaining a high level of morale and personnel efficiency in the operating unit.

7. Planning for continued growth, diversification, and profitable operation of the operating unit.

13
Corporate Policies for Higher Productivity

Corporate policies form the fundamental thinking that shapes the business and sets the pace of progress that is to be made. They determine what the business stands for and how it is to operate in the broadest sense. Very often a policy statement is followed by a procedure that interprets how the policy may be implemented to achieve business objectives, goals, and forecasts. Corporate policies are so important to the success of the business that they should be thoughtfully formulated by top management and then carefully expressed in written form. In this way, all levels of management and supervision can be made to understand the way in which the business is to be conducted. Further, written policy statements serve as a ready reference. This helps to prevent the organization from drifting from its basic theme and, of course, provides the foundation for "breaking in" key personnel as organizational changes are made. The most persuasive reason for putting policies on paper, however, is that this tends to sharpen top management's thinking in formulating the policies. In time, changes in policies may be necessary. Again, when these occasions occur, the impact of the changes can be given careful consideration by top management before the revisions are adopted. In this way the board of directors, the chief executive officer, and the chief operating officer can establish firmly the modus operandi and the pace of the business.

MANAGEMENT, A CREATIVE FUNCTION

Management is much more than just solving problems or responding to challenges. In fact, the most important function of management is to forecast and anticipate conditions and then plan the operation of the enterprise so as to minimize negative influences and maximize positive factors. Thus, management can and should be a creative function. There is no question but that management must react to situations as they arise. But if management's full time is devoted to reacting, there will be little or no stability built into the operation of the business, and costs will be excessive. This is because too many mistakes will be made, too much time and effort will go into trying to catch up to elusive opportunities and fleet-footed competitors. Unprofitable products will be added, or the introduction of new models will be delayed, or loss contracts will be sought and accepted, or any of hundreds of actions will take place that may impair the business. Reacting keeps the organization busy but not necessarily profitable, *and productivity suffers.*

POLICIES SHOULD GUIDE, NOT LIMIT

Corporate policies are guidelines. Each policy should clearly and definitely guide the organization to a course of action adopted as most prudent. A simple way to establish policies and ensure that the business will be operated within the policy structure set by management is to preface every standard practice with a statement of the policy that the standard procedure is designed to carry out. This encourages, and perhaps forces, members of management to anticipate the shortcomings and problems the policy may precipitate. By doing this, management is more able to plan for the most effective course of action.

A word of caution, however, on the strict use and interpretation of written policies and procedures. A company that is too rigidly organized with complete documentation and enforcement of standard practices will slow down gradually to a pace that inhibits creativity and constructive change, and in this way it can "miss the target" also. Thus, top management really has a twofold obligation:

1. To establish well-conceived policies and procedures

2. To allow the organization and the employees to use initiative and creativity, take calculated risks, and make timely decisions

The organization must be made to respect the established policies and procedures and to appreciate the reasons for conforming to them, but at no time should the employees feel that they are unduly limited or constrained by the standardized policies and practices. A philosopher coined a thought that expresses this concept. It is: "Home should be the center but not the boundary of one's life." This idea can be paraphrased for business this way: "Policies should set the central theme but not the limit of corporate thinking and action."

The condition to be avoided is to have poor decisions made and action taken or not taken in the name of "it's company policy." Employees are not thinking when they use this excuse. Thus, all managers should strive to give their employees some guidelines with which to make appropriate decisions and with which to coordinate activities and functions so that the highest possible degree of creative teamwork can be directed toward realizing company objectives, goals, and forecasts. The teamwork and spirit of a football team exemplifies this point. In football after the play is called, the line is supposed to open a specific hole for the ball-carrying back to run through. But if the hole is not there, nothing is gained by running into a stone wall just because that was the plan. The back is expected to use his judgment and skill to roll around the blocked hole, reverse his direction, sidestep, dive over, or do anything to move the ball toward the goal. This is why football is no longer a game of just brawn. Today it is a contest of muscular strength and physical fitness with fast-action thinking and maneuverable speed added. As a result, the game is much more entertaining for the customers and decidedly more interesting and rewarding for the participants. For best overall results corporate policies and procedures should be used this way also.

THE OVERALL VIEWPOINT

Essentially, the policies that apply overall to the entire company should spell out how the company in total is to operate and by doing this should have a salutary influence on the productivity of the employees and the corporation. The first two would include the following:

1. General Corporate Policies—This standard practice represents a succinct summary of the vital, primary policies of the corporation, for example: "To establish the management purposes, the organization structure, the management objectives, the operating principles and practices, the management result areas, and in broad terms the management duties, management approvals, and the custody of property requirements of the corporation." Obviously, this standard practice could be spread out into eight or more standard practices. However, there is a value to concentrating these management philosophy policies in one convenient standard practice where each executive and each manager can readily grasp the total picture of how the corporation is expected to function.

2. Written Corporate Policies—This policy should be designed to establish standard practices as the basis for disseminating policies and procedures to all levels of the corporation. It should lay down the format that in general is to be followed in preparing and issuing standard practices stating the purpose of the standard practice, the policy that is covered, the distribution of the standard practice, and the procedure by which the standard practice is intended to fulfill its purpose and implement the policy.

THE FIRST TWO STANDARD PRACTICES

Following are examples of these first two standard practices. These examples are intended to illustrate the general composition and the content of policy and procedure statements developed and applied by top management. Both have general application in business, industry, and commerce. However, in practice, the standard practices should be tailored specifically for each corporation by its top management.

	STANDARD PRACTICE	SUBJECT
CORPORATION	NUMBER C-1　　　PAGE 1 OF 6	GENERAL CORPORATE POLICIES
	EFFECTIVE　　　REVISION DATE	

ISSUED BY	APPROVALS		

PURPOSE

To establish the management purposes, the organization structure, the management objectives, the operating principles and practices, the management result areas, and in broad terms the management duties, management approvals, and custody of property requirements of the corporation. This primary corporate policy is basic to the operation of the corporation and of each operating unit.

POLICY

It is corporate policy to describe its operating practices and procedures in writing to communicate them to all employees.

DISTRIBUTION

Corporate officers
Corporate managers
Operating unit general managers
Operating unit managers

Management Purposes

The fundamental business purpose of the corporation is to achieve and maintain a high return on investment with continuous growth in sales and profits.

The fundamental marketing purpose of the corporation is to serve appropriate markets as an outstanding supplier of proprietary products, specially designed systems, and machined, fabricated, and assembled components. Outstanding in terms of service and economic value given to the customers as measured by price, quality, delivery, and technical superiority. The emphasis is to be placed on selected high-value, high-volume products for which there are continuing market potentials.

The fundamental planning purpose of the corporation is to evaluate industry trends, to anticipate potential opportunities, and to formulate programs for development, expansion, acquisition, and spin-off designed to achieve the best total result.

Organization Structure

The corporate organization chart (see Exhibits 12-1 and 12-2) is attached. The management principles upon which the organization of the corporation is based are:

CORPORATION	**STANDARD PRACTICE**	SUBJECT
	NUMBER C-1 PAGE 2 OF 6	GENERAL CORPORATE POLICIES
	EFFECTIVE REVISION DATE	

ISSUED BY	APPROVALS		

1. The corporate management group is to be small and effective.

2. The organization structure and the operating climate are to be established so as to inspire creativity, encourage calculated risk taking, and reward achievement.

3. The importance of change is to be recognized with provision for the creation of constructive changes and the prompt, orderly conversion of "discovery into effective use."

4. Authority, responsibility, and accountability are to be delegated to the operating units so that:

   a. Most decisions are made at the operating unit level by those management employees closest to the vital data and who comprehend it thoroughly and who can act adroitly and effectively.

   b. Entrepreneurial management is emphasized and expected of the general manager and the management staff of each operating unit.

   c. A simple system of quantitative objective-setting, both immediate and long range, and measurement of results is implemented for each operating unit with periodic review by corporate management.

5. Each operating unit is to be headed by an appointed general manager assisted by functional managers reporting directly to the general manager. The general plan of organization is that each functional manager will manage a specific key function of the operating unit such as sales, engineering, manufacturing, industrial engineering, quality assurance, accounting, and employee relations. Each functional manager will be expected to be expert in a specific field of responsibility, to train and direct his or her organization, and to make decisions and initiate action within his or her function. The general manager will work with the functional managers, both individually and as a group, to direct and coordinate their efforts for most effective achievement and results. In addition, the general manager will devote considerable time and attention to the marketing activities of the operating unit. The general manager will develop working relationships with major customers. He or she will review all customer inquiries and requests for quotation, and will review and approve all quotations and proposals before being submitted and all customers' orders before being accepted.

The general manager with the functional managers will make up the man-. agement staff of each operating unit. A major and most difficult job for each management staff will be to formulate sound, workable plans. This will require that the general manager and the functional managers be well informed, factual, realistic, and view operations with complete objectivity in setting high, attainable goals.

6. The prime objective of the operating units will be to place the corporation in a top position as a supplier of precision components, products, and services to its customers by:

  a. Building a reputation for service
  b. Building profits
  c. Building sales volume

Management Objectives

The management objectives for the corporation and each operating unit will be established to highlight the significant factors that serve to measure the progress of each profit center. Quantitative objectives will be preferred over qualitative goals, and each objective, after careful analysis and selection, will be defined and described so as to be readily understandable, concise, and attainable. Management attention, thought, and effort at all levels are to be focused on producing results. The basic objectives will be tailored to each operating unit's unique conditions. Basic measurement indices common to all profit centers include:

1. $\% \text{ profit on sales} = \dfrac{\text{net profit before taxes}}{\text{net sales}} \times 100$

2. $\text{Turnover} = \dfrac{\text{net sales annualized}}{\text{gross assets employed}}$

  where gross assets employed is defined as book assets − receivables from corporate + cost of leased real estate + book depreciation.

3. $\% \text{ return on investment} = \% \text{ profit on sales} \times \text{turnover}$

4. $\% \text{ sales growth} = \left(\dfrac{\text{net sales for period}}{\text{net sales for prior period}} - 1.00 \right) \times 100$

5. $\% \text{ gross profit} = \dfrac{\text{net sales} - \text{total cost of sales}}{\text{net sales}} \times 100$

	STANDARD PRACTICE	SUBJECT
CORPORATION	NUMBER C-1 PAGE 4 OF 6	GENERAL CORPORATE POLICIES
	EFFECTIVE REVISION DATE	

ISSUED BY	APPROVALS		

6. $\% \text{ S,G\&A} = \dfrac{\text{selling, general and administrative expense}}{\text{net sales}} \times 100$

7. $\text{Inventory turnover} = \dfrac{\text{net sales annualized}}{\text{total inventory}}$

8. Dollar working capital in relation to planned working capital

9. $\% \text{ employee performance} = \dfrac{\text{standard hours produced}}{\text{hours on standard}} \times 100$

10. $\% \text{ on standard} = \dfrac{\text{hours on standard}}{\text{hours on standard} + \text{daywork production hours}} \times 100$

Operating Principles and Practices

The management and direction of all operating units in the corporation will be based on the following fundamental operating principles and practices:

1. Engineered pricing of quotations and proposals predicated on detailed estimates of standard direct labor hours modified by appropriate learning curve factors, and the application of current hourly wage rates, factory overhead and S,G&A rates, and full profit markups.

2. Thorough industrial engineering preparation of all factory orders including detailed methods descriptions with gaging, tooling, speeds and feeds, and setup and unit time standards specified.

3. Soundly conceived and consistent time standards established from engineered time studies and elemental standard time data.

4. The establishment of effective incentives for direct and indirect employees based on increased productivity as measured by time standards.

5. Incentives for management employees based on an evaluation of achievement related to specific performance objectives, and the total profit performance of the operating unit.

6. Budgetary control of all elements of cost and expense, and profit planning projected at the end of each quarter for the next 12 months ahead.

7. Quality assurance programming that emphasizes "do it right the first time" achieves quality levels permitting effective use of sampling plans, and reduces scrap, rework, and returned goods to acceptable limits.

CORPORATION	**STANDARD PRACTICE**	SUBJECT
	NUMBER C-1 PAGE 5 OF 6	GENERAL CORPORATE POLICIES
	EFFECTIVE REVISION DATE	

ISSUED BY	APPROVALS		

8. Schedule control designed to obtain minimum manufacturing cycles and inventories with a high degree of on-time deliveries.

9. The continual upgrading of facilities and capabilities through the installation of new and latest-generation equipment, tools, and processes, both in the factory and in the office, as justified by analyses indicating adequate returns on investments.

Management Result Areas

The key result areas that are to be foremost in the thinking, planning, and action of all officers, directors, general managers, and managers are:

1. Profitability
2. Productivity
3. Market standing
4. Innovation
5. Manager performance and development
6. Employee performance and attitude
7. Physical and financial resources
8. Public responsibility

Management Duties

The management duties that are important and common to all officers', corporate managers', general managers', and functional managers' responsibilities are to:

1. Identify opportunities
2. Evaluate potentialities
3. Establish prices
4. Make plans
5. Coordinate action
6. Review results
7. Take corrective action
8. Develop personnel

Management Approvals

The one-over-one rule is to be followed in authorizing and approving all personnel and salary and wage changes, and any other specified matters. This rule requires the immediate supervisor making the decision to obtain the approval of his or her superior before announcing or implementing the action.

	STANDARD PRACTICE	SUBJECT
CORPORATION	NUMBER C-1 PAGE 6 OF 6	GENERAL CORPORATE POLICIES
	EFFECTIVE REVISION DATE	

ISSUED BY	APPROVALS		

Custody of Property

The officers, corporate managers, general managers, and functional managers are responsible for the custody of all funds and property under their supervision. This responsibility includes keeping proper records and identifying, using, storing, and maintaining property in good, clean, efficient, operating condition. The controller of each operating unit, while reporting to the general manager of the operating unit, also has a responsibility to the corporate controller to audit and make certain that the funds and assets allocated to the operating unit are properly managed.

CORPORATION	**STANDARD PRACTICE**	SUBJECT
	NUMBER C-2 PAGE 1 OF 3	WRITTEN CORPORATE POLICIES
	EFFECTIVE REVISION DATE	

ISSUED BY	APPROVALS		

PURPOSE

To establish standard practices as official written descriptions of corporate policies and procedures.

POLICY

Economic conditions and practices within the competitive environment of the free enterprise system strongly indicate the need for maximum operating effectiveness throughout the corporation at all times. Toward that objective, it shall be regular policy to put into writing and to publish existing and future policy and procedure directives to those who have a need for guidelines and basic reference information for sound decision making and for directing the operations of the corporation. All operating units, whether a subsidiary, a division, or a distribution center, shall establish and maintain a written standard practice program to describe, implement, and supplement corporate policies.

This policy is designed to promote:

1. Improved communications for better understanding of, and closer conformity to, existing and future corporate policies.

2. Increased use and effectiveness of individual initiative by employees who are properly informed of job boundaries and overall goals and objectives.

3. Reduced costs for the training and orientation of new or transferred employees who can more quickly and with less assistance acclimate themselves and become fully productive.

4. Improved working relationships between operating units of the corporation as a result of improved communications.

DISTRIBUTION

Corporate officers
Corporate managers
Operating unit general managers
Operating unit managers

	STANDARD	SUBJECT
CORPORATION	**PRACTICE**	WRITTEN CORPORATE POLICIES
	NUMBER C-2 PAGE 2 OF 3	
	EFFECTIVE REVISION DATE	

| ISSUED BY | APPROVALS | | |

PROCEDURE

1. Issue

   a. Corporate

   The office of the vice president of administration shall generate standard practices from time to time on appropriate subjects and make distribution to applicable operating units of the corporation.

   b. Operating Units

   Each subsidiary or division shall generate standard practices to implement the policies described in the corporate standard practices. In addition, each operating unit shall explain its local policies in written form for distribution to its own personnel. In all cases, the standard practices issued by the operating units are to be prepared within the guidelines and limitations established by the corporate standard practices.

   Each operating unit shall promptly send a copy of each of its standard practices to the office of the vice president of administration.

2. Numbering

   Each corporate standard practice shall be identified by C followed by a hyphenated number, the first two digits of which shall be the number of the originating department. The subsequent digits represent the actual number of the particular standard practice being issued. For example: the twenty-fourth standard practice issued by Department 03 would be written C03-24. The standard practice numbering sequence begins with "1" for each department and progresses consecutively as required. Corporate numbering of departments shall be made to coincide with those issued by the vice president of finance's office in connection with the corporate chart of accounts.

3. Distribution

   The office of the vice president of administration shall make distribution of all standard practices to each operating unit except for those with subjects which have limited application or a specialized interest. That type will be sent only to those operating units which are affected.

4. Revisions

When standard practices are revised, they will bear the same number as the original except that the identifying number will be suffixed to indicate a revision and the timing involved.

Example: The twenty-fourth standard practice issued by Department 03 and revised August 1976 would be numbered as follows: C03-24 (R. 8-76).

5. Supplements

When the subject of the standard practice requires more elaboration, or new information becomes available, a supplement will be issued. The supplement will bear the number of the original standard practice plus the suffix *Sup.* followed by the next numeral in the suffix sequence.

Example: When the twenty-fourth standard practice issued by Department 03 requires a supplement to add new information, it would be numbered and revised as follows: C03-24 (R. 8-76) Sup. 1

6. Cancellations

When a corporate standard practice is rescinded, a written notice will be sent to all holders of that particular instruction with appropriate directions for making disposition. Cancellation notices will reference the original standard practice number for easy identification by each operating unit.

14

Operating Controls for Higher Productivity

Operating controls are tools for management. They are useful when the control information is timely, reliable, consistent, and understood by the executives, managers, and supervisors who are directing the activities. All controls to be helpful should be designed to assist management in achieving any one or any combination of the following desirable results:

1. Higher employee productivity

2. Increased yield from materials, machines, and facilities

3. Lower total costs per unit of product

4. More profit in relation to sales volume

5. Growth in sales volume

ACCOUNTING STATISTICS

The usual accounting system provides some of the data needed to measure progress in these areas. The balance sheet and the profit and loss statement along with supplementary reports on cash flow, backlog, inventories, and cost of goods sold contain what is needed to calculate indices commonly followed by management. These indices include the following:

1. *Percent profit on sales,* the net profit before taxes related to net sales

2. *Turnover,* the ratio of net sales annualized to gross assets employed

3. *Percent return on investment,* obtained by multiplying percent profit on sales by the turnover

4. *Percent sales growth,* determined by comparing net sales for related periods

5. *Percent gross profit,* calculated by subtracting the cost of sales from net sales and relating the resulting margin to net sales

6. *Percent S, G&A,* computed by relating the selling, general, and administrative expenses to net sales

7. *Inventory turnover,* the ratio of net sales annualized to total inventory

8. *Working capital dollars* in relation to the planned basic working capital dollars

In addition, the usual accounting system provides for profit planning. This is a method of combining forecasted sales with budgeted costs to indicate projected profits by accounting periods for the year ahead. Later the actual sales, costs, and profits are compared to the profit plan by periods and on a cumulative year-to-date basis. Variances are computed and reported, and management focuses its attention on the negative variances in a hopeful but, too often, hopeless desire to correct the conditions and reduce or eliminate the unfavorable variances. This tends to become a management exercise in frustration. There are several reasons for this. First, the reports are issued from 5 to 20 days after the close of a period. Certainly, this is too late for any action in the period being reported and almost too late for attention in the current period. Thus the controls, instead of helping management steer the business, become interesting, historical statistics. When the numbers are good, everyone is happy. When the statistics are contrary to expectations, management calls after-the-fact meetings and demands action. This doesn't correct the conditions or change anything very much, any more than shaking a tree produces fruit.

Second, most accounting budgets are related to sales dollars. Sales dollars are subject to all the vagaries of competitive and inflationary forces, and shifts in product mix. Thus the base to which the budgets are keyed is unreliable and inconsistent. Let's assume that the budgets are reasonably correct for the forecasted sales volume and product mix. In practice, however, actual sales volume will vary from that forecasted, often by small amounts, but sometimes the differentials are large. Further, the product mix in the actual sales almost never is identical to that forecasted. In fact it is safe to say the actual mix in a free economy is never the same as that projected. Now think of the impact on costs and their relationships to budgets when either or both sales volume and product mix vary from the plan. It's fairly well known that some products contain a high purchase content whereas others are labor intensive. A shift from one to the other obviously will distort the budgeted costs and the forecasted profits. A more reliable common denominator than sales dollars is needed for controlling costs.

Third, the average accounting system relates operating overhead costs to direct labor dollars. Sometimes direct labor hours are used. Too often, however, the accounting system loosely defines direct labor and then accepts anything and everything the operating departments report as direct labor. This, of course, encourages all department managers, supervisors, and foremen to charge as much as possible to direct labor. This practice inflates the direct labor base used for overhead absorption and reduces charges to overhead. The compounding effect of this distortion results in significantly lowered overhead rates or creates a misleading euphoria of favorable overhead absorption. Either is wrong and leads to improper and seriously weakened budgetary controls.

Another fallacious "control" in popular use is to calculate the ratio of direct employees to indirect employees on the premise that if this index is held constant or increased, costs are under control. Such a ratio is meaningless and takes the management profession back a hundred years. Those employees classified as direct labor will be found to be performing all sorts of indirect work and charges such as waiting, setup, bad work, rework, tool and machine repairs, moving materials, running errands, first aid, instructing, union business, and more. Again, this rule-of-thumb index tells management nothing about employee productivity and the control of costs. *The management that uses such an index for control purposes is running a high-cost operation.*

Still another unreliable "control" is the ratio of sales dollars per employee. Some managers happily compare this rule-of-thumb ratio from period to period and company to company with almost complete disregard for differences and changes in prices, product mix, and the fixed costs that are inherent in every enterprise. Obviously, the sales per employee ratio has nothing to do with costs and to be usable must assume that the material content in a sales dollar is constant. This ratio is not a measure of cost control or of productivity. It is just a simple device for misleading management. It is a snare and a delusion.

Essentially, the foregoing points up the conditions whereby management people are limited by the control information developed by the accounting system. The usual accounting system is not designed to provide real operating controls. The reason for this seems to be that accounting systems are concerned primarily with assigning charges to established accounts, adding the totals, and from this information preparing the balance sheet and the profit and loss statement. Control is a secondary issue and as such is given left-handed thought and treatment. A true cost control system is very different from an accounting system. Both are needed.

WHAT IS NEEDED FOR CONTROL?

The very first thing a cost control system requires is a sound measure of the volume of product being produced. This then becomes the base, the common denominator, to which all elements of cost can be related for control purposes. The only sound measure of volume of product is the standard hour of salable product produced. This is a consistent measure of the productive work required to convert materials or services into a product that the customers can be expected to purchase, keep, pay for and use, consume, or enjoy. It is a measured amount of work that must be performed regularly to each part, assembly, or unit of output in order to transform raw materials and know-how into *salable products and services.* This is *measured direct labor,* and it is very different from the *actual direct labor* the usual accounting system willingly accepts. For example, in a company or a department where the employees are paid for the time they put in, the actual direct labor hours are highly erratic and greater in relation to output than in a business where the employees are paid for the standard hours of work they turn out. This is because the actual direct labor on an unmeasured basis includes low employee performance, getting materials and supplies, looking for tools, waiting for instructions, receiving instructions, training, repairing tools and machines, bad work, extra operations, and an assortment of other overhead activities.

The *standard hour of direct labor* on the other hand, represents a definite amount of work because it is based on a *normal performance* by the employees doing the work and contains specific allowances for the employees' personal needs and fatigue. There is no other measure of output that consistently, reliably, and predictably lets management know what is required to produce and how much is produced on an operation, a process, a part, an assembly, a product, a product line, or a series of unrelated product lines or services. In setting standards for setup and production, the method is defined in terms of the sequence of the elements of work required for completion of the setup or the operation. This is followed by selecting and applying standard elemental time values to the elements required. From this, the standard minutes or standard hours for completing a setup or for producing an operation, a part, or a unit of product or service is developed. In the standard setting procedure, full consideration is given to effectively utilizing both the employees and the machines, tools, and processes. This is achieved by specifying the optimum machine speed and feed or the process time for each set of conditions and by sorting the elements of work that must be done *externally* from those that should be performed *internally* to the *power machine time* or the *automatic process time*. With this analysis, the work of the employee and the cycle time per unit can be calculated when the machine or machines or process is operated by the employee at the proper machine efficiency. Thus, the standard time to make and remove a setup is separated from the productive time. This setup time and cost go into overhead. And the standard time to complete a unit of product or services is calculated. This productive standard time is pure direct labor. When the productive time standards are multiplied by the respective number of acceptable pieces or units produced and then totaled for the work produced by an employee, a group of employees, a department, a product, or a company, a true measure of volume of output is obtained. This is the common denominator necessary for control of costs. All other activities and costs go into overhead where they rightfully belong. Now, the costs that make up variable overhead can be measured and controlled in relation to the standard hours of salable product produced. The fixed components of overhead and expense require special management treatment.

MEASURE AND REPORT EMPLOYEE PERFORMANCE

Salaries, wages, and fringe benefits compose the major portion of controllable variable costs in most companies. All of this cost relates to people. How effectively the people use their time in producing a product or providing a service determines their productivity, both individually and in total. Time standards provide the means for measuring productivity, or employee performance as it is more commonly called.

The very first control, then, is to calculate individual performances every day for all employees performing direct labor and for all whose indirect work can be measured with time standards. This encompasses almost all work in the factory and a substantial portion of office and service activities. The following three standard practices illustrate how the time standards are applied and administered for properly reporting and controlling employee and departmental labor and supervisory productivity and costs. The three standard practices cover timekeeping and counting, payroll and cost calculations, and the labor analysis sheet. In practice, employee and departmental performances are summarized each day along with the hours worked on standards, on daywork production, and on indirect activities. This information is given to each department foreman or supervisor the following day. Thus, immediate action can be taken by supervision to improve substandard performances and to reduce the time spent off standard, the objective being to measure a high percentage of the work performed by each employee and to encourage the employees to perform at standard or better. In this way supervision is given fast feedback that is timely and factual. When the employees and the supervisors are trained how to use this information effectively, the resultant improvements in productivity and labor costs can be very substantial.

REGULARLY REVIEW DEPARTMENT EFFECTIVENESS

The labor analysis sheet described in Standard Practice OU-5 summarizes departmental activities and payrolls each week. This is factual information for use by supervision and management in directing department, plant, and company operations more efficiently. Again, these reports are issued several days after the close of each weekly period. The significant controls shown on this report include the standard hours of salable product produced, the percent performance, the percent on standard, the percent capacity used and cost per standard hour of salable product for direct labor, direct labor excesses, indirect labor, and total labor. Overall progress is measured by the extent to which the actual cost per standard hour of salable product continues to be reduced and approaches established objectives. Controls of this kind are factual, reliable, up-to-date and are related directly to the wage rates, skills, machines, facilities, and supervision used in each cost center. For example, Table 14-1 shows several actual control figures reported for a machine shop operating with time standards and wage incentives:

TABLE 14-1

| | Cost per standard hour of salable product | | | | | |
Period	Direct labor	Direct labor excess	Indirect labor	Total labor	Reduction in cost, %	Increase in productivity, %
Reference	$7.09	$0.50	$5.37	$12.96	0	0
Current	4.94	0.32	2.33	7.59	41	71
Objective	4.80	0.14	2.11	7.16	45	81

Results of this magnitude are achievable, because with a standard hour equivalent to a 100 percent performance, experience has demonstrated that the average daywork employee produces at less than 70 percent of standard, the average measured daywork employee at less than 85 percent of standard, and the average wage incentive employee at more than 125 percent of standard. These differences in output are very significant in terms of utilization of the workforce, money, and facilities and point to the standard hour as the only reliable base to which other elements of operating costs should be related and controlled. As Phil Carroll has said: "Correct labor measurement is much more vital to the profitable operation of a business than simply to supply an incentive to operations. It is the foundation for managerial control."

Here are the three standard practices referred to earlier.

PURPOSE

To establish the procedure for timekeeping and counting to be used in conjunction with the work measurement and wage incentive plan.

DISTRIBUTION

The management staff
Chief accountant
Supervisor, cost accounting
Supervisor, standards

POLICY

It is company policy to administer the work measurement and wage incentive plan in strict accordance with Standard Practice OU-2. This policy requires that the timekeeping and counting be performed by personnel trained to conscientiously follow established and authorized procedures. This is important in order to ensure that the work measurement and wage incentive plan is administered in a fair and consistent manner, both initially and in the future.

PROCEDURE

The timekeeping and counting function is the responsibility of the cost accounting section of the finance department. The supervisor, cost accounting, will assign a timekeeper to each manufacturing department.

The timekeeper will compile for each employee, each day, a daily time sheet, form #STD-01, as follows (see Exhibit 14-1):

1. Record the employee's number and name, sheet 1 of 1, the date, and the department number in the spaces provided at the top of the daily time sheet, and clock-in the start time in position 0 in column 18, entitled "Start/Stop."

2. Record the first job or activity assigned to the employee on line 1, making the following entries:

   a. Column 1—Job order or account number. The job order number must be the number of the production shop order, tool work order, maintenance work order, or rework order on which the employee is working. When the employee is not working on one of the above type orders and is assigned by his or her foreman to other activities, the employee's time must be charged to the proper account number listed under the heading "Chargeable Account Numbers." These are the only accounts authorized for use by hourly rated employees in the production departments.

EXHIBIT 14-1

DAILY TIME SHEET FOR RECORDING EACH EMPLOYEE'S ACTIVITIES AND FOR CALCULATING PAY, PERFORMANCE, AND COST.

FORM NO STD-01

DAILY TIME SHEET

EMPLOYEE NO.   EMPLOYEE NAME   SHEET   OF   DATE   DEPT. NO.

| JOB OR ACCT NO. 1 | PART | | MACH. NO. 6 | GOOD PIECES COMPL. 7 | STANDARD MIN PER PIECE | | STANDARD MINUTES | | | | % NWT 13 | ACTUAL HOURS | | | | START STOP |
| | NUMBER 2 | NAME 3 | OPERATION | | | PROD. 8 | EXP. 9 | PROD. 10 | EXP. 11 | SETUP 12 | | ON STD 14 | D.W. PROD 15 | IND. LABOR 16 | D.L. EXC 17 | 18 |

OPERATION: NO. 4   DESCRIPTION 5

TOTAL STD. MINS   TOTAL COST

TOTAL HOURS   TOTAL COST

ATD HRS   %OT   OT HRS

0 1 2 3 4 5 6 7 8 9 10 11 12 13 14 15 16 17 18

CHARGEABLE ACCOUNT NUMBERS

04 SPARE CLEANING	22 PERSONAL MEDICAL
06 SOCIAL SECURITY	23 UNION MEETING
08 HOLIDAYS	41 MATERIAL HANDLING
09 OTHER INDIRECT BY DIRECT	44 LEADMAN
	11 TOOL MAINTENANCE
	12 TOOL PROOFING
	15 MACHINE
	19 INVENTORY
	21 INDUSTRIAL ACCIDENT

DIRECT LABOR EXCESS COSTS   INDIRECT LABOR COSTS

EXPENSE STANDARDS	SETUP	
IDLE TIME	SUPERVISION AND CLERICAL	
UNEARNED GUARANTEE	INSPECTION	
REWORK	MAINTENANCE	
SCRAP	MATERIAL HANDLING	
	O.T. PREM AND SHIFT DIFF.	
	OTHER INDIRECT BY DIRECT	
TOTAL	TOTAL	

TOTAL STD. MINS

TOTAL MINS ON STD.

% PERFORMANCE

REWORK CHARGE

SCRAP CHARGE

SHIFT DIFFERENTIAL

OVERTIME PREMIUM

INCENTIVE EARNINGS   PER MIN

DAY RATE EARNINGS   PER HR

TOTAL EARNINGS

GUARANTEED DAY'S PAY   PER HR

INCENTIVE PREMIUM

UNEARNED GUARANTEE

STRAIGHT TIME PAY

TIME-KEEPER

EX-TENSION

CHECK-ER

STANDARD PRACTICE	SUBJECT
CORPORATION NUMBER OU-3 PAGE 2 OF 4 EFFECTIVE REVISION DATE	TIMEKEEPING AND COUNTING

ISSUED BY	APPROVALS		

b. For job orders, record the following:

Column 1—Job order number.

Column 2—Part number.

Column 3—Part name.

Column 4—Operation number.

Column 5—Operation description.

Column 6—Machine or work station number, when applicable.

Column 8—Standard minutes per piece when a production standard has been issued (see Exhibit 14-2).

Column 9—Standard minutes per piece when an expense standard or a rework standard has been authorized and issued (see Exhibit 14-3).

Column 12—Standard minutes per setup when a setup standard has been issued.

Column 13—% NWT when applicable. Special instructions will be issued for this.

EXCEPTION: Record the job grade in this column when a leadman works on standard.

Column 18—When the first job or activity is completed clock the stop time in position 1. This time is automatically the start time for the second job or activity. The daily time sheet is designed to record as many as eighteen jobs or activities per employee per shift. In the event it becomes necessary to use a second sheet, clock the stop time for the eighteenth job order or account in position 18 and clock the same time in position 0 on sheet 2, complete the heading on sheet 2 identifying it as sheet 2 of 2, and change sheet 1 to read sheet 1 of 2.

Column 14—For all jobs performed on standard, calculate the actual hours on the job by subtracting the start time from the stop time and record the actual hours on standard in column 14.

Column 15—For jobs performed on daywork production, calculate the actual hours on the job by subtracting the start time from the stop time and record the actual hours on daywork production in column 15.

Column 16—For jobs performed on daywork on tool work orders and maintenance work orders, calculate the actual hours on the job by subtracting the start time from the stop time and record the actual hours indirect labor in column 16.

EXHIBIT 14-2

STANDARDS SHEET USED TO DESCRIBE THE WORK TO BE PERFORMED AND TO ISSUE THE SETUP AND PRODUCTION TIME STANDARDS FOR THE OPERATION.

STANDARDS SHEET

Part No.	B/P Chg.	Part Name		Opr. No.	Date
Oper. Desc.	Jig/Fixt. No.		Material	Mach. No.	
Std.Min./Set Up	Std.Min./Piece		Job Grade	% N.W.T.	By

Operation Description	Feed	Speed	Tooling

STANDARDS DEPARTMENT

EXHIBIT 14-3

EXPENSE STANDARDS SHEET USED TO DESCRIBE EXTRA WORK TEMPORARILY REQUIRED AND TO ALLOW ADDITIONAL STANDARD TIME FOR THE EXTRA WORK.

EXPENSE STANDARDS SHEET

Part No.	B/P Chg.	Part Name		Opr. No.		Date	
Oper. Desc.		Jig/Fixt. No.	Material		Mach. No.		
Std.Min./Set Up	Std.Min./Piece		Job Grade	% N.W.T.		By	
Operation Description				Feed	Speed	Tooling	

STANDARDS DEPARTMENT

	STANDARD PRACTICE	SUBJECT
CORPORATION	NUMBER OU-3 PAGE 3 OF 4	TIMEKEEPING AND COUNTING
	EFFECTIVE REVISION DATE	

ISSUED BY	APPROVALS		

Column 17—For rework performed on daywork on rework orders, calculate the actual hours on the rework by subtracting the start time from the stop time and record the actual hours direct labor excess in column 17.

c. For indirect account charges record the following:

Column 1—Indirect account number.
Column 5—Title of indirect account.
Column 16—Calculate the actual hours on the work by subtracting the start time from the stop time and record the actual hours indirect labor in column 16.

d. For direct labor excess account charges record the following:

Column 1—Direct labor excess account number.
Column 5—Title of direct labor excess account.
Column 17—Calculate the actual hours on the activity by subtracting the start time from the stop time and record the actual hours direct labor excess in column 17.

3. Calculate the employee's attendance hours by subtracting for the full shift the employee's start time from his or her stop time, subtract 0.5 hour for the lunch period when applicable, and record the total hours in the attendance hours block. Calculate the overtime hours and record the time-and-one-half overtime hours in the block entitled "½ OT Hours" and record the double-time overtime hours in the block entitled "1 OT Hours."

4. During the shift at the completion of each job order and at the end of the shift, count and record in column 7 the good pieces completed on each job order. Following this for all jobs performed on standard multiply the "Good Pieces Completed" (column 7) by the "Standard Minutes per Piece" (column 8) and record the "Standard Minutes Production" (column 10). In addition, when an expense standard or a rework standard has been authorized and issued, multiply the "Good Pieces Completed" (column 7) by the "Expense or Rework Standard Minutes per Piece" (column 9) and record the "Standard Minutes Expense" (column 11).

5. At the end of the shift add and record the "Total Standard Minutes Production" (column 10), "Expense" (column 11), and "Setup" (column 12). In addition, add and record the "Total Actual Hours on Standard" (column 14), "Daywork Production" (column 15), "Indirect Labor" (column 16), and "Direct Labor Excess" (column 17). Then add the totals in these four columns and make certain that the total of the total actual hours equals the attendance hours recorded in the block at the bottom of column 18.

	STANDARD	SUBJECT
CORPORATION	**PRACTICE**	TIMEKEEPING AND COUNTING
	NUMBER OU-3 PAGE 4 OF 4	
	EFFECTIVE REVISION DATE	
ISSUED BY	APPROVALS		

6. Initial each daily time sheet in the block entitled "timekeeper."

7. CLASSIFICATION OF CHARGEABLE ACCOUNT NUMBERS
   The chargeable account numbers are classified for timekeeping and cost purposes as follows:

      05 Idle time
      13 Sick leave
      22 Industrial accident
      25 Personal medical
      33 Union meeting

    INDIRECT LABOR COST ACCOUNTS
      04 Spare cleaning
      06 Field service
      07 Other indirect by direct
      11 Tool maintenance
      12 Tool proofing
      15 Inventory
    497 Material handling
    498 Leadman

	STANDARD PRACTICE	SUBJECT
CORPORATION	NUMBER OU-4 PAGE 1 OF 5	PAYROLL AND COST
	EFFECTIVE REVISION DATE	CALCULATIONS

ISSUED BY	APPROVALS		

PURPOSE

To establish the procedure for payroll and cost calculations to be used in conjunction with the work measurement and wage incentive plan.

DISTRIBUTION

The management staff
Chief accountant
Supervisor, cost accounting
Supervisor, standards

POLICY

It is company policy to administer the work measurement and wage incentive plan in strict accordance with Standard Practice OU-2. This policy requires that the payroll and cost calculations be performed by personnel trained to conscientiously follow established and authorized procedures. This is important in order to ensure that the work measurement and wage incentive plan is administered in a fair and consistent manner, both initially and in the future.

PROCEDURE

The payroll and cost calculation function is the responsibility of the cost accounting section of the finance department. Payroll and cost calculations are to be made daily and then summarized for each weekly payroll period. The supervisor of cost accounting will assign a payroll clerk to process the daily time sheets from each manufacturing department.

DAILY PAYROLL CALCULATIONS—The payroll clerk will calculate the performance and the earnings for each employee each day on the employee's daily time sheet, form #STD-01, as follows (see Exhibit 14-1):

1. For all jobs performed on standard multiply the "Good Pieces Completed" (column 7) by the "Standard Minutes per Piece" (column 8) and confirm or correct the "Standard Minutes Production" (column 10). In addition, when an expense standard or a rework standard has been authorized and issued, multiply the "Good Pieces Completed" (column 7) by the "Expense or Rework Standard Minutes per Piece" (column 9) and confirm or correct the "Standard Minutes Expense" (column 11).

	STANDARD	SUBJECT
CORPORATION	**PRACTICE**	
	NUMBER .	PAYROLL AND COST
	OU-4　　　PAGE 2 OF 5	CALCULATIONS
	EFFECTIVE　　　REVISION DATE	

ISSUED BY　　　　　APPROVALS

2. Confirm or correct the totals recorded as "Total Standard Minutes Production" (column 10), "Expense" (column 11), and "Setup" (column 12). Then add the totals in these three columns and record the total in the block entitled "Total Standard Minutes."

3. Confirm or correct the totals recorded as "Total Actual Hours on Standard" (column 14), "Daywork Production" (column 15), "Indirect Labor" (column 16), and "Direct Labor Excess" (column 17). Then add the totals in these four columns and make certain by confirmation or correction that the total of the total actual hours equals the attendance hours recorded in the block at the bottom of column 18. Confirm or correct the overtime hours recorded in the blocks entitled "½ OT Hours" and "1 OT Hours."

4. Multiply the "Total Actual Hours on Standard" (column 14) by 60 to convert hours into minutes and record the result in the block entitled "Total Minutes on Standard."

5. Divide the total standard minutes by the total minutes on standard, multiply the result by 100 to convert into percent, and record the result in the block entitled "% Performance."

6. Record the employee's personal hourly rate within the blocks entitled "Day Rate Earnings _____ per Hour" and "Guaranteed Day's Pay _____ per Hour."

7. Divide the employee's personal hourly rate by 60 and record the rate per minute within the block entitled "Incentive Earnings _____ per Minute." There are two exceptions to this. When an employee's personal hourly rate exceeds the maximum for his or her job classification, then the maximum of the rate range will be used in establishing the rate per minute. Also, the maximum of the rate range for the highest job grade of work performed by a leadman will be used when a leadman works on standard.

8. Multiply the rate per minute by the total standard minutes and record the result in the block entitled "Incentive Earnings."

9. Multiply the employee's personal hourly rate by the total of the "Total Actual Hours on Daywork Production" (column 15), "Indirect Labor" (column 16), and "Direct Labor Excess" (column 17) and record the result in the block entitled "Day Rate Earnings."

10. Add the incentive earnings to the day rate earnings and record the result in the block entitled "Total Earnings."

11. Multiply the employee's personal hourly rate by his or her attendance hours and record the result in the block entitled "Guaranteed Day's Pay."

12. Subtract the guaranteed day's pay from the total earnings and record the result in the block entitled "Incentive Premium." In event the guaranteed day's pay exceeds the total earnings, subtract the total earnings from the guaranteed day's pay and record the result in the block entitled "Unearned Guarantee."

13. REWORK CHARGES—The work measurement and wage incentive plan provides, when the employee is responsible, for charging the cost of rework against any incentive premium earned by the employee within the weekly pay period during which the work was performed. The employee is credited with good pieces completed only. And the employee is to be given credit for the rejected pieces when they are reworked and accepted as good pieces.

Rework charges, then, are handled in the following manner:

a. No special charge is required when the employee reworks his or her own rejected pieces while still clocked in on the job. In this case the time to rework the rejected pieces increases the time on standard and automatically reduces the incentive premium.

b. However, when the rejected pieces are discovered after the employee has clocked off the job or when the rejected pieces must be reworked by another employee, the employee is given credit for the pieces but the standard labor cost, or the actual labor cost in the absence of a rework standard, is to be charged back against any incentive premium earned during the weekly payroll period by the employee responsible for the rework cost. In this case the rework cost is to be entered on one of the employee's daily time sheets in the block entitled "Rework Charge."

14. SCRAP CHARGES—The work measurement and wage incentive plan provides for paying for good pieces completed only. In the event the employee is credited with pieces that are subsequently rejected and scrapped, the standard labor cost for the work performed on the scrapped pieces by the employee responsible for the bad work is to be charged back against any incentive premium earned during the weekly payroll period by that employee. All scrap charges against the employee are to be entered on one of the employee's daily time sheets in the block entitled "Scrap Charge."

DAILY COST CALCULATIONS—The payroll clerk will calculate the direct labor, direct labor excess, and indirect labor costs for each employee each day on the employee's daily time sheet, form #STD-01, as follows (see Exhibit 14-1):

1. Multiply the rate per minute by the total standard minutes production, expense, and setup and record the results in the corresponding blocks entitled "Total Cost."

2. Multiply the rate per hour by the total hours daywork production, indirect labor, and direct labor excess and record the results in the corresponding blocks entitled "Total Cost."

3. Transfer the total costs of expense standards, setup, and unearned guarantee to the summary section at the lower left side of the daily time sheet.

4. Review the account numbers charged during the shift, multiply the rate per hour by the hours charged to each account, and record in the proper place in the summary section.

5. Add the direct labor excess costs in the summary and record the result in the "Total" block.

6. Add the indirect labor costs in the summary and record the result in the "Total" block.

7. Initial each daily time sheet in the block entitled "Extension."

WEEKLY PAYROLL AND COST CALCULATIONS—At the end of the weekly payroll period, the payroll clerk will total for each employee the items of pay, performance, and cost from each employee's daily time sheets for the weekly payroll period and will record these totals in the lower section of a "weekly summary" daily time sheet. Then, the payroll clerk will proceed as follows (see Exhibit 14-4):

1. Divide the total standard minutes by the total minutes on standard, multiply the result by 100 to convert into percent, and record the result in the block entitled "% Performance."

2. Multiply the attendance hours by $0.24 per hour for employees working the second and third shifts, and record the result in the block entitled "Shift Differential."

3. Then in column 18, record the incentive premium in block 1, any rework charge in block 2, and scrap charge in block 3, the guaranteed week's pay in block 5, and any shift differential in block 6.

4. Subtract the rework charge and the scrap charge from the incentive premium and record the result in block 4 entitled "Net Incentive Premium." NOTE: If the rework and scrap charges exceed the incentive premium for the payroll period, enter 0 in block 4.

EXHIBIT 14-4

"WEEKLY SUMMARY" DAILY TIME SHEET USED TO SUMMARIZE EACH EMPLOYEE'S PAY AND PERFORMANCE AND RELEVANT COST DATA EACH WEEK.

FORM NO. STD-01

"WEEKLY SUMMARY" DAILY TIME SHEET

EMPLOYEE NO.	PART			EMPLOYEE NAME						SHEET	OF	DATE				DEPT. NO.	

Incentive Premium — $1\ AD$
Less Rework Charge — $2\ T$
Less Scrap Charge — $3\ U$
Net Incentive Premium — $4\ AT = AD-T-U$
Plus Guaranteed Weeks Pay — $5\ AC$
Plus Shift Differential — $6\ V = N \times .24$
Straight Time Pay — $AU = AT+AC+V$
Plus Overtime 1/2 OT @ AV — $8\ W = OXAV$
Plus Overtime 1 OT @ AV — $9\ AW = FxAV$
Gross Pay — $AX = AU+W+AW$

$11\ AU$
(WEEKLY AVERAGE HOURLY EARNED RATE) — $12\ AV = \dfrac{AU}{N}$

Net Incentive Premium — $14\ AT$
% Performance — $15\ S$
Hours on Standard — $16\ D$

				STANDARD MIN PER PIECE		STANDARD MINUTES				% NWT	ACTUAL HOURS						START STOP

TOTAL STD. MINS.
TOTAL COST

	A	B	C	D	E	F	G
	H	I	J	K	L	M	

CHARGEABLE ACCOUNT NUMBERS

PERSONAL, MEDICAL, UNION MEETING, MATERIAL HANDLING, LEADMAN

TOOL MAINTENANCE, TOOL PROOFING, IDLE TIME, INDUSTRIAL ACCOUNT

DIRECT LABOR EXCESS COSTS

		INDIRECT LABOR COSTS	
EXPENSE STANDARDS	I	SETUP	J
IDLE TIME	AJ	SUPERVISION AND CLERICAL	AM
UNEARNED GUARANTEE	AE	INSPECTION	AN
REWORK	AK	MAINTENANCE	AO
SCRAP	AL	MATERIAL HANDLING	AP
		O.T. PREM. AND SHIFT DIFF.	V+W+AW
		OTHER INDIRECT BY DIRECT	AQ
TOTAL	A R	TOTAL	AS

INCENTIVE EARNINGS — Q
DAY RATE EARNINGS — R
$S = \dfrac{Q \times 100}{R}$ % PERFORMANCE
TOTAL EARNINGS — T
INCENTIVE PREMIUM — U
UNEARNED GUARANTEE — V
STRAIGHT TIME PAY — W
OVERTIME PREMIUM $1/2\ OT$ — $\dfrac{1}{1\ OT}$

		PER MIN	Z
		PER HR	AA
			AB
		PER HR	AC
			AD
			AE
			AF

CHECKER — AI
TIME-KEEPER — P
EXTENSION

TOTAL

CORPORATION	**STANDARD PRACTICE**	SUBJECT
	NUMBER OU-4 PAGE 5 OF 5	PAYROLL AND COST
	EFFECTIVE REVISION DATE	CALCULATIONS
ISSUED BY	APPROVALS	

5. Add the "Net Incentive Premium" (block 4), the "Guaranteed Week's Pay" (block 5), and the "Shift Differential" (block 6), and record the total in block 7 entitled "Straight Time Pay."

6. Divide the straight time pay in block 7 by the attendance hours shown at the bottom of column 18 and record the employee's weekly average hourly earned rate on the lines entitled "Overtime ½ OT @_____" and "Overtime 1 OT @_____."

7. Divide the ½ OT hours shown at the bottom of column 18 by 2 to obtain the overtime premium hours and multiply the overtime premium hours by the employee's weekly average hourly earned rate and record the overtime ½ OT pay in block 8. EXCEPTION: When an employee works 40 hours or less in a weekly payroll period, calculate the overtime ½ OT pay at the employee's personal hourly rate instead of his or her weekly average hourly earned rate.

8. Multiply the 1 OT hours shown at the bottom of column 18 by the employee's weekly average hourly earned rate and record the overtime 1 OT pay in block 9. EXCEPTION: When an employee works 40 hours or less in a weekly payroll period, calculate the overtime 1 OT pay at the employee's personal hourly rate instead of his or her weekly average hourly earned rate.

9. Add the straight time pay in block 7, the overtime ½ OT pay in block 8, and the overtime 1 OT pay in block 9, and record the total in block 10 entitled "Gross Pay."

10. Continuing in column 18, record the net incentive premium in block 14, the percent performance in block 15, and the hours on standard in block 16.

11. Form 6, containing the record of the employee's earnings and deductions for the weekly payroll period, is to be compiled from the employee's "weekly summary" daily time sheet. In addition to the usual information shown on this form, the following items are to be reported:

    Net incentive premium $_____

    Performance on standard _____%

    Hours on standard   _____

12. Transfer the cost of shift differential and overtime premium to the summary section at the lower left side of the "weekly summary" daily time sheet and adjust the total cost shown in the block entitled "Indirect Labor Accounts Total" accordingly.

13. Initial each "weekly summary" daily time sheet in the block entitled "Checker."

CORPORATION	STANDARD PRACTICE		SUBJECT
	NUMBER OU-5	PAGE 1 OF 6	LABOR ANALYSIS SHEET
	EFFECTIVE	REVISION DATE	

ISSUED BY	APPROVALS		

PURPOSE

To establish a method of reporting departmental activities for review and analysis that directs attention toward improvement in operating costs.

DISTRIBUTION

The management staff
Chief accountant
Supervisor, cost accounting
Supervisor, standards

POLICY

It is company policy to continually improve the operating effectiveness of the company and of each of its departments. One program designed to implement this policy is the work measurement and wage incentive plan, Standard Practice OU-2. This plan provides engineered time and cost standards for measuring, reporting, and controlling departmental activities. It establishes the standard hour of salable product produced. This is a measure of good salable production to which direct labor, direct labor excess, and indirect labor costs can be related. The labor analysis sheet serves to summarize this operating control information in a readily usable, up-to-date form for management attention and action.

PROCEDURE

Essentially, the labor analysis sheet is designed to set department supervisors in business for themselves. It is a profit and loss statement of all labor costs within the control of the supervisor of the department being measured. There are no charges or allocations to or from the department. The labor analysis sheet is compiled from the daily time sheets of the employees in the department. It reports for each week in a quarter, the actual production, performances, and costs in relation to known objectives.

The cost accounting section of the finance department is responsible for the preparation and distribution of the labor analysis sheets. The supervisor of cost accounting will assign a payroll clerk to prepare the labor analysis sheets for each manufacturing department in which the time standards are applied. Exhibit 14-5 shows the design of the labor analysis sheet and outlines how the sheet is compiled from the "weekly summary" daily time sheets, Exhibit 14-4, indicating the calculations used to compute the control information.

EXHIBIT 14-5

LABOR ANALYSIS SHEET USED TO REPORT DEPARTMENTAL PRODUCTION, PERFORMANCE, AND COSTS EACH WEEK FOR A CALENDAR QUARTER.

LABOR ANALYSIS SHEET

FORM NO. STD-03 QUARTER YEAR SUPERVISOR DEPARTMENT

WEEK ENDING		PRODUCTION						EFFECTIVITY				DIRECT LABOR COST				DIRECT LABOR EXCESS COST					
		STANDARD HOURS			ACTUAL HOURS		STD HRS OF SALABLE PRODUCT	% PERF	% ON STD	% SETUP	% CAPAC USED	STD PROD	DAYWORK PROD	TOTAL ACTUAL	EXP STD	IDLE TIME	UNEARN GUAR	RE-WORK	SCRAP	TOTAL ACTUAL	% EX OF D L PROD COST
		PROD	EXP	SETUP	ON STD	DAYWORK PROD															
		2	3	4	5	6	7	8	9	10	11	12	13	14	15	16	17	18	19	20	21
A		A/60	B/60	C/60	D	E						H	K		I	AJ	AE	AK			
B	ACCT																				
C	OBJ																				
1																					
2																					
3																					
4																					
5																					
6																					
7																					
8																					
9																					
10																					
11																					
12																					
13																					
14																					
QUARTER																					

WEEK ENDING		INDIRECT LABOR COSTS										COST PER STANDARD HOUR OF SALABLE PRODUCT				COST SUMMARY			
		SETUP	SUPV & CLERICAL	INSP	MNT	MATL HAND	OT PREM AND SHIFT DIF	OTHER	TOTAL ACTUAL	TOTAL STD	% EX ACTUAL TO STD	DIRECT LABOR PROD	DIRECT LABOR EX	INDIRECT LABOR	TOTAL	TOTAL ACTUAL	TOTAL STD	EXCESS ACTUAL TO STD	% EX ACTUAL TO STD
	22	23	24	25	26	27	28	29	30	31	32	33	34	35	36	37	38	39	40
A		J	AM	AN	AO	AP	V+W+AW	AQ											
B	ACCT																		
C	OBJ																		
1																			
2																			
3																			
4																			
5																			
6																			
7																			
8																			
9																			
10																			
11																			
12																			
13																			
14																			
QUARTER																			

CORPORATION	**STANDARD PRACTICE**	SUBJECT
	NUMBER OU-5 PAGE 2 OF 6	LABOR ANALYSIS SHEET
	EFFECTIVE REVISION DATE	
ISSUED BY	APPROVALS	

In compiling the labor analysis sheet for a manufacturing department, the payroll clerk will proceed as follows:

1. Enter the proper account numbers in the block at the top of each column entitled "Acct." These account numbers will be supplied by the supervisor of standards.

2. Enter the proper objectives in the block at the top of each column entitled "OBJ." The objectives will be supplied by the supervisor of standards.

3. WEEK ENDING, columns 1, 22—Enter the ending date of the weekly payroll period being reported. These entries should be made on the lines that coincide with the number of the week in the accounting quarter, such as 1, 2, 3, 4, 5, 6, 7, 8, 9, 10, 11, 12, and 13. The fourteenth line is to be used to total and summarize the results for the 13 weeks in the accounting quarter.

4. The capital letters, such as A, B, C, D, AJ, AK, et cetera, referred to in the following paragraphs and shown on the labor analysis sheet, Exhibit 14-5, indicate the data to be totaled and transferred from the "weekly summary" daily time sheets, Exhibit 14-4, of the employees working in the department during the weekly payroll period being reported.

5. PRODUCTION SECTION, columns 2, 3, 4, 5, 6, and 7

   a. STANDARD HOURS PRODUCTION, column 2—Total the "Total Standard Minutes Production" (block A), divide by 60 to convert into standard hours, and record the result in column 2.

   b. STANDARD HOURS EXPENSE, column 3—Total the "Total Standard Minutes Expense" (block B), divide by 60 to convert into standard hours, and record the result in column 3.

   c. STANDARD HOURS SETUP, column 4—Total the "Total Standard Minutes Setup" (block C), divide by 60 to convert into standard hours, and record the result in column 4.

   d. ACTUAL HOURS ON STANDARD, column 5—Total the "Total Hours on Standard" (block D) and record the result in column 5.

   e. ACTUAL HOURS DAYWORK PRODUCTION, column 6—Total the "Total Hours Daywork Production" (block E) and record the result in column 6.

    f. STANDARD HOURS OF SALABLE PRODUCT, column 7—Convert the "Actual Hours Daywork Production" (column 6) into equivalent standard hours by multiplying the actual hours by the performance factor and add the result to the "Standard Hours Production" (column 2). Record the total in column 7. The performance factor to be used for each manufacturing department will be supplied by the supervisor of standards.

6. EFFECTIVITY SECTION, columns 8, 9, 10, and 11.

    a. PERCENT PERFORMANCE, column 8—Add the "Standard Hours Production" (column 2), "Expense" (column 3), and "Setup" (column 4), and divide the total by the "Actual Hours on Standard" (column 5). Multiply the result by 100 to convert into percent and record the "% Performance" (column 8).

    b. PERCENT ON STANDARD, column 9—Divide the "Actual Hours on Standard" (column 5) by the total of the "Actual Hours on Standard" (column 5) plus the "Actual Hours Daywork Production" (column 6). Multiply the result by 100 to convert into percent and record the "% on Standard" (column 9).

    c. PERCENT SETUP, column 10—Divide the "Standard Hours Setup" (column 4) by the "Standard Hours of Salable Product" (column 7), multiply the result by 100 to convert into percent, and record the "% Setup" (column 10).

    d. PERCENT CAPACITY USED, column 11—Divide the "Standard Hours of Salable Product" (column 7) by the "Standard Hours of Capacity," multiply the result by 100 to convert into percent, and record the "% Capacity Used" (column 11). The standard hours of capacity to be used for each manufacturing department will be supplied by the supervisor of standards.

7. DIRECT LABOR COSTS SECTION, columns 12, 13, and 14.

    a. STANDARD PRODUCTION COST, column 12—Total the "Total Cost Standard Minutes Production" (block H) and record the result in column 12.

    b. DAYWORK PRODUCTION COST, column 13—Total the "Total Cost Daywork Production" (block K) and record the result in column 13.

    c. TOTAL ACTUAL COST, column 14—Add the "Standard Production Cost" (column 12) to the "Daywork Production Cost" (column 13) and record the total in column 14.

8. DIRECT LABOR EXCESS COSTS SECTION, columns 15, 16, 17, 18, 19, 20, and 21.

    a. EXPENSE STANDARDS, column 15—Total the "Total Cost Standard Minutes Expense" (block I) and record the result in column 15.

    b. IDLE TIME, column 16—Total the cost of "Idle Time" block AJ and record the result in column 16.

    c. UNEARNED GUARANTEE, column 17—Total the cost of "Unearned Guarantee" (block AE) and record the result in column 17.

    d. REWORK, column 18—Total the cost of "Rework" (block AK) and record the result in column 18.

    e. SCRAP, column 19—Select the proper scrap charge for each manufacturing department from the monthly scrap analysis report, Schedule S-1, issued by the finance department, divide the charge by the number of weeks (4 or 5) in the accounting period, and record the result for the same number of weeks (4 or 5) ahead in column 18. NOTE: Add any cost of "Scrap" (block AL) to the average weekly scrap cost recorded above.

    f. TOTAL ACTUAL COST, column 20—Add the cost of "Expense Standards" (column 15), "Idle Time" (column 16), "Unearned Guarantee" (column 17), "Rework" (column 18), "Scrap" (column 19) and record the total in column 20.

    g. PERCENT EXCESS OF DIRECT LABOR PRODUCTION COST, column 21—Divide the "Total Actual Direct Labor Excess Cost" (column 20) by the "Total Actual Direct Labor Cost" column 14, multiply by 100 to convert into percent, and record the "% Excess" (column 21).

9. INDIRECT LABOR COSTS SECTION, columns 23, 24, 25, 26, 27, 28, 29, 30, 31, and 32

    a. SETUP, column 23—Total the "Total Cost Standard Minutes Setup" (block J) and record the result in column 23.

    b. SUPERVISION AND CLERICAL, column 24—Total the "Supervision and Clerical Cost" (block AM), add the foreman's salary averaged on a weekly basis, and record the result in column 24.

    c. INSPECTION, column 25—Total the "Inspection Cost" (block AN) and record the result in column 25.

d. MAINTENANCE, column 26—Total the "Maintenance Cost" (block AO) and record the result in column 26.

e. MATERIAL HANDLING, column 27—Total the "Material Handling Cost" (block AP) and record the result in column 27.

f. OVERTIME PREMIUM AND SHIFT DIFFERENTIAL, column 28—Total the "Overtime Premium and Shift Differential" (block V + W + AW) and record in column 28.

g. OTHER, column 29—Total the "Other Indirect by Direct" (block AQ) and record the result in column 29.

h. TOTAL ACTUAL COST, column 30—Add the cost of "Setup" (column 23), "Supervision and Clerical" (column 24), "Inspection" (column 25), "Maintenance" (column 26), "Material Handling" (column 27), "Overtime Premium and Shift Differential" (column 28), and "Other" (column 29) and record the result in column 30.

i. TOTAL STANDARD COST, column 31—Multiply the standard indirect labor cost per standard hour of salable product by the "Standard Hours of Salable Product" (column 7) and record the result in column 31. The standard indirect labor cost per standard hour of salable product for each manufacturing department will be supplied by the supervisor of standards.

j. PERCENT EXCESS ACTUAL TO STANDARD, column 32—Subtract the "Total Standard Cost" (column 31) from the "Total Actual Cost" (column 30), divide the difference by the "Total Standard Cost" (column 31), multiply by 100 to convert into percent, and record the "% Excess" (column 32).

10. COST PER STANDARD HOUR OF SALABLE PRODUCT, columns 33, 34, 35, and 36.

a. DIRECT LABOR PRODUCTION, column 33—Divide the "Total Actual Direct Labor Cost" (column 14) by the "Standard Hours of Salable Product" (column 7) and record the result in column 33.

b. DIRECT LABOR EXCESS, column 34—Divide the "Total Actual Direct Labor Excess Cost" (column 20) by the "Standard Hours of Salable Product" (column 7) and record the result in column 34.

CORPORATION	STANDARD PRACTICE	SUBJECT
	NUMBER OU-5 PAGE 6 OF 6	LABOR ANALYSIS SHEET
	EFFECTIVE REVISION DATE	
ISSUED BY	APPROVALS	

c. INDIRECT LABOR, column 35—Divide the "Total Actual Indirect Labor Cost" (column 30) by the "Standard Hours of Salable Product" (column 7) and record the result in column 35.

d. TOTAL COST, column 36—Add the "Cost per Standard Hour of Salable Product Direct Labor" (column 33), "Direct Labor Excess" (column 34) and "Indirect Labor" (column 35) and record the result in column 36.

11. COST SUMMARY, columns 37, 38, 39, and 40.

a. TOTAL ACTUAL, column 37—Add the "Total Actual Direct Labor Cost" (column 14), the "Total Actual Direct Labor Excess Cost" (column 20), and the "Total Actual Indirect Labor Cost" (column 30) and record the result in column 37.

b. TOTAL STANDARD, column 38—Multiply the "Direct Labor Standard Production Cost" (column 12) by the direct labor excess factor, add the "Direct Labor Daywork Production Cost" (column 13) multiplied by the direct labor excess factor and by the performance factor. Then add to the above the "Total Standard Indirect Labor Cost" (column 31) and record the result in column 38. The direct labor excess factor and the performance factor to be used for each manufacturing department will be supplied by the supervisor of standards.

c. EXCESS ACTUAL TO STANDARD, column 39—Subtract the "Total Standard Cost" (column 38) from the "Total Actual Cost" (column 37) and record the result in column 39.

d. % EXCESS ACTUAL TO STANDARD, column 40—Divide the "Excess Actual to Standard Cost" (column 39) by the "Total Standard Cost" (column 38), multiply by 100 to convert into percent, and record the "% Excess" (column 40).

15

Work Measurement and Wage Incentive Plans for Higher Productivity

Money is the most attractive incentive there is. This is probably because there are so many things people want that money will buy. But today, more than ever before, too many people are being given more money for nothing. To just give money away is wrong. It's wrong because when it is not earned the effect is to feed inflation. And the ultimate consequence of inflation is to make money worthless. Someone has to produce the food, the materials, the fuels, the housing, the conveniences, and the services that all of us need and desire. We all want to improve our way of life. We want a better standard of living, more education, a healthier environment, extra recreational opportunities, and greater security. These are worthwhile individual and national objectives. We can enjoy all of them if we work to produce these hallmarks of civilization.

If money is such a powerful incentive, why don't we use it on a national and international scale to accomplish more. Well, as a matter of fact, we have been using money on a grand scale but in a mistaken way. In effect, the politicians literally have been bribing individuals, each other, and countries. This achieves nothing but debt and promotes the corrupt art of blackmail. If money is to serve as an incentive, the rewards must be awarded in direct relation to what is accomplished. This can only be done with measurement as the foundation. Measurement and incentive must go together. When they do, there is no limit to what can be gained. Howard K. Smith, the noted news commentator for the American Broadcasting Company, in his commentary on December 11, 1975, pointed this out clearly when he cited the example of the Lincoln Electric Company of Cleveland, Ohio, as follows:

> Lincoln has just paid its 2300 employees their annual bonuses. The bonuses average nearly 12,000 dollars a worker—on top of high weekly wages, not to be sneezed at.
>
> Lincoln has a system. It began in the depression in 1934. Mr. Lincoln told his workers business was bad so he couldn't pay. They said, "If we produce more, more cheaply, will you pay us the benefit gained?" He said, "Yes."

So a productivity scale was set for each worker. All produced more at cheaper cost. Contracts came in. The increased income was parcelled out in bonuses, reaching nearly 12,000 dollars per worker this year.

Nothing is simple in economics. But that's the simplest model of how the national economy should be run. Pay each, not unearned benefits won by corporate or union clout, but by what he contributes.

A thousand firms living on government subsidies, overt or hidden, would howl at the loss of unearned income. As would a hundred unions.

But productivity would rise, costs and prices fall, sales increase, inflation decline as would the Recession it caused.

In an economy gone wrong, somebody is doing something right: The Lincoln Electric Company of Cleveland.

A CHALLENGE INSTEAD OF A CHORE

Sound measurement is needed to consistently recognize accomplishment. Employees want recognition, executives thrive on recognition, and companies prosper on recognition. Providing the opportunity to earn monetary rewards based on measured achievements is one of the most tangible forms of recognition. Pride of performance must be revived. Good incentives based on sound measurement can help to redevelop a constructive attitude in the minds of our people—an attitude or a "job conscience" that directs them to do their best and "to do the job right the first time." We must put a lot of "purpose" in their thinking and their work. And we will get the best results when we make their work a challenge instead of a chore. How better to do this than to tangibly reward their achievements in meeting important, meaningful, measurable objectives.

USE MEANINGFUL, MEASURABLE OBJECTIVES

The measurable objectives should be established so as to focus attention and emphasis on the job to be done. Top management is there to produce a profit and to develop the growth of the enterprise. Thus, profit should be the prime factor for measuring and rewarding the management staff. Not much is gained by trying to stimulate a billing clerk or a drill press operator by using profit as the basis for rewarding their achievements. Profit is too remote for them. The connection between their efforts and the result is so indirect and so nebulous as to have almost no impact on their attitudes and efforts. This is not to say it will have no affect, but rather that other measurements can be more meaningful and therefore much more effective in stimulating them to improve their productivity. Direct measurement of their daily and weekly output with the earned incentive premium paid weekly will inspire these employees to the greatest degree. In fact, it is axiomatic that *the more direct the measurement and the shorter the interval between effort and reward, the more effective the result.*

Many activities are of such nature that direct measurement and reward are not economical because of the administrative cost required to maintain the measurement properly. Engineering, quality assurance, production control, and toolmaking are good examples. Such functions are there to serve the departments that are producing the products or services the company sells to its customers. A simple and meaningful way to ensure good service from these functions and to control their cost of operation is to relate the total of their salaries and wages to the standard hours of salable product produced by the departments they serve. This provides one factor, the degree to which these functions control and reduce their cost in relation to company output, that can be used to measure and reward their efforts and effectiveness. However, since these functions have additional impact on the success of the company, it may be desirable to use cost of operation as only one of several factors for measuring and rewarding their contribution. Percent on-time shipments and percent on-time order intake are possible factors, also, depending upon the nature of the business and the extent of the influence of these functions in these areas.

Department supervisors and foremen and the indirect employees in departments and sections utilizing direct measurement can be measured by several factors, all of which are related to carrying out their responsibilities effectively. Factors normally used include percent performance, percent on standard, percent excess total cost to standard cost, and percent capacity, as reported for each group.

PROVIDE EQUAL INCENTIVE OPPORTUNITY FOR ALL EMPLOYEES

The incentives at all levels in the organization should be designed to provide an opportunity to earn a premium or bonus of 25 to 35 percent of base salaries or wages when established objectives are achieved. Opportunity of this magnitude is necessary in order to gain the full pull of the incentives in increasing productivity and in improving the operation of the enterprise. When several factors are used, they should be weighted according to their importance and in combination should provide the same total incentive opportunity as when only one factor is employed. In this way all employees in the company enjoy the same incentive opportunity and are rewarded by factors that best measure their individual and collective contribution to achieving company objectives. This is total measurement motivation. It is a necessary part of our economy if we are to expect significant inflation-stopping increases in productivity to be realized in the future.

THE BASIC WAGE INCENTIVE PLAN AND RELATED PLANS

Following are a series of typical wage incentive plans. These plans are intended to illustrate how measurement and incentive can be applied to all employees within a company. Standard Practice OU-1, entitled "Measurement Motivation Program," outlines the total concept. Standard Practice OU-2, "Work Measurement and Wage

Incentive Plan," describes in detail the principles, techniques, and calculations used to measure and apply wage incentives to the work of direct employees and those indirect employees whose work can be measured directly. This plan is basic to most other plans, since it establishes the standard hour and the standard hours of salable product produced to which overhead and expense should be related for cost control purposes. This write-up has special significance because it was the first wage incentive plan approved by the National Labor Relations Board (NLRB) in 1950, when wage and price controls were placed in effect due to the Korean war. The plan was approved tentatively until it could be demonstrated that it was noninflationary. The company where the plan was installed first was the Metal Textile Corporation, which has since become a division of General Cable Corporation. Metal Textile was required to submit monthly reports to the NLRB. These reports, compiled department by department as the plan was installed, showed very substantial increases in employee productivity and earnings accompanied by significant reductions in unit labor costs. About 6 months later the NLRB was satisfied the plan was noninflationary and that the improvements in productivity more than offset the increased earnings of the employees. The plan was given complete approval and was established as the criterion for subsequent approval of proposed wage incentive plans for other companies. Metal Textile employees were represented by the International Brotherhood of Electrical Workers (IBEW). This union accepted and supported the program and helped facilitate the installation of the time standards and the wage incentive plan. Metal Textile has administered the program well over the intervening years and has used it as the basis for continual improvement in productivity. The plan still is operating effectively, and management's relations with the IBEW union and the employees are excellent.

In 1972, General Cable decided to discard an old piecework plan in its Canadian plant, Gencab, Limited, and to replace it with the same wage incentive plan that proved so successful in its Metal Textile Division. The plan was equally effective in Canada. Productivity improved considerably, employee earnings increased significantly, unit labor costs were reduced substantially, and plant output was almost doubled with essentially the same labor force. The Canadian employees are represented by the United Electrical, Radio, and Machine Workers of America. Here again the union accepted and supported the program. In both instances, Metal Textile Division and Gencab, Limited, the local managements decided they wanted the plan and then took the steps necessary to ensure the plan was introduced properly and administered carefully. The result is the plan has functioned well and the managements have used the information and momentum derived from the plan to generate continued improvement in operations.

This work measurement and wage incentive plan is based on fundamentals that have universal application. The plan has been applied successfully to numerous companies producing many different types of products. It has been used in the United States of America, West Germany, Belgium, England, Ireland, and Canada. It has been accepted and supported by AFL-CIO international unions and others, including the United Steel Workers; the International Association of Machinists; the Teamsters; the International Brotherhood of Electrical Workers; the United

Electrical, Radio, and Machine Workers of America; workers' councils; independent unions; and by employees not represented by unions. The plan is designed to be fair to the employees and to the company. The time standards are carefully engineered from studies made in each company by employees who have been given intensive training in standard data timestudy techniques and in wage incentive administration. In every instance the plan has been installed successfully because of the cooperation and combined efforts of the management, the supervision, the employees, and the union involved.

This work measurement and wage incentive plan must be installed first, because it establishes the foundation, the standard hours of salable product produced, upon which most of the wage incentive plans for other indirect employees, supervisors, and managers are based. Standard Practices OU-6 through OU-10 outline typical multifactor plans covering other groups of employees. The write-ups describe the incentive factors to be used, the rules that govern the implementation of each plan, the base and objective indices for each factor, the percent incentive premium assigned to each factor when the objectives are reached, the maximum that can be earned on each factor, and the percent incentive premium per index point for each factor for improvement over the established base. These wage incentive plans serve to illustrate for each group the factors that may be used and the relative weight for each that might be considered. Obviously, in practice each plan should be designed to best meet the needs of each situation. The following examples cover incentive plans for these groups:

1. Management staff

2. Staff employees in:

   Accounting
   Employee relations
   Engineering
   Industrial engineering
   Maintenance
   Marketing
   Material control
   Purchasing
   Quality assurance
   Receiving and shipping

3. Manufacturing managers

4. Production supervisors

5. Indirect hourly employees

IDEA AWARD PLAN

Also, at the end Standard Practice OU-11, entitled "Idea Award Plan for Direct and Indirect Employees," is included. This plan can be used in conjunction with the

"Work Measurement and Wage Incentive Plan," Standard Practice OU-2, and in which case it would supersede the use of the regular suggestion system for all employees whose work is measured directly by time standards. Employees have many good ideas. The purpose of this plan is to encourage the employees to think about their work and to turn in their ideas for improving productivity. The plan provides for rewarding the employees on a formula basis for their ideas that are implemented by the company. Keep in mind it is imperative to the continual success of the work measurement and wage incentive plan that the time standards be revised every time a change in method is made. This maintains the consistency and fairness of the time standards and helps to ensure that the plan will not deteriorate over the years. This award plan rewards the employees for bringing worthwhile changes to management's attention.

The typical wage incentive plans follow.

PURPOSE

To provide motivating incentive plans based on measurable factors for rewarding all employees in relation to improvements achieved in meeting individual, group, departmental, and company operating objectives.

DISTRIBUTION

The management staff

POLICY

It is company policy to recognize and reward employees for outstanding performances and extraordinary contributions to the success of the company. Also, it is policy to establish objectives and rules for measuring, determining, and distributing incentive premiums so that the awards are timely, fair, and continue to be a motivating factor for improved operation of each of the departments within the company. Further, it is policy to provide each and every employee with an opportunity to earn incentive premiums.

PROCEDURE

These company policies are to be implemented through a series of incentive plans briefly described in this standard practice.

The guiding principles upon which the incentive plans are to be established and are to function are as follows:

1. OPERATING PROFITS are to be the base for management incentives.

2. STANDARD HOURS PRODUCED are to be the foundation for incentives for direct employees and those indirect employees whose work is measured directly.

3. STANDARD HOURS OF SALABLE PRODUCT produced by direct employees are to be the foundation for incentives for supervisory employees and for those indirect employees whose work is not measured directly.

4. The incentive premiums are to be closely related to each employee's base pay and to the employee's effectiveness in achieving and surpassing measured objectives.

5. The incentive plans, as nearly as practical, are to be designed to "put each employee in business for himself" with his or her rewards and recognition related to:

a. The effective implementation of his or her ideas, plans, and efforts.

b. A high degree of well-coordinated action among employees, departments, and operating units.

c. Continual improvement in:

Reducing costs
Improving quality
Meeting schedules
Shortening production cycles
Lowering inventories in relation to sales
Developing and implementing constructive changes

d. Continuous progress in the growth and utilization of company:

Profits
Sales
Products
Facilities
Operating controls
Working capital

The principles and practices outlined in Standard Practice OU-2, entitled "Work Measurement and Wage Incentive Plan," apply to all employees whose work is measured directly by time standards.

A series of incentive plans will be prepared to provide other indirect, supervisory, and management employees with opportunities to earn incentive premiums. These incentive plans will describe the factors that are used and the percent incentive premiums that will be earned when the objectives or the maximums are achieved. The definitions of the factors that may be used are as follows:

1. % OPERATING PROFIT—As reported on the profit and loss statement for the period.

2. % EXCESS COST—Actual total salaries and wages for the group related to standard hours of salable product produced in the period divided by the respective standard labor cost per standard hour of salable product.

3. % ON-TIME ORDER INTAKE—Actual order intake in dollars divided by the forecasted order intake in dollars from the profit plan on a cumulative year-to-date basis through the period.

	S T A N D A R D **P R A C T I C E**	SUBJECT
CORPORATION	NUMBER OU-1 PAGE 3 OF 3	MEASUREMENT MOTIVATION
	EFFECTIVE REVISION·DATE	PROGRAM
ISSUED BY	APPROVALS		

4. % ON-TIME SHIPMENTS—Two percentages are calculated and then combined into one composite factor as follows:

    a. % ON-TIME DOLLAR SHIPMENTS

$$= \frac{\text{ACTUAL OVERDUE AND SCHEDULED SHIPMENTS IN DOLLARS}}{\text{OVERDUE DOLLARS + SCHEDULED DOLLARS}}$$

    b. % ON-TIME ORDER SHIPMENTS

$$= \frac{\text{ACTUAL OVERDUE AND SCHEDULED SHIPMENTS IN NUMBER OF ORDERS}}{\text{OVERDUE ORDERS + SCHEDULED ORDERS}}$$

    c. % ON-TIME SHIPMENTS $= \dfrac{\% \text{ DOLLARS (a)} + \% \text{ ORDERS (b)}}{2}$

5. PRODUCTION FACTORS—As reported on the departmental and plantwide LABOR ANALYSIS SHEETS, see Standard Practice OU-5:

    a. % PERFORMANCE
    b. % ON STANDARD
    c. % EXCESS TOTAL ACTUAL COST TO STANDARD COST
    d. % CAPACITY USED (Modifier)

A standard practice will be issued to explain in detail the incentive plan to be applied to each group or department. Each write-up will define the specific factors to be used, the incentive opportunities assigned to each factor, and will describe how the incentive plan is designed to function.

	STANDARD PRACTICE	SUBJECT
CORPORATION	NUMBER OU-2 PAGE 1 OF 6	WORK MEASUREMENT AND WAGE INCENTIVE PLAN
	EFFECTIVE REVISION DATE	

ISSUED BY	APPROVALS		

The future growth and success of our business depends on providing three "musts" to our customers:

1. Competitive prices
2. Good service
3. High quality

We are making a careful study of our company in order to find ways by which we can better serve our customers and thus bring in more business. One result of our study is a decision to provide work measurement and wage incentive for the direct employees.

The employees and the company will benefit from the work measurement and wage incentive plan we have developed. The employees will gain through substantially increased earnings; the company through increased production and lower costs.

Further, the work measurement and wage incentive plan will produce information that will assist in analyzing, planning, and directing plant operations. This will help to improve our cost estimating and control.

A. PRINCIPLES

1. The company guarantees that no employee can earn less than his or her personal hourly rate multiplied by the number of hours worked per day, plus overtime provisions and shift differentials.

2. Incentive earnings will be paid 100 percent to the employee for all good production. It is expected that the average skilled operator, fully qualified, working at incentive pace, will earn about one-quarter more than the job rate. No limit will be set on incentive earnings.

3. Time standards will be set from standard data developed by detailed timestudy analyses of the operations required. Under certain conditions, direct timestudy may be used.

4. Each time standard will be guaranteed so long as no change is made in the operation except for obvious clerical errors. When changes are made in material, methods, speed and feeds, tooling, equipment, processes, and quality, the standards will be reviewed and revised as necessary. Changes in time standards are to be made as nearly concurrent as possible with these types of changes, and the revised standards will become effective when applied.

5. The time standards will be set for performing the work to acceptable standards of quality. Incentive earnings will be penalized for all work not conforming to operation quality specifications.

CORPORATION	**STANDARD PRACTICE**	SUBJECT
	NUMBER OU-2 PAGE 2 OF 6	WORK MEASUREMENT AND
	EFFECTIVE REVISION DATE	WAGE INCENTIVE PLAN

| ISSUED BY | APPROVALS | | |

6. Correct allowances will be made for extra work which is temporarily required because conditions are not standard.

7. All daywork, which is work not done on standard, will be paid for at the employees' personal hourly rates.

8. The employees will be compensated at their personal hourly rates for all lost time resulting from delays beyond their control.

9. Incentive earnings will be calculated on a daily basis except when the type of work makes it necessary to perform the computation on some other basis.

B. TIME STANDARDS

The following is a step-by-step description of the procedure by which time-studies will be taken, standard data developed, and standards set and applied:

1. Timestudy

The operations performed in the several departments will be time-studied in detail by trained timestudy people. Simultaneously with the recording of the elemental times, the performance of the employee will be rated. These timestudies will provide basic information from which standard data will be developed.

2. Rating

Variations in the rate of performance of the employee must be con-sidered in order to determine fair incentive standards. In this way, the actual time taken for each element will be adjusted to that time which a normal qualified employee working at normal speed would take. Thus, if an employee performs at a rate faster than normal, the ele-mental time will be increased proportionately so as to represent the time required at normal speed. Conversely, if an employee's perform-ance is slower than normal, the elemental time will be decreased proportionately. For example, the normal performance will be termed a rating of 100 percent, which represents 60 minutes of work per hour. Assume the actual time for an element was 0.16 minutes at 125 percent rating, the time would be increased as follows:

$$0.16 \times 125\% = 0.20 \text{ minutes}$$

or, if the actual time taken was 0.25 minutes at an 80 percent rating, the time would be adjusted as follows:

$$0.25 \times 80\% = 0.20 \text{ minutes}$$

STANDARD PRACTICE	SUBJECT
CORPORATION	
NUMBER OU-2 PAGE 3 OF 6	WORK MEASUREMENT AND
EFFECTIVE REVISION DATE	WAGE INCENTIVE PLAN
ISSUED BY APPROVALS	

3. Relax Factor

In addition to adjusting the actual time to normal time for each element by means of rating, it is necessary to compensate the employee for fatigue, personal needs, and unavoidable delays. This is done by adding a percentage, termed a *relax factor*, to the normal time. In all cases, personal time will be allowed at the rate of 5 percent and unavoidable delays at 2 percent, for a total of 7 percent. In most cases, a fatigue allowance of 8 percent will be applied, resulting in a total relax factor of 15 percent. Where it is very clear that physical demand is abnormally high or extremely severe, fatigue factors of 13 and 18 percent will be used. The resulting relax factors of 20 and 25 percent respectively are necessary sometimes in machine shop and assembly work.

4. Standard Data

The actual elemental times, when adjusted to normal by means of rating and increased to include the relax factor, become what are termed *element standards*. These element standards will be compiled suitably in the form of tables, charts, and curves to compose standard data. The standard data will be used to set time standards on all work coming within the range of the data.

5. Setting Standards

Each standard will be set by selecting from the standard data the element standards for those elements of work which are required to be performed in order to complete the operation satisfactorily in accordance with specifications, such as dimensions, tolerances, and finishes.

Operation standards will be separate from setup standards in order to provide equal opportunity for incentive earnings at all quantities of production. The operation standards will be set in terms of standard minutes per piece. The setup standards, expressed in standard minutes per setup, will include all work necessary in the preparation and teardown of an operation for the production of good pieces in the standard time.

6. Power Machine Time

Incentive should be paid on physical work only. This is done by computing a normal working time factor for each job involving power machine time. This factor represents the fraction (expressed decimally) of the total normalized cycle time during which the operator is actually doing physical work. Time on standard is computed by multiplying the total time spent on the job by the normal working time factor. The remainder of the time is considered to be available idle time and is paid for at the personal hourly rate.

This procedure has the advantage of providing a greater incentive opportunity for employees whose jobs require a higher percentage of physical work. It is unduly restrictive, however, when power machine cuts are so short that an operator could not logically be required to do additional work during the cutting time. It is also unduly restrictive in cases where power machine time is substantial, but where additional work assignments cannot be made. Because of this, normal working time factors will be used only in cases when multiple machine or multiple job assignments are definitely contemplated. In all other cases, machine time will be rated at 125 percent with no relax factor, thus protecting the operator at full incentive pace. In order to make this concession, however, the company must require that the greatest possible amount of work be assigned during the power machine time.

7. Revising Standards

Each standard will be guaranteed so long as the operation is not changed. The standards will be reviewed and revised as necessary when changes in material, methods, speeds and feeds, tooling, equipment, processes, quality, and obvious clerical errors are made in order to maintain fair and consistent standards. Such changes may result in either an increase or a decrease in the standard. In all cases, however, the revised standard will provide equal opportunity for incentive earnings consistent with the work involved. The employees will be notified when such changes are made.

In order to provide incentive while changes are being made, it may be necessary in some instances to set temporary standards. However, all temporary standards will apply only to current job lots and will be returned to the standards department upon completion thereof. Reapplication will be made only upon the specific approval of the manager of standards.

8. Expense Standards

Expense standards will be set to provide correct allowances for extra work resulting from irregularities which are required temporarily but are not included in the standards. For example, if a lot of castings contains excess stock which requires an extra cut to be taken, an expense standard will be set for the extra work. The expense standard will be allowed only so long as the irregularity exists.

9. Lost Time

The employees will be compensated at their personal hourly rates for all lost time resulting from delays beyond their control. It is important that the lost time be reported separately, so that the incentive earnings of production employees will be protected and also so that the lost time can be properly analyzed and reduced. Lost time includes such delays as waiting for material, tools, orders, machine breakdowns, and engineering changes.

10. Quality

The time standards will be set for performing the work to established standards of quality. Incentive earnings will be paid for good work only. No credit will be given the employee, in calculating incentive earnings, for pieces which do not conform to operation quality specifications. When such pieces are subsequently reworked to conform to specifications, they will be credited to the original operator, but the direct labor cost of the rework will be charged against the incentive premium of the operator. Standard cost will be used if the rework operation is measured, and actual cost will be used if this is not the case. Rework will be done on standard wherever possible. However, in all cases involving defective workmanship, the employee cannot earn less per day than his or her personal hourly rate multiplied by the number of hours worked per day, plus overtime provisions and shift differentials.

The value of materials and labor contained in our products makes it imperative that scrap losses be reduced and controlled. The time standards are set to include adequate time to perform all of the elements of work required to produce good pieces, including time for inspection and observation.

Accordingly, all scrap losses will be reviewed by management and where, in management's opinion, the scrap is excessive or caused by operator negligence, the full value of scrapped pieces will be deducted from any incentive premiums earned during the week. Each case will be discussed with the employee involved and decided on its own merits.

C. EARNINGS

1. Personal Hourly Rate

Each employee's personal hourly rate multiplied by the hours worked each day, plus overtime provisions and shift differentials, represents the minimum wage that will be paid to the employee.

<table>
<tr><td rowspan="3">CORPORATION</td><td colspan="2" align="center">STANDARD PRACTICE</td><td>SUBJECT</td></tr>
<tr><td colspan="2">NUMBER
OU-2   PAGE 6 OF 6</td><td rowspan="2">WORK MEASUREMENT AND
WAGE INCENTIVE PLAN</td></tr>
<tr><td colspan="2">EFFECTIVE   REVISION DATE</td></tr>
<tr><td>ISSUED BY</td><td>APPROVALS</td><td></td><td></td></tr>
</table>

Earnings for time worked not on standard will be computed at the personal hourly rate.

2. Computation

Incentive earnings will be computed on a daily basis and will be based on the standard minutes of work produced and the job rates. An example of the calculation of a day's wage is as follows:

Assume the employee's personal hourly rate equals $4.80 per hour and the employee worked a total of 8 hours.

JOB NO.	PIECES COMPLETED	STANDARD MINS. PER PIECE	STANDARD MINS. PER SETUP	STANDARD MINS. PRODUCED	JOB RATE PER MIN.	INCENTIVE EARNINGS	ACTUAL HOURS
1	Setup		30.0 =	30	× $0.08 =	$ 2.40	.4
	50 ×	1.8	=	90	× 0.08 =	7.20	1.3
2	Setup		43.8 =	44	× $0.08 =	$ 3.52	.5
	10 ×	17.1	=	171	× 0.08 =	13.68	2.3
3	Setup		40.0 =	40	× $0.08 =	$ 3.20	.5
	20 ×	7.5	=	150	× 0.08 =	12.00	2.0
				525		$42.00	7.0

4 Daywork   1.0

Total Time Worked   8.0

$$\% \text{ Performance on Standard} = \frac{\text{Standard mins. Produced}}{\text{Actual hrs. on Standard}} \times \frac{100}{60} = \frac{525}{7.0} \times \frac{100}{60} = 125\%$$

TOTAL INCENTIVE EARNINGS ·	$42.00
TOTAL DAYWORK EARNINGS = 1.0 hrs. × $4.80 per hour =	4.80
TOTAL DAY'S WAGE	$46.80
GUARANTEED DAY'S WAGE = 8.0 hrs. × $4.80 per hour	38.40
INCENTIVE PREMIUM	$ 8.40

Overtime payment will be computed at the weekly average earned rate. The job rate per hour used for converting standard minutes into incentive earnings will be employee's personal hourly rate except as follows:

1. The maximum of the rate range will be used in the event an employee's personal hourly rate exceeds the maximum for his or her job classification.

2. The maximum of the rate range for the classification of the work performed by a leadman will be used when a leadman does productive work on standard.

	S T A N D A R D	SUBJECT	
	P R A C T I C E		
CORPORATION	NUMBER	MANAGEMENT STAFF	
	OU-6 PAGE 1 OF 2	INCENTIVE PLAN	
	EFFECTIVE REVISION DATE		

ISSUED BY	APPROVALS		

PURPOSE

To provide a measurable basis for rewarding members of the management staff in relation to improvements achieved in meeting and surpassing company operating objectives.

DISTRIBUTION

The management staff

POLICY

It is company policy to recognize and reward managers for outstanding performances and extraordinary contributions to the success of the company. Also, it is policy to establish objectives and rules for measuring, determining, and distributing incentive premiums so that the awards are timely, fair, and continue to be a motivating factor for improved operation of the company and of each of its departments.

PROCEDURE

The plan is designed to reward each member of the management staff in relation to the improved operation of the company as measured by a single factor as follows:

% Operating Profit

A. RULES

1. The plan is designed to provide each member of the management staff with an opportunity to earn an incentive premium of about 25 percent of his or her base salary when the company achieves the operating objective. In addition, a maximum limit has been set. The maximum provides opportunity for earning greater incentive premiums when the company exceeds the operating objective.

2. The percent incentive premium earned by each member of the management is to be calculated and reported for each quarterly accounting period. The amount of incentive premium earned for the period will be paid by the end of the month immediately following the end of the quarter.

3. The amount of premium earned is to be obtained by multiplying the percent incentive premium by each manager's base salary for the period.

	STANDARD PRACTICE	SUBJECT
CORPORATION	NUMBER OU-6 PAGE 2 OF 2	MANAGEMENT STAFF INCENTIVE PLAN
	EFFECTIVE REVISION DATE	

ISSUED BY	APPROVALS		

4. The factors, the base, and the objective for each factor, and the percent incentive premium assigned to each factor, will be reviewed prior to the beginning of each fiscal year and will be modified or revised to shift emphasis or to meet changes considered necessary by the president of the corporation.

B. INCENTIVE FACTORS

A base and an objective will be established for each incentive factor. The *base* is the point beyond which the manager begins to earn incentive premiums, and the *objective* is the expected operating point. The percent incentive premium allocated to each incentive factor is distributed proportionately over the span between the base and the objective. A maximum percent incentive premium will be set for each incentive factor also. The incentive factor to be applied for the fiscal year ending June 30, 1977, and the base, objective, and percent incentive premium assigned to the incentive factor will be as follows:

INCENTIVE FACTOR	INDEX			% INCENTIVE PREMIUM AT			% INCENTIVE PREMIUM PER INDEX POINT
	BASE	OBJEC-TIVE	MAXI-MUM	BASE	OBJEC-TIVE	MAXI-MUM	
% operating profit	5.5	17.0	22.0	0	25	36	2.18

PURPOSE

To provide a measurable basis for rewarding employees in the staff departments in relation to improvements achieved in meeting and surpassing departmental and company operating objectives.

DISTRIBUTION

The management staff

POLICY

It is company policy to recognize and reward employees for outstanding performances and extraordinary contributions to the success of the company. Also, it is policy to establish objectives and rules for measuring, determining, and distributing incentive premiums so that the awards are timely, fair, and continue to be a motivating factor for improved operation of the company and of each of its departments.

PROCEDURE

The plan is designed to reward each employee in each staff department (except the manager) in relation to the improved operation of the company and the department as measured by a combination of all or some of the following factors:

1. % Operating profit
2. % Excess departmental cost
3. % On-time shipments
4. % On-time order intake
5. % On standard

A. RULES

1. The plan is designed to provide each employee in each staff department with an opportunity to earn incentive premium of about 25 percent of the employee's base salary when the department and the company achieve the operating objectives set by management. In addition, a maximum limit has been set. The maximum provides opportunity for earning greater incentive premiums when the department and the company exceed the operating objectives.

2. The percent incentive premium earned by each employee in each staff department is to be calculated and reported for each monthly accounting period. The amount of incentive premium earned for the period will be paid by the end of the following month.

3. The amount of premium earned is to be obtained by multiplying the percent incentive premium by the employee's base salary for the period.

4. The factors, the base, and the objective for each factor, and the percent incentive premium assigned to each factor, will be reviewed prior to the beginning of each fiscal year and will be modified or revised to shift emphasis or to meet changes considered necessary by management.

B. INCENTIVE FACTORS

A base and objective will be established for each incentive factor. The *base* is the point beyond which the staff employees begin to earn incentive premiums, and the *objective* is the expected operating point. The percent incentive premium allocated to each incentive factor is distributed proportionately over the span between the base and the objective. A maximum percent incentive premium will be set for each incentive factor, also.

The incentive factors to be applied, and the base, objective, and maximum percent incentive premium assigned to each incentive factor will be as follows:

A. ACCOUNTING EMPLOYEES

	INDEX			% INCENTIVE PREMIUM AT			% INCENTIVE PREMIUM PER INDEX POINT
INCENTIVE FACTOR	BASE	OBJEC-TIVE	MAXI-MUM	BASE	OBJEC-TIVE	MAXI-MUM	
1. % operating profit	5.5	17.0	22.0	0	10	14	0.87
2. % excess departmental cost	25.0	0	(10)	0	15	21	0.6
3. TOTAL % INCENTIVE PREMIUM EARNED				0	25	35	

STANDARD PRACTICE

CORPORATION

NUMBER
OU-7   PAGE 3 OF 7

EFFECTIVE   REVISION DATE

SUBJECT

STAFF EMPLOYEE
INCENTIVE PLAN

ISSUED BY

APPROVALS

B. EMPLOYEE RELATIONS EMPLOYEES

INCENTIVE FACTOR	INDEX			% INCENTIVE PREMIUM AT			% INCENTIVE PREMIUM PER INDEX POINT
	BASE	OBJEC-TIVE	MAXI-MUM	BASE	OBJEC-TIVE	MAXI-MUM	
1. % operating profit	5.5	17.0	22.0	0	10	14	0.87
2. % excess departmental cost	25.0	0	(10)	0	15	21	0.6
3. TOTAL % INCENTIVE PREMIUM EARNED				0	25	34	

C. ENGINEERING EMPLOYEES

INCENTIVE FACTOR	INDEX			% INCENTIVE PREMIUM AT			% INCENTIVE PREMIUM PER INDEX POINT
	BASE	OBJEC-TIVE	MAXI-MUM	BASE	OBJEC-TIVE	MAXI-MUM	
1. % operating profit	5.5	17.0	22.0	0	10	14	0.87
2. % excess departmental cost	25.0	0	(10)	0	5	7	0.2
3. % on-time shipments	95.0	105	109	0	5	7	0.5
4. % on-time order intake	95.0	105	109	0	5	7	0.5
5. TOTAL % INCENTIVE PREMIUM EARNED				0	25	35	

D. INDUSTRIAL ENGINEERING EMPLOYEES

INCENTIVE FACTOR	INDEX			% INCENTIVE PREMIUM AT			% INCENTIVE PREMIUM PER INDEX POINT
	BASE	OBJEC-TIVE	MAXI-MUM	BASE	OBJEC-TIVE	MAXI-MUM	
1. % operating profit	5.5	17.0	22.0	0	7	10	0.61
2. % excess departmental cost	25.0	0	(10)	0	10	14	0.4
3. % on standard (all production)	75.0	95.0	100	0	8	10	0.4
4. TOTAL % INCENTIVE PREMIUM EARNED				0	25	34	

E. MAINTENANCE EMPLOYEES

INCENTIVE FACTOR	INDEX			% INCENTIVE PREMIUM AT			% INCENTIVE PREMIUM PER INDEX POINT
	BASE	OBJEC-TIVE	MAXI-MUM	BASE	OBJEC-TIVE	MAXI-MUM	
1. % excess departmental cost	25	0	(10)	0	15	21	0.6
2. % on-time shipments	95	105	110	0	10	15	1.0
3. TOTAL % INCENTIVE PREMIUM EARNED				0	25	36	

F. MARKETING EMPLOYEES

| | INDEX | | | % INCENTIVE PREMIUM AT | | | |
INCENTIVE FACTOR	BASE	OBJEC-TIVE	MAXI-MUM	BASE	OBJEC-TIVE	MAXI-MUM	% INCENTIVE PREMIUM PER INDEX POINT
1. % operating profit	5.5	17.0	22.0	0	10	14	0.87
2. % excess departmental cost	25.0	0	(5)	0	5	6	0.2
3. % on-time order intake	95.0	105	110	0	10	15	1.0
4. TOTAL% INCENTIVE PREMIUM EARNED				0	25	35	

G. MATERIAL CONTROL EMPLOYEES

| | INDEX | | | % INCENTIVE PREMIUM AT | | | |
INCENTIVE FACTOR	BASE	OBJEC-TIVE	MAXI-MUM	BASE	OBJEC-TIVE	MAXI-MUM	% INCENTIVE PREMIUM PER INDEX POINT
1. % excess departmental cost	25	0	(10)	0	15	21	0.6
2. % on-time shipments	95	105	110	0	10	15	1.0
3. TOTAL% INCENTIVE PREMIUM EARNED				0	25	36	

ISSUED BY	APPROVALS		

H. PURCHASING EMPLOYEES

INCENTIVE FACTOR	INDEX			% INCENTIVE PREMIUM AT			% INCENTIVE PREMIUM PER INDEX POINT
	BASE	OBJEC-TIVE	MAXI-MUM	BASE	OBJEC-TIVE	MAXI-MUM	
1. % operating profit	5.5	17.0	22.0	0	7	10	0.61
2. % excess departmental cost	25.0	0	(10)	0	10	14	0.4
3. % on-time shipments	95.0	105	109	0	8	11	0.8
4. TOTAL % INCENTIVE PREMIUM EARNED				0	25	35	

I. QUALITY ASSURANCE EMPLOYEES

INCENTIVE FACTOR	INDEX			% INCENTIVE PREMIUM AT			% INCENTIVE PREMIUM PER INDEX POINT
	BASE	OBJEC-TIVE	MAXI-MUM	BASE	OBJEC-TIVE	MAXI-MUM	
1. % operating profit	5.5	17.0	22.0	0	12	17	1.04
2. % excess departmental cost	25.0	0	(10)	0	5	7	0.2
3. % on-time shipments	95.0	105	109	0	8	11	0.8
4. TOTAL % INCENTIVE PREMIUM EARNED				0	25	35	

CORPORATION	STANDARD PRACTICE	SUBJECT
	NUMBER OU-7 PAGE 7 OF 7	STAFF EMPLOYEE
	EFFECTIVE REVISION DATE	INCENTIVE PLAN

ISSUED BY	APPROVALS		

J. RECEIVING AND SHIPPING EMPLOYEES

	INDEX			% INCENTIVE PREMIUM AT			% INCENTIVE PREMIUM PER
INCENTIVE FACTOR	BASE	OBJEC-TIVE	MAXI-MUM	BASE	OBJEC-TIVE	MAXI-MUM	INDEX POINT
1. % excess departmental cost	25	0	(10)	0	15	21	0.6
2. % on-time shipments	95	105	110	0	10	15	1.0
3. TOTAL % INCENTIVE PREMIUM EARNED				0	25	36	

PURPOSE

To provide a measurable basis for rewarding the material manager and the production manager in relation to improvements achieved in meeting and surpassing operating objectives established for the departments under their supervision.

DISTRIBUTION

The management staff
Material manager
Production manager

POLICY

It is company policy to recognize and reward managers for outstanding performances and extraordinary contributions to the success of the company. Also, it is policy to establish objectives and rules for measuring, determining, and distributing incentive premiums so that the awards are timely, fair, and continue to be a motivating factor for improved operation of the company and of each of its departments.

PROCEDURE

1. The material manager will be measured and will be given an opportunity to earn an incentive premium based on the composite results achieved by the departments under his or her supervision, using the same factors, indices, and percent incentive premium values set by management in the departmental incentive plans.

2. The production manager will be measured and will be given an opportunity to earn an incentive premium based on the composite results achieved by the departments under his or her supervision, using the same factors, indices, and percent incentive premium values set by management in the departmental plans.

3. The plans are designed to provide the material manager and the production manager with an opportunity to earn an incentive premium of about 25 percent of their base salaries when their respective departments in total achieve the operating objectives. In addition, maximum limits have been set. The maximums provide opportunity for earning greater incentive premiums when their respective departments in total exceed the operating objectives.

CORPORATION	**STANDARD PRACTICE**	SUBJECT
	NUMBER OU-8 PAGE 2 OF 2	MANUFACTURING MANAGEMENT
	EFFECTIVE REVISION DATE	INCENTIVE PLAN

ISSUED BY	APPROVALS		

4. The percent incentive premiums earned by the material manager and the production manager are to be calculated and reported for each monthly accounting period. The amount of incentive premium earned for the period will be paid by the end of the following month.

5. The amount of premium earned is to be obtained by multiplying the percent incentive premium by each manager's base salary for the period.

6. The factors, the base, and the objective for each factor, and the percent incentive premium assigned to each factor, will be reviewed prior to the beginning of each fiscal year and will be modified or revised to shift emphasis or to meet changes considered necessary by management.

CORPORATION	**STANDARD PRACTICE**		SUBJECT
	NUMBER OU-9 PAGE 1 OF 3		PRODUCTION SUPERVISION INCENTIVE PLAN
	EFFECTIVE REVISION DATE		
ISSUED BY	APPROVALS		

PURPOSE

To provide a measurable basis for rewarding production foremen in relation to improvements achieved in meeting and surpassing departmental and company operating objectives.

DISTRIBUTION

The management staff
Production manager
Foremen, production

POLICY

It is company policy to recognize and reward employees for outstanding performances and extraordinary contributions to the success of the company. Also, it is policy to establish objectives and rules for determining and distributing incentive premiums so that the awards are timely, fair, and continue to be a motivating factor for improved operation of each department within the company.

PROCEDURE

The production supervision incentive plan has been established by management in recognition of the importance of each foreman's efforts in increasing productivity and production, reducing costs, eliminating wastes, encouraging and implementing methods improvements, improving yield and quality, and meeting schedules.

The plan is designed to reward each foreman in relation to the improvements made in the operation of his or her department as measured by selected production and cost factors. In general, these factors include:

1. % performance
2. % on standard
3. % excess total actual cost to standard cost
4. % capacity used
5. % on-time shipments

The following describes the operation of the plan in detail.

A. RULES

1. The production supervision incentive plan is applicable in departments that are operating with the work measurement and wage incentive plan, Standard Practice OU-2; timekeeping and counting, Standard Practice OU-3; payroll and cost calculations, Standard Practice OU-4; and the labor analysis sheet, Standard Practice OU-5.

2. The plan is designed to provide each foreman with an opportunity to earn an incentive premium of approximately 25 percent of his or her base salary when the department achieves management's operating objectives. In addition, a maximum limit has been set. The maximum provides opportunity for earning greater incentive premiums when a foreman exceeds the objectives set by management.

3. The percent incentive premium earned by each foreman is to be calculated and reported each week. However, the total earned premium will be paid once each month on the payday immediately following the end of the month.

4. The amount of premium earned is to be obtained by multiplying the percent incentive premium earned by the foreman's base salary for the period. EXCEPTION: The maximum of the salary range will be used in the event a foreman's salary exceeds the maximum for his or her position classification.

5. The factors, the base, and the objective for each factor, and the percent incentive premium assigned to each factor, will be reviewed once each year and will be modified or revised to shift emphasis or to meet changes considered necessary by management.

6. The factors and the percent incentive premium assigned to each factor may be different for various departments in order to direct attention to those conditions of most significance in each department.

B. INCENTIVE FACTORS

A base and an objective will be established for each incentive factor in each production department. The *base* is the point beyond which the foreman begins to earn an incentive premium, and the *objective* is the expected operating point. The percent incentive premium allocated to each incentive factor is distributed proportionately over the span between the base and the objective. A maximum percent incentive premium will be set for each incentive factor also. In general, the incentive factors to be applied and the base, objective, and percent incentive premium assigned to each incentive factor will be as follows:

INCENTIVE FACTOR	INDEX			% INCENTIVE PREMIUM AT			% INCENTIVE PREMIUM PER INDEX POINT
	BASE	OBJEC-TIVE	MAXI-MUM	BASE	OBJEC-TIVE	MAXI-MUM	
1. % performance (*column 8)	100	125	130	0	10	12	0.4
2. % on standard (*column 9)	75	95	100	0	8	10	0.4
3. % excess total actual cost to standard (*column 40)	50	0	(10)	0	10	12	0.2
4. SUBTOTAL				0	28	34	
5. % capacity used—modifier (*column 11)	0	72	100	0	0.72	1.00	
6. MODIFIED SUBTOTAL				0	20	34	
7. % on time shipments	95	105	115	0	5	10	0.5
8. TOTAL % INCENTIVE PREMIUM EARNED				0	25	44	

*See labor analysis sheet, form #STD-03, described in Standard Practice OU-5.

	STANDARD PRACTICE	SUBJECT
CORPORATION	NUMBER OU-10 PAGE 1 OF 2	INDIRECT HOURLY EMPLOYEE INCENTIVE PLAN
	EFFECTIVE REVISION DATE	

ISSUED BY	APPROVALS		

PURPOSE

To establish and provide wage incentive plans for rewarding indirect hourly employees in relation to improvements in meeting and surpassing departmental and company operating objectives.

DISTRIBUTION

The management staff
Supervisors
Foremen

POLICY

It is company policy to continually improve the operating effectiveness of the company and each of its departments. This program, applied in conjunction with the work measurement and wage incentive plan, is designed to implement this policy. The indirect hourly employees and the company will benefit. The employees will gain through substantially increased earnings; the company through lower costs and improved service to the production departments.

All work that is performed regularly to each part, subassembly, or assembly will be classified as direct labor. This could include some inspection, cleaning, touch-up, and packing operations, for example. Production standards will be established and applied on this type of work and the employees performing the work will be given an opportunity to earn an incentive premium in accordance with the principles and practices outlined in Standard Practice OU-2, entitled "Work Measurement and Wage Incentive Plan."

Indirect hourly employees performing other types of work such as toolmaking, maintenance, truck driving, expediting, and material handling will be given an opportunity to earn an incentive premium in accordance with the plan described by this standard practice, OU-10.

PROCEDURE

The plan is designed to reward each indirect hourly employee in relation to the improved operation of the company and the department in which he or she works or services as measured by two factors as follows:

1. % on-time shipments
2. % excess actual cost to standard cost

A. RULES

1. The plan is designed to provide each indirect hourly employee with an opportunity to earn an incentive premium of about one-quarter more than the job rate.

2. The percent incentive premium earned by each indirect hourly employee is to be calculated and reported for each monthly accounting period. The amount of incentive premium earned for each period will be paid once each month on the payday immediately following the end of the month.

3. The amount of premium earned is to be obtained by multiplying the percent incentive premium earned by the employee's base wages for the period.

4. The factors, the base, and the objective for each factor, and the percent incentive premium assigned to each factor, will be reviewed once each year and will be modified or revised to shift emphasis or to meet changes considered necessary by management.

B. INCENTIVE FACTORS

A base and an objective will be established for each incentive factor. The *base* is the point beyond which the indirect hourly employee begins to earn an incentive premium, and the *objective* is the expected operating point. The percent incentive premium allocated to each incentive factor is distributed proportionately over the span between the base and the objective. A maximum percent incentive premium will be set for each incentive factor also.

The base, objective, and maximum and the percent incentive premium assigned to each factor are as follows:

INCENTIVE FACTOR	INDEX			% INCENTIVE PREMIUM AT			% INCENTIVE PREMIUM PER INDEX POINT
	BASE	OBJEC-TIVE	MAXI-MUM	BASE	OBJEC-TIVE	MAXI-MUM	
1. % excess actual cost to standard cost	25	0	(10)	0	15	21	0.6
2. % on-time shipments	95	105	110	0	10	15	1.0
3. TOTAL % INCENTIVE PREMIUM EARNED				0	25	36	

CORPORATION	STANDARD PRACTICE	SUBJECT
	NUMBER OU-11 PAGE 1 OF 3	IDEA AWARD PLAN FOR DIRECT AND INDIRECT EMPLOYEES
	EFFECTIVE REVISION DATE	

ISSUED BY	APPROVALS		

PURPOSE

To provide a measurable basis for rewarding employees for suggestions for improved methods that result in cost reduction.

DISTRIBUTION

The management staff

POLICY

It is company policy to reward nonsupervisory employees for submitting acceptable cost-saving suggestions. This idea award plan is applicable only to those employees working under the work measurement and wage incentive plan, Standard Practice OU-2. All other nonsupervisory employees are encouraged to submit constructive suggestions through the regular suggestion system.

PROCEDURE

The idea award plan is to be administered by the industrial engineering department. All improvement ideas are to be submitted in writing, preferably on a suggestion form available at the suggestion boxes in each building. The improvement ideas may be deposited in the locked suggestion boxes or may be delivered to the industrial engineering department. Assistance in writing up the improvement ideas may be obtained from the foremen or the industrial engineering department personnel.

The procedures and rules under which the idea award plan is to function are as follows:

1. Only nonsupervisory employees working under the work measurement and wage incentive plan are eligible to participate.

2. Each employee's improvement idea must be related to the type of work the employee normally performs and must be identified by part number, operation number, or shop order number. If the improvement idea is applicable to more than one part number or operation number, the employee must include the additional numbers when submitting the suggestion.

3. Each idea must suggest an improvement in an operation on which a time standard has been set by the industrial engineering department.

4. Each improvement is accepted by the company when a new time standard is issued for the improved operation or combination of operations, as suggested by the employee.

5. The dollar improvement achieved by the idea is to be calculated by multiplying the reduction in standard minutes allowed per piece or per setup for the operation or combination of operations by the job rate per minute.

6. A projected 6-month reduction in cost is to be determined by multiplying the dollar improvement per piece or per setup by the number of pieces or setups forecasted to be made during the next 6 months.

7. The forecasted number of pieces or setups to be made during the next 6 months is to be determined by the production control department by a review of order backlog.

8. The dollar award to be paid to the originator is to be equal to one-half the projected 6-month reduction in cost.

9. Each dollar award is to be paid by check to the employee suggesting the improvement idea within 30 calendar days after the new time standard is issued.

10. When several employees submit an improvement idea jointly, the dollar award will be divided equally among the several employees.

11. When two or more employees independently submit the same improvement idea, the dollar award, when determined, will be paid to the employee whose suggestion is first received. The improvement ideas will be date stamped and logged into the industrial engineering department when received.

12. When an improvement idea is not accepted by the company, the employee will be notified and the reason for not using the idea will be explained to the employee. If at a later date conditions change and the idea is accepted, the originator will be paid the dollar award after the new standard is issued.

13. It is the function of the engineering, quality control, and industrial engineering departments to reduce costs continually through improved product design, quality requirements, processes and methods, and equipment and tools. In the event an employee's improvement idea is identical with an improvement already under consideration by one of these departments, no dollar award will be made to the employee. However, the situation must be explained to the employee and tangible evidence that the improvement was initiated prior to submission by the employee must be provided by the company. When tangible evidence of prior consideration is not available, the employee will be paid the dollar award as outlined above.

CORPORATION	**STANDARD PRACTICE**	SUBJECT
	NUMBER OU-11 PAGE 3 OF 3	IDEA AWARD PLAN FOR DIRECT AND INDIRECT EMPLOYEES
	EFFECTIVE REVISION DATE	
ISSUED BY	APPROVALS	

14. EXAMPLE—The following example illustrates the calculation of a dollar award under this idea award plan. Assume the improvement idea relates to:

   a. Part no. 12345, operation no. 20.

   b. The current operation standard is 10 standard minutes per piece.

   c. Based on the improvement idea, the standards department issues a new operation standard of 8 standard minutes per piece on July 15, 1976.

   d. The job rate is $4.80 per hour, equal to $0.080 per minute.

   e. The dollar improvement is $0.16 per piece calculated by multiplying the reduction in standard minutes per piece ($10 - 8 = 2$) by the job rate per minute ($0.080).

   f. The production control department forecasts 1000 pieces will be made during the next 6 months.

   g. The projected 6-month reduction in cost is $160.00 calculated by multiplying 1000 pieces by the dollar improvement of $0.16 per piece.

   h. The employee receives a check prior to August 16, 1976, for a dollar award of $80.00, one-half the reduction in cost.

   i. The company retains $80.00, the other one-half of the reduction in cost, to partially offset the cost of tool changes and additions and the cost of implementing the change.

16

Management Commitment and Involvement for Higher Productivity

Two ingredients will determine more than anything else the progress that will be made in improving productivity in the future. They are people and electronic technology. Both hold great promise, and it will be up to management to put them to work on worthwhile endeavors. Management reduced to fundamentals is the development of people. What really determines whether productivity is improving or retrogressing, whether costs are low or high, controlled or not controlled, is how effectively our people use their time and talent to develop new methods, new processes, new products, new markets, new systems, and new businesses. People — develop not by concentrating on themselves but by becoming absorbed fully in a challenging project, one that consumes all their skills, energies, and determination. Everything we have, we see, we know, originated in the past. The only thing certain about the future is continual change. Those managements who can influence the changes constructively to their advantage will move ahead. First, management must have confidence in its objectives. Then, management must face the future with the conviction that there is always a way to do things that must be done or are worth doing. Improving productivity by large amounts year after year after year must be the prime objective. It is the single objective that will make all other goals possible to attain. In effect, raising productivity substantially and regularly is the "fountain of youth" for citizens, companies, countries, and the world.

PEOPLE AND TECHNOLOGY

Management is there to manage people and technology so that good things happen. It is there to get more results from our human and physical resources. We should expect management to take the steps necessary to check inflation and to make certain that supply does meet demand. One of management's major tasks is to expand the markets for current products and services and to develop markets for new products and better services. Lower prices are needed to accomplish this task, and

higher productivity is the forerunner of lower prices. The Bendix Corporation is a
good example. This company, through management direction and expertness in
applying advanced technology, has held the leadership in growth, profits, and capability in a variety of fields for many years. Some years ago, Bendix was faced with
the problem of producing cams for jet engine controls. The cams were complex, requiring precision machining to intricate contours and exacting finishes and tolerances. It took weeks of concentrated effort by a skilled toolmaker to produce one
master cam from which others could be patterned. Bendix engineering was called
in to try to solve this bottleneck. By combining the technical know-how of Bendix
engineers in electronics, digital computers, hydraulics, and servomechanisms, Bendix developed a numerical control system. This system proved to be workable and
practical and reduced the machine time to make the master to a few hours. Thus,
the bottleneck was eliminated, costs were reduced, but most important, Bendix
management recognized an opportunity to enter a new industry—the numerically
controlled machine tool industry. Today Bendix industrial controls division is a
leader in developing and producing numerical control contouring systems for machine tools. Four very significant management principles were employed in this
situation:

1. The application of advanced technology to solve problems.

2. The concept of transfer and interchange of knowledge to bring the latest
   capabilities together in solving problems.

3. The ability of management to grasp the business opportunities in problem
   areas and to exploit them effectively for future growth and profits.

4. The extension of productivity-improving ideas to serve multipurpose uses.

This is dynamic management in action. The application of these four principles
ensured that the capabilities of the company were utilized fully.

Technological advances in the laboratory, in the office, and in the factory have
produced an abundance of things we want and need. However, alert management
should be concerned with its ability to maintain the rate of technical advancement.
Without question, we need to accelerate the pace of progress. But there is every
indication the United States as a country will be facing a technical manpower crisis
within the next decade. There is a pressing need for higher productivity, urban
renewal, pollution control, improved public transportation, energy conservation,
adequate defense capabilities, and exploration into new areas of science. We will
be competing in world markets, and this competition promises to be severe. Russia
is graduating 140,000 engineers per year, one-third of whom are women. Japan is
educating 200,000 engineers per year, about 17 percent of their graduating classes.
The United States is awarding about 45,000 engineering degrees per year. This is
approximately 2 percent of the total students graduated by our colleges. These numbers are significant and point up the action required. The United States maintained
the gold standard for years. This now is shattered, but we are easily surviving its
demise. We still set the technological pace for the world, a position we cannot
relinquish. Gold is meaningless, but technological progress is the very foundation

of our economy and of our position of leadership in the world. Technological advancement and to a large degree improvement in productivity are dependent upon having an adequate supply of capable engineers and scientists. Management must set the conditions for growth in this area. This is necessary not only for the well-being of the United States but for the good of the entire free world.

The S&S Corrugated Paper Machinery Company of Brooklyn, New York, is doing something about it. S&S's president, Mitchel Flaum, was asked how the company was keeping its ideas fresh. His answer:

> Creative momentum! It's our main thrust for growth and it has never been stronger. New machines are on the drawing boards. We're deeply involved in electronics. Our numerical preset control for Flexos is unique in the industry. Everywhere we are modifying, simplifying and improving. By changing the configuration and relative position of parts, we have reduced the number of gears in the JS and JST triple knife by seventeen. The result? Fewer parts and improved accuracy because there are fewer interconnecting parts. Not only is the corrugated boxmaker getting more accurate cuts but the machine maintains its accuracy over a longer period of time.

> How are we keeping the good ideas coming? By encouraging original thinking. We listen to every proposal, no matter how far-fetched. We share opinions at lunch, at the drawing boards, in meetings, in each other's homes, while driving to work in car pools. An idea can happen anywhere, anytime.

> Then there are the new ideas brought in by new designers who join our staff. In a sense, our Engineering Department is like the faculty club of a university, with specialists in many different fields.

Mitchel Flaum was asked about the philosophy of S&S management. He responded:

> First, to manage our own destiny. Our growth, our job security comes from satisfying customer needs. We are an important part of the world economy. Corrugated boxes are essential to domestic and international marketing. Each of us is involved. Each of us contributes. First, we define the need, then we seek the best solution. It's all very deliberate but our thinking is uninhibited, we exercise full freedom in exploring new approaches.

> So if we design good machines, sell at a fair price, provide proper service, if we do all of these things, the result will be profit, and the amount of profit will reflect just how well we have each done our jobs.

> Two axioms should apply to each of us in everything we do for S&S. First, never compromise with quality, only the very best is ever acceptable. Second, strive always to be reliable. Build a reputation for dependability.

Asked to comment on machines in general, Mitchel Flaum continued:

> Not only are we investigating new machines to build and sell, we are acquiring more highly sophisticated machine tools for both our Brooklyn and Dundalk

plants. We are operating with two quarter million dollar Giddings and Lewis numerically controlled boring mills, the flagships in the fleet of other S&S machine tools that now include two Warner & Swasey N/C turret lathes, a N/C Carleton horizontal drill, a N/C Pratt & Whitney sensitive drill and a Giddings & Lewis N/C Numericenter with a capacity of forty random access cutting tools. To augment our existing numerically controlled machine tools we have just added Warner and Swasey Sc15 4-Axis turret lathes and a Kearney & Trecker 200 machining center that will have electric eye sensing, automatic tool changing and fifty-two positions for tool storage. With random selection capability, the Kearney & Trecker 200 will mill, bore, drill and tap parts in one setup.

We've had this modernization program for ten years and thank heaven for it. We believe if we are going to tell our customers they should have modern, high speed machinery we had better practice it ourselves and keep our plants up to date. Another point, the new machine tools use the identical system of numerical controls we've engineered into our S&S machines—namely, that of employing a computer, as opposed to the so-called hard-wire setup that exists in older tape-controlled machines. Both the S&S machines we design and sell and the new machine tools we are buying employ the very latest concepts.

When asked if S&S machines in the field can be updated to take advantage of these innovations, Mitchel Flaum replied:

We attach great importance to giving present owners of our machines the advantage of new concepts we develop. This always puts an extra burden on Engineering, but it's worth it. We want any purchaser of a new S&S machine to know he is buying future as well as present performance, and that he will almost certainly be able to retrofit to his machine any improvements we may develop. This is something that doesn't just happen. It's not merely a matter of saying "Okay, we'll design things that can be retrofitted." All down the line, from inception of the idea in the Engineering Department to the erector who installs and services the advanced part or unit, each man must be conscious of the role he plays and its implications. *We are all involved in anything that relates to any S&S machine.*

In managing our business we are not trusting to luck. We're planning ahead. We are an essential part of an industry basic to the world economy. We make machines that make corrugated boxes in which tens of millions of "things of living" are shipped. We help make it happen. The ideas we've discussed today afford a glimpse of the kind of thinking required to assure the future of our company and all those associated with it.

Thus, the S&S organization is working diligently to improve its own productivity and that of its customers. This is compounded improvement that produces double-digit gains in productivity. A good example of the way S&S has helped to increase productivity for their customers revolves around design improvements made in its line of Flexo Folder-Gluers. This type of machine makes the boxes from corrugated cardboard. Eight years ago this part of the process was performed by two machines. One machine creased, slotted, and printed the corrugated cardboard, the second machine folded, glued, and delivered the box flats to a stack. To set up and run the two machines required about 0.3 man-hours per 1000 square feet of corrugated board. With the development of the fast-drying flexographic inks, which incidentally made possible finer definition and more vivid colors with a semigloss finish, S&S engineers combined these two machines into one. The single machine slots, creases, prints in two colors, folds, glues, and delivers corrugated box flats in counted bundles. Initially, the new Flexo Folder-Gluer reduced setup and run time to 0.13 man-hours per 1000 square feet of corrugated box production. Further improvements in design and the introduction of electronic controls have simplified and speeded up the process to the point where currently only 0.08 man-hours per 1000 square feet of boxes are required. Thus, in the past 8 years, the productivity of the Flexo Folder-Gluers has been increased approximately 275 percent. In addition, less floor space is needed and a scheduling problem has been eliminated. Today, for a typical-size corrugated box, one Flexo Folder-Gluer produces about 18,000 boxes per hour. It is interesting to note that historically the folder-gluer operations were the bottleneck in the total process. This is no longer true. Presently, it takes about two corrugating machines to match the output of one folder-gluer. Engineering attention now is directed to increasing the output of the machines that make the corrugated board and to improved mechanical devices for handling the output of the folder-gluers.

Technology and design are necessary for advancement. But nothing really happens until someone sells the product. Marketing makes the total process regenerative on a widening scale.

THE IMPACT OF MARKETING

Marketing has a tremendous influence on the direction each company and the economy in total pursue. By expanding existing markets and by creating new demand, marketing enlarges volume. Normally, this increases productivity, reduces unit costs, and brings lower prices to the ultimate consumer. During the past decade, however, this process slowed down and finally reversed itself. The automative industry is the prime example. It almost priced itself out of business. In 1974, in two issues, only a fortnight apart, of the *Los Angeles Times,* one automobile company announced the highest earnings in its history and that it was increasing prices across the board on its new models. This is arrogant management policy that runs contrary to the best interests of both the company and its customers. The energy crisis is another case in point. The Arab countries didn't do anything more than precipitate a situation that the automobile companies created because they allowed the dollar sign to blur their vision. Their marketing people and their managements were on a joyride, with the attitude "Let costs go up, push prices up, accelerate, accelerate, accelerate with the mistaken idea that the helpless public would continue to buy, buy, buy. Ignore gas mileage. So what if it continues to go down. Blame it on the ecologists." It took a full-scale depression to change their thinking.

Marketing people are paid to guide the company on all these points. Marketing must think of the customer again, must have confidence in its conclusions and recommendations, and then must be forceful and persuasive to the point where top management takes appropriate action to satisfy the mood and the needs of the consumers and, in so doing, protects the long-range interests of the company and the economy. Obviously, these interests should be to grow steadily in unit sales volume and profits in an orderly and constructive manner. This has a greater meaning than just sales and profits. Every time we have a depression, productivity dips and the proponents for a planned economy, socialism, and communism move forward.

In addition, marketing people can help to improve productivity by being more discriminating. The constant proliferation of new packages, new colors, and new styles must add to the cost. When they add to volume which more than offsets this cost, they are economically justified. But if all of this effort just adds cost and forces price increases, nothing is gained and inflation shifts into high gear. Marketing is not a game to amuse people or to keep them occupied. It should be a serious appraisal of the marketplace.

Further, the company that raises the price and reduces the content fuels inflation at a mad pace. Last month the package contained 16 ounces, this month 13½ ounces. Apparently, this is supposed to be clever marketing strategy. Let's call it what it really is. It's legalized cheating, and it's revolting and disenchanting to the consumers. Marketing is there to satisfy customers, not play weird games with them or arouse their ire. Again, why do publicly regulated utility companies advertise in newspapers, periodicals, and on TV? The stated reasons are to attract venture capital and to encourage the public to conserve energy. Whatever the reason, in a regulated industry this is a misuse of the customers' dollars. No wonder consumerism is growing and government regulation over consumer products and services is expanding. Marketing has not been doing its job. The customer is no longer paramount in marketing and management thinking. Even the recent depression did not alter the situation significantly. A complete change is necessary if we are to revitalize our economic growth.

One other facet of marketing that needs attention is the cost of distribution. This cost has skyrocketed to the point where serious study needs to be given to establishing more strategically located plants, warehouses, and distribution centers. And more companies should give thought to finding ways to minimize transportation costs. Postal rates and freight tariffs continue to climb, with no end in sight. Some companies will be forced to establish or expand their own transportation media. The validity of any analysis of this sort depends largely on marketing's ability to correctly anticipate and forecast the markets by product line and area. This is not easy to do, but it is necessary if management is to make the best decisions. Moving materials and products from place to place and storing them adds nothing to their value to the customer. Reducing and controlling these costs per unit of product can improve overall productivity. The railroads may once again become the favored low-cost mode of transportation for many businesses.

THE TECHNOLOGICAL ECONOMY

For almost a century, scientists and engineers have lead us into new worlds. First, machinery, then the automobile, followed by radio, the airplane, air conditioning, television, jet aircraft, computers, space capsules, lasers, and now a myriad of miniaturized solid-state electronic devices. Not too many years ago, the consensus was that mechanical and hydraulic systems were more reliable and cheaper to operate, control, and maintain than electrical and, especially, electronic systems. The advent of solid-state electronics has changed all that. The solid-state devices are cheaper, faster, more reliable, take less space, use less material and energy, and enlarge man's horizon a thousandfold.

Patrick E. Haggerty, chairman of the board of Texas Instruments, Incorporated, Dallas, Texas, in accepting the Henry Laurence Gantt Medal for 1975 awarded by the American Management Association and the American Society of Mechanical Engineers, explained it this way:

> Most of us are acquainted with the immense power of contemporary data processing machines and their peripherals. But I believe that the basic technology represented has just begun to impact the productivity of our society. Computers depend for their functioning on elements of logic and memory that can be manipulated electronically to store and process information and to initiate and control action. Semiconductor technology has just begun to make available at very low cost extremely complex assemblies of logic and memory which also are very powerful.

> I am convinced that the significance of these very powerful, very low-cost assemblies of logic and memory is far beyond the obvious and presents a technological force which inherently has the capacity to improve the productivity of our industrial societies over the long run to a degree at least equivalent to the burden placed upon those same societies by scarcer resources and more costly energy.

> First of all, logic elements are simply electronic assemblies which can be programmed to make choices or cause actions when inputted by specific signals. Similarly, memory units are electronic units in which information can be stored and from which that same information can be recovered on demand. Because of the extraordinarily small mass of the electron (on which the functioning of these solid-state electronic logic and memory elements depends), they operate at speeds measured in millionths of a second and require incredibly small amounts of energy.

> The TI SR-52 programmable calculator is easy to program even for someone who has not had previous programming experience. It will allow 224 program steps to be specified in 20 different addressable memory locations. Thus, the hand-held SR-52 can evaluate a complicated algebraic expression such as

$$Y = X_1 \ (X_2 + X_3 \ \sqrt[X_5]{X_4})$$

> Even if all of the quantities shown—X_1, X_2, X_3, X_4, and X_5—are expressions in themselves of the same complexity as the one shown here for Y, the SR-5 would

evaluate all of the individual quantities, X_1 through X_5, and obtain Y without the necessity of storing any intermediate results in the unit's addressable memory. Further, if these expressions are to be evaluated repetitively, the user can build his own program on magnetic strips so the sequence of operations can be performed automatically with only the variables inserted as desired by the user. The SR-52 depends upon seven integrated circuits. The SR-52 logic integrated circuit alone (1 of the 7) contains approximately 10,000 devices interconnected to provide 3,000 functions. If desired, this little hand-held calculator can be inserted in a small printing cradle that will print out not only the results but as many of the intermediate steps leading to them as the user desires.

In a very real sense, this pocket-size programmable calculator has more computing power than the room-size computers of 20 to 25 years ago, such as that great general purpose computer of the 1950s, the IBM 650. While the operations of this special-purpose, hand-held calculator are not completely equivalent to those of that machine, the comparison is still a valid one. The IBM 650 occupied 45 square feet of floor space, weighed almost 3 tons and required 5 to 10 tons of air conditioning. The SR-52 requires 1/20,000 of the power of the IBM 650. It executes its principal functions from 5 to 10 times as fast, and it sells for $395, (1976 dollars) against the IBM 650's $200,000 (1955 dollars).

Because it provides true computer capability to the engineer, salesman, or businessman without the expense or delay of accessing a large-scale computer facility, the SR-52 and the even more powerful small calculators and computers to follow will change the way people approach their everyday problems.

The SR-52 at $395. is, in fact, already very low-priced for its power, but I am firmly convinced that units of equivalent or more power and flexibility will be available in a few years at about one hundred. of today's dollars. At that price and power, the units will become common tools in our high schools, colleges, and universities. Through their use, the young men and women of a few decades hence will be as accustomed to using and as innovative in the application of logic and memory as the generations of the 20th Century have been in applying mechanisms and gasoline engines made familiar to them by the automobile and farm machinery, or the electric motors made so universal by readily available and low-cost electric power.

Further, because these powerful packages of logic and memory are exceedingly small, very reliable, consume miniscule amounts of energy, and are low in cost, they need not be assembled into large data processing centers to attain power in processing and reasonable cost.

I suggest that, thus far, most of the gains proceeding from the industrial revolution have fundamentally multiplied man's muscle and improved his mobility. With the widespread availability of inexpensive and powerful logic and memory, we are, in fact, multiplying man's mind. When one adds the ability to transmit the information processed or the control impulses generated from one end of the world to another, or out into space at 186,000 miles per second, and to display the information at another location as a veritable reconstitution of reality, surely the ability to multiply not just our muscle but our ability to think, to remember, to describe, to imagine, to create, must imply that the possibilities for continued future gains are boundless.

Engineers tend to be ingenious in the ways they contribute to higher productivity. Several examples taken from Industrial Nucleonics Corporation's experience in designing, applying, and installing computerized controls in process industries serve to illustrate some of the potential opportunities for cost reduction and productivity improvement. Two years ago, the Simpson Lee Paper Company of California installed Industrial Nucleonics' AccuRay 800 system on one of its paper machines. Simpson Lee's system engineer Ray Root says: "Today our quality is better than it has ever been at this mill, and we're running at nearly maximum throughput. The advanced control strategies have enabled us to optimize the machine. We've improved quality and increased throughput, thanks to faster machine speeds and substantially shorter grade change times."

The mill's grade pattern encompasses 6 different types of paper, pyramiding into about 132 product types, all of which are stored in the system's multimemory. Says Root:

> We've reduced grade change time from 20 down to a maximum of 13 minutes, and most often we're doing it in six. We've cut basis weight and moisture variations by 50%, resulting in variations of less than one pound. We've also achieved a high level of uniformity and capitalized on fiber savings. The system is there, up and operating when we need it, 99.9% of the time. With the AccuRay system we're able to place some variables surrounding papermaking in a quantifying situation and that's something we've been waiting for. Overall, I'm quite enthusiastic about what Industrial Nucleonics' engineers have done to make the traditional art of papermaking much more of an exact science that we can use day after day, machine after machine, mill after mill.

The AccuRay 800 control system is being used also to monitor and control the extrusion of plastic films and sheets. One minicomputer system is capable of controlling eight extruders. In addition to measurable quality improvements, such as greater uniformity in film thickness, the controls are reported to have attained and maintained material savings of 5 to 8 percent plus improvement in productivity per extruder of 5 to 10 percent. Improved yield and output of this magnitude result in from $50,000 to $100,000 additional annual profit contribution per extruder. Interestingly, these gains are in addition to the $25,000 to $50,000 obtained earlier using closed-loop analog controls.

Industrial Nucleonics proudly points to computer applications in the tire and rubber and other process industries as follows.

> The AccuRay 2000 system extends capability far beyond initial function of continuous process measurement and control. The engineered operator station enables production and supervisory personnel to interact to maximum effectiveness with the computer. Advanced computer control programs optimize use of raw materials, maximize throughput, and maintain desired quality standards. Hard copy reports generated by the system allow management personnel to assess production levels, raw materials usage, and product quality. Results from these computer applications have shown 20% increases in production output, 40% reduction in machine downtimes, 50% reduction in quality variations and scrap materials, amounting to system payback within a year.

The AccuRay system for the synthetic fabric industry includes multiline monitoring of heatsetting operations and continuous control over fabric yield, weight variations, productivity, and width characteristics. Specially developed measurement systems continuously monitor fabric variables while advanced controls multiplexed over several lines readily adjust machine conditions to fabric variations. Returns-on-investment of 100% and paybacks in less than one year are common from increased throughput, reduced scrap, and greater yield.

The AccuRay computer system for the mining industry automatically monitors and controls horsepower and water and ore fed into the grinding mills, constantly adjusting to optimum grinding conditions and compensating for the wide fluctuations in process variables. The system also controls the work load between grinding operations so that the maximum flow of materials is achieved through the process. An important result of these efficiency and productivity improvements is more effective fuel consumption. Management information provided by the system consists of video displays for immediate operator information, hard copy reports for summary and historical statistics, and data logging capability for further process evaluation.

TECHNOLOGY IN THE OFFICE

The scientists and engineers have been working creatively in the office too. This is a fertile field. Experts report investment in capital equipment per employee in the office is approximately $2500 compared to about $25,000 per employee in the factory. This relationship is due for a change. Costs in the office have risen steadily and sharply during the past 10 years. This area now needs substantial improvement in productivity. Perhaps the paperless office is coming. In any event, the attention and efforts of large office-equipment companies are being directed to reduce paperwork in spite of the ever-increasing demand for more information. Addressograph Multigraph Corporation expresses it this way: "We make you look better on less paper." International Business Machines, Xerox, Litton Industries, Hewlett-Packard, Lexitron, Daconics, Redactron, Digital Equipment, and many other companies already have machines and systems available, with more coming. It will be management's role to keep abreast of these paperwork-eliminating machines and methods and to judiciously apply those that best suit each business' operations. Productivity improvement of substantial magnitude will be the reward.

In effect, the office is about to be automated. Until recently, a variety of individual office machines has been developed and used. These machines perform designated operations with no immediate direct relationship to one another. Gradually, these machines are being merged into well-synchronized office systems. The basic components for this are the dictating terminal, the editing typewriter, the computer, the laser printer, and the magnetic and optical disks for information storage and retrieval. *Word processing,* the handling of words, sentences, paragraphs and numbers by electronic hardware, is beginning to facilitate and accelerate the movement of information in the office, between offices and departments, among divisions and subsidiaries of a company, and with other companies. The potentials for productivity increases will be generated by quicker and more effective use of information, greater accuracy, and almost instantaneous correction of errors and inclusion of changes.

Hewlett-Packard already has introduced its 3000CX Mini DataCenters. This concept provides a combination of hardware and software that can be applied to all functional areas of a company. The system is designed to make available problem-solving capability with immediate access by the people who need it. This can be in the office, on the production floor, in the laboratory, and in engineering, accounting, sales, and the field operations. The system can be arranged to suit one or any combination of demands by placing interactive terminals wherever they can be used to advantage. The system can expand and contract to adapt to conditions readily and adequately. For example, in a small business one Mini DataCenter may handle all the diversified needs. In a large company separate Mini DataCenters may be installed in engineering, manufacturing, marketing, and finance and then be linked in a network to operate as a total overall system. The big advantage of a network system of this kind is the speed of immediate access and the use of data base information that ensures everyone is working with the very latest input. Here again the entire office and problem-solving process can be improved to the point where the gains in employee productivity and coordination bring about very tangible results in timeliness of decisions and reductions in operating costs.

THE UNCOMMON DENOMINATOR

Managers will be required to make correct decisions on much more complex issues in the future. Better measurement of all sorts of parameters—productivity, costs, markets, energy—will be needed to properly distinguish between opinion and fact. Measurement will be fundamental to their understanding and to the logical, analytical solution of the problems they will face. Good judgment will be needed too. But sound measurement will provide a solid background to which their judgment can be applied. The entire process of decision making is facilitated when our facts are straight. Measurement by definition compares with established standards. Just having lots of numbers can be misleading. True measurement, however, can help managers grow more exact, and this will make their efforts to steer the right course more effective and more useful.

In all operations involving people and machines, a measure of the volume of output is needed in order to plan for and schedule the activities and to control the cost of the enterprise. The sales dollars and direct labor dollars commonly used for this purpose are erratic bases at best. They wander and meander off course and tend to be inflated. Management needs a much more reliable and more consistent measure of output. The standard hour of salable product or service produced is the one common denominator that meets this need. Management, however, must insist that this uncommon denominator be adopted as the standard criterion. The accountants on their own will never make this transition. Accountants are concerned with financial reporting; management is interested in controlling. And correct measurement of volume is the basis for control.

Some companies already are using the standard hour of salable product produced as their common denominator for directing and controlling operations. For example, S&S Corrugated Paper Machinery Company operates its plants in Brooklyn, New York, and Dundalk, Ireland, with work measurement and wage incentives. Its operating controls and wage incentives are based on the standard hours produced. Interestingly, S&S has programmed all input from the data collection terminals located in the operating departments directly to their Honeywell Computer. The computer makes all calculations for payroll, cost, and production control purposes, and computes the incentive premiums earned by the employees and their supervisors. All this information is compiled into reports by the computer. The printout for each department relates all control statistics to the standard hours of salable product produced.

THE PERSUASIVE MANAGER

Management has a fine array of things to work with, and the technological promise for the future is many times greater than in the recent past and the present. However, every single technical device and all systems must be developed and programmed or used by people. Thus we quickly come back to the truism: *Management is the development of people.* Managers will have to be very versatile in the art of directing people in order to inspire all to produce more units of product and services with fewer man-hours; less materials, supplies, and energy; and with economically justifiable investment in facilities, machines, tools, and inventories. The emphasis in the preceding statement should be on "to produce." This is because there is a world of difference between working and producing. To work carries with it all of the connotation of drudgery. But to produce means to make, to sell, to create, to change, to build, to achieve, to accomplish. People may not all like to work but they can be inspired to enjoy producing. Management must provide this inspiration. Another thought very basic to our purpose is that management must resurface the desire to serve. Government is there to serve the citizens; private enterprise to serve the customers. Again, the emphasis should be on "to serve." A company is not in business to beat competition or to out-manage competitors or to provide employment or just to make a profit. A company is there to serve the customers. Profit is the reward but not the reason for the business. Similarly, power and self-perpetuation are not the reasons for government. Managers by their very actions must filter "to serve" and "to produce" into the attitudes of all employees including their own.

What makes people like to come to work or to enjoy working as a team? There is no single answer or panacea to these questions. There are some generalizations that help, but for the most part management must continue to think up ways to make producing interesting and exciting. For example, when employees do not enjoy their work and do not consider their jobs important, absenteeism usually runs high. Absenteeism alone is an expensive hidden cost. This is because fringe benefits today are 30 percent and more of salaries and wages; in Belgium they are running about 70 percent of payrolls. When absenteeism is high, a company must add people or over-time in order to fill the orders. Both add cost. Exhibit 16-1 is a multivariable chart that gives some idea of the extent to which payroll costs are increased by fringe benefits, shift differentials, and overtime premiums when extra people or hours are required to make up for absenteeism. For example, if absenteeism causes a depart-ment to hire 10 percent more people than are actually required in order to meet commitments to customers, the extra cost with fringe benefits at 30 percent is ap-proximately 2.7 percent of the total departmental payroll on the first shift. On the second shift with a shift differential of 5 percent, this excess cost increases to 3.2 percent. The third shift with a 10 percent shift differential will run about 3.6 per-cent. If, instead, the department makes up the lost hours and production with 10 percent overtime hours at time and one-half, the extra cost is 4.5 percent of the payroll. Thus, absenteeism adds to cost and reduces productivity. This must be the concern of every manager.

Exhibit 16-1 was designed originally to give a manager a quick means for determining the cost differential among the alternatives of adding people, adding shifts, and using overtime to meet increased demand. The dotted lines on the chart illustrate how it is used for the following example:

Assume these departmental conditions:

1. Output to be increased 50 percent

2. Fringe benefits total about 30 percent

3. Second shift differential is 10 percent

4. Overtime premium is 50 percent

In using the chart, begin at the three indicated starting points and follow the dotted lines to the above factors. These alternatives would add to payroll costs as shown in Table 16-1:

TABLE 16-1

Alternative	Cost differential, %	Extra cost, %
1. Add employees to first shift	10.0	0
2. Add employees to second shift	13.3	3.3
3. Add overtime	16.7	6.7

The differentials relate only to salaries and wages in the department. The impact of the increased output on total unit costs is not included. The example reveals that enlarging a second shift will cost 3.3 percent, and using overtime 6.7 percent, more than adding employees on the first shift. The example also assumes that the work in the department is measured with high coverage of standards, per-haps including wage incentives. With reference to a daywork department where the work is not measured, the best way to increase departmental output would be to install time standards and operating controls. In the typical daywork department, the application of work measurement and wage incentives, as described in Chapter 15, can be expected to increase output by as much as 100 percent with the same labor force. Improvement of this magnitude would reduce departmental payroll costs in relation to output by as much as 40 percent and would eliminate the need for adding employees or overtime. And this would contribute between 10 percent and 20 per-

EXHIBIT 16-1

MULTIVARIABLE CHART FOR DETERMINING EXTRA COST ASSOCIATED WITH ADDING EMPLOYEES, OVERTIME, OR SHIFTS TO INCREASE OUTPUT.

EMPLOYEES VERSUS OVERTIME
% Differential in Departmental Salary and Wage
Cost per Standard Hour of Salable Product

2 START (% Fringe Benefits)					1 START (% Increase in Total Hours or Employees over the Basic 40 Hour Shift)									
10	20	30	40	50	10	20	30	40	50	60	70	80	90	100
0					.9	1.7	2.3	2.9	3.3	3.8	4.1	4.4	4.7	5.0
5					1.4	2.5	3.5	4.3	5.0	5.7	6.2	6.6	7.1	7.5
10	0				1.8	3.3	4.6	5.7	6.7	7.5	8.2	8.9	9.5	10.0
15	5				2.3	4.1	5.8	7.2	8.3	9.4	10.3	11.1	11.8	12.5
20	10	0			2.7	5.0	6.9	8.6	10.0	11.3	12.3	13.3	14.2	15.0
25	15	5			3.2	5.8	8.1	10.0	11.6	13.2	14.4	15.5	16.5	17.5
	20	10	0		3.6	6.7	9.2	11.4	13.3	15.0	16.5	17.8	18.9	20.0
	25	15	5		4.1	7.5	10.4	12.8	15.0	16.9	18.5	20.0	21.3	22.5
		20	10	0	4.5	8.3	11.5	14.3	16.7	18.8	20.6	22.2	23.7	25.0
		25	15	5	5.0	9.2	12.7	15.7	18.4	20.7	22.6	24.4	26.0	27.5
			20	10	5.4	10.0	13.8	17.1	20.0	22.5	24.7	26.7	28.6	30.0
			25	15	5.9	10.9	15.0	18.5	21.7	24.4	26.8	28.9	30.7	32.5
				20	6.3	11.6	16.1	20.0	23.4	26.3	28.8	31.1	33.4	35.0
				25	6.8	12.5	17.3	21.4	25.0	28.2	30.9	33.3	35.5	37.5

(Left axis: % Shift Differential)

3 START — % OVERTIME PREMIUM

	10	20	30	40	50	60	70	80	90	100
50	4.5	8.3	11.5	14.3	16.7	18.8	20.6	22.2	23.7	25.0
100	9.1	16.7	23.1	28.6	33.3	37.5	41.2	44.4	47.4	50.0

EXAMPLE:

			DIFF.	EXTRA
Increase Output	50%			
Fringe Benefits	30%			
2nd Shift Differential	10%	1. Add Employees to 1st Shift	10.0%	0 %
Overtime Premium	50%	2. Add Employees to 2nd Shift	13.3%	3.3%
		3. Add Overtime	16.7%	6.7%

cent more savings, because the additional cost of fringe benefits, shift differentials, and overtime premiums would not be incurred. With wage incentives the employees would earn about 25 percent more for their increased productivity. Every time a manager finds a way to help employees excell and thereby reduce costs while increasing their earnings, he or she is making "producing" more interesting and exciting. Work measurement with wage incentive is one of the ways.

INCENTIVE MANAGEMENT

The modern manager must develop and implement sound policies. People are more confident when they have a guide to the direction they should take. Working within the framework of carefully established policies and guidelines should facilitate decision making, should make the decisions better and more consistent with achievement of desired objectives, and should provide more time for planning and executing the short- and long-range goals of the business. All of this is pointed toward running the business more effectively.

Incentive management as practiced by the Lincoln Electric Company is the business philosophy upon which that entire company operates. It's a policy that is understood and accepted at all levels in the organization. It is a philosophy that the employees believe in and one that motivates by making all employees feel that *their best interests are served when they serve the company best.* Charles Herbruck of Lincoln Electric says:

> This philosophy shapes the hundreds of decisions and actions undertaken every day; it determines the manner in which the more or less standard operating techniques are used; it sets the standard by which is determined what is worth doing and what is not worth doing; and in many cases the things that are not done contribute more to efficiency than do the things that are done. *Incentive management is the esprit de corps,* the key to the relationship between individuals; it is the regenerative source of the will to produce.
>
> Incentive management is an expression of basic economic freedom. It creates a rising spiral in which as costs and prices are reduced, the market is expanded; and, as the market expands, the opportunity for cost reduction increases.
>
> The key is to give people responsibility, to let them work out their problems within the framework of company policy.
>
> Everyone must be rewarded in proportion to what he contributes. This, of course, is the prime incentive in any cooperative endeavor: *Just recognition of contribution.*

James F. Lincoln, founder of Lincoln Electric, in answer to the question of what it is that causes people to strive so mightily for success said:

> The answer is recognition of our abilities by our contemporaries and ourselves. The gaining by our skills of the feeling that we have desirable abilities that others covet. The feeling that we are different in some way or ways that others admire

and wish to emulate. The feeling that we are outstanding and are so recognized by our fellows.

Lincoln Electric uses a combination of job evaluation, time standards, and merit rating to recognize each employee's contribution each year. The employees are rated individually every 6 months. Their immediate supervisor or manager is responsible for all ratings. However, assistance in rating each employee may be requested from other departments. The inspection department rates quality performance. The production control department rates quantity output. And the time-study and methods department evaluates contribution to improvement through cost reduction ideas that have been implemented. All this information is combined into an annual performance rating for each employee. The employees then share in a bonus fund in proportion to their base wages and their performance ratings. The bonus fund is what remains of the company's annual earnings after taxes, reserves, and a dividend are subtracted from the total. The bonus fund historically has been in the range of 100 percent of the total payroll. This is powerful incentive and it works. Productivity remains high, the employees are recognized for their individual and combined contribution, and the company prospers. Everyone is involved, everyone is rewarded.

MANAGEMENT INVESTMENT

Every company and every country could afford today's wages and tomorrow's wage increases if they were organized to increase productivity commensurably. In any event, profit is an important adjunct for the future. Helmut Schmidt, chancellor of West Germany, is looking forward. He says, "Today's profits are tomorrow's plants and next year's wages." Capital investment at a high rate in the best and very latest facilities, machines, tools, and equipment has to be one of management's prime objectives. In the long run, this is the low-cost way. These "tools" make it possible for people to be more productive. In turn, the improvement in productivity pays for the investment. The added output helps to meet demand, and this tends to keep prices in line, which in turn adds to demand. If the available capital is not fully invested, it will be lost in inefficiencies and there will be nothing to show for it. It will be wasted. Thus, for management there is no alternative to investing in new plant, additional sources of energy, more advanced products, and better services.

Management will have to invest in people also. Training has been neglected for almost a generation. Education has advanced; now we are faced with a young population that possesses higher levels of knowledge but less specific know-how. Does management have the ability to train and channel this talent into productive activities? Of course management is equal to the challenge, but the time for action is immediate. The labor force in total grows rapidly every day. New plant and new training capabilities must be made available to absorb these young citizens productively. What are the critical skills? Machine maintenance is one area needing more well-trained people. Today's mechanical, hydraulic, electronic, and laser systems are complicated. Proper maintenance is an important part of keeping these machines and systems operating at peak efficiency. The Metal Textile Division of General Cable Corporation, for instance, has a capable maintenance crew. These men know their business. They are up to date on the latest machinery installed in the plant, but even more important, they make periodic reviews to prevent downtime. They keep good maintenance records and maintain adequate stocks of replacement parts. They are organized to do their job, and plant productivity shows they are producing results. It's management policy that they give the physical plant the detailed, dedicated attention it deserves.

Management must give more attention to the new employee also. Too often the new employee is allowed to drift, which develops bad habits. The very first day is the time to put the new employee to work. He or she wants to make good and is most responsive at the very beginning. This enthusiasm should be used to develop good work habits. Management must set the stage—the policy—for pointing the new employee in the right direction and for ensuring that he or she will become a productive member of the team.

The new employees should be given every opportunity to make good. On the very first day give them clear instructions, put them on standard, tell them what the standard is. Explain that the important thing is to learn how to do the job right. Reassure them that they are not expected to attain standard performance immediately but that by measuring their output, their progress in learning the job can be followed. The Bureau of the Census found that good instructions with measurement reduced training time by 75 percent. The result: new employees quickly develop a sense of achievement and become much more interested in the work.

Every job becomes monotonous if an employee performs it long enough, because the work no longer challenges his or her ability. This is not conducive to improving productivity. A management-sponsored policy for job change and employee development or upgrading is basic and good for both the employees and the company. And this applies equally to production and service employees, office personnel, clerks, supervisors, and managers. In other words, it should be an across-the-board kind of program designed to satisfy and excite employees to want to grow in stature, talent, skill, and value. Their response and progress is favorably intensified when they know that management believes in this and in them.

Perhaps the one thing management strives for most in leading an organization is control. But really what is control? Control consists of many things. In essence, it means achieving objectives efficiently and effectively. It is present when each manager:

1. Trains his or her people to do their jobs well and on time.

2. Plans and assigns work in advance.

3. Checks to make certain everything needed is available and in good working condition.

4. Explains and issues instructions so that the employees have a clear idea of what is to be done, when, and how long it should take.

5. Follows up to lend assistance and to ensure that the work or project is being completed according to plan.

6. Reports regularly and accurately the action taking place in his or her department.

7. Gives special attention to the low performers, the latecomers, and the chronic absentees.

8. Replaces those employees who have insufficient aptitude, ability, or desire to learn the skills necessary to become good producers.

9. Rewards his or her people for extraordinary accomplishment.

10. Generates a feeling of importance and growth toward the objectives that are being pursued.

Bendix Corporation is a good example of a company that continues to control its activities effectively. W. Michael Blumenthal, the former chairman, president, and chief executive officer, summed up the reasons for his company's success and gave a concise definition of modern management when he said, "No doubt some of our success must be ascribed to our ability to anticipate problems before they become serious, to our success at trimming costs early and effectively, to our policy of planning our various product lines, and to our continued investment in technology and people."

PRODUCING ABUNDANCE

Modern management has a creative assignment. It is not enough for a company to just earn a profit. Management must direct its attention and the efforts of the enterprise to producing more for all. The modern definition of "more" is higher real salaries and wages, cleaner air and water, better and healthier living and working conditions, greater educational and recreational fulfillment, and increasing opportunities for individual and group expression. This is a huge but a necessary and wholesome responsibility. Time, energy, and materials literally have to be created by discovering and implementing new ways to make more effective use of these basic components of living and advancement. A new value must be placed on successful producers of ideas, services, and products; each and every individual must be given an opportunity to grow and to enjoy a real sense of achievement. And management must establish the environment and set the pace. Rewarding for results must become the popular theme. Inspiration and enthusiasm must be generated and directed by management in such a well-organized, skillful manner that all of us will want and will enjoy seeking and pursuing ways to increase our productivity. "Our" is no longer just individual or national. Now it is international!

THE LIMITS FOR PRODUCTIVITY IMPROVEMENT
ARE OUT OF THIS WORLD

Index